D1476978

A Pilgrim Soul

THE LIFE AND WORK OF ELISABETH LUTYENS

Meirion and Susie Harries

Michael Joseph
LONDON

To Lettice Cooper

MICHAEL JOSEPH LTD

Published by the Penguin Group
27 Wrights Lane, London W8 5TZ, England
Viking Penguin Inc., 40 West 23rd Street, New York, New York 10010, USA
Penguin Books Australia Ltd, Ringwood, Victoria, Australia
Penguin Books Canada Ltd, 2801 John Street, Markham, Ontario, Canada L3R 1B4
Penguin Books (NZ) Ltd, 182–190 Wairau Road, Auckland 10, New Zealand

Penguin Books Ltd, Registered Offices: Harmondsworth, Middlesex, England

First published in Great Britain 1989

Copyright © Meirion and Susie Harries 1989

Made and printed in Great Britain by
Richard Clay Ltd, Bungay, Suffolk
Filmset in Monophoto Ehrhardt

A CIP catalogue record for this book is available from the British Library
ISBN 0 7181 2547 9

Contents

List of Illustrations

Acknowledgements

We should like first of all to thank Elisabeth Lutyens's trustees for giving us unrestricted access to all her papers – letters written and received, manuscripts, notebooks, diaries, programmes, press cuttings: the core of the book. We should also like to thank her husband Ian Glennie and her children (Sebastian Glennie, Rose Abdalla, Teresa Fetherstonhaugh and Conrad Clark) and Edward Clark's son James for giving us all help and encouragement throughout.

We should like to acknowledge the help we have received from the staff of the British Library Manuscripts Collection; the library of the Royal Institute of British Architects; the National Sound Archive; the National Film Archive at the British Film Institute; the National Museum of Photography, Film and Television; the library of the Royal College of Music; the Performing Rights Society; the Arnold Schoenberg Institute at the University of California; the University of Texas at Austin; the Music Division of the Library of Congress; the Sound Archives of the BBC and the Department of Transcripts and Tapes at Broadcasting House. Particular thanks to John Jordan and the BBC's Written Archives Centre at Caversham.

We interviewed a large number of Elisabeth Lutyens's relations, friends, colleagues, pupils and sparring partners. All contributed a good deal to the detail of the book; none is responsible for the whole of it. We should like to thank: Mrs Mary Alwyn, John Amis, Rufina Ampenoff, Denis ApIvor, Malcolm Arnold, Mike Ashman, Francis Bacon, Lady Eve Balfour, Anne Balfour-Fraser, Carol Barratt, Alison Bauld, Richard Rodney Bennett, Tony van den Bergh, Gilbert Biberian, Leo Black, Russell Blacker, Professor David Blake, Robin Bone, James Bowman, Jane Bown, Glyn Boyd-Harte, Susan Bradshaw, George Braithwaite, Neville Braybrooke, Mike Bremner, Anthony Burton, Ken Cameron, Elias Canetti, Simon Carrington, Jeremy Caulton, Nicolas Chagrin, Levon Chilingirain, Bill Colleran, Arnold Cooke, Jill Craigie, Cusson's UK Limited, Hugh David, Philippa Davis, Richard Deering, Norman and Pauline Del Mar, Patric and Sheila Dickinson, Georgina Dobree, Shula Doniach, Freda Dowie, David Drew, the Duke of York's Theatre, Howard Ferguson, Mrs Xenia Frankel, James Gibb, Sydney Giebel, Anthony Gilbert, Mrs Betty Glennie, Sir William and Lady Glock, Professor Alexander Goehr, Livia Gollancz, Sidonie Goossens, Janet Graham, Michael and Ellen Graubart, Paul Griffiths, Miron Grindea, Sally Groves, Carol Hall, Iain Hamilton, Caragh Hanning, Dr Iorwerth Harries, Jonty Harrison, Howard Hartog,

Frank Hauser, Daphne Henghes, Robert Hewison, Peter Heyworth, Jenni Hicks, Jessie Hinchliffe, Sally Hine, Antony Hopkins, Bruce Hunter, Barrie Iliffe, Michael Imison, Joan Ingpen, Georgina Ivor, Lucy Jebb, Stuart Jones, Brian Kay, Milein Keller, Nicholas Kenyon, Lee Langley, Robert Layton, Iris Lemare, Mair Lewis, Caroline Loeb, Andrew Lyle, Candia Lutyens, Anne Macnaghten, Elizabeth Maconchy, Jane Manning, Sir Neville Marriner, Phil Martell, Mrs Hermione Mathieson, Nicholas Maw, Sheila McCrindle, Constance McKerrow, Professor Wilfred Mellers, Dr Jonathan Miller, Anthony Milner, Bel Mooney, Dorothy Morland, Andrew Motion, Thea Musgrave, Bea Musson, Helen Scott Nearing (née Knothe), Jeremy Noble, Buxton Orr, the late Manoug Parikian, Anthony Payne, Anna Phillips, Stephen Plaistow, Robert Ponsonby, Andrew Porter, Alan Poulton, Deborah Price, Isobel Quigly, Rosalind Rajagopal, Joyce Rathbone, Isabel Rawsthorne, Edith Renwick, Lord Revelstoke, Sir Adam and Lady Ridley, Viscountess Ridley, Catherine Roma, Frans van Rossum, Francis Routh, Robert Saxton, Pat Sharland, Sally Swing Shelley, Paul and Mary Silverthorne, Robert Simpson, Rodney Slatford, Daniel Snowman, Nicolas Soames, Yolanda Sonnabend, Fritz Spiegl, Mrs Bertha Stevens, Donald Swann, Sarah Tenant-Flowers, John Theocharis, Hazel Thomas, David Thompson, Andrew Thomson, Virgil Thomson, Wendy Toye, Susan Tyrrell, Ursula Vaughan Williams, Michael Vyner, John Wallace, Kenneth Waller, Michael Blake Watkins, Margaret Williams, Malcolm Williamson, Katharina Wolpe, Hugh Wood.

We are especially grateful to Clayre Percy for her help with Ursula Ridley's papers; to Anthony Besch, who will be developing his ideas on Elisabeth Lutyens's stage works in his forthcoming book on his experiences in opera; to Ian Caddy, who made available to us his own extensive collection of Lutyens material, and lent us many tapes; to John Patrick Thomas and Brian Elias, who allowed us to see particularly valuable collections of letters; to Glyn Perrin, who endured endless queries patiently, and consistently helped and cheered us; to Jennie Orchard, who got the book off the ground; and to Anne Askwith, who edited it. We should also very much like to thank the Phoenix Trust for its help towards the book.

Above all, we should like to thank Peter Day, who suggested we write the biography; and Mary Lutyens and Joe Links, whose kindness, tolerance and enthusiasm for the book made the work a pleasure.

Quotations from the Lutyens Collections Add. Mss. 64456, and from Add. Mss. 5226, are made by kind permission of the British Library.

Quotations from the correspondence of Arnold Schoenberg to Edward Clark are made by kind permission of Lawrence Schoenberg and the British Library.

The quotation from Cecil Gray, *A Survey of Contemporary Music* (1924) is made by permission of Oxford University Press.

The quotation from Brigid McConville, *Sisters*, is by permission of Pan Books, London, Brigid McConville and Anthony Sheil Associates Ltd. Copyright © *Sisters* by Brigid McConville.

All quotations from BBC correspondence are by kind permission of the BBC Written Archives Centre, Caversham.

The quotation from Igor Stravinsky and Robert Craft, *Dialogues and a Diary*, is by permission of Faber and Faber Ltd.

The quotations from Donald Mitchell and Hans Keller, *Music Survey, New Series 1949–52* and Paul Griffiths, *New Sounds, New Personalities*, are reproduced by kind permission of the publishers, Faber Music Ltd.

The quotations from Sir Arthur Bliss, *As I Remember*, are by kind permission of Lady Bliss.

The quotation from *Under Seige* (revised editon) Methuen, 1988, is by permission of Robert Hewison.

The quotation from Quasimodo, *Selected Poems*, translated by Jack Bevan, copyright © Jack Bevan 1965, is by permission of Penguin Books Ltd.

The quotation *Paris and the New York Diaries*, copyright © 1983 by Ned Rorem, published by North Point Press, is reprinted by permission.

The quotation from *The Complete Poems of D. H. Lawrence* is by permission of William Heinemann Ltd, London, and Viking Penguin Inc.

The quotation from Arthur Koestler, *The Yogi and the Commissars*, is by permission of Jonathan Cape Ltd.

The quotation from Barbera and McBrien, *Stevie*, is by permission of William Heinemann Ltd, London.

The quotation from Geoffrey Grigson, *Recollections*, is by permission of Chatto and Windus Ltd.

The quotation fron Virginia Woolf, *A Room With a View*, is by permission of the Executors of the Virginia Woolf Estate and the Hogarth Press.

The quotation from Dylan Thomas, *The Collected Letters of Dylan Thomas*, edited by Paul Ferris, is by permission of the Trustees of the copyrights of Dylan Thomas and J. M. Dent.

Prologue

'NEVER SPOIL A good story with the truth.' It was one of Elisabeth Lutyens's favourite lines, and a principle she observed faithfully in the last twenty years of her life when she was preparing the version of herself she wanted to be remembered. As she got older, word got round that Sir Edwin Lutyens's daughter, 'the mother of British serialism', provided good copy, and in interview after interview the same persona was paraded: 'Twelve-tone Lizzie', woman in a man's world, veteran pioneer ploughing a lifelong lonely furrow, Bohemian aristocrat, game old bird, worldly-wise yet young at heart, battered but indomitable.

At the heart of this carefully constructed character, underpinning it, was a single belief. 'Myths grow like crystals,' writes Arthur Koestler. 'As soon as a suitable core is found, they group themselves around it.' [1] Elisabeth Lutyens's core was the conviction that she had never received her due – her due of love and understanding from her parents, appreciation from her peers, support from her husbands, opportunity and recognition in the music profession.

Her life as she looked back on it seemed to her a series of interlinked battles, fought without allies and without remission. Rebellion against a background of privilege and what she portrayed as the rankest philistinism; interminable years in the cultural wilderness, a lone voice proclaiming a new musical gospel before its time; struggle for survival in habitats almost exclusively male – the pubs of Fitzrovia, the Features Department of the BBC, the film industry of the 1950s; heroic attempts to combine music and motherhood; and the long crusade to vindicate a husband victimised by the musical establishment. '*Mother Courage*,' she once said, 'was too much like a busman's holiday to me.' She would have been intensely irritated by the suggestion that to some degree she had deliberately made fighting an art form. Her life ran on indignation and defiance, and without them momentum might have petered out.

Elisabeth Lutyens's version of herself took shape in the letters she wrote to her mother between the ages of ten and forty, and it began to set solid in the public lectures of her middle years. Polished by repetition, it was presented to the world in her autobiography *A Goldfish Bowl* in 1972.[2] And then in the decade leading up to her death in 1983 it was revolved endlessly on the gramophone record of her grievances, until its outlines disappeared in a blur of anecdote and bile.

'Elisabeth Lutyens is an outrageous 76-year-old,' wrote the *Evening Standard* in 1982. 'Bent fingers clutch at the air in brave expansive gestures, red nails flash as her often shocking language takes another iconoclastic swipe at the establishment. . . . She has been described as the most radical composer of British music of her generation, her capacity for composition only equalled by her appetite for life. She has weathered two husbands, four children, nervous breakdowns, alcoholism, widowhood and now rheumatoid arthritis. But still the pen and score are on the sofa next to her.'[3]

'Outrageous', 'brave', 'shocking', 'iconoclastic', 'radical' – the description must have delighted her. It is both accurate in every detail and utterly misleading. The 'fucks' and 'shits' which peppered her conversation, delivered in an accent so upper-crust that it made them comic rather than simply crude, were balanced by an insistence on the niceties of English usage and an acute sensitivity to the nuances of social class. The intellectual practitioner of the most cerebral brand of composition, who chose to set Wittgenstein, Joyce and Beckett, poured music on to paper with reckless haste as a release from the pressures of guilt, envy, anger, loneliness and fear.

The tough, seasoned professional, wise to all the tricks of the music trade, was an anxious, affectionate, romantic person, whose aspiration was to hear sounds heard by no one else quite like that before and pass them on as truthfully as she could, in a way that would be worthy of a musical tradition of which she felt very much a part. In the 1960s she wrote,

> Songs break; sing down my limbs; shout through my
> body,
> shaking me;
> Sound streaming, singing!
> *My* own,

my own songs;
songs that are *mine*
of my *making*, echoing; echoing round the curves
and crevices of all
my myriad worlds.
I live in my songs.
My songs live through me.[4]

The lines were intended for one of her stage works, for a character with distinctly autobiographical features. In the end she left them out, having embarrassed herself, perhaps, by writing so openly about her aspirations. This may not be very accomplished verse; but it is not the utterance of a cynic or a musical time-server.

'I have always disliked myself at any given moment,' Cyril Connolly once wrote. 'The total of such moments is my life.'[5] Lutyens spent less time than Connolly in self-analysis, but there was much about herself she wanted to change. Rather like Philip Heseltine, who invented for himself a louder, brighter, less inhibited and more resilient identity as Peter Warlock, she evolved a personality with which to take on the music world. With the connivance of a press which had little interest in or comprehension of her music but put a very high premium on 'personality', in her sixties and seventies she made herself a stock character whose 'brave expansive gestures' and well-rehearsed epigrams obliterated much that was original, vulnerable and attractive.

The caricature has slipped easily into other people's mythologies; 'Liz' stories bob about the arts world like 'Dylan' or 'Constant' or 'Stevie' stories. But too many people now remember only the unhappy last years when the wit and epic party-giver, the inspired teacher and intuitive friend, was frequently overpowered by a musical Ancient Mariner who bought company with champagne and never drew breath in a monologue of frustration and rancour.

Of the friends of her youth and middle age, many drank heavily and died early; there were few left to summon up the young Betty (or Agnes or Lizzie or Elisabeth or E.L. – to different people she was all these), set her beside the old Liz and relate the two in a single personality. In the heat of the barrage thrown up by the old Liz, one much younger friend observed, 'I wasn't thinking much about *why* she was doing it, I was thinking about how the hell she was getting away with it, and wishing she'd stop.'[6]

It is not uncommon for a life to telescope towards its close, leaving only a flattened, over-bright cartoon in people's minds. The more glaring the personality at the end, the deeper the shadow into which it casts the past. But in Lutyens's case the distortion threatens to affect the future as well, because it has shaped the way her music is regarded.

Very few people survive in the public memory as personalities alone; achievement is the eventual touchstone, and hers has quietly submerged in a sea of anecdote. The 'controversial', hard-bitten figure of the 1970s, whose compositions sometimes seemed to be musical V-signs mechanically executed at a profession which would rather she had stopped writing, blots out the author of a significant number of pieces which are intensely lyrical, enthusiastic in every sense of the word, breathing passion not anger, and as beautiful as she could make them. This was the composer Elisabeth Lutyens always wanted to be. Very rarely in her life was she allowed to realise that she had succeeded.

CHAPTER ONE

'Bowling Wides at Jesus'

SIR EDWIN LANDSEER LUTYENS always claimed to believe in filial criticism; failure to look hard and clear at one's parents amounted to 'bowling wides at Jesus'.[1] Nevertheless, even he might have been taken aback by his third daughter's judgement of the family in which she grew up. In her autobiography Elisabeth Lutyens presented her life as lived in a series of 'goldfish bowls' – distinct worlds, each with its own population, its own rules and conventions, and its own scheme of rewards and penalties. The inhabitants of the first world of her childhood are as vulnerable and exposed to her scrutiny as any goldfish circling under the eye of a cat; and the picture she presents is as distorted in its way as the image seen through the convexity of a goldfish bowl.

Her father, Sir Edwin, appears in a protective aura of glamour and legend; Elisabeth idealised him for his genius and his jokes. But her book is dedicated not to him but to 'the two people I have most loved in my life: my mother, in spite of some of the things I say about her, and my husband, Edward Clark, in spite of so many things I have had to leave out about him'.

Her mother, Lady Emily Lytton, mercilessly criticised in the book, was nevertheless at or near the centre of her daughter's emotional life for nearly fifty years. It was her mother whose love and approval Elisabeth wanted, her mother who received all her confidences and was blamed for disappointment and disaster. Not her mother alone, however, made Elisabeth's childhood what it was, the crucible of her adult personality, but the relationship between Lady Emily and her husband.

The marriage of Edwin and Emily Lutyens could be taken as a paradigm of incompatibility and selfishness, and yet it survived for forty-five years, opening and closing in a devotion both romantic and touching. Their letters are riddled with traces of egocentricity, mis-understanding and bitterness, but they were exchanged virtually every day when the couple were apart, and with very few exceptions are phrased in terms of great intimacy and affection, even ardour. Had Lutyens and Lady Emily been the only people involved in their drama, one might say that they brought it to a happy, even triumphant ending – but they had five children, of whom Elisabeth was perhaps the least able to avoid the emotional fall-out.

The relationship was constantly under strain from the lives each led outside the home. By the time of Elisabeth's birth, the demands of a career as the foremost builder of houses for the rich of Edwardian England had shaped and in some respects constricted her father's personality. Edwin Lutyens was eventually to become the most success-ful architect of his day, entrusted with some of the most prestigious of public commissions, including the imperial capital at Delhi, but he made his early reputation with classic country houses. In him artistic ability was coupled with ambition, and to succeed and survive in what was socially an alien environment he evolved the persona of the perfect weekend guest: lovably whimsical and acceptably outrageous – a chubby, benevolent figure, pipe-smoking, port-drinking, *bon viveur*, punster and wit. Significantly, this is the picture of him that Elisabeth paints in her autobiography.

Behind this façade sheltered an anxious, obsessively hardworking man, uncomfortable in his lack of a public-school education, and unable or unwilling to talk seriously about the things he valued most. Intellectually austere, he was also withdrawn in crucial ways from the family for whom instead he devised the puzzles, jokes, irresistibly funny drawings and 'vivreations' which have become famous.

Lutyens's family was by no means ordinary, but nor was it high-born; he was the first to bear a title, when he was knighted in 1919. His ancestors came to England in the late seventeenth century by way of Hamburg, where the first traceable Lutyens had been a barber. They established themselves in trade and then the army. His great-uncle Engelbert acted as intermediary between Napoleon and the British Military Governor on St Helena, and his grandfather was Commissariat Officer to Sir John Moore at Corunna.

Edwin's father, Charles Henry Augustus Lutyens, disturbed the pat-tern by retiring from the army at the age of twenty-eight to paint. He was a pupil of the great Landseer, Edwin's godfather, and contributed to the design for the Trafalgar Square lions, but his speciality was horses and hounds, with a particularly profitable sideline in portraits of

Derby winners. While the supply of wealthy clients lasted he made a living quite handsome enough to support his fourteen children. But hearty realism eventually fell from fashion, and he retired to Thursley, a village near Guildford in Surrey, to spend a long old age brooding on the 'Venetian Secret' – a method of achieving uniquely rich tonal perspective by underpainting in a particular shade of red.

Progressive blindness did not stop him painting, but his subjects became more unorthodox. In 1910, five years before his death, he was preoccupied with a painting of a black Venus, designed 'to elevate the blacks in the eyes of the whites'. Venus was Edwin's sister Aileen, 'black all over laying up against a Surrey bank with a parrot in a nutbush and some geraniums under the hedgerow to give colour'.[2]

Edwin's mother Mary Gallwey was a gentle but determined woman, profoundly devout, whose opening words to a guest were liable to be 'Are you saved?' (Not surprisingly, her son found Edmund Gosse's *Father and Son* highly evocative.) A nervous, lonely child, Edwin was kept away from school by illness, and his relationship with his mother was unusually close. When Lady Emily first met him, for months he gave her the impression that he was the only son of a widowed mother, as perhaps he would have liked to have been.

Apart from the need to appear other than he was, Lutyens brought two noticeable characteristics away from his childhood. Throughout his life he had an almost neurotic fear of poverty; as his father's income became increasingly inadequate, family life verged on the squalid, with newspapers used as tablecloths and one plate for all courses. (Charles added to the overall effect by dipping his roast potatoes in tea to soften them.) And he had an equally compelling desire and need for a dominant, protecting mother-figure – someone who would give him the support he required for his work without making reciprocal demands on him. Both these characteristics were to make themselves felt in his marriage.

The eccentricity in Lady Emily's family was better bred and partially disguised by power and privilege, though not in her generation by wealth. Her father was a Lytton, her mother a Villiers, so she could boast among her forebears Oliver Cromwell and the Earls of Essex, Clarendon and Jersey. Her grandfather, the statesman and Gothic novelist Bulwer Lytton, expanded even further on the quality of the lineage, having a portrait of the Emperor Charles V copied to hang at Knebworth, the family seat, under the title of 'Sir Roland de Lytton', and in more extravagant moments claiming that the name 'Bulwer' was a title of the god Odin.

Bulwer's main legacy seems to have been a pronounced melancholy and a disregard for convention. His son Robert Lytton – Lady Emily's father – was by inclination a poet (under the name of Owen Meredith) and only of necessity became a career diplomat. Although he achieved the rank of Viceroy of India (1876–80), he hardly conformed to the traditional picture of a Victorian imperialist. Extravagant and indiscreet, with a weakness for roller-skating and flirting with the wives of his staff, he was fond of forecasting policy in accordance with the behaviour of hot-air balloons.

His wife Edith Villiers, however, measured up far more closely to the notion of a diplomatic wife. '*Charm*,' she wrote, 'and a power of adapting themselves to their husbands, *we* consider far more essential [in women] than great study which might only ruin their healths.' Edith refused to read the work of the new novelist Charles Dickens – 'so dreadfully vulgar, and the people seem to do nothing but drink' – preferring the luxury and ceremony of colonial life. She minded very much the steep decline in the Lytton fortunes after Robert's death in 1891: henceforward, according to her youngest son Neville, the motto at Knebworth was to be 'Stucco and Stinginess'.

It was not long before Emily, the fourth child of Robert and Edith, found herself reacting against her environment. She was shy, clumsy, brusque and earnest, with a mother she adored but who, in her words, 'discouraged intimacy'. 'I was a large, ungainly girl still wanting to cling round her neck.' Her greatest pleasure, besides a fervent religious faith, was reading – but for private satisfaction rather than public display. Her elder sister Betty, who married Gerald Balfour (brother of the Prime Minister A. J. Balfour), was a leading member of the intellectual coterie called 'the Souls', and much against her will Emily was forced to mix with them. Though she was intellectually equipped to compete, she detested their conversation radiant with self-conscious 'intelligence', the savage, point-scoring party games and the bogus 'liberated' morality which stopped well short of risk. 'If the Souls could but have their thin coat of paint scraped off,' she wrote when she was seventeen, 'what poor wooden blocks they would be. . . .'

She found Wilfrid Scawen Blunt far more appealing. He was a close friend of her father, a poet, landowner and adventurer, married to Byron's granddaughter, equally unorthodox, who introduced Arab horses to Britain and devoted much of her neglected life to her stud farm. Some forty years older than Lady Emily, Blunt was still extremely attractive, and had his own distinctive views on the best way of liberating Victorian womanhood.

Lady Emily, convinced of her own ugliness and social shortcomings, was immensely flattered by his attentions, and at eighteen embarked on a highly charged flirtation which only ended, three years later, when her doorhandle started rattling in the night. (Blunt boasted to his daughter that 'it would have done Emily all the good in the world – she wasn't pretty enough to get much of a husband and wasn't likely to get such a chance again'.)

In the aftermath of the affair, she decided to take up what she described as 'the last resource of the desperate' – social work. And in this frame of mind, in 1896, she met Edwin Lutyens, a promising and already fashionable young architect, with a blossoming practice in picturesque country houses. Neither was quite what they seemed; each was possibly attracted by the element of the unusual in the other, but in their marriage these were the very elements that were to conflict.

Their courtship was highly romantic, beginning one evening when Lady Emily arrived home from a day spent bicycle-racing in Leslie Stephen's garden with his daughters Virginia and Vanessa and their half-brother Gerald Duckworth. Lutyens was waiting, anxious to take her to see a house he was building near by, and that night they broke in so that he could show her his work by moonlight. The next day it was supper with Gertrude Jekyll and her cats, an impromptu meal of mutton chops, tipsy cake, bullseyes and hot elderberry wine which enchanted Lady Emily, already impatient of Victorian etiquette.

Lutyens then offered his love what became known in the family as 'the Casket'. This small, beautifully designed chest contained the symbols of what he hoped would be their life together – a tiny anchor, for permanence; a pipestopper, representing the fireside; a heart; a Bible; a long, desperately romantic poem he had written; and the drawings for a 'little white house', whose ground plan was based on their shared initials intertwined. Dismayed at first by the disapproval of her family, Lady Emily gradually broke down their resistance and accepted his offer of marriage.

But romance was under pressure from the start. From the family's point of view, this was a disappointing, even hazardous match for Lady Emily, and they insisted on Lutyens taking out as security a £10,000 life insurance policy. In doing so, he effectively committed himself to earning over £1000 per year, a huge amount for the 1890s. Lutyens objected briefly but strongly on ethical grounds – such a manoeuvre went, he said, against his mother's principle of trusting in the Almighty. More honestly he revealed later that it was a significant financial burden he resented all his life. Twenty years on he wrote sadly to Lady Emily,

'I think, believe, and hope I have achieved security for you but I seem to have lost more than it was worth.'[3] In her eyes, they had both paid too high a price. The consuming devotion to his work which had seemed so noble when they first met had expanded as his reputation grew and the work increased, and it left little room in his life for her, for her interests, for their children.

The stresses of money worries, family pressures, conflicting temperaments and diverging interests were apparent in their marriage long before Elisabeth, their fourth child, was born, nine years after their wedding. In the Lytton family, the birth of Agnes Elisabeth Lutyens, on 9 July 1906, was received with restraint. They had been hoping for another boy, but as Betty Balfour wrote: 'There are compensations. No circumcision, for one!'[4]

Lady Emily herself had no reservations. At nine pounds six ounces the new baby was endearingly tubby, with bracelets of fat, long lashes and 'a mass of soft black hair like a golliwog – the image of Ned', in Emily's eyes. In fact, like all the Lutyens children, Elisabeth had inherited her father's prominent forehead – 'the knee', as she unkindly described its appearance in one of her sisters – but her nose came straight from the Lyttons.

At three weeks the baby distinguished herself by frightening away burglars with the vehemence of her demands for her 2 a.m. feed. Six months later she was getting about at a tremendous pace 'by rolling over and over till she meets a wall and can get no further'. When she was fourteen months old a photographer called her 'the little boy', and Lady Emily commented, 'I am afraid they have all inherited the Lytton grimaces'. When her original ample shape persisted, her father labelled her 'Buddha'.

In the correspondence between her parents over the next few years she appears in various guises – eating six cold potatoes at a sitting; trying unsuccessfully to turn somersaults; 'a fat lump of independance [sic] and pure joy'; 'solemn and passionate – defiant – sometimes very happy and then very cross'; the belle of the ball at a Knebworth fancy-dress party as a four-year-old nun; happy in the role of a maid carrying the chamber pot for an older sister's teddy.

Betty, as her family called her all her life, though it was a name she detested, was the fourth of five children and third of four daughters, an awkward position to occupy in the family hierarchy. The eldest child, Barbara (Barbie), born in 1898, was exceptionally pretty, with extraordinary blue eyes. Much courted as a VAD in the First World War, she was sophisticated and socially ambitious – 'not made to be a poor man's wife', her mother remarked.

The second child, Robert, five years older than Betty, had the double misfortune of being the only boy, supporting the full weight of his father's expectations, and of having inherited the Lytton melancholy. He had a strong sense of being Bulwer Lytton's 'spiritual heir' – in his teens he put 'B.L.' after his name like a kind of degree – and felt his natural home to be Knebworth, rather than Bloomsbury. But with this legacy came what he described as 'the mortal disease of discouragement'. He was strikingly handsome in the Byronic style, which he cultivated, ravished adults with his charm and succeeded at almost everything he tried; as a child he danced well, recited well, and painted ably enough for Henry Tonks to offer him a provisional place at the Slade on the basis of a precocious watercolour of the Crucifixion.

But he lacked discipline and was readily deterred by criticism, a mixture, in his own words, of insecurity and egotism. To his younger sisters, he was a cruel tease, who would seek them out in the nursery in order to reduce them to tears; often his mere appearance in the doorway was enough for Betty.

Then there was Ursula, two years older than Betty, and for almost half a century her particular bugbear; talented, attractive, discontented and critical, she could neither be successfully emulated nor entirely ignored. As an adolescent she would be a rival for parental affection; as a young wife and mistress of a country estate, she would be a critic of Betty's very different style of life; as a mother, an oracle pronouncing freely and unfavourably on Betty's methods of child-rearing. The relationship between the two girls was irretrievably distorted from the start by the fact that Ursula was her father's favourite. He made no attempt to hide his feelings, and Ursula, not unnaturally, made the most of them. She was a delicate, sensitive child on whom Edwin could expend all the protective feelings that were sometimes wasted on his wife, and in return Ursula was effusively anxious to please him – a quality he felt singularly lacking in the rest of his family. Her winning ways with adults infuriated her younger sisters, who were unable to deny her charm, intelligence and looks – alone of the five she had natural curls – but also suffered from her bullying and constant competitiveness. 'Ursula always wanted to be top at everything and she was,' wrote the youngest Lutyens, Mary.

But Betty's greatest grudge against Ursula was that she was allowed to stay up to supper, 'to crack the nuts: have a sip of Father's port and be fussed over' while she herself was packed off ignominiously to bed with Mary, although she was closer in age to Ursula. And then – crowning injustice (which rankled, ludicrously, until she died) – when

Betty in her turn was promoted to the dining room, Mary, more than two years younger, received the privilege at the same time and was not made to wait.

Despite this *casus belli*, Mary was Betty's best friend in the nursery. Rounder as a baby even than Betty – 'like a rising sun with a very red face', wrote Lady Emily – Mary grew up to be placid, persevering, entertaining and above all happy. She gave no trouble because she felt none. 'The world is my kingdom,' she observed at the age of four, and Betty was an admired and beloved figure in that kingdom.

In this configuration of children, there was no distinctive role for Betty to claim for herself. She was neither oldest nor youngest, neither the only boy nor anyone's favourite. (With the ruthless age snobbery of the under-tens, she did not count Mary, her junior.) And in an uncommonly handsome family, she was the only one without conventional prettiness. A face which could look beautiful, and in old age was mesmerising, could also look sullenly plain, and she herself only ever saw the unattractive features, wildly exaggerating her lack of good looks.

Lutyens's family never lived in the 'little white house' whose plans were in the Casket, a fact which bitterly disappointed Lady Emily, who never ceased to hanker after a life on a small and simple scale. It was Lutyens who insisted on elegance and a certain level of grandeur. 'If I were a Duke,' he had written to her the year they married, 'I should love to take my Emy to live in 29 Bloomsbury Square', a house which had been used as an office by his great predecessor Norman Shaw. In the end he took her there anyway, to a large, light house which had the beautifully proportioned rooms he could not resist – and which required seven servants for its smooth running. From the very first day of their marriage, Lady Emily's hopes for their life together were confounded.

In 29 Bloomsbury Square the children all spent their early years in comfortable, picturesque, privileged conditions, the provision of which absorbed the greater part of Lutyens's income. Their day-to-day existence was in the hands of Nannie Sleath and, from 1911 onwards, the nursery maid Annie, who came, like Nannie herself, from the home for motherless children with fathers in the Guards regiment. (Annie's real name was Constance McKerrow, but in order to avoid confusion with Lady Emily's sister Constance, a regular visitor to the house, she was obliged to change it.)

There were expeditions to Gorringe's toy department, to a drinking-chocolate shop in Bond Street, to the British Museum every Saturday morning under the tutelage of a governess. There was the annual ritual of *Peter Pan* – but Barrie was a friend of the family, and with inside knowledge Betty commented dourly in her diary 'Peter and Wendy too old'.[5] Even less satisfactory was *Chu Chin Chow*; Betty was already passionate in her sympathies, and Lady Emily wrote angrily afterwards, 'One rather disgusting and wholly unnecessary scene in the slave market where the slaves were nearly nude. There was also a scene in the robbers' cave too much for Betty's feelings and I had to take her out till the excitement was past.'

At home, every Wednesday morning the little girls performed physical jerks to a piano accompaniment. Theatrical entertainments from the dressing-up chest were popular, and ballets were choreographed and danced by Ursula and Mary, with Betty as Musical Director. For this role she styled herself 'Milhoff', chosen as 'a good masculine and Germanic name', and was dashed to find it already the property of a Piccadilly cigar importer.

Christmas was usually spent in the grand style at Knebworth House, with its battlements, towers, maze, statues, minstrels' gallery, spiral staircase, haunted room, suits of armour and shades of Bulwer Lytton. The house and title of Earl of Lytton had passed to Victor, Lady Emily's younger brother, and the younger Lutyens children had good friends among their cousins – with the exception of Betty, who was either too old or too young for any of them.

She was far happier at Homewood, the house which Sir Edwin had built on the Knebworth estate for his mother-in-law. Here for the first time, when she was about six, Betty heard music other than the barrel organs and Salvation Army bands in Bloomsbury Square, and when the drawing room was empty she discovered new sounds on the piano.

At least two months of every year were spent at the seaside. These could hardly be described as family holidays, however, because Lutyens never came. Happiest when working, he never really appreciated holidays. He disliked the sea; he and Lady Emily had spent much of their honeymoon at Scheveningen on the Dutch coast (chosen because it was cheap) sitting back to back in high basket chairs, she looking out to sea and he inland. In particular, he detested the desolate east coast which she favoured for its bracing climate. One year at Felixstowe the problem was the cats of which the house smelt; all had fleas, and Lady Emily reported blithely, 'Poor little Betty wriggles about in a most comic manner.' But Betty was well compensated by the cornelians on the beach; all her life one of her favourite pastimes was what she called 'seeking', beachcombing in silence for pebbles, shells, driftwood in strange shapes, and anything else that seemed worth keeping.

This impasse over holidays was just one sign of the increasing strains in her parents' marriage. With the best will in the world – and the affection between Lutyens and Lady Emily never faltered, however profound their misunderstandings – neither was supplying what the other needed.

Lutyens had had visions of a wife who would understand and inspire his work. He seems to have seen Lady Emily's strength of character – her 'high moral fearlessness' – as a resource on which he might draw to give his work 'the serious touch'. But in practice she was ill-equipped to give him the kind of support he demanded. She had virtually no visual sense at all, a fact of which she had been acutely conscious ever since the day when, in an attempt to please him, she had gathered up the loose photographs in his room, stuck them in an album and labelled it carefully 'The Works of Edwin Lutyens'. Tragically, these photographs were far from being the works of Edwin Lutyens – simply odds and ends, advertisements and 'awful warnings' to himself, and Emily, out of love, had given away the fact that in the world where her husband was most completely himself, she had no bearings.

Now, afraid of being 'shown up to your artistic friends', she found it better 'rather brutally perhaps to disclaim all knowledge about your work'. And brutal she sometimes was, as when she informed him that hot-water pipes had been installed for Edith Lytton at Homewood, a building of which he was proud, and that the work had been done clumsily. 'After all, her comfort is more important than the look of the house.'[6] He did try perfunctorily to find a language in which they could discuss architecture. But about his work he was almost completely inarticulate. 'As regards what I design and how I do it, I don't know. It just comes because I want it to, and if it don't I have to grip inside and make or force it and there is no speech that can describe it.' To attempt to crystallise these intuitions might be to destroy them altogether. 'I can think better of things when unsaid and unspoken than the driftwood of words that spoil reflections in the water and blot out the skies therein.'

It did not really matter if his wife failed to share in his work, as long as she helped further it – and here again in his terms she failed him. Lutyens saw cultivating the client as part of the job – 'like stroking a cat to make it purr' – and looked on parties rather as professional engagements. Despite her background, Lady Emily was no happier in the social circles from which Edwin drew his clients than she had been with the Souls, and argued infuriatingly, 'If I don't help you by society touting and planning, it is because it is unworthy of us both, and you know it too in your real moments.'

She had the disregard for appearances of the extremely well-born, the single-mindedness of the natural fanatic, and at times the insensitivity of both; on occasion, title or no, she could be a liability. His friend 'MacSack' (Lady Sackville, mother of Vita Sackville-West) recorded disapprovingly that she 'had absurd little vegetarian meals brought specially for her and looked so bored and McNed [Edwin] anxious and fussed'.[7]

In the first flush of their courtship Lutyens had visualised, how seriously it is hard to tell, a homemaker in the best homespun William Morris tradition. 'Emy to her accounts shall go and write in her nutbrown ledgers the moneys of the day. Peerless mistress; with apron and a bunch of keys that chime of home and honey in the store and to the kitchen where the pots range and glisten in the light.' This Emy was, however, a figment. The woman he had actually married had never needed to learn to cook, nor even instruct someone else what to cook; she did not know how to run a household, and had no desire to learn. *Her* ideal habitation was small, bare and functional – 'everything very clean, easily washed and yet rather stern' – and 29 Bloomsbury Square, for all its Lutyensian grace, met none of these criteria. She enjoyed not a single aspect of keeping house, and her considerable energies were directed elsewhere.

'The beauty that appeals to me,' she wrote defiantly in 1907, 'is moral beauty, moral principles, moral ideals, traits of character,' and her first outlet was the social work she had abandoned when she first met Lutyens. She joined the Moral Education League and organised evening discussion groups on such subjects as 'Heredity versus Environment' – this, she wrote happily, was her idea of 'an interesting and inexpensive social life'. With dazzling optimism, she accompanied her bosom friend 'Pussie', wife of the cricketer A. J. Webbe, on regular visits to the Lock Hospital to read fairy stories to prostitutes suffering from venereal disease. (One wonders sometimes what had happened to her sense of humour. She told Lutyens once that she considered her humour 'really rather superior' to his. 'Mine is of the type of *Cranford*, yours of Mark Twain' – to which he retorted, 'You keep it in airtight compartments: you can lock them up and lose the key, can't you?'[8])

Almost inevitably, given her temperament and the climate of the times, her interest in social issues overflowed into political involvement. She joined Mrs Pankhurst's Women's Social and Political Union, and for one holiday the whole family's swimming was disrupted by efforts to sell the magazine *Votes for Women* on the beach. It was in fact Lady Emily who initially brought into the movement her older sister Constance Lytton, later one of the best known of the suffragettes.

In 1910 Con was jailed for throwing a stone wrapped in paper bearing the slogan 'Votes for Women', but was released as soon as the authorities discovered that she had both a title and a weak heart. Outraged by this condescension, she promptly cut her hair, changed her name to 'Jane Wharton', and threw another stone, this time in Liverpool. Jane Wharton's heart was not tested, and when she was subjected to forcible feeding, she suffered an attack which left her partially paralysed for the rest of her life. Lady Emily was hugely proud of Con (as Elisabeth was later to be), although she herself had left the WSPU in 1909, unable to subscribe to its militant violence.

Lutyens, on the other hand, could perhaps best be described in political terms as a romantic conservative, with a sentimental attachment to the ideals of feudal loyalty and *noblesse oblige*. 'A house with the soul of a Wilton gives me a choke of veneration,' he enthused after a visit there. In reply Lady Emily pointed out with some force that the aristocratic ethos had a darker side, with which she was all too familiar, 'for I lived in it half my life and it is oppressive – difficult to be natural'.

Although she rarely enjoyed her contacts with the lower classes – fellow travellers on trains and boats were invariably 'common' – she liked to think of herself as a socialist, and progressed far enough to be asked to stand as Labour candidate for Luton in 1920. Lutyens found even Lloyd George's Liberals 'a government of super-educated cads', and must have been aggravated as well as disappointed by his wife's response to the news that he had been chosen to design the new Liverpool Cathedral, one of the most prestigious commissions of his career: 'I do wish it had been model dwellings and not a church!'

To many of his friends and admirers, Lady Emily seemed eccentric, dreary and humourless, her activities an embarrassment to a 'good fellow' who deserved better. MacSack commented, 'Emmie shocked me greatly with her Bolshie views about everything. . . . Her gestures were those of a mad woman.' What they failed to understand, because they were not used to thinking in these terms, was that he was falling just as far short of meeting *her* needs.

Above all Lutyens was not offering her the company she had hoped for. To her, intellectual companionship was easily the most important aspect of marriage. She was not physically cold; she told Mary later that she had been a passionate girl, and a significant part of Wilfrid Blunt's attraction for her, though she may not have been conscious of it, was undoubtedly sexual. But she never enjoyed her husband's love-making. When they married, he had had no experience and she no advice except the chilling injunction from her mother never to refuse and always to keep cold cream by the bed. 'Girls . . . are taught that everything is wrong,' she wrote, 'and then suddenly plunged right into the middle of it.' His physical desire was a constant threat, even when she was pregnant, as she so often was, and his advances were all the less appealing because of his incessant pipe-smoking. The intimacy she longed for was of quite a different kind.

But Lutyens shared so few of her interests. Lady Emily was very well-read and delighted in talking about books; the only terms in which she might have been able to discuss his work were literary. But he, largely self-educated, was incurably suspicious of articulacy and the written word. To read poetry, which again she loved, seemed to him positively damaging. Better to avoid it, because then 'you have to get your eventual quota of it through and in your work and not be doped with other folk's adjectives'.

His posture in their relationship was often that of a child, 'little Nedi', lovable, fey, clowning to amuse the 'grown-ups' who had the power to reward or punish him – an abnegation of responsibility which had the advantage of allowing him to concentrate his mental energies on his work. In his youth, to overcome shyness, he had decided to behave like a puppy which rolls on its back and relies on helplessness for its charm: 'I now say whatever comes into my head and hope that no one will kick my round, soft tummy.' The 'Nedi' persona was endearing, and he used it as a social tool, writing what he described as 'ultra Nedi' letters. The technique had some success, particularly with outsiders, who succumbed readily to the patter and the cajoling, the *enfant terrible* routine. But Lady Emily had enough children, and though at the beginning of their courtship she had encouraged his pose – 'my sweetest little boy man' – at heart she wanted to be led. If he could have taken the role of master to her pupil, he could have saved himself a great deal of pain; but in choosing to be child to her mother-figure – she even looked much like his mother – he left the position of master vacant.

In July 1905, a year before Betty's birth, Lady Emily had given him fair warning of the dangers in the way their marriage was developing. 'You always manage to make time for what you *really* want to do – fishing, patience . . . but you have *never* time for me. . . . I just ache and crave for sympathy and understanding, and have it I must – and I want so that you should give it to me – and not let me find it outside my home.'

Lutyens's response is entirely characteristic – 'You must help me and be patient with me and take me by the hand as though I were a little child . . . I can only come to you on my knees and beg you to make me better.' Having effectively transferred the onus back to her again, he concluded, 'All the work in the world would count as nothing whilst you are unhappy and lost to me. . . . I long to get back tonight but have to meet people here tomorrow.'

Paradoxically, it was in the one area where they might have had most in common that they ultimately drew furthest apart. '*Au fond* somewhere,' Lutyens once wrote, 'I am horribly religious.' He believed strongly in absolute values, eternal verities and a notion of divinity, just as Lady Emily did; but he could reach out for them only in his work, where his faith was combined with a formidable intellectual discipline that ruled out all that was vague, mystic and deliberately obscure in religion. Any hint of the occult was anathema – and it was precisely towards this sphere that his wife was being drawn.

Interestingly her spiritual aspirations may have been less 'pure' than his in the sense that they always had a highly personal focus. 'I am one of those people to whom hero worship is the greatest joy of life,' wrote Lady Emily. 'I want to be always at someone's feet.' She had originally been confirmed in her Christian faith by her friendship with the Reverend Whitwell Elwin, an Anglican clergyman almost fifty years her senior with whom she exchanged a remarkable sequence of letters throughout her adolescence. Now she was led to a new spiritual home, the world of Theosophy, by the charismatic figures of Annie Besant, Bishop C. W. Leadbeater and, most compelling of all, Jiddu Krishnamurti. For the twenty years at the heart of her forty-seven-year marriage, throughout the growing-up of her children, Lady Emily, as she had warned she might, turned the focus of her attention away from her family.

Theosophy was one of many creeds heavily tinged with the occult and psychic which blossomed at the end of a determinedly rational and humanistic century. Its fundamental tenet, now as then, is a belief in the universal brotherhood of man, and the essential unity of all religions as different manifestations of the same central Truth. Christianity, for instance, is not denied, but its exclusivity is rejected; it is not the whole truth in itself, but a single facet of a broader faith, which also incorporates elements of Eastern religions.

Within this framework, the role of the individual Theosophist is self-perfection, achieved through a series of incarnations – and it is here that the Theosophy of the late nineteenth century began to take on its occult or 'esoteric' flavour. It was felt that the quickest route to initiation into a higher state of existence was to be chosen by a being who had already achieved perfection and release from *karma* (the universal law, found in Hinduism and Buddhism, by which all men reap inexorably and exactly what they have sown). There was believed to be an extensive occult hicrarchy of such superior beings, but Lady Emily was concerned with only three – the Bodhisattva or Lord Maitreya, and two of the many Masters beneath him. A few Masters chose to remain in human form specifically to assist the evolution of those just entering on the Path. Of these few, two – Morya and Kuthumi – had special responsibility for the Theosophical Society, and it was the latter whose pupil Lady Emily hoped to become.

The procedure was that the aspirant should first be put on 'probation' for an unspecified period, during which time he or she was educated on a higher plane, not directly by the Masters but by an older pupil who claimed to communicate with them on the astral plane. Once sufficient progress had been made, the pupil was 'accepted' by the Master and linked directly with his consciousness. Under his guidance the pupil would then attempt to pass through five successive Initiations to become an *arhat* and be released from *karma*.

Running alongside the creed of the Masters was the belief that at intervals of about two thousand years the Lord Maitreya manifests himself in human form, taking possession of a body specially prepared for this honour, and founding a new religion in order to shape the civilisation and moral heritage of the age. In his two previous manifestations the Lord Maitreya was believed to have taken the bodies of the Hindu religion's Sri Krishna and of Jesus. By 1909 an influential group within the upper echelons of the Society claimed to have discovered that another manifestation was imminent, and that it was to be through the body of Jiddu Krishnamurti, the fourteen-year-old son of an Indian member of the Theosophical Society. Krishna, as his friends called him, was accordingly being prepared for the coming of the Lord Maitreya by the Society's leaders, Mrs Annie Besant and her colleague C. W. Leadbeater.

It was this Messianic element in Theosophy which appealed strongly to Lady Emily. As a child she had had the firm conviction that she would witness the Second Coming, and now as an adult she was offered an opportunity of seeing her dream realised. 'In my early youth I poured out all the devotion of my being on the thought of the Christ, and now the thought, the hope, the belief of His return absorbs me sometimes to the exclusion of everything else.'

Her introduction to the Society, however, came through politics and 'Mrs B.', as Lutyens called her. Annie Besant, who became the President of the Theosophical Society in 1907, had also been a leading campaigner for free-thinking, women's rights, Fabian socialism, birth control and the early trades union movement, and in later years she was to be a most ardent and influential champion of Indian Home Rule. She was an extraordinary, inspiring woman, and it was after reading her books that in 1910 Lady Emily became a Theosophist.

At first, following the faith was simply a matter of attending and, rather to Lutyens's horror, hosting meetings – all talk and Marmite sandwiches. Then, gaining confidence, Lady Emily founded the Central London Lodge of the Society with the aim of applying the principle of the brotherhood of man to the social problems in which she was interested. Gradually she turned herself into an accomplished public speaker on Theosophy, and while her husband was visiting the stately homes of England, she found herself staying with a family of Sweden-borgians in Birkdale, a tailor in Charlton, a geography teacher in Wakefield, and was overwhelmed simultaneously by the kindness of 'ordinary' people and what she described as the fusty atmosphere of doyleys, antimacassars and string fringes, 'none too clean'. Wisely, she reported to Lutyens little of the content of her lectures, but communicated with relish the fact that few northerners seemed to have their own teeth.[9]

At the end of 1910, to recruit her strength, she retired to a health farm for a course of skipping and 'air baths', an English winter version of sunbathing. 'I feel as if I was growing at such a pace I can hardly keep up with myself,' she wrote. Lutyens replied miserably, 'You are not advancing by great leaps and bounds along your new Road and leaving me behind: are you? Don't leave me darling, sweet darling.' But the following year Lady Emily met Krishnamurti, and then there was no turning back.

At the beginning of 1911 a new group, the Order of the Star in the East, was founded in India to draw together those within the Theosophical Society who believed in the imminent coming of the Lord Maitreya. Lady Emily was one of the first to enrol in England, her glowing enthusiasm fanned to flame by her first encounter with the chosen vehicle. In 1911, when Betty was five years old, Krishnamurti arrived in London to study for his Oxford entrance examinations; Lady Emily was on the platform at Charing Cross to meet him.

Over the next fifteen years, her complex relationship with Krishna was to give her much pain as well as pleasure. For his part, he looked to her as a substitute for the mother who had died when he was ten. He and his younger brother Nitya were more familiar figures in the Lutyens nursery between 1911 and 1921 than either Barbie or Robert – a clear indication of Lady Emily's status within the Theosophical Society in England. Annie the nursery maid saw a good deal of them, and seventy years later she remembered, 'He was supposed to be the incarnation of Christ. Well, I took some spots off his coat for him.' Lady Emily, with Mrs Besant, helped him through emotional and spiritual crises to which he was no more immune than any other boy of his age, but for her the relationship was not so simple.

Krishna needed her, as her children needed her, but he was also her teacher and the object of her veneration as the coming Lord. The combination of authority and dependence was intoxicating, and Lady Emily was overwhelmed. 'Krishna became my entire life, and for the next ten years I suffered all the difficulties of trying to sublimate a human love.' This was essentially a romantic, emotional love, not a physical one. Mary, who was closer both to Krishna and to Lady Emily at this time than any of the rest of the family, believes that 'if he had wanted her as a man she would have given herself to him with joy'. But Krishna had a horror of sex, which may in fact have been one of his attractions for Lady Emily. After 1913, she wrote, 'I was never really happy away from Krishna. My husband, my home, my children faded into the background.'

At the same time as their mother's emotional detachment was increasing, the children were seeing very little of their father. In 1912 he was given the biggest commission of his life, the building of New Delhi, and for seventeen years this kept him abroad for at least five months of every year. Then, as his letters show, with their disproportionate amount of space devoted to train times and the handwriting distorted by the swaying and bumping of the carriages in which he was writing, much of his time in England was spent travelling from one building or one potential client to another.

Lutyens could be an enchanting father. Out of the depths of a troubled relationship, his son Robert wrote, 'He hadn't any clear notion of responsibility except towards his work. But it was very heaven for the children of such a man to have their lives infiltrated by the constant flow of fun and nonsense.' It was Robert who remembered his parting gesture as he sailed from Tilbury in the early days of the First World War; solemnly blowing up the lifebelt with which he had been issued for fear of submarine attack, he sent it home with the injunction that if he were torpedoed, his wife and children should stand in reverence while it was deflated, listening to 'Father's last breath'. For Mary, on the day of George V's coronation, he cut crowns out of orange peel; and Betty took particular pleasure in his French irregular verb – 'Je pense, Two pense, Three pence, Pensions, Rendezvous, Restaurant'.

But it was nearly impossible to be consistently close to five children whom he met only in fits and starts and whom he could not help seeing as rivals for such attention as Lady Emily could spare. Too often the fun hardened into a routine; no pun ever bears repeating, and some of his were no more than nervous reflexes. Visiting children noticed a certain lack of appreciation among his family. Betty's cousin Eve Balfour detected a code operating at mealtimes. 'When he made a joke they would put a knife across their drinking glasses, which meant "I've seen the point but I can't be bothered to laugh."'

It was not true, as Lady Emily often alleged, that he had no interest in their upbringing. He worried painfully about the effect which contact with her odder friends might be having on them, and was terrified beyond reason lest any of the girls embark on an affair with an Indian. 'There is one limit,' he wrote, 'beyond which I should prefer death'.[10] But he was aware that their affection for him depended largely on his wife's mediation; and, frank as ever, she told him, 'It is difficult to put you much into our lives when you are never there.'

CHAPTER TWO

One Apart

To GAUGE THE effect of one person's unhappiness on another is always difficult; and it would be over-simplifying to suggest that Elisabeth Lutyens's childhood was clouded and her life shaped by the extraordinary stresses within her parents' marriage. Mary, who grew up in the same situation, denies having been adversely affected by it at all. Children of that class and time were rarely close to their parents in the business of day-to-day living. For the details of washing, dressing, eating, illness, going to school, going to bed, they looked to Nannie for help – and, if they were lucky, she met their emotional needs as well.

To Mary, secure in the love of Nannie Sleath and Annie, whom she felt to be her own particular property, Lady Emily seemed, despite her distance, the perfect mother, ready to share with her children all that was most precious in her own life. 'I never felt that she neglected us or was not there when we wanted her.' As for her father, Mary had always been aware of his preference for Ursula, considered it reasonable, and expected little of him.

But Betty was born a different creature – more volatile, more anxious, subject to greater extremes of rage and grief, and less insular. People were more important to her, and she made greater demands on them – not surprising, then, if her childhood needs, unlike Mary's, went largely unanswered, and if, during the years when her parents' relationship was at its most troubled, Betty was becoming a thoroughly 'difficult' child. Annie, who loved her but saw her clearly, says now, 'It must have been her nervous system.' By the time she was six or seven, she threw regular screaming fits; she also once threw a knife at her mother across the dining table, and tried to brain Mary with a golf club. On Sunday nights, while Nannie was at Evensong, the younger children took turns to go to sleep in her bed; when she came home, the favoured one was lifted back into her own chill sheets, and Nannie climbed into warm ones, invariably finding as she did so a note on her pillow from Betty, begging forgiveness for the day's sins. 'My own darling Nannie and Mummie, I am going to be good to please you too darlings ones, you are such pets, for farth and Annie too.'

It was Betty who always burst her buttons during physical jerks on a Wednesday morning. Getting a decent dress on her, Annie remembered, was always a struggle; and Mary, who loved clothes, could never wear her cast-offs, hopelessly battered. 'If she got anything new, she wore it at once, and ruined it.' Anriette Mallet, daughter of one of Lady Emily's Theosophist friends, always cherished a mental picture of Betty bicycling. She preferred to ride Robert's bicycle, standing on the pedals and zig-zagging, but if thwarted was reduced to her own undersized machine. One afternoon at teatime she disappeared, and was spotted by her father pedalling furiously round Bloomsbury Square in a nun's outfit (used for fancy dress at Knebworth the previous Christmas), singing the Marseillaise. Sent to retrieve her, Lutyens stood in the middle of the square and lit his pipe. 'Nothing could have been more comical than that tiny wild nun whose legs worked incredibly fast, her veil flapping behind her. Her father waved, and each time she extended a jerky arm in return, so intent and indomitable that we were speechless.' [1]

If drama did not exist Betty created it. 'My own darling Mummy,' she wrote from the country, 'I am very sad to say that we have all got the mumps, tell berne [her governess Miss Bernau] that we will not be abell to come back tell 7 weeke. I am to bad to say eny more.' On the back of this letter Nannie had commented severely, 'My Lady, Betty has written this to frighten you, they are much better.' It was Betty's misfortune that she did not get on with Nannie Sleath. The other children loved her, and celebrated the date on which she had first arrived in the family in 1898 – Lutyens called it 'the nannieversary'. But Betty could not relax with her, claiming that they were both too highly strung – even at this age she was acutely aware of her own physical and mental states – and so forfeited the emotional ballast that she provided.

Nor could Betty share the principal nursery treat of being read to. When she was at home, Lady Emily would go up after tea and read out loud for an hour – Dickens, Austen, the Brontës, Thackeray, Bulwer Lytton. Annie used to rush through washing up the tea things to take her seat – but Betty hated being read to, even by her mother. Later she explained this as a rejection of the second-hand experience. At the time she simply disliked seeing the reader's face from underneath, upside down and distorted, and found it next to impossible to sit still, because she suffered badly from growing pains in her legs. So instead she fidgeted in the corner with her fingers in her ears.

As she got older, her main desire was privacy and some territory of her own. Her most successful hideout was to be the cistern cupboard in a downstairs lavatory; she painted the walls glossy black in imitation of her father's colour schemes, laid in supplies of dog biscuits and retired from the fray. 'To this day,' she wrote in her autobiography, 'I find the sound of running water soothing.'

But in 1913, by her seventh birthday, Betty was 'in a dreadful state of nervous irritability', according to her mother. 'Every word spoken by the other children makes her wildly cross.' In Lady Emily's view, the solution was to take her to the healer whom she herself was consulting for colitis and migraine. She described the treatment which he provided:

> I find myself in a large room from which the daylight and noise are shut out. Electric light veiled in transparent alabaster – lovely sprays of white lilac or lilies. I proceed to don white silk pyjamas and a green silk dressing gown and sit wrapped in an eiderdown while he rubs me – the heat from his hands is like a glowing fire.

An experience such as this, she felt, did both her and Betty good. But it could do little for Lady Emily's ailing marriage, which in the following year reached perhaps its lowest ebb.

In 1914 the lease on 29 Bloomsbury Square expired, and the family moved to 31 Bedford Square, a large house, damp to fungus-point, which nobody liked except Mary. She took great delight in the big day nursery with its fine view of the YMCA tower in Tottenham Court Road, and the night nursery overlooking the square, where wounded soldiers from the Front played bowls. The Lutyens night nursery was the inspiration for the one from which the Darling children escape in *Peter Pan*. Below it, somewhat incongruously, was the prayer room which Lutyens had made for his wife, with a floor of dark blue lino and, one of his pet hates, a picture rail, from which depended large photographs of portraits of the Masters. Here, wrapped in the yellow shawl which denoted membership of Mrs Besant's inner circle, Lady Emily sat cross-legged and burned incense before a statue of Buddha. Every day the younger children came to her to recite: 'I am a link in a golden chain of love which stretches round the world, and I promise to keep my link bright and strong.'

Prayers or no, the house had an atmosphere oppressive enough for Lady Emily to feel it needed exorcising. Annie remembered indignantly how she and Nannie came back early with the children from a walk in the park to encounter an 'awful smell' of incense on the stairs, where Lady Emily was swinging a censer, and 'a sort of clergyman with robes and mitre coming upstairs murmuring . . . When he got to our nursery he was dabbing the water all over my furniture . . . He was driving the evil spirits away, but he didn't come over to the staff rooms, so we got them all.'

Thirty-one Bedford Square, to Lady Emily's dismay, was another huge household to run. Money was beginning to worry Lutyens; Lloyd George's 'People's Budget' of 1909, with its steep rise in income tax in the upper brackets and the introduction of death duties, had struck hard at his clientele, and already it contained a higher proportion of the *nouveaux riches* and Liberal politicians he despised. But Lady Emily insisted on a full quota of seven servants. He could not ask her to live in a big house and 'pig it' as his father had done, she argued, her dreams of a 'little white house' dashed again. This was a low blow, and a sign that they were beginning to exhaust each other's patience. Each repeatedly offered to go away – Lady Emily, characteristically, to volunteer herself 'at the Front in some capacity'.

Then in September 1914 she formalised the growing gulf between them by declaring an end to their sexual relationship. Just one year after their marriage she had warned him that she was not happy in this side of their love. Thirteen years and five children later, in 1911, she spelled out her message:

> Remember that I married you, loving you and wanting you physically as much as you wanted me, every bit. . . . You can't believe the nightmare the thought of my honeymoon is to me. . . . I was in constant and unceasing pain and discomfort and you never left me alone. We tramped about all day sightseeing when I ought to have rested and at night I lay beside you crying with pain, weariness and disappointment.

Now she was hoping to be 'accepted' as a disciple of the Master Kuthumi, a step which required complete purity, and this gave her the excuse she needed. A terrible exchange of letters followed.

> I have done my duty to you and my country as regards children. . . . I believe and hold firmly that a woman has the right over her own body. Where she gives it willingly the relationship is beautiful – where she gives it because she *must* it becomes prostitution whether in or out of

marriage. . . . Shall it cease now while I love you dearly or will it continue till my love for you is dead?

A week later she added, 'How you could ever have found pleasure in what you knew I hated. . . .' He replied in anger and agony,

How could I all this time do those things you hate and loathe? How could you, darling, be intimate and petting with the Krishnaji party. . . . How I have hated the large photographs, the constant chuckle at my discomfiture when what I hated was introduced into my house and home. I think the plane – if true – on which you and others occupy each other's minds and bodies is just as immoral – to me nauseous and horrid – as anything else. . . . Heaven knows where . . . your absorbing 'follies' will lead you. Further from, not back to me.

Besides the physical frustration, Lutyens was deeply distressed by the cloud which his wife's gesture threw on their past life together, and he could no longer bear to recall even the happy times. Though he was prepared, for appearance's sake, to get in beside Lady Emily on Christmas morning when the children brought their presents to be opened, he could no longer bring himself to share a bed where he could expect only 'a child's kiss and the grateful warmth of a Nannie', and he had a room prepared for him on the first floor, where he did not have to look at the Casket. Now he hardly ever went up to the bedroom floors, and this meant he saw even less of Betty and Mary, who were still in the nursery, not yet promoted to the drawing room.

Still he persevered with his marriage. Mary believes that had he put his foot down about Lady Emily's involvement in Theosophy, by this time she would have left him, and perhaps he sensed it too. But in 1916 it seems to have been he who was contemplating separation, driven to it when what had been a private emotional problem became a threat to his professional life. Four years into his work on New Delhi, with negotiations over the budget at a delicate stage, Lady Emily originated the English Home Rule League in order to campaign for Dominion status for India. Even Mrs Besant considered this tactless; and Lutyens wrote, 'Your politics, religious and educational, have beaten me. . . . If my wishes and principles as regards our children are ignored – then I must make some arrangement towards finality.'

By this time the ten-year-old Betty had gone away to school – the only one of the children to do so. Up until then, while Barbie and Robert had gone to King Alfred's, Hampstead (a Montessori school and one of the first coeducational schools in England), Ursie, Betty and Mary, still in the nursery, had shared a governess, Miss Bernau. The curriculum that 'Bernie' administered has a strong flavour both of her personality and of the time. In the first weeks of the First World War, when Betty was eight and a half, she was preoccupied with Natural History – 'Inmates of my House and Garden'; Picture Study – Titian and Tintoretto, sticking black-and-white postcard reproductions into an album; Geography – 'The World: Shape, etc.'; and Repetition – 'Ye Mariners of England'. The war was not ignored: besides 'Grecian Exercises and Breathing', Drill included 'Marching', at which Betty was particularly good, and Handicrafts for the term comprised a knitted scarf for the soldiers. Her conduct report was 'much improved', with one qualification – 'She talks too much.' [2]

As the war extended past Christmas, the patriotic temperature of lessons rose. Betty was reciting 'Rule Britannia', 'Hearts of Oak' and 'The Charge of the Light Brigade', and reading *The Life of Lord Roberts*. And by the summer of 1915 the unfortunate soldiers were destined to receive a handicraft bag, while she was singing 'The British Grenadiers' and learning to drill with the rifle and light pole.

After a brief experimental stay at King Alfred's, learning 'to express myself in clay', as she scornfully put it, Betty went in 1916 to Worcester Park School, Westgate on Sea, Kent. Worcester Park was a small, select establishment with no more than sixteen or seventeen pupils and a wide range of 'activities' other than education. Betty always claimed she had been packed off to boarding school, an 'adoring victim' of some educational theory of her mother's. As Mary remembers it, she urgently wanted to go, despite Lutyens's determination that none of the girls should go away. Certainly, removed from the competition of the nursery and armed with her white Pekinese, Kamu, she very much enjoyed this period as an orthodox schoolgirl.

Her life was undoubtedly made easier by her mother's title. At home Betty had been, like the other children, a fairly strict vegetarian (though eggs were permitted on the grounds that this was birth control rather than murder); she was allowed to stick to this diet at school, and was even informed by the headmistress that she recovered from illness quickly 'because my blood was so pure being a Vegetarian'. She was granted immunity from having her letters home read; and sixty years later the music mistress at Worcester Park revealed that all the staff had been warned against scolding her, as

you had been at a Montessori school previously, and were not to be corrected for a month to give you time to adjust yourself to English discipline. . . . You were the first pupil to whom I taught Walter Carroll's 'Farm Scenes', and I can see you now in the little music room next to Miss Walsh's study, struggling with them. I was a bit nonplussed when you made a mistake and said 'Oh my God'.[3]

In fact Betty discovered that routine and discipline suited her. In tennis and hockey, and what she described as 'dulcrows' (Dalcroze exercises), she found an outlet for her restless energy. Getting into the hockey team gave her intense pleasure at the time, though she was later to disparage this achievement by pointing out that there were eleven players in a hockey team and only seventeen girls in the school – and two of them crippled.

She did not excel in lessons but was not shamed, and was able to devote much of her time to her own writing, which she enjoyed. Barbie was favoured with an early poetic effort – 'The Lion, the Lion he dwells in the waste. He has a big head and a very small waist.' Lady Emily received a more ambitious play, entitled 'Captain Riddly's Reward', in which Betty, as the Captain, is captured by the enemy but refuses to become a slave. 'So I sing Rule Brittania etc. and dive away risking live [sic] because the sharks are in the sea and so I get the VC.' In another intriguing fragment, the cast list features Prince Joshua, Robin Hood and the villain of the piece, Lord Homo, whose dialogue curiously resembles that of Good King Wenceslas.

She threw herself with relish into all the school's extra-curricular activities. For the 'topsy-turva [sic] dance', a regular event, the pupils dressed as grown-ups and the teachers as little girls; less peculiar was the fancy-dress ball which Betty graced as Peter Pan. 'I was dressed in a little brown pair of nickers and a brown coat and a pair of brown stockings that came write up my legs over my nickers and I had my hair cliped with a little horn.' The other girls came as Shylock, Bluebeard, Shock-Headed Peter, 'Fry Tuck' and 'Knight of Auther', the teachers, with less verve, as Red Cross nurses.

She took a keen interest in magic-lantern shows – 'about Microbes how they get about to get inside people. . . . Microbes live in Durt'. Later it was Digestion – 'When ever our electric bell of nature rings we should never wait. We can only eat as much as our power can turn into blood. If we eat more . . . our food gets stuck in our bowels and results in an operation. It all depends if we thoroughly chew our food.'[4] Not surprisingly, as a Girl Guide she was anxious to do 'Domestic and

Hygean', but she was also skilled in Morse and semaphore and, Miss Bernau's patriotic efforts bearing fruit, revelled in drilling her patrol.

It is symptomatic of her attitude to herself and her past that Betty later described the schoolgirl she was as 'plain, unpopular and a nailbiter'. Neither her letters home nor her teachers' reports suggest anything other than an orderly and conventional school career. The discipline and routine of school life seem to have put paid to the temper tantrums. But back at home nothing had changed, and in the summer of 1918, Lady Emily wrote anxiously to her husband,

> Betty seems so much one apart – and to have no place at home and she feels it very much – and gets to feel lonely and depressed which is bad for her – and increases the morbid self-consciousness which is her curse. She is very devoted to me and clings to me – but I wish she got on better with the others. . . . She is a sweet little girl and more unselfish and helpful than all the others put together.

But it was the others who were absorbing most of Lady Emily's attention by 1920 when Betty, now fourteen, exercised her option to leave Worcester Park. Barbie had been a member of the Voluntary Aid Detachment during the war in the Charles Street Hospital for the War Wounded run by her aunt Pamela, Countess of Lytton, and then a hugely successful débutante. She was very much embarrassed by her mother's eccentricities, and resented the economies that were increasingly necessary in the Lutyens household.

'We never seem to know where we are,' Lady Emily had complained in 1917, 'and we jump from poverty to wealth in a most disconcerting manner.' In 1917 and 1918, when no work was done on Delhi, Lutyens's income had dwindled accordingly, while he spent much of his time working for the War Graves Commission, largely unpaid. Lady Emily campaigned ceaselessly for a smaller house, and in 1918 31 Bedford Square, much to everyone's relief, was sold – but Lutyens promptly succumbed to a beautiful Adam house, 13 Mansfield Street, which was even larger and employed even more servants.

Despite his eminence – he was knighted in the New Year's Honours List of 1919 – over the next few years his finances became ever more precarious. His overdraft at times reached £6000, a colossal sum for the 1920s, and in his anxiety he could be quite sharp with his wife. 'I don't think you a bit realise what a struggle for life is and means. . . . I saw father's profession fail him and fortune vanish at the same time.' Cecil Baring's daughter Daphne, to whom he was 'Uncle Ned', noted that he spent nothing on himself; his suits were shiny, his hands grimy, and he cut his own hair. 'He once demonstrated the procedure to us; he would twist a strand of his curly hair into a tight little rope and chop it off with nail-scissors.'[5]

Barbie suggested that cooks were chosen during this period of austerity immediately before and after the end of the war on the basis of their culinary skills in a previous incarnation. She tried to change the oak refectory table for mahogany, and the brass pestle and mortar which acted as a centrepiece for a shallow bowl of water with flowers floating on the surface, in line with current fashion. Cheese, which constituted a major part of everyone's meals except Sir Edwin's, was to be cut into comely slices and handed round in a triangular bowl, not left on a board on the table. Throughout her campaign for gracious living she was rude and disobedient, living a far more riotous social life than her father could condone or afford; and Lady Emily was thoroughly relieved when in 1920 she married Euan Wallace, a Captain in the Life Guards with two small sons by his first wife, Idina, daughter of Muriel, Countess De La Warr. (Euan was kind, rich and respectable, Idina less so; the model for 'the Bolter' in Nancy Mitford's *The Pursuit of Love*, she was eventually to have six husbands, one of them Lord Erroll, who was murdered in the 'White Mischief' scandal in Kenya.)

At the same time Robert was making a match which Sir Edwin at least found far less acceptable. Robert's adolescence had been difficult. The freedom of King Alfred's had not really suited his insecurity, and had not prepared him academically for Cambridge, which he entered without examination as an ex-serviceman. (He had falsified his age to serve as a cook on a mine-sweeper, precisely with a view to getting exemption from university entrance.) Unable to cope with the work, he spent most of his time and his allowance on drink, smoking and gambling, true to his namesake Robert Lytton, who had greatly annoyed Bulwer Lytton by doing much the same. Almost worse, in Lady Emily's view, he took to studying psychoanalysis and reading Russian novels, with the result that he informed his mother he was 'a degenerate and super-sexed'. Of one of his literary choices she protested, 'It is not a wholesome book and neither do I think it true of England – tho it may be of Russia. I do not believe that every man looks at every girl only to imagine her naked and himself raping her.'

In 1920 Robert fell in love with Eva Lubryjinska, a niece of Chaim Weizmann, who was to become the first president of the state of Israel. Sir Edwin disliked almost everything about her. She was a research chemist, seven years older than Robert, with red nails, high heels, a pronounced wiggle, an unpronounceable name which she insisted on writing cummings-style entirely in the lower case, and a Polish accent. Sir Edwin refused to give his permission for their engagement and threatened to make Robert a ward of court, whereupon the couple promptly eloped. Amidst all the excitement, there was little attention to spare for Betty.

Against this background – out of a web of family rivalries, ambitions, jealousies and prejudices – Betty's music grew. She was impelled, at the start at least, less by an obvious natural talent or irresistible urge towards music than by the need to attract attention and press her claim for affection and admiration. Mary has always felt that Betty wanted to be different, Betty insisted that she simply wanted to fit in. In a sense both statements are true: she wanted to distinguish herself, and so establish her place within a talented family. To do it, she felt she had to turn to a *métier* where she would have neither the 'visual' Lutyens family nor the literary Lyttons looking over her shoulder – another version of the retreat to the cistern cupboard and the longing for territory. All her life she was to be reluctant to compete.

Yet her family background was not quite the musical desert she was later to suggest. One of Sir Edwin's sisters was a professional pianist, and Lady Emily's sister Con, a grand-pupil of Clara Schumann, could also have been, in the days before she entered the suffragette movement, had she not been obliged to help her mother with her social duties as the wife of an ambassador. (Lady Emily's father Robert Lytton ended his diplomatic career as British Ambassador to Paris in the 1880s.) Lady Emily herself played the guitar, though this was no more than a parlour accomplishment, and Sir Edwin liked to sing (even if he claimed to know only two tunes, 'God Save the Weasel' and 'Pop Goes the Queen'). Barbie played the cello, which for some reason she called 'Thomas'. More significantly, Robert had real musical talent, and could play fluently by ear; he played both piano and violin well, and had a harmonium in his bedroom with which, in his words, he 'made a fine art of monotony'.

This was not, however, a 'musical family' like those of Betty's near-contemporaries Benjamin Britten or William Walton, where music was recognised as a profession as well as a principal source of entertainment, and there was unquestionably an element of defiance in her choice. 'I became involved in something the family neither knew of nor cared for,' she wrote, 'so that no one could spoil it for me.' There was also a more positive incentive. She loved and admired her aunt Con for her humour, courage, radical politics and romantic past, and, perhaps more, for the fact that Con was the only person to single her out for special affection and interest. Con encouraged her in the first little pieces she wrote, and this was a greater spur than almost anything else could have been.

The family myth was that Betty's music started when she was encouraged at seven or eight to learn the violin as an antidote to nailbiting. Robert had already begun lessons, and she inherited both his miniature fiddle and, in the school holidays, his teacher. Marie Motto was a good violinist, with a quartet in which Frank Bridge played the viola. She was a plump, prim woman whose Italian descent was perhaps reflected in her clothes; Betty described them unkindly as 'artistic', 'of the black cape variety'. Lessons were held in a room which had something of the atmosphere of a monk's cell – empty of furniture except for piano, music stand and a beautifully polished table with a bowl of fruit. 'Every lesson was as quiet and difficult as a prayer.'

Miss Motto played Betty the Bach violin partitas, which impressed her deeply; and by going to the quartet's concerts over the years, she gradually became familiar with the classical repertoire. The only problem was her teacher's fondness for Robert. 'I always feel,' wrote Betty, 'that Miss Motto resents my going [to the concerts] when she loves Robert so.' In the struggle to be taken seriously in her music, she found her main obstacle to be constant comparison with Robert – the very thing she had hoped to avoid in her choice of calling. Robert, who was said to have perfect pitch; Robert, who had been presented to Paderewski at Edward VII's funeral, to be told that he had a pianist's hands. 'It is indeed possible,' he wrote stuffily and sadly in later years, 'that such casual condescensions, among other things, did something to foster the conviction – or more precisely, the implicit understanding, as it were – that I was selected for a special destiny.'

'Robert thinks me a fanatic,' Betty wrote furiously to her mother in 1922. 'Everyone thinks I'm frightfully unmusical. It seems hard that Robert who is settled in life [he was to be a journalist] ... should try to take away my one joy and hope and *life* in life. He thinks it is a phase of a "silly girl of 15". But I will prove to the contrary. He has talent, ear and passion for music – far more talent and ear than I, as he says, but for all that I do not think him musical.'

By this time she was also learning the piano, with Polyxena Fletcher, a friend of Miss Motto but a different and more congenial personality – volatile, emotional, enthusiastic, with a visible sense of humour which Betty seems to have preferred to monastic austerity. These lessons were as much talk as teaching, ranging over the whole history of music and its practice, and Miss Fletcher soon became a major influence in Betty's life, the yardstick for all new musical and intellectual experience. She was going to concerts quite often now, usually with Annie, whose father had been a drum-major in the Guards; they went regularly to the Proms and other performances at the Queen's Hall, standing in the gods so that they could see the conductor's face, and here Betty encountered orchestral music in performance for the first time.

Unfortunately, Betty played the piano badly, and always would, but with Miss Fletcher's encouragement her efforts at composition took root. Her scope was not over-ambitious. Unlike Britten, who at the age of twelve was writing an overture in B flat minor for full orchestra which ran to ninety-one pages, she confined herself to solos for violin and piano, with the occasional duet – minuets, gavottes, and once a Morris dance for the flute. At sixteen, however, she was working on a ballet, and her mind was made up. There was a certain resistance to her music in the house; Nannie thought it unladylike to practise so furiously, and the other children simply resented the noise. 'It is hard on her,' wrote Lady Emily, 'having to practise with every one cursing her.' But Betty was unmoved. 'I know that later anyhow I can compose and I'm willing to work oh so hard for it.'

CHAPTER THREE

Fighting for the Faith

BETTY WAS GOING to have to fight harder than she knew for the sake of her music, but her most dangerous antagonists were not her family but conflicting desires within herself. She was now sixteen, and the 'difficult' child was turning into an anxious, intense adolescent who saw in her own earnestness a tool with which to attract the attention of her mother, and accordingly gave it full rein, at the cost of her health and happiness. Had it had a single focus, had she been able to concentrate her mental and emotional energies on her music, she might have been safe, might even have developed faster than she did. But the natural intensity of her temperament found two outlets – not just composition, which was to some extent an effort of will, but also an instinctive and fervent religious enthusiasm. Her adolescent years became a misery because of her tendency to confuse the two, and in the process her music only narrowly escaped being submerged.

In retrospect Betty's sympathies in the battle between her parents were with her father, yet at the time it was Lady Emily's approval she craved. She was confronted with a mother who was able to write, 'Had he [Krishna] called me to give up everything and follow him into the wilderness, I would have done so unhesitatingly; it was, I think, what I was really longing for.' Threatened, however indirectly, with being abandoned, Betty set out to explore and develop the elements in herself she felt to be most like Lady Emily, twisting and forcing her own instincts and interests into the mould of her mother's obsession, in a pathetic attempt to anchor her at home.

Betty's letters between 1922 and 1926 illuminate her total inability to do anything by halves. They show her lurching from one enthusiasm to another – God, music, nature, Theosophy, dogs – looking for a secure foothold. Throughout this time she was trying to make sense of the Theosophical beliefs which, slowly but surely, Lady Emily had been transmitting, and reconcile them with the Christianity in which she had originally been brought up.

'I used to make such a friend of "my" God when I was at school,' she wrote. 'No one can understand what he was to me – terribly personally mine.' Her mother might have understood: as a girl, under the tutelage of Whitwell Elwin, Lady Emily had herself evolved a fervent, intimate Christian piety. But while she had not needed to reject that faith, because of the all-inclusiveness of Theosophy, gradually it had been overlaid by the more esoteric Theosophical doctrines. Her reverence for Krishna could not simply be substituted for her worship of Christ without some change of ethos and emphasis – and now the same was happening to Betty.

While she was away at school, she did her best at Lady Emily's suggestion to keep in daily contact with home through 'thought forms'. Theosophists believed that, with sufficient focus and concentration, thoughts could be transmitted from one mind to another on the astral plane. Betty, in moments of homesickness, took great comfort in what she felt to be the forms of love and reassurance that her mother was sending her, and every night in bed she would try to return them, if sleep did not overcome her first. (The receiver did not have to be consciously attuned; shortly after Dr Crippen's arrest, Lady Emily consoled Barbie, overcome by compassion, with the thought that they could send him uplifting forms.)[1]

Lady Emily had told Betty of the Coming of the Lord Maitreya, and Betty produced her own version of it in a little hand-made book entitled 'The Teachings of Theosophy by A. E. Lutyens'.[2] Inscribed firmly on the flyleaf, 'This book is for the purpose of teaching, not for pleasure', the teachings relate how 'Jesus was like a match and the world the wick of a candle. . . . The wick of the candle (the world) was of no use to anyone till the match (Jesus) came and lit the wick and made a light, and when the light dies out . . . another match will come again.' By 1922, although she would soon be confirmed in the Church of England, she was calling herself a Theosophist.

What she found lacking in the new faith, however, was the personal contact with the divine. The Theosophists' Great Being was an impersonal deity; and Krishna could not supply an emotional focus as he did for Lady Emily, because to Betty he was still just a friend from the nursery. Instead of the intimate conversation with God which had given her such pleasure at school, she now made music her 'path to God', a means of exploring her spiritual feelings and 'realising' the divine, whatever form it took.

'Beethoven considered all his works not as an expression of himself but as a divine revelation and I am sure it is so. . . . The language and art of Music . . . I think is that world or atmosphere which one reaches by meditation and which I feel I see on the Buddha's face.' The other arts are 'but an expression . . . outward signs of invisible things but to me at any rate Music is the invisible things themselves. . . . Now I could yell with joy and I feel that God is so near I long to sing. . . . I feel as a lark singing – up – up – up – nothing to stop.' 'I am such a crank – such a crank,' she wrote, staking her claim to kinship with her mother. 'Shake hands darling. For I am now considered a real crank still being a vegetarian and with my music.'

This quasi-religious approach to music stayed with her during the first six months of 1923, which she spent in Paris. Her stay there was not the usual 'finishing' process for young ladies; in theory she had already undergone this in 1920 at Miss Wolff's Academy in South Audley Street, where she observed with scornful incredulity the preparations for 'coming out', and won a volume of Charles Lamb for an essay on moral courage – useful preparation, perhaps, for the moment when she informed her parents that she wanted to go abroad to study music instead.

In her autobiography she made it sound as if she had had to wage a war of attrition, and depicted herself playing the violin outside Lady Emily's door at dawn as a negotiating ploy. All her life she thrived on opposition; but in this case it hardly existed – surprisingly perhaps, in view of her age and upbringing. Sir Edwin had been quick to squash Ursula's less daring proposal to study in London as a dancer. Instead, Lady Emily wrote wearily at the end of 1922, 'Betty and Ursula had a good old quarrel. They so much dislike each other and it is a bore. I think it will be good for Betty now to get away.' And when she succeeded in finding somewhere for Betty to stay, she was triumphant. 'It is such a marvellous chance for Betty to be right in the heart of French life. I believe she is going to make something big of her music – and this will give her the needed opportunity.'

Betty was to stay at 85 rue la Fontaine, Auteuil, near the Bois de Boulogne, with the young composer Marcelle de Manziarly – one reason, perhaps, for Lady Emily's enthusiasm, because 'Mar', as she was known then, was the daughter of a prominent member of the Theosophical Society, and a devotee of Krishna. She was also an early pupil of Nadia Boulanger, and a published composer – a feat Betty regarded with awe.

Betty went twice a week to the Ecole Normale for instruction in harmony, counterpoint and solfège, subjects that were all new to her. The grounding was thorough, if uninspiring. 'All the rules make me feel – My God – what *is* allowed!', she complained to her mother, 'but till you know all the rules made and approved of by many great musicians then only can you know what rules are best broken for your special expression.' She supplemented the theory with long talks to Mar about music and the musical profession, grateful and proud to be treated as an equal.

Paris in 1923, as Betty liked to emphasise in later years, was the Paris of Picasso, Braque and Juan Gris, of Stravinsky and the other Russian emigrés. But in fact whatever she later claimed, she saw little of it, as she was chaperoned, even while staying with Mar, ironically by a Russian lady of middle years with a sentimental disposition and a limp. 'The maid left her on a seat when a baby,' reported Betty unsympathetically, 'and someone sat on her.' Mademoiselle Janetska irritated Betty fearfully by trailing her round Paris gazing fondly and holding her hand at the least provocation. She also insisted upon tidying the chaos of books, music, a bust of Beethoven, and innumerable shoes which was Betty's room.

But in April 1923 Betty had to move out, taking Beethoven with her. She was now boarded with a Russian widow and two grown-up sons at 3 rue Théodore Banville, Wagram, and she began to enjoy Paris less. The two sons, in their early twenties, made her acutely self-conscious. 'I wish I wasn't so shy,' she wrote, 'especially in French. In English as long as I talk or make puns I don't notice my shyness. It's more difficult in French' (though Sir Edwin had provided her with at least one French pun, of a sort – *'Barley-vous français? Wheat, wheat'*). The impact she made on the evening she wore her first evening dress of dull blue and silver satin was marred for her by the frequency with which she dropped her handkerchief, a large square of red and white polka dots.

Romantic to the core, she would have loved to have had looks to match. Mary remembers her, in fact, as very pretty at this time, looking suddenly grown-up. But in her own eyes, compared with Barbie and Ursie (who was soon to make an excellent marriage to the third Viscount Ridley) she was irredeemably the ugly sister. At school she had had to wear glasses for reading, and was much troubled by spots. Above all she was painfully sensitive about her nose, a particularly pronounced version of the Lytton profile; as a child her best party trick was to touch the end of it with the tip of her tongue. Useless for Mary to point out that she could only do this because of the shortness of her upper lip, a highly desirable feature; to Betty the nose seemed to her to grow out of proportion to the rest of her face, and the best she could do was make nervous little jokes about elephants and fellow-feeling.

She also suffered agonies of embarrassment over an ailment which was to plague her until she was at least eighteen, adding a great deal of anguish to an already difficult adolescence. Whether it was caused by anxiety and emotional disturbance, or a physical weakness aggravated by cold weather, she often found herself wetting the bed. She herself was inclined to see it as an emotional problem. 'There is I am sure some disturbance of which I am unconscious. I am always thinking of music and I think sometimes I get worried and think in bed, which is not good.'

Either way she found the affliction almost impossible to bear. 'I don't care what you arrange,' she burst out when she was thirteen, 'as long as I'm released from this filthy curse and can be like the rest. I don't seem ever to get rid of it and I shudder whenever I think of it – and it seems so dirty – how can one ever be clean in mind living in a dirty body?' Neither electric treatments nor the Coué method of self-help – repeating 'Every day in every way I am becoming better and better' – had any effect whatsoever. It had always made going away for the weekend a torment; and now to her horror she found that her hostess had, without comment, put a macintosh sheet under her bed. So great was her misery, she was even glad to be visited by Ursula who, at her best in a crisis, was kind and funny and took her out to buy a hat.

Humiliation may account for the near-hysteria of a tirade she launched against the Russian widow. This lady had suggested that Betty lacked sophistication and an *intelligence ouverte*, and should not have been allowed to specialise in music so early. Never one to accept criticism gracefully, Betty exploded, 'I dream I get mad with joy or pain – am very nervous and queer . . . I couldn't see *her* go mad with the beauty of a dark sky. . . . She thinks of music as a charming, interesting thing, not as a thing enormous with a fire and strength.'

In spite of everything, Betty brought a great deal away from Paris with her. She had had her first taste of falling in love – an attachment which would last for years and, though unrequited and intermittently painful, made her feel romantic, French, worldly. Early in 1923 she was introduced to the family of the painter Charlot Geoffroy-Dechaume, the greatest friend of her uncle Neville Lytton – a meeting which transformed her social life in Paris. Charlot's daughter Anne, later Lady Glock, was to be Betty's lifelong friend; and his son Antoine – in Betty's words, 'extremely beautiful' – was her first love.

Antoine Geoffroy was, and is, a composer and organist, and Betty's feelings for him fuelled her ardour for music, which by the time she left Paris looked set to become her ruling passion. Marcelle had taken her to concerts of new music, introduced her to several composers, and given her the run of her own library. It was at Mar's that Betty had come across a photograph of Stravinsky for the first time – 'a face like a very piercing Dachshund with glasses . . . and a squint' – and read an account of his style, which she said 'gave me an idea of modern rhythm'.

She had also, more crucially, encountered the music of Debussy, the first composer seriously to influence her work. Cecil Gray has pointed out that Debussy embodies feelings everyone has experienced when young. 'It is impossible to forget those early days of our youth when he seemed to represent our innermost and dearest ideals, to express our most intimate thoughts and most personal experiences.'[3] For Betty it meant the evoking of a new musical atmosphere. 'I went after tea to Mar's piano and read some of Debussy's *Pelleas and Melisande*,' she told her mother, 'and improvised on the excitement with pink cheeks in the dark . . . I got several themes for the quartet I'm writing. They are probably effused [sic] with my excitement over the Debussy, but I don't mind – it is a lesson to try.'

At sixteen Betty was over-emotional, incoherent, often comic in her earnestness. 'It makes me hot to think how thick and vulgar I used to be,' she wrote solemnly. But in the midst of the effusions was a genuine passion for music and the sense of a vocation. Later in her life she was to claim that she had no natural musical talent, that her music was purely the result of an effort of will, but this was in a sense a betrayal, a selling-short of her sixteen-year-old self. 'What music has given me is extraordinary,' she wrote in 1923. 'I know as well as I know anything that my work here is music. It was only last night that I fully realised that I was to have a special message to give.'

Ever since those violin lessons with Miss Motto had been 'as quiet and difficult as a prayer', Betty's music had been almost a religion to her. In music she found a way to express her inchoate ideas about God – and the resulting exaltation itself buoyed up the music. In Paris musical aspirations and spiritual energy seemed to run together and reinforce each other, so that it was unnecessary to distinguish them. But after she left in the summer of 1923, it was only a matter of weeks before the claims of religion, in the form of Theosophy, became too pressing to be reconciled with music, and threatened instead to stifle 'the lark singing'.

While Betty had been battling to understand, Lady Emily's commitment to Theosophy had been escalating steeply, reaching a peak in 1921 with her first visit to India, the Society's spiritual home and the birthplace of Krishna. Sir Edwin, preoccupied with the need to keep in with officialdom in order to see his plans for New Delhi fulfilled, was in an agony of apprehension lest his wife 'suddenly thought it right or comfortable to wear vegetable sandals and your hair down'. He knew only too well that she was prone to denounce the colonial administration which her father had headed as 'the relic of prehistoric barbarism', adding for good measure that General Dyer, author of the Amritsar massacre, should be shot.

His fears were entirely justified. For Lady Emily the real India was one Sir Edwin never saw, and on arrival she spent only a few days with him before leaving to join Mrs Besant in Benares, sleeping on station platforms, sitting cross-legged, eating Indian food. Another brief period behaving herself in Delhi, and she was off to the Theosophical Society's headquarters at Adyar on the Coromandel coast, the place where she was perhaps happier than anywhere else on earth.

In 1922 Lady Emily had finally been 'accepted' as a pupil of the Master Kuthumi, and she was anxious to share her happiness with her children. Barbie and Robert, though full of spiritual potential according to the Theosophist leaders, had outgrown it, and Ursula was too sensitive to her father's feelings. But little by little, Betty and Mary had gradually been offered and had absorbed ever more Theosophical doctrine, and for the next few years they were to accompany Lady Emily on her Theosophical travels all over the world.

In the summer of 1923 all three went to join Krishna and his younger brother Nitya at Ehrwald in the Austrian Tyrol, where Krishna was to undergo the painful preparation of his body to receive the Lord Maitreya. For his disciples it was a time of swimming, sunbathing, forest picnics and simply being close to him. With all this Betty tried to combine her music, to consolidate the discoveries she had made in Paris. She irritated her mother by lugging round a tin trunk full of music, and unearthing a German professor to give her lessons. But already she had a despairing sense of relinquishing music to Theosophy; she wrote later, 'I gave up the joys of creating to It, though I hoped to create under Its orders.'

Back in London she made another, near-disastrous attempt to reconcile her two enthusiasms by going for private composition lessons to John Foulds. Foulds, born in 1880, made his living for many years as a cellist in the Hallé Orchestra, but he also composed. He shared many of the philosophical ideas of Scriabin, and cultivated an interest in Indian music.[4] When Betty first met him, his most famous piece, the *World Requiem*, was about to be given its first performance. It was an enormous two-hour work commemorating the war dead of all nations, in a mixture of Biblical texts, passages from *The Pilgrim's Progress* and Hindu poetry, which was mounted that autumn of 1923 by the British Legion as the centrepiece of the Festival of Remembrance.

Foulds was an unusual and interesting musician, and his preoccupations may have had an indirect influence on some of Betty's later work. He was fascinated, as she was later to be, by the relationship between music and other forms of expression – painting and the spoken word in particular. But he was also a Theosophist, and his teaching was heavily tainted with 'spiritual' dogma. At this point Betty was finding it hard enough to use and develop what she had learned about music in Paris – he told her that she was creative but had neither technique nor 'Innitiative' (her expression). Trying simultaneously to assimilate esoteric Theosophical concepts was more than she could handle.

She had left school at fourteen, after an education which was perhaps stronger on social accomplishments than rigour of thought. It is revealing to compare her intellectual development with her mother's, let alone with that of a male contemporary receiving a full-blown public school education – Cyril Connolly or Anthony Powell, say. She had read neither as widely nor as ambitiously; she had no guiding influence, like the Reverend Whitwell Elwin or an Eton beak; she had not been trained to think clearly or objectively. To expect her to be able to progress in one bound from Dalcroze, nature study and *Black Beauty* to theology and metaphysics was unreasonable, and her incoherent, emotional, repetitious efforts to formulate a personal creed make pathetic reading. 'These then are my mad wanderings,' she wrote hopelessly to Lady Emily. 'I have been looking at books to help me – I think that probably I am wide of the mark.'

Throughout that winter of 1923, the seventeen-year-old Betty was much alone. Lady Emily, Ursie and Mary were all in India, Barbie and Robert married, and Sir Edwin travelling. 'I feel too *inside*,' Betty wrote, 'rather like living on the moon alone. . . . It would be a rest to see someone [sic] of you.' Even allowing for her tendency to self-dramatise, it was a time of miserable unhappiness.

Following the path of Theosophy – and by this time Betty seems to have been tackling the fully fledged doctrine of the Masters – entailed a degree of self-examination that had the worst effect possible on what ten years before Lady Emily had called 'the morbid self-consciousness that is her curse'. Foulds was primarily interested in the occult side of Theosophy. His stated aim as a composer was to 'transcribe in physical-plane terms . . . the variety and glory that may be contacted in the inner realms of man's consciousness',[5] and he spent much of his time trying to 'bring through' musical messages from the higher plane. In her autobiography Betty's misrepresentation of this process as one of taking musical dictation from St Michael is very entertaining, but there was nothing funny about the way in which, under his influence, she strained to become psychic.

Sir Edwin, who despite himself believed in the existence of psychic forces and was very afraid of them, once wrote, 'I would rather a child of mine went tigershooting on foot than dabble with brain magnetism.' But he seems to have been unable to help Betty now, and at the age of seventeen she suffered what she later described as a bad nervous breakdown. The language of a letter she wrote on 30 December 1923 is histrionic and cliché-ridden, but the distress, confusion and sense of being unclean and inadequate are all painfully genuine.

> I am going through more Hell than I thought it possible for anyone to experience. I have followed *It* till now with all its pains, its wearinesses, its ecstasies and adventures with the joy of youth and the love of struggling, worshipping the hand that cut and healed. . . . But the nightmare of this hell sweeping and taking everything with it. . . . I can feel no one, can hear nothing – can see nothing. All that I hate most in myself rises up and mocks me. . . . I feel things monstrously ugly in their suggestiveness, mocking and jeering at me from the dark. . . . I'm terrified as if I'm lost in a fog on the top of a precipice. . . . All the ecstasie of real life – when you can listen and hear the world tuning up for the Fulfillment of the Promise – it's all wrapped in a dark veil. . . . Of course my personality takes the opportunity of thinking itself everything and it is positively hateful. . . . Even Music and Art appear as demons tempting me. I long to wash and burn away my obstinacies. . . . Rest is a stranger to me now.

Betty's use of the term 'nervous breakdown' may have been a loose one – Mary Lutyens once observed affectionately that Betty was the kind of person who never had a temperature of 99 degrees, it was always 104. Nevertheless, it is still surprising to find that Lady Emily, far from hurrying home when she received this cry for help, actually extended her stay in India so that she could visit Adyar.

'I am too delighted to think of you at Adyar,' wrote Betty pitifully. 'It's stupid making a tragedy out of nothing, besides being awfully tiresome depending on someone. Even if you were never coming back it would be stupid to mind.' Thirty years later, in a draft of her autobiography, she betrayed some of the bitterness she must have felt. 'With all her love I know now [Mother] never understood nor tried to.'[6] The 'bond' of their shared spiritual fervour, the 'intimacy' to which Betty staked a claim with her frequent letters to her mother were, it seemed, illusory.

For all her misery Betty was not yet ready to break with Theosophy. Krishna had suggested that in order to progress faster along the Path of Discipleship, Lady Emily, Mary and she should go to Bishop Leadbeater in Sydney, to stay at the Manor, the greatest of the occult forcing-houses (a venture to be financed, like the rest of the family's travels, by the long-suffering Sir Edwin). 'The loneliness and sense of ostracism that would have resulted from standing apart,' she wrote, 'was not to be contemplated.' She decided to struggle on.

> In the midst of hell quivering with strain and fear with all one's 'guts' pulling, there gently comes the thought of the Masters – like the scent of the lotus – and even though our mind laughs with sckepticism [sic] . . . one's whole being inhales the beauty of that scent and one pushes on singing with all the youth of the world as a thrilling chorus.

'The youth of the world' was represented in practice by what even Lady Emily called the 'travelling circus' which now surrounded Krishna. Its members were mostly young girls, dubbed the 'gopis' after the milkmaids who danced with Sri Krishna in the forest of Brindaban. The circus next pitched camp in the summer of 1924 at the village of Pergine, near Trento in the foothills of the Dolomites. 'Camp' was actually an eleventh-century castle converted into a hotel, two of whose towers were occupied by the Theosophical party. Krishna, his brother Nitya and the most favoured of the disciples, including Lady Emily, lived in the square tower where, after a day of readings, an address, and rounders by way of relaxation, Krishna would retire to undergo the same kind of intense preparation as at Ehrwald.

The others, in the round tower, could not help feeling excluded – and Betty felt more strongly than this. Overwrought and insecure after her earlier breakdown, she gradually succumbed to her jealousy of the unique place Krishna occupied in her mother's affections.

Part of Krishna's role as the World Teacher was to help aspirants along the path to the Truth which he had already so nearly attained. For the gopis that summer, his guidance took the form of private conversations in which he pointed out their individual shortcomings and suggested remedies. Nobody was immune, and almost all, including

Lady Emily, were reduced to tears. Mary was informed that she was 'too damned calculating and like an iceberg' – a state Krishna diagnosed as a reaction against Betty's over-emotionalism and hasty temper.

Certainly none of the others reacted as violently to his criticisms as Betty. Krishna had been her nursery companion. With Mary she had chanted 'Cowardy cowardy custard, your face is the colour of mustard', and for Krishna's benefit put a cube in the lavatory which made the water froth and turn green when disturbed. In her diary entry for Christmas Day 1918, she had recorded happily his present of 'lovely swad gaiters or leggins'. Now she found it hard to accept his spiritual promotion; to her his dreamy remoteness seemed like slow-wittedness and a squeamish lack of warmth, failings she particularly despised. Possibly his extraordinary beauty made her nervous, self-conscious as she was about her own looks. She was quick to accuse him of exploiting his appearance and his status to gather a circle of female devotees, encouraging emotional attachments which he then self-righteously destroyed once he had had time to sublimate his own feelings.

But his real crime in her eyes was to undermine what little confidence she had left. For all her reservations, she badly wanted his approval; he was, after all, a central figure of great authority in the world she was trying to enter. But for her alone he seemed to have no comfort. To Mary, after the reprimand, he said that 'when he saw me it was like some beautiful rose that was being maltreated every day . . . that from morning till night he was thinking of me – how he could help me'. Not surprisingly, Mary swallowed the sugared pill and benefited by the treatment. 'I compared myself to an empty gourd from which all the rottenness had been scooped out and which was now ready to be filled with the waters of life.' To Betty he simply seemed like a cat playing with a mouse.

While they were at Pergine, Leadbeater gave his permission for Lady Emily and the girls to come to the Manor. So at the end of October 1924 – a matter of days after Ursie had married Matthew Ridley with a maximum of conventional ceremony – the trio set sail for Sydney with Krishna and Nitya. On the way they stopped in India for four months, dividing their time somewhat schizophrenically between Calcutta (where Lady Emily's brother Victor Lytton was the Governor of Bengal), Delhi with Sir Edwin, and Adyar. On their way to follow the Masters, the Lutyens party were not dressed for Anglo-Indian social life, and Betty remembered her time in Calcutta primarily for the longueurs of hours spent standing dowdily about in an agony of new shoes.

Both here and in Delhi the girls were living in the shadow of Ursie, who had been a huge success the previous year with her curls, charm and a galaxy of social accomplishments which included accompanying herself on the ukelele in 'On the Beach at Waikiki',[7] and executing a Cossack dance in red leather boots. Betty nevertheless blossomed in Delhi, conspiring with her father to alleviate the 'church-all-day' atmosphere generated by Mrs Besant, who was there on an extended visit. Betty took over the housekeeping and improved immeasurably on the tepid Graves and tired cheese which was often all that Lady Emily could be bothered to produce. Sir Edwin designed and made a blackboard top to cover the dining table, with a piece of chalk by each plate for the moments – quite common in colonial society – when conversation flagged.

But back in Adyar the demolition of her personality continued. She was sloppy, untidy, hectic, Krishna said. 'I was noticing just now when you were typing – your legs fidgeting, your mouth twitching – papers all over the place.' She would be desperately controlled for ten minutes and then flop; her unselfishness was forced, not natural. She was jealous and bad-mannered – 'Give up thinking of the Master . . . and learn ordinary common politeness.' Compared with Mary, whom everybody preferred, she had little character, and she was guilty of 'bourgeoiseness', which she must have picked up at school. Being bourgeois, he felt, encouraged 'all that sex stuff'. (She had confessed that she had 'difficulties in this last direction', being sometimes distracted, not unnaturally at eighteen, by sexual feelings.) If she felt it coming on, she should think of something else, 'for it is chiefly mental, isn't it?' A fruit diet might help, or perhaps she could transmute the urge and 'use it for art or something'.[8]

Betty acknowledged that Krishna's objective was her spiritual advancement, and she did not really suspect malice. But the conclusion he allowed her to draw was that she was 'a freak – not normal', and this showed, as she said, an utter lack of understanding of her mental state at that time. She had neither the energy nor the confidence to profit from such bracing treatment, and she left Adyar obsessed with her own failings, tormented by jealousy of her mother's apparently unquestioning admiration and obedience towards Krishna, and burning to retaliate. Almost half a century later, she did: *A Goldfish Bowl* is consistently disparaging and unfair about Krishna and without libel lawyers would have been harsher.

Her personal dislike of Krishna was significant because it meant that one crucial aspect of Theosophy was vitiated for her – the messianic element which gave both Lady Emily and Mary such emotional and spiritual satisfaction for so long. Alienated from the figure who was to be the Lord in his new incarnation, she concentrated harder on the other, more exotic strand of Theosophical practice, the doctrine of the Masters as interpreted by Bishop Leadbeater.

C. W. Leadbeater – a figure whose authenticity is still hotly debated – was born in 1854, not in 1847 as he claimed, wishing to identify himself with Mrs Besant who was born in that year. His father was a railway clerk in Stockport, and not the director of a railroad in Brazil as Leadbeater liked to suggest. His brother was not murdered by Brazilian bandits for refusing to stamp on the Cross; nor did C.W. seek out the killers, only to be restrained from revenge by a vision of the martyred one – in fact he had no brothers. He was not forced to leave Queen's College, Oxford, when the family fortunes failed; the records of the diocese of Winchester, where he was a candidate for ordination, reveal that he never went to university at all.[9]

But the ordination was authentic enough. In 1878 Leadbeater took Holy Orders and became the curate – rather high – of St Mary's, Bramshott, Hampshire. Six years later he left the Church of England, and travelled with Madame Blavatsky to India. In the interim he had joined the Theosophical Society, taking a particular interest in its occult side. But in 1906 he was forced to resign from the Society over accusations of homosexuality and corruption of youth. He never denied that he had encouraged boys to masturbate as a means of relieving physical feelings which could ruin their spiritual concentration, and he may even have demonstrated – this at a time when masturbation was believed to make one mad and blind. But homosexual practices were never proven – in all the time she knew Leadbeater, Mary Lutyens saw no evidence of them whatsoever – and in 1908 when Mrs Besant became President of the Society she reinstated him.

It was Leadbeater who in 1909 identified Krishna as the vessel of the Lord, struck by the beauty of his aura. It was also Leadbeater who took the boy on the astral plane to meet the Masters and got him put on probation to Kuthumi. His authority in astral affairs was absolute within the Society, acknowledged even by the future World Teacher himself.

The figure which greeted Lady Emily and her daughters in Sydney was a spectacular one – to Lady Emily 'a mixture of Wilfrid Blunt, Bernard Shaw and his Rev [Whitwell Elwin] rolled into one', with all that this implied. In 1916 Leadbeater had been consecrated a Bishop in the Liberal Catholic Church, a breakaway sect of Catholicism which refused to subscribe to papal infallibility, and he now often wore a purple cape, scarlet cassock, and amethyst cross and ring. What impressed

Betty most forcibly, however, were his booming voice and long yellow dog-teeth, almost fangs, bared very often in a beaming smile.

Leadbeater's sincerity is not really in doubt, and to those who believe in psychic powers it is almost certain that he was generously endowed with them. Genuine or bogus, he was a magnetic personality, and life at the Manor revolved around him, strongly resembling modern cults in some respects. (It was, for instance, largely financed by the disciples, who paid according to their means; Lady Emily, with a title and a private income, was expected to subscribe generously.)

The manor itself was in the northern suburb of Mosman, a hideous house with a beautiful view of the harbour. Several of its rooms, including Leadbeater's own, were lined with beaten copper, originally 'decorative' but now regarded as ideal for occult purposes, charged as it was with magnetism. Lady Emily and the girls, however, shared a small bare room, whose only advantage was its proximity to that of 'Brother', as Leadbeater liked his disciples to call him, so their auras could mingle.

For a good part of the time, the mingling of auras was all that went on at the Manor. In 1925, fifty-two people, most of them between fifteen and twenty-five, were training for the service of the Masters, but this seemed to entail little more than typing envelopes for the Society's correspondence or sitting around aimlessly 'like an inactive stock exchange', as Betty put it, 'waiting for another message to come through on the astral ticker tape'. True, 'Brother' would sometimes emerge to talk to them of the nature spirits that were everywhere; the Coming was making itself felt even in minerals, and he told them of a rock in the National Park which had become enamoured of an earlier Manor inmate and warmly welcomed his sitting on it.

There was also a variety of religious services, some with the names of the Catholic liturgy, others more esoteric. Betty went often to the services of healing, finding them 'quaint and medievil' [sic], and once thought she saw the healing angel and the hilt of his sword, though it was very hazy. Another time she felt her ring, which 'Brother' had magnetised for her, pulling towards 'a little idiot boy'.[10]

Leadbeater was in the habit of magnetising his disciples' personal possessions with the qualities he felt each most lacked. Mary he felt needed a keener sense of joy, Betty, significantly, a sense of balance. In fact, despite her retrospective account in *A Goldfish Bowl*, whose tone is one of unrelieved sarcasm, the months at the Manor were a time of some happiness for Betty. As at Worcester Park, she enjoyed the regimentation and the certainties, and as part of the services she was able to play more music than for some time past.

She also had friends, unlike Mary, who was lonely and bored at the Manor, where Krishna's role seemed to be secondary to the cult of the Masters. Leadbeater's particular favourite, a strikingly handsome Australian boy called Theo, took Betty up, a mark of distinction in which she revelled, and they spent much of their time together, swimming and playing duets. (Theo was killed on his motorcycle at the age of sixteen.) She also played the violin and sang with Helen Knothe, an American gopi.

For once it appeared to be Betty and not Mary who was making spiritual progress with ease. Both were baptised in the Liberal Catholic Church, but Betty took the further step of becoming a Co-Mason – a fresh batch of services to attend, this time in honour of Osiris, Ra and Rameses. 'Brother,' she reported proudly, 'said I drank in the force beautifully . . . He kept his sword on me a few moments.'

But there were frequent moments too of acute misery and tension. The Manor community was, at its worst, rife with spiritual snobbery and competitiveness, the disciples all vying with each other to attract Leadbeater's attention, and to 'get on' up the ladder of holiness. To some extent the two were synonymous; with all advancement taking place on the astral plane, 'Brother' was the only one qualified to judge when it had occurred, and he was particularly slow to detect the promotion of disciples who had offended him.

Betty, reluctant to relinquish her individuality and her creative gift, ran the risk of offending him constantly, for both were anathema to the impersonal, self-sublimating ethos of Theosophy. 'I am sure it is not a good idea doing music at the present time,' she wrote unwillingly. 'It seems to get me back into my old emotional, individualistic mood and attitude. . . . It seems to be when things are beginning to go well I get "thrilled" and . . . I start trying to become intense, or consciously realise a feeling which came naturally, and so overbalance.'

Krishna's 'pi-jaws' had made her very sensitive to her own failings, and she detected unworthy feelings all the time – streaks in her aura which the Masters, constantly on the watch, could see, and which might at the last disqualify her from sharing in the Coming. Mary described the atmosphere at the Manor as 'like being blind and deaf inside a power station . . . shaken and stupefied by unseen, unheard vibrations.' Betty started to suffer from terrible headaches and spells of depression, which 'Brother' diagnosed helpfully as 'generally indigestion. . . . It is of course sometimes an astral influence, probably someone you have been helping during the night. . . . Whilst you are going about doing your various duties during the day, these people are still clinging on to you for help.' 'A sword must be put into us,' she wrote near-hysterically. 'This is the truest Compassion. Compassion must hurt if it is to arouse the Divinity within.'[11]

In this state of mind, she was finally put on probation to the Master Kuthumi, with Mary, in May 1925. At the same time Lady Emily succeeded in taking her first Initiation, and having achieved her aim, decided to go home for the birth of Ursie's first child, leaving Betty and Mary in Sydney without her until the end of the year. As it turned out, this was the time when the divergence between the two factions within the Society became too great to be concealed or remedied, and the Theosophical adventure as Lady Emily and her daughters knew it was soon to be ended.

As Krishna's spiritual development proceeded and he became more convinced of his own calling as a world teacher, he became correspondingly suspicious of those who claimed to be interpreting the wishes of the Masters. For a few weeks in Holland, while Krishna was in California nursing Nitya, who was desperately ill, the astral plane was humming with news of psychic advancement as the Society's leading officials bounded up the ladder to perfection and release from *karma*, taking two or more steps in a week. It was decreed that the more senior among them should wear silk underwear and no hats, while the most senior of all should eat no eggs. One was discovered to be in his very last incarnation; 'henceforth he would be sent all over the universe and not attached to any one planet'. Without Krishna being consulted, the names were 'brought through' of the twelve apostles (including Lady Emily) whom the Lord had chosen to work with him when he came.

Krishna's sceptical reaction to this dubious spiritual explosion really marked the end of Lady Emily's whole-hearted involvement with Theosophy – and it was against this background that in Sydney Betty and Mary were informed they had been taken to the Master Kuthumi on the astral plane and accepted as his pupils.

Both were aware of having been wide awake and firmly rooted in the human plane for more or less all of the night in question. 'The crickets in the garden kept up a terrific clatter,' wrote Mary. 'The ferries hooted; other bodies lying out on the verandah snored abominably; and at two o'clock the Greek fishermen round the bay began to sing "I Found a Rose in the Devil's Garden". Betty got up soon after this and had a bath and then lay down again with cold wet towels wrapped round her legs in an attempt to get the blood down from her head.' But there was no arguing with 'Brother', and they were deemed to have achieved what they had been aiming at through all the months in Ehrwald, Pergine, Adyar and Sydney. There was no excuse to offer Sir Edwin for staying at the Manor any longer, and in November 1925 Betty and Mary left Australia, to come home by way of the jubilee Convention of the Theosophical Society at Adyar.

On the journey from India to England, Betty was ill, as she had been on the passage out, with head pains, fever and earache. Lady Emily ascribed it to a 'rare tropical germ', admitting blithely that none of them had taken even the most elementary health precautions in India, 'such was my faith in the protective influence of the Masters', and without vaccination had drunk tap water on station platforms and unboiled milk. Mary was more inclined to attribute the pains to the violence with which Betty meditated, as she did everything. Most likely perhaps was the ship's doctor's diagnosis of a chronic ear infection, aggravated by swimming in rough seas.

Betty herself again described her illness as a nervous breakdown, a reaction to the strains of life at the Manor. This is overlooking the fact that if Sir Edwin had not at last put his foot down, she would have gone back the following winter; this was at least her intention when she left Sydney. But by the time Lady Emily announced her intention of following Krishna to America at the end of 1926, Betty had decided to stay behind.

Music and religion still occupied overlapping spheres in her mind; that summer, when she was twenty, she wrote a piece for voices and orchestra to the words 'Mary Mother of God, be with us now and in the hour of our need', and *pace* John Foulds, announced her intention of writing 'something to St Michael'. But she was finding that at last she had the power to distinguish the two enthusiasms and to choose between them, and this time she chose music. She had not yet progressed very far along the path – the pieces that survive are earnest and childish – but she had come far enough to know it was the path she wanted to follow for the rest of her life. While Mary went with her mother to Krishna's retreat at Ojai, California, Betty enrolled for the autumn term at the Royal College of Music.

In 1929 Krishna would repudiate the Theosophical Society; Lady Emily finally resigned in 1934. Krishna too was moving away from her; though she never ceased to love and admire him, she was not capable of the emotional and intellectual independence he now urged on those who had been his followers. Lady Emily was a born disciple, and could not move forward on her own; so instead she moved back, to her husband.

> After twenty years of constant activity and feverish excitement my life had suddenly become empty. My eyes were suddenly opened to the fact that my absorption in Theosophy and Krishna had largely separated me from a very wonderful human love. . . . He welcomed me back without a single reproach or reminder of how much of our lives together I had wasted.

Lady Emily's frankness was always endearing, but it did not stretch as far as considering what she – and Sir Edwin – had done, albeit unintentionally, to Betty. In *A Goldfish Bowl* Betty was to remark ingenuously, not to say untruthfully, 'I have no criticism of her for her desertion of Father, disruption of the home and the great harm her beliefs had on my health and life.' The Theosophical episode did not alienate her affections from her mother, who remained the central point of her emotional reference for another thirty-eight years, but did leave a residual bitterness. 'She adores me and yet hates everything about me,' Lady Emily wrote later to Ursie. 'She is bitterly resentful of Theosophy and Theosophists or anything bordering on religion. There is a very good reason for this. She plunged into it all too deeply and strained herself and got ill and now it frightens her to look back on.'[12]

And this critically affected her attitude to music. Betty's confusion of spiritual enthusiasm and musical inspiration was replaced by an almost equally complete and artificial disjunction between them. Theosophy, she wrote, 'left me with a horror, fear and dislike of the amorphous, slovenly, dishonest, muddled, stupid and narrow-minded "mystic" attitude to life, things and people, and especially art', which to her was 'a precision instrument'.

The invocation to 'Mary, Mother of God' was virtually the last overtly religious text she ever set on her own initiative. And by the age of twenty, against her instincts and despite a temperament that was naturally romantic and demonstrative, she found herself moving towards the Stravinskian view that composing is primarily a question of organising the musical material available, not exploring and exposing soul and personality. In self-defence, she made music become for her, in theory at least, less an expression of feelings than an antidote to them. In choosing the Royal College of Music rather than Krishna and California, she had to some extent been taking refuge from feelings that were too strong to be endured. 'I know from experience,' she wrote later, 'that sanity . . . lies in applying the *conscious* mind objectively and allowing the "unconscious" – "inspiration", "soul". "spirit" . . . to look, as an adult, after itself.'[13]

CHAPTER FOUR

Anchoring the Heart

IN 1925, THE YEAR before Betty entered the Royal College of Music, *Wozzeck* was given its first performance in Berlin; in England the most noteworthy première that autumn was Vaughan Williams's *Flos Campi*. There is no real point of comparison between the two works, just as there was little between the stages musical development had reached generally in Europe and Britain. In Vienna Schoenberg, Berg and Webern were already using the twelve-tone technique; elsewhere the neo-classicism of Stravinsky and Hindemith was ascendant. *The Rite of Spring*, *Pierrot lunaire*, *Duke Bluebeard's Castle* and Webern's Five Pieces for Orchestra were already a decade old.

In Britain, on the other hand, between 1926 and 1930, the years Betty spent as a music student, the English Renaissance was nearing its peak, and 'for those who cared about English music triumph was thrilling in the air'.[1] Unfortunately for Betty, she did not care about it, or not about the composers who were then triumphant: Vaughan Williams, John Ireland, Arnold Bax, Gustav Holst and others whom she was later sweepingly to dismiss as 'the cow-pat school' of English pastoral – 'folky-wolky modal melodies on the cor anglais'.[2] In this she took her cue from Constant Lambert, whose contempt knew no bounds. He wrote in *Music Ho!*:

> There is about this music something both unbearably precious and unbearably hearty. Its preciosity recalls the admirably meant endeavours of William Morris and his followers to combat the products of those dark satanic mills with green and unpleasant handwoven materials while its heartiness conjures up the hideous *faux bonhomie* of the hiker . . . singing obsolete sea shanties with the aid of the Week-End Book.[3]

Betty's idol was Debussy whose experiments 'assumed an almost political quality as a revolt against the tradition of German romanticism, and became a convenient handbook of revolution'.[4] But Debussy's influence in England had to some extent been limited by his association with the aesthetic movement, itself in eclipse since the trial of Oscar Wilde; and the tradition of German romanticism was still firmly entrenched at the Royal College of Music, where, according to Betty, *Brahms* was considered the great modern.

She was exaggerating, of course. Brahms was a good model to use when teaching composition, because his musical procedures were easy to follow, but since the retirement of the previous Director of the College, Sir Charles Villiers Stanford, undoubtedly a force for reaction, he had hardly been held up as an exemplar of modernity. The visits to London between 1911 and 1925 of Diaghilev's Ballet Russe, if nothing else, would have made it hard to ignore Continental developments entirely.

Nevertheless it was true that the then Director, Sir Hugh Allen, was an organist and choral conductor firmly rooted in the English tradition, a close friend and admirer of Hubert Parry; and to some extent 'the shades of Stanford and Parry hung like a pall' over the College in 1926, as she alleged. Excluded from the curriculum were any composers before Haydn or after Sibelius, and beyond the pale lay progressives like Schoenberg, of whom Parry was reputed to have said, 'I don't mind the fellow when he is loud, but it's when he's soft that he's so obscene.'[5]

Allen, whom Grove described as an enterprising conservative, was not the ideal mentor for Betty. She maintained that he did not believe she had even the vestiges of a talent for composing, and wanted her to concentrate on the viola as her first subject. When she persisted, although he gave in he would not let her study with Vaughan Williams or Ireland, the most prestigious of the composition teachers, but sent her to Harold Darke who was primarily an organist and teacher of harmony and counterpoint (though his church music is still frequently used).

She came to be very grateful for Allen's choice. Dr Darke, delighted to diversify into teaching composition, promoted her music vigorously, and ensured that almost every piece she wrote was performed at some level or other within the College. He taught her to play the organ, and introduced her to Bach's choral preludes – like the violin partitas, a profound experience. But being assigned to him did mean that she was set slightly apart from the other student composers, male and female.

The proportion of women students at the College had increased dramatically after the First World War, a reflection of wider changes in women's status. Many were undoubtedly dabblers, who could equally well have studied art or dancing while waiting for marriage, but they decorated the fringes of what was the first full generation of professional women musicians in Britain. The composers alone included, besides Betty, Elizabeth Maconchy, Phyllis Tate, Grace Williams and Dorothy Gow.

Betty's career at the College was satisfactory, if not startling. She played in the second orchestra and in chamber groups; she sang in the chorus as a contralto (joking that with her voice growing gruffer all the time, she might have felt happier in the basses); she took home friendly, not to say ingratiating reports at the end of each term. For Christmas 1929, Allen wrote, 'Music prospers at her hands', a sentiment Lady Emily found 'most poetical'.

The term she left, she won the Alfred Gibson Memorial Prize (five guineas) for violin and viola players; but throughout her time at the College it was Elizabeth Maconchy and Grace Williams who won the composition prizes and scholarships. Elizabeth Maconchy herself felt that Betty had not yet found a distinctive voice. The passion and commitment were there, but not the means of expressing them.

During Betty's student years, from the age of twenty to twenty-three, the house in Mansfield Street was her principal base, though the family, with the exception of Mary, was scattered. Ursula was now mistress of the Ridley estate at Blagdon, outside Newcastle-upon-Tyne. Robert lived near by in London with Eva, had vague aspirations to become an architect and, once the rift with his father had healed, drifted in and out of Mansfield Street; occasionally he and Betty reached temporary accord playing duets, but they were never to be close. Barbie was one of the more successful young society matrons, dividing her time between a large town house, a hunting box in Leicestershire and the Scottish estate.

It was Barbie's bedroom which Betty appropriated in the early days of her student career, at the same time turning the day nursery on the ground floor into a studio. She then set about overhauling her mental state, which in the aftermath of Sydney she described as 'quite frozen emotionally . . . incapable of any spontaneous reaction'. Her remedy, as it was so often to be in the future, was a routine, religiously observed. She drew up a timetable which divided her day equitably between composition, violin and piano and still left time for cold baths and walks with the new dog. Before long the results were perceptible. 'Music was beginning to take over again and I was surely, if very slowly, thawing. It was like waking from an anaesthetic, shaky but glad to be alive.'

Amongst Betty's papers there is a single page, smudged and torn, which appears to be a fragment of emotional autobiography.[6] In *A Goldfish Bowl* she attributes it to 1925 and the time of Krishna's 'pi-jaws' in Adyar, but there is much to suggest that she wrote these notes, fraught and disjointed, some time later and with hindsight. Certainly there are sentences which throw light on her attitude to life during these early years as a composer.

> Religious ecstasy instead of young men's arms. . . . Travel for pleasure, so they say, and go to Bombay. . . . The precipice of thought and growing terror. . . . We are but twenty-one, have pity on our age and give us youth or silly sense of humour. The breakdown and no hand to help. Just years of timetable to tame our fears, and gradual normality. Brahms the best, boredom's best than madness. A little love and little pain – Anchor your heart in kindness and pay the toll.

In 1927, at twenty-one, she was still suffering from occasional depression. Her mother, who had also been afflicted as an adolescent by periodic fits of gloom, might have had more sympathy had she not been preoccupied with the schisms in the Theosophical Society; as it was, Betty learned to extricate herself from troughs in her mood which would open up increasingly frequently as she got older.

She was also scourged by intransigent acne; her father told her unkindly that she resembled 'the leopard who never changed his spots'. On Barbie's advice and at her expense, she took a beauty treatment at Elizabeth Arden. 'On my way to becoming a perfect peach', she wrote optimistically, but the spots persisted for years, and she later blamed them for a characteristic which was both vice and virtue. 'I am a great talker or gabbler and actually remember the long-ago-moment in my extreme youth and excessive shyness when I decided that I would "talk" in an attempt to distract the grown-ups from an acne-ed face.'

In the circles where Barbie and Ursie were at home, the worlds of riding, shooting and weekend house parties, she was utterly out of place. Ursie wrote to her mother despairingly:

> Betty leads an entirely independent life from the rest of the community, gets up at different hours and goes to bed at different times . . . and only appears at meals to talk so fast that no one can understand her. She is very sweet and funny – but entirely absorbed in her own thoughts. She

has got a very morbid mind – hums the most mournful tunes, and goes crazy over a gloomy poem – thinks there is nothing more beautiful than the account of a woman being kicked by her husband with the pains upon her, and likes all the dampest darkest saddest spots in the garden.[7]

Gradually, though, she developed a circle of acquaintances in London with whom she went roller-skating, and a much smaller number of close friends. Dorothy Gow was the first in the long line of musical *confidants* who were indispensable to her all through her life. 'Dorrie' Gow was greatly respected as a composer by her peers, but was too shy, frail and lacking in ambition to push herself or her work, which has been almost completely neglected, despite Betty's efforts on her behalf. They met regularly to discuss what each was writing and thrash out technical problems, and Dorrie, slightly the older and more experienced, steered Betty around the major landmarks of the contemporary music scene.

At home, in the spring of 1927, while both Lady Emily and Mary were still with Krishna in Ojai, California, Betty started entertaining for her father, as she had done two years before in Delhi. 'He's been so sweet and friendly,' she wrote happily, 'nicer than he's ever been, and brings home queer friends.' The 'queer friends' included W. B. Yeats, William Nicholson, Alfred Munnings, George Moore and William Orpen, and Betty had her first taste of being a hostess.

Munnings she found a bore, given to reciting an interminable Masefieldian ode to a pig. Yeats, whose poetry she greatly admired and later often set to music, was a disappointment in all but his appearance. Humourless and greedy, he positively slavered over the Lobster à l'Américaine that appeared when the vegetarian contingent was away, and was much taxed by the question of how to house his OM (Sir Edwin told him to put it in his bottom drawer). Orpen, on the other hand, won points by playing amicably with the dog and asking intelligent questions about musical calligraphy. For a treat, Sir Edwin took her on several Ladies' Days to the Garrick, his favourite haunt; thrilled, she met Arnold Bennett, Frederick Lonsdale and E. V. Lucas, and gained a vivid impression of the milieu in which her father was at home, so dramatically different from the ambience of Krishna, 'Brother' and Mrs Besant.

How highly she prized the opportunity to draw closer to him is reflected in the fact that all her life she exaggerated the length of this happy time as his hostess; she made it sound like months, even years, when in truth it lasted no more than a few weeks. She was now cast in the role of his ally against the Theosophical faction, and it was with a certain relish that she reported to Lady Emily his reaction to the rumour that Mary had become engaged to Krishna. 'Swore that if it was [true] he'd give up Delhi and all his work, turn us out of his house and never see any of his family again. . . . Poor Father, he has such incredible family pride which none of us have inherited. It's very funny but we daren't laugh here.' From now on, if the house was full of her mother's devotees, Betty simply complained that she could not get near the piano.

Later she was to claim a unique sympathy with Sir Edwin, conveniently overlooking Ursula's unswerving devotion. 'After years of loneliness,' she wrote, 'he was slow to realise that it was possible for one of his family to need him and respect him as a great artist.' In retrospect, she idealised their relationship; at the time, it was not quite the meeting of minds she would have loved it to be.

She would have liked above all things to have been able to discuss his work with him, to feel that he was interested in hers, and to establish common ground which might have given some significance to the inevitable tag 'daughter of the architect'. In the most abstract terms they did have ideas in common. 'One could not better define the sensation music produces,' wrote Stravinsky, 'than by saying it is identical with that evoked by contemplation of the interplay of architectural forms.' [8] Increasingly Betty was to subscribe to the Stravinskian notion of music as 'achieved order', satisfying for the beauties of its construction; and Sir Edwin was fascinated by the idea that music, like architecture, was built on structural principles stemming from the Greek. Both in principle shared a temperamental distaste for the mystic and the vague.

But in practice neither enjoyed trying to articulate their own art in words. Betty might have liked to have argued and speculated and learned about architecture, but Sir Edwin had already confessed, 'I can think better of things when unsaid.' And while he liked pieces that made him cry, especially 'Land of Hope and Glory', and enjoyed Purcell's music because it was quintessentially English (though he could not distinguish it from Handel), he appreciated contemporary music not at all.

As a conversational gambit, he might bait her in later years about her experiments with twelve-tone technique, which he referred to as her 'scale'. But at heart he did not take her career seriously. 'Father did not attach much importance to what daughters took up,' she wrote in a clear-sighted moment. 'He felt marriage and babies their real function and hoped they would marry well as a justification for his achieved position in the world, and to conform with the attitudes and life of his friends and clients. He remarked to me once that he would not have allowed a son to become a professional musician.'⁹ The vocation to which he attached the greatest importance he simply assumed to be closed to women; asked about 'the Future for the Woman in Architecture,' he replied, 'It depends on which architect she marries.'¹⁰

Beyond doubt he loved Betty, as he loved all his children. During those weeks in 1927, they made a start at overcoming their inhibitions and he told her of his past life with her mother. When Lady Emily returned from America and the ménage came to an end, Betty moved out, ostensibly to avoid any more damaging exposure to Theosophy, perhaps simply out of jealousy, and Sir Edwin wrote to her, 'I am not much of a father in a fatherway [sic], but you make it up by being a perfect daughter in a daughterly way as I think you aughterly should do.'

But they did not recapture the closeness, even though Betty's excursions into digs never lasted long. A scruffy room in Abingdon Road in Kensington with brown wallpaper and 'an appalling orange frieze' was quickly followed by another in Holland Street rendered uninhabitable by bellringing practice in the church next door. Her last refuge, just behind Paulton's Square, in Chelsea, was next to a family of dwarfs and had no lavatory, which gave her a reasonable excuse for spending much of her time in Mansfield Street.

Eventually she moved back for good, when her parents, anxious to economise, reduced the number of their servants and vacated the old kitchen quarters in the basement. Betty knocked down the maze of partitions, revealing an Adam pillar in the centre of a large hall, and turned the kitchen itself, a vast room with a vaulted roof and charcoal stove, into a studio. The walls she painted in Lutyensian black gloss (as once she had painted the cistern cupboard). The floors were scarlet, and the old bread ovens housed her music. Sir Edwin designed the gas fires for her in grey and white marble, flush with the wall, and she appeared in her first ever public photograph in the *Gas Gazette*.

Unfortunately her father was better at expressing his emotions at a distance; at close range over a period of time she got on his nerves. She was violent in her affections. Lady Eve Balfour, Betty's cousin, remembered Betty telling her how, invited to greet Sir Edwin, she had flung herself into his arms and knocked him over. 'Did he fall absolutely flat?' Eve asked. 'Don't be absurd – how could Father fall flat, you know what shape he is.'

She was quixotic in her sympathies: 'Betty says she passed an old woman who sleeps in a doorway,' Lady Emily told Ursie, 'and now that she has two rooms she will have to invite her to sleep in one!' [11] She was also unpunctual – 'Betty late than never,' her father remarked – and chaotic, 'full of a cheerful restlessness', in her own words. Nor was she any tidier than she had been in Paris. 'Darling old Betty,' observed Sir Edwin, with his passion for elegance and order, 'has not much consideration for things she uses – save perhaps her violin.'

The violin itself was a bone of contention, likewise the piano. 'Publish it not,' he wrote, 'her playing on the piano was very irksome – noise and no music, for no sense at all – and her fingernails click-click.' This was leaving out of the account the 'excruciating' concertina, the zither ('a pleasant wailing'), and later the accordion, 'an instrument only possible out of doors'. 'Angel Betty's accordion is very discordant,' he informed his wife miserably, 'and grates the nerves.'

As she grew more confident, she decided to enlarge her circle of acquaintances by asking each of her dozen or so friends to bring ten of their friends to a party. She chalk-polished the floor, set up small separate tables lit by candles in bottles, commissioned the parlour maid to supply a crude but effective fruit punch, and hired a band of street musicians whom William Nicholson was using as models. She supplemented the entertainment with her accordion, which often served more usefully as protection from assault; dancing with Lord Sandwich, she wore the accordion as a garter ribbon, and was delighted when, in attempting to pinch her bottom, he inadvertently broadcast his intentions by hitting a low B flat.

Sir Edwin referred to these occasions as 'Dartmoor' for the rich variety of guests one might encounter in the dark, but Betty's parties were hardly debauched. Nevertheless, they were noisy; and her post-Theosophist personality, gradually emerging, made him nervous. She was unconventional and combative as his other children had not been, already relying heavily on the shock tactic as a social weapon. She was also a romantic, sometimes with a capital 'R'. 'The human being part of me,' she exclaimed, 'wants to lead a regular life and work, and order my future, whilst the artist in me wants to live at a rate and depth that my health won't stand – to be more lonely, more free, more strong, more titanic.' Sir Edwin reported to Lady Emily in alarm:

> Betty and I went to the Berkeley Grill. . . . Betty eat [sic] and talked a good deal of you, me and herself. The latter was rather terrifying – I hope a pious or impious wish and not true – that all experience is the

right of the young to indulge in – nor would she believe that when I was young I was not as practically inquisitive as she purports to be herself.

'Purports' was probably the right word. When not trying to impress her father, Betty was quite unworldly for her age and thoroughly inexperienced with men. 'So shy, and so hard to please,' commented her mother. Much later she told an interviewer, 'When my generation was young, nobody did the last fence, we were too terrified before birth control.'[12] Her emotional life in the late 1920s was centred for all practical purposes on her dog, a mongrel named Hoover for his habit of dragging his bottom along the carpet. But her horizons were widening.

In her late teens Betty had often stayed with Eve Balfour on the dairy farm she ran with a friend at Haughley in Suffolk. The first time she visited Newbells, she was greeted at the door by Eve (who was known as the 'Compost Queen' for her early experiments with organic farming methods) in breeches and a red spotted handkerchief, and in this garb she sat down to a supper of Welsh rarebit and stewed lettuce. Betty was enchanted by the informality, the log fires, nasturtium bed and fox terriers, and the constant flow of company. She got on well with Eve's great friend Beb (who had once commented that the world seemed to be divided into men, women and Theosophists), and sometimes played jazz with her, though she did not always approve of Beb's musical tastes. 'She's orchestrated a Brahms song,' she told Lady Emily, 'which meant giving parts to saxophone, banjo and drum . . . gruesome.'

Now she asked Eve for a corner of a field in which to build her own cottage, which she achieved for less than £100 – a Suffolk-style timber-framed barn/hut with an asbestos roof that soon weathered to the colour of thatch. Inside, the cottage – which she called 'Braughles' – consisted of little more than one room large enough to house all her instruments, which now included a spinet and a Dolmetsch clavichord; a stepped fireplace vaguely reminiscent of a Lutyens interior at Lindisfarne or Lambay accommodated her collection of clay pipes, which she would occasionally smoke for effect. A kitchen, bedroom and tiny bathroom were supplied, according to Betty, with whatever water was left when the cows had finished, and there was room for guests in the loft.

Over a period of about five years she went down to Braughles almost every weekend as an escape from the music world, which she was already beginning to find oppressive. The pose of the freak and the loner which she had adopted for her family quickly became a habit, and she was wary and afraid of cliques in music; singers, she noted suspiciously, always stuck together.

Her cottage offered her refuge both from the pressures of competition and from her family – though it was not as much a change of scene as it might have been. In 1922 she had informed Lady Emily seriously, 'It's amazing what a tremendous lot one can learn by nature and the country.' Eight years later she was not one for the outdoor life. 'She didn't like to be out of the smell of cigarettes,' commented one friend; and Eve Balfour noticed a tendency to keep urban hours, particularly in the morning – 'but she managed to lie in bed with vigour'. She treated the cottage, from the domestic point of view, 'as though it were a houseboat – everything was just thrown out of the window', and Newbells Farm benefited later from a splendid apple tree which had sprung from one of Betty's cores.

Occasionally she invited musical friends down, but she spent most of her time alone with her instruments. For pocket money she obliged the mother of a local vicar by giving her music lessons almost exclusively centred on the 'Moonlight' Sonata, with the difficult pages pasted together. This helped to finance the rota of choirboys who had to be bribed with acid drops to pump the organ at nearby Woolpit, where she was the organist for a while. Here in the evenings in the little church with its magnificent hammer-beam roof she explored not only the organ works of Bach, to which Dr Darke had introduced her, but also the pre-Bach 'old stuff' with which very few organists of his generation bothered.

In the mid-1920s, with the inauguration of the Dolmetsch Festival at Haslemere in 1925 and the publication of Peter Warlock's *The English Ayre* (1926), the awakening of enthusiasm for ancient music was well under way. But Betty's interest was largely, if not entirely, attributable to Antoine Geoffroy, who was already a specialist in early music. He introduced Betty to the work of another composer she was often to cite as an influence – Girolamo Frescobaldi, in whom she found poignant emotion combined with complete formal control, 'every interval and "tension" *necessary* and deliberate'. The need for control was to be impressed upon her again when she returned to Paris in 1931, after finishing at the Royal College, to study counterpoint briefly with Georges Caussade. 'Il faut être maître de votre pensée', he told her, and taught her how to use the simplest combination of lines and make them sound like people singing.

Antoine visited Newbells from time to time, and in 1930 he was the 'foreign man' with whom the newspapers reported her to have had a car accident on the road to Bury St Edmunds, where he was to play the organ. Betty was a passionate driver, with a two-seater Alvis of which she was extremely proud, and accelerating too fast past a lorry, she skidded and turned the car over. The crash reduced her legs to 'bloody shreds, with white-as-Persil bones showing through'.[13] Even if there are shades here of her reporting of the mumps ('I am to bad to say eny more') it was a serious accident which left her lame for two months, and she was aggrieved at the equanimity with which her mother received the whole incident.

During the early 1930s, a more promising relationship was developing. In 1929, at a musical evening convened by one of her piano teachers, the twenty-three-year-old Betty met a young baritone named Ian Glennie, and by winter, Lady Emily was recording with interest the presence of 'a man friend'. 'She is really coming out of her shell a bit.'

Ian Glennie, the son of a minor canon and prebendary of Hereford Cathedral, was educated at Marlborough and Oriel College, Oxford, though he came down early, suffering from nervous strain. Tall, quiet, good at crosswords and writing verse, he was already established as a professional singer. Most of his engagements were for the light classical repertoire, but he also performed twentieth-century music, and one of his contemporaries remembered him as 'an intellectual, intelligent, sympathetic singer'.[14]

He had all the gifts Betty felt she lacked – obvious musicianship, a good ear and sight-reading skills – and in what she considered her plain and spotty state, his interest was surprising and flattering. Later she wrote:

> I still remember how abominably I played that night, put off and made agonisingly shy by this huge young man who appeared so superior, singing everything when asked by sight with effortless confidence. . . . By the end of the evening I was in a thoroughly bad temper with myself. Ian Glennie offered to see me home, which made me crosser. I could only presume that it was politeness on his part and against his inclinations. Even his payment of my bus fare made me suspicious, as if I had sold twopence-worth of my independence.

The feeling of independence – symbolised by the excursions into digs, however brief – was important to Betty. She needed a little breathing room to develop an individual style – entertaining, sharp-tongued, often outrageous, seemingly holding herself aloof and yet still governed by impulse, swayed by enthusiasms and prejudices of equal violence. At the same time she badly needed security and reassurance, to be found partly at Mansfield Street, partly in social success, and male admiration in particular. (In her first terms at college she claimed she had no male friends at all – 'I only knew a few "holy men" likely to retire, after a supper of raw carrot, at nine p.m.') Her mother wrote shrewdly to Ursula at this time, 'Betty is a rebel – but I think it is to some extent a defence. At heart she craves for love and friendship, she longs passionately to be *first* with some one.'

When Ian Glennie rang a few days later to ask her out, she agreed to meet him one evening in the Six Bells in the King's Road – an occasion distinguished by the behaviour of Hoover, who fought with other dogs all night under her chair. The courtship survived the mêlée, and Ian's affection survived all the tests to which Betty could subject it. Over the next four years she would hanker intermittently for Antoine; during her second visit to Paris in 1931 she shared a flat with him and a plump, melancholy Italian acquaintance – a peculiar but entirely Platonic ménage which 'contributed towards a wished-for reputation for greater sophistication than I actually possessed.... I was incredibly naïve, ignorant and *en arrière* for my age.'

She also had what she described forty years later as 'the usual quota of affairs and romances, all ending almost as soon as they began, in bitter experience and heartache'. The basement parties escalated to the point where Sir Edwin seriously considered moving out of Mansfield Street. But always in the background was the comforting knowledge of Ian's admiration and devotion, the feeling of 'being first' with him, an essential prop to her self-esteem and spur to her confidence.

It was for Ian that she wrote many of her earliest works – though happily for him, he was not implicated in her very first adult effort, a setting of the entire book of Job in the style of Brahms, for soloists, double chorus and a large orchestra, which even Dr Darke could not get played. The first piece to be given a semi-public performance was a setting of Keats's sonnet 'To Sleep' for contralto and an orchestra conducted by Darke at one of the College's Patron's Fund concerts in 1929. The Patron's Fund was utilised to have students' works thoroughly rehearsed by professional orchestras, conditions which were virtually unobtainable elsewhere, and Betty was grateful for the opportunity to have her work brought off the page. At the same time, she was bitterly disappointed. 'I think I had expected "a sea change / Into something rich and strange",' she wrote. 'But no – it was exactly as I had originally heard it.'[15] In later years she would undoubtedly have settled for that.

Some vocal quartets survive from her student days – solidly tonal, rather static settings of Robert Bridges, Walt Whitman, George Herbert and Robert Herrick, moving mostly in unison, with every appearance of having been written for examinations. Her next performed piece, however, was more sprightly, a ballet on Wilde's 'The Birthday of the Infanta'. The score received its first performance at the College in 1932, again courtesy of the Patron's Fund; Betty was convinced that Allen had programmed the work without reading it, simply to please her father, and she muttered darkly about corruption.

Penelope Spencer, the leading light among the College's dance students at that time, had already choreographed *Infanta* for use in classes when she was approached by the Camargo Society. The Society, which had been founded in 1930 to keep alive the interest in ballet aroused in England by Diaghilev, asked her to mount a production; she suggested *Infanta*, with a very young Wendy Toye in the title role, and Betty provided Rex Whistler, a friend of Barbie's, to do the designs as his first stage commission.

His inexperience showed; the design was based on Velasquez, which should have meant hooped dresses, but he was seduced by sateen, which dangled limply. He also interpreted the character of the Funambulist as a nun with an umbrella. This offended the ballerina Tamara Karsavina, in whose honour the ballet was to be given a special performance, and the Funambulist's dance was reconceived for Eve, the contortionist from a Cochran revue, whom it was believed would be a draw. The results were peculiar; but the music for the Dwarf at least was praised as 'good *gesture* music' by no less than Dame Ethel Smyth, who shouted herself hoarse from the balcony in her support for a younger woman's effort.

Other critics were less generous. 'Banal and derivative,' remarked the *Daily Mail*, 'it is what comes of bringing up babes on *Petroushka*', and in the event, Betty was not pleased with her first stage work. Diffident, she sought advice from too many people and later regretted taking it. On the other hand, she irritated everyone by refusing to accept more practical help. Lady Emily had persuaded Sir Edwin to approach Maynard Keynes, who was both a friend and a member of the Camargo board, for advice on promoting the ballet. Keynes, predictably enough, suggested that Sir Edwin put £100 into the production, but Betty refused point blank to let him, afraid that this would conjure up the spectre of a rich man's daughter buying her way into the arts. She was to remain a purist about this sort of patronage all her life.

The episode, though, calls into question the image which Betty liked to project of her mother as a philistine totally indifferent to her music. Lady Emily treasured the favourable reports which filtered out of the College. She shared evenings huddled over the wireless in Mansfield

Street. 'Betty has succeeded,' she told Sir Edwin, 'in getting many foreign stations and we just hear Italian opera, then French and German orchestras, intermingled with an English lecture on the habits of the mosquito, and atmospherics.' She even offered her room to Miss Motto for a concert, 'really to please Betty who feels so much, and rightly, that one should help artists. No cost to me. There were about fifty people and an even funnier crowd than my Theosophists! Most motheaten! I got the giggles at the sight of two Catholic dignitaries sitting beside my Buddha!'

The opportunities for public performance of contemporary British music in the 1930s were very limited. Besides the Patron's Fund concerts, which were not public, the College mounted very few performances of students' work. Betty claimed, with only slight exaggeration, that in her time at College only two composers – Elizabeth Maconchy and Leonard Isaacs – were given public concerts; and remarkably, Britten had only one piece performed during his years there. Sir Henry Wood had made some bold experiments at the Proms, but there was still a huge backlog of the music of the past twenty years to be tackled. In the 1920s a few individuals had staged isolated concert series in London featuring modern works, most notably Eugène Goossens and someone called Edward Clark. Clark had also helped to infiltrate contemporary music into the BBC, but with more emphasis on the continental avant-garde. And when Betty sent him some music on spec, the parcel came back from the BBC apparently unopened.

The only solution appeared to be for composers to stage their own concerts – a point Betty made to Anne Macnaghten, a young violinist with a quartet in search of work. She said much the same to Iris Lemare, who was studying at the College as a conductor, timpanist and organist, and together the three of them set out to create a new platform for modern music.

This was not an overtly feminist venture. Despite the influence of Aunt Con, Betty was never interested in feminism as an organised movement. In contexts where she wanted to emphasise the difficulty of her life, she would mention the added handicap of being a woman, but she felt it was one that each woman had to overcome for herself, as she had done. She could rarely resist the offer of a performance, so her works did appear in concerts devoted to 'women's music', but she consistently refused to take part in discussions or workshops which treated women as essentially separate from men. Her aim, and that of Anne Macnaghten and Iris Lemare, was to improve conditions for *all* young composers.

None of them would have denied, however, that women were likely to be the most grateful. There had been progress from the days when music was purely a social grace and women were confined to writing harp sonatas for parlour performance. In the nineteenth century the conservatories were open to women, who began to play less 'proper' instruments like the cello and clarinet, and to compose in the larger genres. But residual prejudice was very strong, rooted in the belief that creativity was related less to social class or status (and hence training and opportunity) than to biological make-up. The male was rational, the female (courtesy of Goethe and his Eternal Feminine) intuitive and incapable of objectifying emotion, and that was all there was to it. Havelock Ellis produced the argument that women's lack of success in music was both consequence and proof of biological inferiority. And as late as 1928 Cecil Gray was applying to women's composing Dr Johnson's dictum about the woman preacher and the dog walking upright – 'It is not done well; but you are surprised to find it done at all.'[16]

'There is no mark on the wall to measure the height of women,'[17] wrote Virginia Woolf. Betty was conscious of the lack of tradition, which made the woman composer's position a lonely and unconfident one. 'Does a man realise that the achievements of men in all fields,' she wrote, 'enable him to say to himself when young, "What man has done, I can do"?'[18] There was, of course, one precedent which she could hardly avoid – that of Ethel Smyth, who, in the sense that she had had the largest possible work (her opera *Der Wald*) performed in the most conservative possible surroundings (the Metropolitan Opera House), had gone as far as it was possible to go in a male-dominated world.

But the example of Dame Ethel was a mixed blessing, because her personality, if not her music, tended to reinforce prejudices rather than dispelling them. She was mannish in her dress, which was liable to include cigar, tam o'shanter, country tweeds and a tie – usually in the purple, white and green of the Women's Social and Political Union, another nail in her coffin as far as the male establishment was concerned. Almost worst of all in its consequences for other female composers was her widespread reputation as a pest when it came to pushing her own work and complaining of the victimisation of women.

In 1931 Virginia Woolf, herself a leading campaigner for equality of opportunity in the arts, wrote to her sister describing a visitation from Ethel. 'For three hours she nailed me to my chair while she ... went through, with the minuteness and ingenuity of a maniac, the whole history of her persecution for the past fifty years, brought out old letters and documents and read them aloud, beat on my chair with her fists.'

Virginia felt 'like a stoat nailed to a barn door' and finally 'I had to shout that I had such a headache that unless she stopped talking I should burst into flames and be combusted.'[19] (There was a lesson here for Betty, had she but known it.) Dame Ethel's eccentricities confirmed male suspicions about 'artistic females' which, combined with male dislike of women in positions of authority, made scarce the opportunities for women composers, conductors and quartet leaders.

Having contributed the original idea of promoting a series of concerts, in which the young British composer would be cushioned by older contemporaries and rarely heard pre-classical repertoire, Betty was content to leave its organisation (and hence its name, the Macnaghten–Lemare Concerts) to the other two. Anne Macnaghten found the venue – the Mercury Theatre in Notting Hill Gate – and arranged the practicalities of fees, ticket prices and promotion. Composers and performers alike were expected to persuade their friends and relations to buy season tickets (nine shillings), and the audience included few outsiders, but among them were invariably Arthur Bliss and Ralph Vaughan Williams, who took an avuncular interest in younger British composers. (Vaughan Williams even signed his letters to Anne Macnaghten 'Uncle Ralph.')

It was Iris Lemare who involved Benjamin Britten in the project as both composer and back-desk violin, sitting virtually shoulder to shoulder with A. E. Lutyens, viola. The Macnaghten–Lemare Concerts made good the College's omission by giving Britten his first public performance (three settings of poems by Walter de la Mare dating from 1932), as well as the première of *A Boy was Born*; they also gave Alan Rawsthorne his first performance anywhere.

The first concert took place on 3 December 1931, and included five songs by Betty for soprano and quartet (Dora Stevens and the Macnaghten Quartet). The second one followed eleven days later, with a Lutyens string quartet in one movement; this dated from 1927, and Christian Darnton, in his capacity as critic rather than composer, noted a trifle patronisingly that what might then have seemed iconoclastic was now more or less innocuous. (In his own music at this time he was making some radical experiments with dissonance.) The third concert on 28 January 1932 incorporated some unexceptional arrangements for chamber orchestra of organ pieces by Frescobaldi and Titelouse.

Betty was not satisfied with any of her early music. Anne Macnaghten confirms that in comparison with the work that Britten, Maconchy, Rawsthorne and Gow were producing, Betty's had little definite identity. She was diffident and uncertain, and kept altering pieces and withdrawing them, with the result that no more of her work was featured until December 1932, and then it was a set of choral songs, *Winter the Huntsman* (words by Osbert Sitwell), one of which was dismissed outright as 'a small offspring of a young parent', Constant Lambert's *Rio Grande* (words by Sacheverell Sitwell).

In 1935, when Iris Lemare had temporarily taken over the running of the concerts, Betty's contribution was positively bizarre – a setting for tenor, four horns and strings of Austin Dobson's long poem 'The Dying of Tanneguy de Bois'. Miss Lemare now describes it frankly as 'an awful, lugubrious piece'; in *A Goldfish Bowl* details of this concert mercifully 'escaped' Betty – possibly because the individual works were entirely overshadowed in the minds of the press by the fact that all the composers were women. (The others were Elizabeth Maconchy and Grace Williams.) The advance publicity for the concert in the *Glasgow Herald* is a very good example of the condescension to which women composers used to be subjected, and to some extent still are. It suggested that women seemed to be invading

the more remote and superior kind of programme. . . . Two of the most prominent of these cerebrals are Miss Elizabeth Maconchy and Miss Elisabeth Lutyens. . . . Moreover the conductor [Iris Lemare] is of the same serious and mentally burdened sex. Musicians who have been looking on with considerable interest at this branch of the feminist movement are beginning to wonder when a woman composer is going to write some music reminiscent of the sex as it used to be.

Constant Lambert's criticism was both more intelligent and more damning. In an article entitled 'Women composers are so forceful' he wrote:

In the art of the novel, it is true a certain womanliness is cultivated and even flaunted. There the 'feminine instinct' and the 'quiet touch' are allowed full play. . . . But in the visual and audible arts this is not so. Give a woman a chunk of granite or a few trombones and she immediately proceeds to out-Epstein Epstein and out-Holbrooke Holbrooke. . . . Miss Lutyens in her setting of Austin Dobson's very olde-worlde poem 'The Dying of Tanneguy de Bois' is evidently determined that none of the Morris wallpaper atmosphere of the words shall be reflected in the music which is strained, angular and unconvincing. But having chosen this particular text she should at least have paid some slight respect to it and not obscured its form and meaning by the pointless repetition of phrases. A formal poem by Dobson cannot be set as if it were a fragment of modern prose.

This charge was to be levelled at Betty's vocal settings all her life – that she wrote musical prose even where her chosen text was highly poetic – and the home truths must have made her smart, especially coming from Lambert. He had conducted *Infanta*, with various arrogant remarks about her scoring, and at that stage he was handsome enough to make her nervous and suspicious of him. But he was one of the very few critics she ever forgave, and he was to become one of her most highly prized friends.

The unfortunate soloist in *Tanneguy* was Steuart Wilson, who up until 1932 had been one of Britain's leading tenors, despite having lost the best part of a lung in the First World War. But after an untidy divorce, his career had suffered seriously, which doubtless made him more receptive to Iris Lemare's invitation in 1935. Four years later, however, he came to her rescue out of pure philanthropy. The problem was Betty's 'realisation' of Monteverdi's *Lamento e recitativo d'Arianna*, and the audience was treated to the spectacle of Wilson, who was tall and rugged enough to have made a better Minotaur, impersonating instead the forsaken Ariadne to the accompaniment of the full strings of the London Symphony Orchestra. One way or another, it lacked the authentic feel – one critic wrote, 'The fussy accompaniment handicapped the voice part like a dog cart harnessed to a thoroughbred' – and it occupied a disproportionate amount of rehearsal time, at the expense of the première of Alan Rawsthorne's First Piano Concerto, because Betty's score was so messy that several players kept trying to peform ledger lines.[20]

Betty was perhaps right to suspect in her first decade as a career musician that of the attention she received, a large proportion was due to her maiden name, which she retained for professional purposes. An *Evening Standard* entry was typical – 'Sir Edwin Lutyens, President of the Royal Academy, has a daughter who is making a name for herself as a musician. . . . A witty, outspoken conversationalist, an excellent cook, she can play almost any musical instrument.'

The most successful interpreter of Betty's music during the 1930s was almost certainly Ian Glennie. On the advice of his singing teacher, he had decided to become a tenor, and his performance in January 1935 of her four songs for tenor and piano, with words by Emily Brontë, D. H. Lawrence and Shakespeare, was one of the few he undertook while his voice was settling. The critics were kinder to the singer than the songs, which they described as 'incompletely incubated and inconsequential' (Frank Howes), with an ungrateful vocal line and a piano line that was methodical but stiff (Jack Westrup). Other early songs, however, were lush and romantic to a degree that embarrassed her in later years, some of them displaying a lavish helping of Debussy.

By the time she wrote the four songs for him, Betty had been married to Ian Glennie for two years. 'A little love and little pain. . . . Anchor your heart in kindness,' she had written, and for years he had been offering her kindness, constancy and security. The rest of her family were all married, including Mary, two years younger, who in 1930, in a temporary reaction against the way of life urged by Krishnamurti, had married Anthony Sewell, a young stockbroker whom she herself described as 'very worldly'.

Betty badly wanted children of her own, partly in response to Ursula's claim that motherhood was the only true creativity. 'My earlier conviction that babies and music were incompatible,' she remembered, 'was weakened by the realisation that the longing – stimulated by the arrival of Ursula's babies – was occupying as much time in my thoughts as the physical having of them would.' She was aware that her father liked Ian for what he described as his 'modest and simple demeanour', referring to him as 'her master's voice'; and she was herself very fond of him. So she accepted a proposal he had often repeated, and on 11 February 1933, they were married by his father at All Soul's, Langham Place.

By the end of June Sir Edwin was informing Lady Emily, 'I saw Betty who announced to me with gaiety that there was a possible babe and she had been very sick.' On 12 February 1934, as William Sebastian was born, 'with family comments echoing through my gas-blurred head,' she wrote, 'I heard myself roar to the astonished lady doctor miles away at the other end, "And I still want to write music, fuck you!"'

CHAPTER FIVE

The European-looking Gentleman

FROM 1933 TO 1938 BETTY combined music, marriage and maternity happily enough. She and Ian lived in the basement of 13 Mansfield Street with a cook, a housemaid and a charwoman, and Betty remarked blithely, 'I think with about £800 per annum and living rent-free we ought to be very comfortable.'

The Glennies led a sociable life, continuing the accordion parties in the basement and making a widening circle of musical friends. One in particular, the violinist and musicologist André Mangeot, had a profound influence on Betty. He was working on an edition of the Purcell Fantasias, in which she found an intriguing alternative to classical forms. The traditional arrangement of tune at the top, accompaniment in the bass, had irritated her since her days in the RCM's second orchestra, when as a lowly viola she found herself all too often with little or nothing interesting to play. In the Fantasias the instruments had equal voices, a manner of composition which liberated her imagination and prompted her to make a series of experiments in string writing.

She was to claim she found it less 'alarming' to write a sequence of works in the same genre, trying to solve its particular problems from a variety of different angles, rather than attempting to condense her ideas into a single definitive statement. Now she wrote her own Fantasia for five strings, following this with a partita for two violins, a viola sonata and a string quartet.

The shade of Bartók hovered round some of this early string music. Betty's own voice was not yet ringing clear in her head – and now there was a further hiatus, when her second pregnancy in 1936 turned out to be twins, Rose and Teresa (or Tess). 'The following months were fallow for my music,' she wrote later. 'I was exhausted after an almost sleepless pregnancy and horrifying birth. I was also suffering acutely from "Wimbledon headache", brought on by the left-right, right-left turning of eyes and head (as in watching tennis) as I nursed my tiny, premature pair every three hours.'

The staff in the basement at Mansfield Street had been extended to include a nanny, and Betty left the infant twins and the two-year-old Sebastian largely in her care, though not without a pang. Nothing could shake her determination to succeed as a composer, and this included parenthood; but surrounded by sisters who, as she felt, were more attractive and had married more prosperously, she also desperately wanted to succeed as a woman. She was one of those women who feels giving birth to be a crucial part of femininity; the more babies she had, the more essentially feminine she would prove herself. When she was first pregnant, she fervently hoped she would be ample and maternal-looking, but was cured of this particular earth-mother tendency during her second pregnancy when, carrying the twins, her weight shot up from seven to twelve stone and she only dared go out after dark.

Though she had some illusions about motherhood and her own capacity for it, Betty's desire in these early years of marriage to have children was real and urgent, and it began to cause severe strains in her relationship with Ian. He had been far more hesitant to embark on a family, less sanguine than Betty about their financial position, knowing that he would be earning almost nothing while his voice was settling in its new register. But her obstinacy was irresistible, in this as in so much else – 'a whole battalion going on at one', Ian remembers now. She was increasingly critical, contentious and restless, and the end of the marriage might not have been long in coming in any event. But it was painfully precipitated by the appearance in Betty's life of one of the most remarkable characters on the British musical scene.

Since leaving college in 1930 Betty had gradually become aware that wherever she turned in the tiny world of contemporary music, a single figure confronted her. She went to concerts put on at the London Centre for Contemporary Music, and its president was Edward Clark. She listened to concerts on the radio – programmed by Edward Clark. She submitted pieces to Adolph Hallis, who was privately promoting a series of chamber concerts in London, and had her first quartet accepted with the remark that her string writing was admired by the selection committee, especially Edward Clark.

She first met Edward in 1938 at one of his regular haunts – Casa Prada, an Empire Restaurant on the Euston Road. She was lunching with Alan Rawsthorne, already one of her closest friends, and with the film director Basil Wright, when there entered

> an elegant 'European-looking' gentleman in a white silk open-necked shirt and short blue linen coat . . . in his buttonhole the dark red clove carnation he invariably sported. . . . Being an *homme de théâtre* of late nights and continental habits, this was his first *sortie* of the day, I gathered, for breakfast-cum-lunch. I with my background of restaurant meals for 'occasions and anniversaries only' found this full of glamour.

At a party given by Alan Rawsthorne's first wife Jessie some weeks later, there was more chance to talk, and they spent most of the evening in a quiet corner sizing each other up; there was still in Betty's attitude a detectable element of hero-worship for this figure of authority, with his European reference, his vast store of musical names and dates, his easy familiarity with every face on the avant-garde totem pole. 'Having come across him associated with – to me – all the most interesting happenings, I was now meeting and getting to know him personally,' she wrote in *A Goldfish Bowl*, the excitement still in her voice thirty years later. 'Was he, perhaps, all I had been seeking for in a man, all I had been seeking for in a musician?'

Heading some weeks later for a party at the Polish Embassy in Portland Place after a performance of the Webern string trio, they arrived on the doorstep together. Instead of making their entrance, they decided without speaking to go for a walk. 'From that moment to this,' she wrote years after his death, 'he was the all-important person in my life.' As they emerged from the party with friends, Betty spotted an insecurely parked car with its keys in the ignition and took the entire company joyriding, 'heady with the music of Webern, new-found love and Polish slivowitz'. The next two years, so grim in Britain generally, were perhaps the happiest of her life.

Edward was almost twenty years older, surrounded by a certain mystique, and different enough from anyone Betty had ever met to intrigue her. The first time Betty was invited to visit him at his flat, a different facet of the 'European-looking gentleman' was revealed. Fitzroy Street, running between Oxford Street and the Euston Road out of Charlotte Street, had a grimy glamour which made nearby Mansfield Street seem very sedate. Number 12, where Edward lodged, had been the headquarters of the Euston Road school of painters; Sickert had lived nearby, William Coldstream was in residence downstairs and Rex Whistler across the road.

Betty swept up from her Adam flat in her Alvis two-seater, and found herself in a room whose elegant proportions were more or less obliterated by a chaos of books, posters, papers, telephones, typewriters and strangers who ignored her entirely as they prepared for a forthcoming Festival of Music for the People. The scruffy but earnest ambience, and the furious rage which enveloped Edward when his ritual of correct sherry-drinking was thwarted by a recalcitrant cork, were entirely at odds with the carnation, the monocle and the silk shirts. It was to take Betty years to disentangle the threads of his personality, or even to decipher the outlines of his life.

He was born in Newcastle-upon-Tyne in 1888. His father James Clark, a successful self-made coal-exporter, was an avid amateur musician, and their house a centre of local activity. But James had never envisaged music as a career for his son, and did his best, when Edward left the grammar school, to introduce him to banking. Nothing, as it happened, could have been less suitable. The profundity of Edward's failure as a money man was matched only by the depth of his passion for music. On the pretext of preparing to enter the family business, he persuaded his father to pay for a period of study abroad, and at a time when, in Ernest Newman's phrase, England was 'where good foreign music goes when it dies',[1] Edward escaped to 'passportless, happy Europe'[2] at a critical stage in the formation of the twentieth-century aesthetic.

In 1907 he was in Paris in a circle of young composers including Ravel, Roussel and Debussy, whose standard he carried back to England where all three were still virtually unknown. Photographs of him at this time reveal a self-consciously romantic figure, round-faced with drooping moustache and cravat straight out of *La Bohème*. By 1909 he was making regular visits to Vienna to visit Richard Strauss, and to sit at the feet of Mahler (again, almost unplayed in England). He was based, however, in Berlin, where he studied with the conductor Oskar Fried and acted as the Berlin correspondent of the *Musical Times*.

For Edward the moment of truth was his meeting with Arnold Schoenberg, after a performance of Schoenberg's *Pelleas und Melisande* conducted by Fried. Edward's most endearing characteristic was his blazing enthusiasm; for all the cosmopolitan sophistication which so impressed Betty, he was never cynical, and Schoenberg, restless, chain-smoking, haunted, speaking in oracles, embodied for him the higher reality which was music. 'As he talked he looked through you,' he wrote, 'incinerating your doubts or hesitations, making equivocation impossible, and as what he said always involved ultimate attitudes to life or music, he extracted the best and the uttermost from every listener.'[3]

Edward also had one rare and unchallengeable gift – his instinct for the special. Schoenberg was in dire straits in Vienna, penniless and execrated by the conservative Viennese audience; and with other supporters (who included Ferruccio Busoni and Artur Schnabel), Edward now launched a campaign to bring him to Berlin. He drafted a newspaper paragraph advertising Schoenberg's music courses, helped arrange a series of lectures, and found him somewhere to live. He was also one of the only two private pupils who came to Schoenberg when he first arrived in Berlin, to learn 'some of the deep and simple mysteries of the musical craft'.

For Edward the years immediately preceding the First World War were extraordinarily happy ones, by which he tended to measure all others. He was a good linguist – Betty was to wonder whether he actually thought in German, as she waited for verbs which never arrived – and he made a wide circle of friends. One was Anton Webern, for whom he pulled the stops at rehearsals for Schoenberg's *Herzgewächse* where Webern was playing the harmonium; that is, until Webern's irritation at his imprecision became too great.

Schoenberg was puzzled by his pupil-cum-promoter. 'Remarkable; he knows no Wagner operas, nothing by Mozart, nothing by Beethoven. But he wants to be a conductor!! And he has often seen *Elektra*! . . . I thought the young people of today grew up with Wagner! . . . He blames it on musical conditions in England.'[4] But Edward's percipience when it came to his master's music was not in doubt. He was in at the birth of *Pierrot lunaire* – one of his favourite reminiscences in later life was of listening to Kreisler decipher the violin part over Schoenberg's shoulder – and avidly followed its bumpy progress across Europe.

Edward wanted to make his career in Germany, and would almost certainly have been happier if he had. It is fairly typical of his luck and his timing that in mid-1914 he had plans to take German citizenship, and was on his way to Stettin to succeed Webern as principal conductor at the theatre there when war broke out. Adrian Boult, who had been studying in Leipzig, was extricated safely by his parents; Edward was interned with other enemy aliens in the converted racetrack at Ruhleben. Here, according to family myth, he learned the habit of passive acceptance and lost the knack of writing letters.

When he returned to England, it was to a somewhat miscellaneous conducting career. His first job was with a troupe of Polish dancers at the Empress Theatre, Brixton; but in 1919 he joined Diaghilev's Ballet Russe for its English tours. The company was no longer authentically avant-garde; in Constant Lambert's view, it belonged essentially to the 1890s, and its principal adherents were '*fin de siècle* characters born out of their time'[5] (a description which many people were to apply to Edward). But to the general public, in an England which was still a generation behind the Continent in its artistic tastes, the Ballet Russe remained 'the most quickly grasped expression of all that was most aesthetically exciting and new'.

Edward was engaged to supervise orchestral contracts and perform odd jobs – he was the typewriter soloist at the first London performance of Erik Satie's *Parade*. He also acted as assistant to principal conductor Ernest Ansermet, whom he had met in Berlin in 1909. When Ansermet was obliged to quit the season early, Edward was not invited to succeed him, but he supplied the new man Adrian Boult with invaluable advice on the detail of scores, including *Petrushka*, which he already knew well.

He still had a modest private income from his father, and in 1921 at the Queen's and Aeolian Halls he mounted his first contemporary concerts. 'Side whiskers, velveteen dinner jackets, horn-rimmed spectacles, and other symbols of futuristic youth were much in evidence,' according to one newspaper. 'Not for a long time has the "advanced brigade" so thoroughly enjoyed itself', as Edward offered it the first British performances of *Pulcinella*, *The Firebird*, Milhaud's *Le Boeuf sur le Toit*, Schoenberg's *Kammersinfonie*, and Busoni's Clarinet Concerto. 'Blare music,' gibbered the *Daily Mail* nervously. 'The triumph of Nietzsche, with his motto "Let instinct live".'[6] The concerts failed to make as great an impact as a series mounted the previous year by Eugène Goossens – a conductor, according to Edward, 'as profoundly versed as I was at that time innocent in the arts of publicity' – and they accounted for the last of his allowance.

A variety of jobs followed – translating Schoenberg's *Harmonielehre*, taking the Margaret Morris Dancers on a tour of seaside resorts, coaching, copying, developing an encyclopaedic and entirely empirical knowledge of the repertoire. He was Owen Nares's Music Director at the Duke of York's Theatre, his only recorded production being Pinero's *The Enchanted Cottage*, with music by Sir Frederic Cowen, which ran for sixty-four performances in 1922.[7]

He was also music critic for the *Daily Herald*, the newspaper of the Labour movement, and a founder of the Chelsea Labour Choir. Edward, according to his elder son James, was 'a grand old-fashioned Bolshevik', well before socialism became fashionable among the intelligentsia. His communism was of the romantic arm-waving kind, more a gesture against his bourgeois family background than a genuine commitment to hard-core ideology, and he was never a member of the Communist Party.

By now he was married to Frances Dorothy 'Dolly' Stephen, distantly related to Virginia Woolf – 'a tall woman of soft figure and relentless drive', according to Virgil Thomson.[8] Thus for security's sake Edward was glad to be gathered in 1924 – as Betty set off for India and Australia on her Theosophical excursion – to the bosom of the BBC, whose music broadcasts were then in their infancy.

He was recruited by Percy Pitt, a man after his own heart. Pitt, who by 1924 was the BBC's first Director of Music, did not belong to the ring of academics who otherwise dominated English music in the 1920s. Educated abroad, he was in touch with the radical developments which were considered so suspect in England; he also shared Edward's Continental taste for the long lunch hour. Enlisting Edward as an ally, he sent him north as Musical Director of the BBC's Newcastle station.

Here Edward reorganised the orchestra, planned all the programmes and conducted a remarkable mélange of concerts. His tastes, unlike Betty's, were catholic. He programmed Mahler at a time when Brahms was still daring in Newcastle, and conducted the first British performance of Stravinsky's *The Soldier's Tale*; nor did his devotion to the Second Viennese School prevent him featuring Hindemith and Honegger. Almost more interesting, he had a passion for the light classical repertoire. He had learned much of his music from the brass bands of his childhood, and now he played selections from Italian opera, Sousa marches and Viennese waltzes. For this enthusiasm, of course, he had the best of all precedents: on 27 May 1921, Schoenberg's Society for Private Musical Performance had given an entire concert of Strauss waltzes arranged by Berg and Schoenberg for piano, harmonium (Berg) and string quartet (with Webern the cellist).

In 1926 the Newcastle base was demoted to a relay station, and Edward moved to head office in London as a Music Programme Builder. (He never progressed beyond this post, though in his obituaries he was frequently described as the BBC's 'Music Director'.) His career now changed tack, as conducting took second place to administration.

The shortcomings of Edward's conducting have been eagerly seized upon by his critics, and it is worth remembering that in the 1920s he had considerable success. When Boult contrived some conducting dates for him with the Ballet Russe, to the ears of some critics Edward was the more successful of the two in conveying the spirit of Stravinsky.[9] The composer himself was reputed to have asked for him to conduct the Paris première of *Le Rossignol*, and to have been thwarted only by the opposition of the French musicians' union. Koussevitsky certainly invited Edward to go to Boston as his assistant – an offer he must often have regretted refusing, but at the time he did not want to leave England. He kept and prized letters of grateful praise he had received from Arthur Bliss, Bernard van Dieren and Frederick Delius.[10]

But Delius at least had had the advantage of not having *seen* Edward's performances. Contemporary critics objected to his limited range of gestures, eyes riveted to the score, and a beat that was both wooden and over-emphatic. Mr Clark, one paper remarked after the 1921 concerts, should not 'do incessantly with two arms that for which one is sufficient'.[11] He actually gestured more expressively in conversation when, as his friend and protégé Denis ApIvor remarked, he employed 'an emotional choreography of movement more usually associated with foreigners'.[12]

In the lighter music he loved, Edward could still produce entirely satisfying performances. Ernest Newman found his Johann Strauss unequalled in Britain: 'I was made to feel, at last, that Vienna is on the Danube and not on the Irwell.'[13] But in the field of his other passion, contemporary music, he was rapidly overtaken by other musicians with sounder technique and, as the pieces gradually crawled into the repertoire, a more detailed understanding of the scores.

It may have been that his recognition of distinction in a composer was not always supported by a note-by-note knowledge of the works. Even Percy Pitt suspected that sometimes Edward promoted pieces solely on the strength of a composer's name or, worse, a publisher's recommendation. Norman Del Mar was one of the horn players in an early performance of Schoenberg's *Kammersinfonie* which Edward conducted, and remembered witnessing its near-collapse, as Edward, who did not seem to understand the note relationships or tempi changes, refused to listen to the advice of those who did. Again, a performance of a Webern cantata which was lamentably under-rehearsed and largely fictional was hailed by Edward, this time from the audience, as the best he had ever heard. (Given the state of Webern performance at that time, this may of course have been true.)

Nevertheless, Edward's nose for genius had no equal, and he affected the nature and quality of music on the BBC, and thus British music in general, more than has ever been adequately acknowledged. (The British programmes which Betty and her mother heard as they huddled over the wireless in Mansfield Street were in all probability planned by Edward.) Under a Director-General, John Reith, who believed in offering an audience what it ought to like rather than what it did like, Edward was able to ensure that contemporary music was given more encouragement in Britain than anywhere else in the world.

It was also Edward who introduced Bach cantatas, then rarely heard, to the radio. Not everyone was grateful. Hailing a taxi on a Sunday morning, minutes before the weekly broadcast was due to begin, he demanded to be taken quickly to the BBC. Suspiciously the driver asked if he had anything to do with 'those cantatas'; and Edward, modestly accepting responsibility, found himself on the pavement.[14]

He was one of the architects of the system by which the BBC Symphony Orchestra is still run. When the threat of competition from Sir Thomas Beecham prompted the BBC to set up its own orchestra, a triumvirate within the Music Department pushed through a plan for a Comprehensive Orchestral Organisation – a single pool of players supplying five different performing groups: large and small symphony orchestras, theatre, light and popular orchestras. This was almost certainly Edward's concept; he also suggested Adrian Boult as the first chief conductor. But to make the plan workable he needed the administrative skills of his fellow programme builder Julian Herbage and his immediate superior Kenneth Wright. With W. W. Thompson, he made a major contribution to Prom programmes in the 1920s and 1930s, including the double-edged achievement of introducing Ravel's *Boléro*. The first day of these planning sessions, Thompson remembered, never varied; a brisk spell of pencil-sharpening followed by a bottle or two of Châteauneuf du Pape.

Edward worked hard for British composers. He refused to recommend the teenage Benjamin Britten for a BBC job, believing it would ruin his work, but introduced him to the GPO Film Unit, and can claim credit indirectly for *Night Mail* and the other early film scores. He was responsible for most of the BBC's scanty commissions at that time, including one to William Walton for *Nebuchadnezzar, or The Writing on the Wall*. (Confusion over length and fee, which provoked Walton into withdrawing the piece, now entitled *Belshazzar's Feast*, from the BBC, was also attributable to Edward.)[15] He saved Walton's Viola Concerto for the instrument when Walton, disappointed by Lionel Tertis's refusal to perform the piece, threatened to make it over for the violin; Edward suggested sending it instead to Hindemith, who gave it a highly successful première.[16]

Most importantly, Edward kept the BBC in touch with developments on the Continent, where he seemed to know every leading musician. His autograph book (kept, like many autograph books, in his son's name) contains affectionate inscriptions from Ansermet, Bartók, Berg, Cocteau, Eisler, Gerhard, Hindemith, Kodály, Koussevitsky, Miaskovsky,

Poulenc, Prokofiev, Ravel, Richard Strauss, Stravinsky, Stanislavsky, Webern and dozens more; and Adrian Boult remembered, 'If one rang him up and asked what Stravinsky was working on at that moment he would tell you most probably not only what the work was but when it would be ready and when the first performance might be expected and when it would be available for performance in London.' [17]

Between 1928 and 1935 he brought all the leading European composers to Britain. To him the BBC owed Webern conducting his Five Movements for String Orchestra, (his own reworking of his Op. 5), Stravinsky playing his own piano concerto, Hindemith his own viola concerto, Bartók his piano music, and Strauss conducting his *Alpensinfonie*. On Schoenberg's behalf Edward launched a 'violent offensive' which Schoenberg's biographer felt was all that kept him in Europe in the early thirties. He programmed the British premières of *Gurrelieder* and *Erwartung*, and an evening which combined *Music to Accompany a Cinema Scene* with Variations for Orchestra, Op. 31. (This latter was the piece which Ernest Newman introduced live with the words, 'It will last for twenty minutes and you may feel that you might be better employed'.) [18] Berg did not come to Britain, but Edward's greatest achievement, perhaps, was to have virtually all his major works performed: Three Pieces from the Lyric Suite, the Chamber Concerto, the Violin Concerto, symphonic extracts from *Lulu* and, a landmark in the history of serious music on the BBC, in March 1934 a complete performance of *Wozzeck*.

In the days before television, radio personalities could be celebrities, and Edward was now a conspicuous figure on the music scene, usually to be found at Casa Prada, with its simulacrum of European café life. He instituted the practice among the clientele of autographing the tablecloths; the signatures were later lovingly embroidered by Signora Prada as a testimonial to the brilliance of the circle revolving around the restaurant in the Euston Road – Stravinsky, Bartók, Hindemith, Webern, Pablo Casals, Luigi Dallapiccola, Roberto Gerhard, Constant Lambert and Edward himself. Two of Lambert's more printable limericks were written on Casa Prada paper, the first dedicated to 'Nobby Clarke [sic], August 28th, 1930' –

> The first of two camp hippopotami
> To the second said, 'What are you, what am I?
> Though our organs are massive
> As lovers we're passive.
> How can we resolve this dichotomy?'

Mr Westrup tore *Lulu* to pieces,
Declaring it atonal *faeces.*
He said, 'I don't mind
When the canon's behind,
But I can't bear *per arsis et thesis!*'

Later Edward would introduce Betty to Prada's, and in old age she recalled her evenings there with an ingenuous enthusiasm which betrayed all over again her gratitude at having been given the entrée to a world which would otherwise probably have been closed to her under suspicion of being an amateur and dilettante, her pride at having been made, in Edward's wake, an honorary 'insider'. 'Constant Lambert's latest clerihew, Dallapiccola reciting Dante, the discussions and company of visiting composers and artists, the comradeship of friends and Edward's resounding laugh ringing out . . . the best of the café life of Europe.'

On 10 December 1933, in an article headed 'Perpetrator', the *Sunday Express* described Edward as

BBC Curio Collector and Staff Conductor. Highest of highbrows, brilliant linguist and musical historian . . . . Has the faith of a fanatic in acute discord, and, as a prophet, has a good deal of honour at the BBC . . . . Think of him as the perpetrator and prime promoter of all the Hindemith, Schoenberg and Stravinsky that you hear (or don't hear – I've often wondered) and you will want to throw a brick. Meet him, and you will immediately be charmed . . . . Talks well, knows the best and cheapest restaurants and a good wine . . . . Looks foreign, talks foreign, is actually English. Kindly, amused eyes, with wrinkles.

In fact, Edward's position at the BBC was precarious. Adrian Boult, who from 1930 was Director of Music as well as principal conductor, was an ally – an odd couple if ever there was one, Edward with his Châteauneuf du Pape and his Continental airs, and the precise, perfectionist Boult, 'reeking of Horlicks'.[19] But Boult too was an adventurous and eclectic musician, even if, in Constant Lambert's description, he conducted Schoenberg 'with a touch of the embarrassment and circumspection shown by a really polite protestant who has found himself involved in a religious ceremony of some totally differing creed'.[20]

Boult's support, however, was not enough. Contemporary music had no more popular support than it does now, and senior BBC staff worried about falling audiences; Reith himself grumbled. 'Such music does not leave me cold – I wish it did.'[21] Nor was Edward valued as a conductor. After a flying start in the first years, the BBC Symphony Orchestra had declined. One cause was adjudged to be the over-use of inadequate staff conductors – and Edward was specifically cited by his colleague Julian Herbage.

He would have been well advised to tread carefully. But from the beginning he had proved himself constitutionally incapable of playing the game by the BBC's rules. In Newcastle it was noticed that he needed a clerk to maintain any sort of order in the office – and a male one, because his language under stress was 'most unpleasant'. At head office in London he complicated his life and that of others by taking a selection of part-time jobs outside the BBC, inclining to the view that routine was dreary and regular hours for other people. He was as often as not to be found at the Arts Theatre, where he was the Music Director, or out to lunch on a scale which staggered the accounts department. (Quizzed about his expenses, he explained that his digestion was weak, and eating at more modest establishments in the Strand made him ill.) After one period during which he was more than usually *distrait* and untraceable, and wore one arm in a sling, he requested sick leave. This he used to conduct a concert in Prague – and was detected the night before he left conducting another private concert at the restaurant Le Boulestin, where doubtless a good deal of rehearsal had been necessary in preceding weeks.

Like Percy Pitt, Edward irritated his colleagues by conducting transactions on the telephone in foreign languages and making no notes, leaving them to chase the loose ends. He had what Bernard van Dieren referred to as 'graphophobia',[22] finding himself unable to write even to Schoenberg, who complained, 'Dear Friend: it is very distressing that you never write me. We speak often of you – but I miss your response.'[23]

The problems intensified after the BBC moved its headquarters from the Strand and Savoy Hill, which had been in many ways like Edward himself – eccentric, improvisatory, happiest operating on a personal basis. Broadcasting House in Portland Place (still the home of BBC radio, for the present at least) was more pompous, the organisation more bureaucratic, with the stress increasingly on administration and control rather than creativity, and Edward patently failed to fit the new mould.

His political beliefs now came into question. The pianist Lamond wrote only half-jokingly to 'Mr Clark the Communist';[24] and though Edward's politics amounted to little more seditious than a naïve delight in the broadest socialist principles and an emotional championship of the Soviet Union as a counterweight to fascism, the climate within official organisations like the BBC was becoming more repressive as sympathy for communism increased in the country after the Depression. (BBC employees holding socialist beliefs were to complain a few years later of being shadowed as they left Broadcasting House.)[25] It was perhaps typical of Edward that he should have chosen 1934, the year of the Incitement to Disaffection Bill, to visit Moscow and Prague on a conducting tour.

At the other end of the political spectrum Edward's ex-wife Dolly was an additional source of embarrassment as she slid round, during the 1930s, from the pro-Soviet left to the pro-Nazi right. Overtaking Oswald Mosley on the right, she ultimately became a member of the Imperial Fascist League. She and Edward had separated in the mid-1920s, after which in 1929 Dolly had had an affair with the BBC's Chief Engineer, Peter Eckersley, which in its outcome nearly precipitated the downfall of Lord Reith. Eckersley was already married and Reith, in accordance with his well-known scruples, felt impelled to sack him, despite his brilliance and conspicuous value to the Corporation – a move pilloried in the press as self-righteous and dictatorial.[26]

Within a few years of leaving the BBC, Eckersley was working with Mosley, exploring the possibilities of 'black' broadcasting – that is, broadcasting whose source was camouflaged. Mosley wished to be able to transmit, both to England and to selected European countries, broadcasts purporting to be British but in fact originating on the Continent, and Eckersley was prepared to help him. He and Dolly also had a good deal of contact with Germany, and Dolly went there just before the outbreak of war. (Before long she would be working for a German radio station and making a major contribution to the German propaganda machine by recruiting William Joyce, the alleged 'Lord Haw-Haw'. For this she would spend eight months in jail in England at the end of the war.)[27]

Edward had nothing directly to do with Dolly's political enthusiasms – they were divorced in 1930 – but the associations through her with Eckersley would hardly have endeared him to Reith, any more than his temperament would have been congenial. Edward set a good deal of store by appearances, and would pick up a taxi a hundred yards away from a concert hall in order to arrive in style. He was rumoured to have gone through several fortunes, taken two women to the south of France, and gone on a blinder in Paris when he was supposed to have been negotiating with Toscanini. His temper was unpredictable, and stories circulated about papers shredded and telephones thrown out of windows. Without formal qualifications or acceptably British social graces, he utterly failed to get on with the establishment figures who sat on the BBC's Music Advisory Committee.

In this he had the entire sympathy of Boult, who once wrote, 'I value the meetings of the Music Advisory Committee most highly because I consider they are representative of the average or perhaps of the rather more stupid type of professional.'[28] But this helped Edward not at all at the only meeting he attended, where he was taken to task for allegedly giving too many concerts in the coming season to foreigners, who were also his friends. (The 'foreigners' were Ernest Ansermet, Oskar Fried and Herman Scherchen.) Edward left the meeting in despair, was violently sick, and never went to another.

In the end, however, Edward's downfall at the BBC was money. In his early days at the BBC he had been described delicately as 'not quite normal from the financial and economic point of view', a man to whom income tax always came as an unforeseen emergency. Among his papers when he died were bills from tailors in Berlin dated 1910 and unpaid, and he was constantly borrowing from the BBC for one purpose and using the money for another. To the suggestion that he might consider being paid monthly instead of weekly he replied in horror, 'I would have to start doing book-keeping. . . . To embark upon this, which means counting up pennies and shillings, would render my present tormented existence quite insupportable.'

He described his style of economy as 'primitive'. 'My experience is that banks are the merest financial quicksand,' he wrote with feeling. 'There is never any money in them when you want it, and I have reason to know that cheque writing is a veritable snare and delusion. For me the most practical manner of dealing with money is to receive it in small packets at frequent intervals, when by looking in my pocket I know exactly how much I have' – a fairly accurate description of the behaviour of a child of eight.[29]

It was against this background that the end came. The BBC was planning its first foreign tour in the spring of 1936, and Edward wished to visit all the host cities in January to finalise the programmes – Paris, Vienna, Zurich and Budapest, with a trip to Monte Carlo to see Toscanini thrown in for good measure. The Administrative Branch resisted strongly, but Boult and a junior administrator named Richard Howgill campaigned for him, and eventually a compromise was reached, with Edward permitted to spend two days each in Paris and Monte Carlo. But then Berg died, and he felt the BBC should be represented at the funeral – in Vienna. He was away for a week longer than had been agreed, failing to meet Toscanini, missing the Winter Proms at home, and spending approximately twice as much as had been allocated to him.

His stock was not high with the BBC when, without warning, the Music Department decided to alter the programmes he had devised carefully in collaboration with the composers. He had been especially anxious that in Budapest the orchestra should feature a major work of Bartók; but for reasons of box office, Beethoven's Fifth Symphony was substituted. Bartók had to be content with a less significant work, and Edward felt personally responsible for a betrayal.

In the version of the story he gave to the press, these machinations took place while he lay stricken with flu in Sussex. He made his way to London to see Boult, who never appeared. 'It was impossible for me to wait,' said Edward, 'my legs had no strength. I sat down and wrote out my resignation. I was compelled to resign. I have burned my boats, but it is better than burning myself.'[30] Whatever he wrote, it was fatal. Boult too had a temper and Edward, he felt, had shown in that letter a complete misconception of his role in the BBC.[31] He accepted the resignation, and the Administration Branch did not even require Edward to serve out his notice.

A scrap of paper, undated, survives from the BBC days, on which Edward has scribbled desperately,

> For God's sake help me to make a lot of money quick and let's get out of this bloody place. I'm fed up with the buggering about. Can't do anything, get no support, the people we depend on are a lot of c—— and it would be damn good to go and be our own bleeding masters somewhere. Bugger, bugger, bugger, and you can show this to Reith and tell him to stuff it up.[32]

Now he was his own master with a vengeance.

Behind the façade of the suave *homme de théâtre* whom Betty met two years after his departure from the BBC, when he was already in limbo, this was at least part of the reality – a man without a foothold in the music profession, who had thrown himself head first out of the only niche likely to fit him. The BBC needed his flair and his European connections and came nowhere near finding a substitute for over twenty years. But even more acutely did Edward need the BBC for the authority and the administrative support it gave him. From then on, James Clark (Edward's eldest son) has commented dispassionately, 'the word "effective" was perhaps what was missing from his life'.

CHAPTER SIX

Twelve-tone Lizzie

EDWARD'S FOUNDATIONS WERE crumbling, because his eminence in the music world depended heavily on finding the right outlet for his peculiar gifts; he never lost his talent, but he would search desperately for a means of expressing it. When Betty met him, however, his insecurity was to some extent camouflaged by his position as Honorary Secretary to the International Society for Contemporary Music, in which he had been influential for a decade.

Founded in 1923, the ISCM strove to coordinate developments in modern music in Europe and America. Each member country had its own organisation (the London Centre for Contemporary Music acted as the British Section) and a selection committee which chose eight works to forward for the consideration of the International Jury. Winning pieces were played at the annual ISCM Festival.

It was as an international figure that Edward appealed to Betty. He knew everyone she admired, had been everywhere she wanted to go, moved with confidence in a world she longed to penetrate. His milieu was romantic – the room crowded with miniature scores, ancient gramophones, French first editions, orchestral parts for *Lulu*, candles in bottles, posters for his concert in Moscow and another in Paris promoted by Jean Cocteau, drawings of him by Satie and Bernard Meninsky, a cup and saucer of Constructivist design covered with the signatures of progressive Russian composers, the Blaue Reiter album and an issue of *Blast* which included a personal attack on him by Wyndham Lewis, a miscellany of communist pamphlets . . . .

His vague, emotional brand of socialism corresponded with her own. She was never an activist, nor even took a systematic interest in politics, but Aunt Con's influence had been more than simply musical, and all her life Betty's sympathies were fundamentally left-wing and anti-Establishment.

Edward, she felt, was attractive to women. She was inclined to pretend that Dolly had never existed – in her biographical account of Edward there is no mention of a previous marriage – but she was proud of his bachelor reputation for squiring glamorous girls. In a good humour he had the air of a happy cat, and in conversation with someone he liked, he had the great gift of making his listener feel uniquely important. He loved football, a legacy of the years in Ruhleben where he had played with great verve; he went regularly to boxing matches with Ernest Newman,[1] and to the local fleapit on a Saturday afternoon to see and re-see ancient thrillers and Westerns or, best of all, Will Hay comedies.

Most important in Betty's eyes, he was passionately interested, as no one else in her life had been, in the field she had adopted as her own. She loved his enthusiasm for ideas – another friend remembered him arguing about the relative merits of two translations of Beaumarchais with sweat on his brow[2] – and she profoundly admired his knowledge. Above all, he took music seriously, as she did; for him it was a way of life, not the dilettante pastime it was considered in her parents' world. And he took *her* music seriously, nourishing and enriching it at a crucial time. The image she chose to describe their meeting was that of a small stream joining a mighty river and being swept along in it, increasing in volume and speed.[3] However she was later to behave, Edward was, as she said, her great and consuming love.

What Edward loved in her, it is harder to say. He was not given to articulating his emotions; and such letters as he did write to her were destroyed, some in 1951 when their relationship reached its lowest ebb, and the majority after her death, at her express request. The more sceptical of her friends felt he attached himself to her as a source of energy and material support; but this is to discount entirely her very real attractions – intelligence, a wit that was already taking a Rabelaisian turn, generosity, warmth, dedication to music. Most likely of all, perhaps, he responded to her love because she so desperately wanted him to.

Equally difficult to answer is the question of exactly how and how much he influenced her composing. The first years of their relationship embraced the point at which she began systematically to use the serial, or twelve-tone, techniques which made her name. These techniques had been evolved primarily by Schoenberg and developed by Webern, and many have automatically assumed that they were transmitted directly to her in their entirety by Edward, who was after all as familiar as anyone with the work of the Second Viennese School.

Serialism, the twelve-tone method, was a logical extension of the gradual abandonment of tonality (the key system) which had begun long before the end of the nineteenth century. As music progressed towards dissonance and away from tonality, it became obvious that some other source of coherence would be needed, some alternative means of organising the material as effectively as the key system had done.

The key system gave automatic priority to certain notes in the scale; but to those using the serial method, all twelve notes of the octave, black and white, were equally important, and all were used as the basic material of any composition. The fundamental idea of the piece was presented in a series of the twelve notes in a characteristic order, with no note repeated until all the others had been used, to ensure that none had precedence. The whole piece was to be evolved from this basic set, by a process of continuous variation and development, so that every part of the work could in some way be related to the original idea. Both the horizontal and the vertical dimension of the musical 'space' were penetrated by the basic idea, so that not only the melodies but also the harmonies were regulated by the order of notes within the series and the relationships between them. For variety, the series could also be played upside down, back to front, and transposed up or down the scale, as long as the order of the notes was preserved.

Those who used the serial technique felt it vital to explain that it was no more mechanical, no more a formula for automatic writing than the key system with all the rules it possesses. It was not a prescription, but a tool to help different composers express themselves differently, adapting the method to their own ends. 'I do not compose principles,' wrote Schoenberg angrily, 'but music.' [4]

In the years before her meeting with Edward, Betty's music, especially her writing for strings, had been becoming increasingly chromatic and dissonant, but the first formally serial work was her Chamber Concerto I for nine instruments, Op. 8/1, the first of a projected set of six concertos. She began it in 1939, but was still at work on the first movement when Neville Chamberlain made his announcement of war with Germany, and only completed the piece in the following year. The concerto is a short work, no more than nine minutes long, serially based and clearly demonstrating the interest in equal-part writing which Betty had picked up from Purcell. The texture of the music is thin, with every instrument distinct, and in comparison with most of the music being written in Britain at that time, it was startlingly radical.

Betty dedicated the Chamber Concerto to Edward. But then and ever afterwards she firmly maintained that in the beginning she came to serial methods by herself. In 1939, she claimed, she had never even encountered the expression 'twelve-tone'. She had heard only the *Gurre-lieder* of Schoenberg, which she detested, and a limited amount of Webern – the String Trio Op. 20 and possibly the Five Movements for String Orchestra, and his cantata *Das Augenlicht*, performed at the ISCM Festival in London in 1938. This certainly had a devastating impact; her immediate reaction was that here was the 'guiding spirit to all future music'. But she insisted that she had had no opportunity to study a score, and had in fact seen no Webern score until 1948.

It was important for her to stress this, because her Chamber Concerto was compared almost as a matter of course with Webern's Op. 24, the Concerto for nine solo instruments – the *same* nine instruments – which he had written in 1934. The implication was inevitably that hers was a pale imitation, and she was to be at pains to point out that Op. 24 was only published in Britain in 1942, well after her Op. 8 had been completed.

Her detractors have always been irritated by her insistence on her originality. In its most extreme form it led her to say, 'Oh – did Schoenberg use the twelve-tone method too?', which is taken as a fatuous attempt to force her way into the vanguard and equate herself with a revolutionary and a genius. Critics point out that her closest companion was Schoenberg's only English pupil, who had personally seen to it that there were performances of most of the key serial works in the late 1920s and early 1930s. Articles had been written by 1939 on Schoenberg's innovations, many of his scores had been published, and other young British composers had been taking a keen interest in the Second Viennese School since the 1920s – Britten in Berg, and Walton in Schoenberg.

Even senior composers were keeping abreast; in his last years Frank Bridge, for instance, was experimenting with radical textures reminiscent of Berg. As composer and critic Anthony Payne points out, Bridge was one of the few twentieth-century composers about whom Betty had nothing bad to say; though there is no surviving evidence, she is likely to have had some contact with him, as he was the viola player in Miss Motto's quartet which she followed faithfully, and which played some of his music. His late works may perhaps have been a channel for some of the European ideas which interested her.

In the end the question of Betty's independence can only be answered with a balance of probabilities, which seems to tilt in her favour. Almost certainly she had heard more serial music than she implied; and very probably she discussed what she heard with Edward, at least in basic terms. There are forty-eight possible forms of any given series if it is reversed, inverted and transposed; and amongst Edward's papers there are several sheets on which he has laboriously copied out all forty-eight versions of different series [5] – presumably, since he was not composing himself, for the purposes of demonstration: and what audience more likely than Betty? She was not ashamed to say in her autobiography that from 1938 onwards, 'his musical yardstick became mine'.

But none of this makes her a slavish imitator of Webern. Even if scores of the Second Viennese School were published, they were hard to buy in England, especially after the German invasion of Austria. And even if they had been readily available, it is highly unlikely that Betty would have sat down to analyse them methodically; systematic study was never her style. She was not particularly well educated musically – in comparison, say, with William Walton, who was introduced to contemporary music at the age of ten by the enlightened organist of Christ Church Cathedral, where he was a chorister. The fourteen-year-old Adrian Boult was being given the complete edition of Grove's *Dictionary* at a time when Betty's most-requested present was a marmoset and her favourite pursuit hockey on roller-skates. It is only too possible that though concerts and scores existed, she had neither heard nor seen them; after all, it was not until 1949 that she heard *Pierrot lunaire*, almost forty years after its composition. Asked point-blank whether she had heard Webern's concerto before writing her own, she retorted simply, 'I could have done, no doubt, but I didn't.' [6]

Other composers arrived independently at their versions of the serial method – Dallapiccola, for example, working in the Italy of the 1930s where atonal music was discouraged as anti-fascist internationalism, or Milton Babbitt in America. And most important, there are elements tending in the direction of serial technique in her early work, written at a time when she could not plausibly be accused of deriving them from Vienna. As she studied the keyboard works of Frescobaldi and others, and realised them for strings, she would take little cells of music and try them out in different positions. In some of her early songs she appears to be running her melody methodically through the different instrumental lines, as one might treat the series in a twelve-note work; and in *The Night is Darkening*, written in 1934, a fragment of melody is suddenly transposed up and down, never developed but just planted on different levels and twisted in various directions. [7]

She herself traced the origins of her serial techniques to the English tradition. Her five-part Fantasia in the style of Purcell could be seen as an attempt to combine atonal sounds with a technique of writing for equal voices which was three centuries old. 'It was the experience of [the Purcell Fantasias],' she wrote later, 'with their independent string part writing, with their English "sensibility" and vitality and wonderful *linear* counterpoint, coupled with the newly accepted harmonic intervals which pointed for me to new musical possibilities.'[8] It seems most likely that, in her phrase, her ear was already cocked to a new music when she met Edward, but he suggested in detail how she might exploit the sounds she was hearing.

It was not so much that Betty wanted to be the *first* serial composer; until her old age, when she became generally more combative, she was not concerned to establish her priority over other British serialists like Humphrey Searle, who was actually a pupil of Webern, or Christian Darnton, who (as Denis ApIvor has pointed out)[9] was already highly dissonant and epigrammatic in the 1920s. It was that she felt an overwhelming need to be original, not an imitator, to be distinct from other people – and the urge to be different, stretching back into childhood, may by itself explain why she voluntarily struck out along such a particularly bumpy musical path.

She may have had an infinite number of reasons for composing as she did. She complained of feeling nauseated by the cloying diatonicism, 'the everlasting cadence', which permeated much contemporary music. It may simply be that in struggling away from it, these are the sounds she heard, and the serial method was simply a convenient tool with which to express them – in Gerhard's words, 'a kind of cradle of scaffolding which allows the composer to work at certain aspects or levels of the sound fabric, at which he could not get without this scaffolding'.[10]

Some critics, perceiving a certain rigidity in the technique, have suggested that she needed it for support. Foulds had suggested that she lacked 'Innitiative'; the serial method in a sense supplied it by always furnishing the next note. Those who admire her moderately or not at all diagnose a lack of natural inventiveness. Her need and desire to write, they say, were greater than her capacity to do it, or the importance of what she had to say; serialism compensated for these shortcomings. Braque once said that his life's object was 'to bring painting within the reach of my own gifts' – a remark she felt was worth copying out. Among her gifts were clarity and control, and the serial discipline might have seemed a means of bringing music within her reach.

Those who feel Betty underrated her gifts see her serialism more positively – not as an external device for generating music artificially, but as a means of conveying the music she was quite capable of generating for herself. Anthony Payne, one of her most loyal champions, has described the technique as a way of setting down *quickly* the music produced by very rapid mental processes. 'You don't want to have to fight for what the next note's going to be, you want to *know* what it's going to be, because you're thinking about lots of other things, the rhythm, the texture. You can see the thing stretching ahead into the next ten minutes and you want to get it down quickly, not mess about inventing every single aspect. If you have that kind of mind, the twelve-note system is something which just gives you an ever-spawning series of notes to flesh out what you can hear.'

Most likely of all is that Betty wanted to be and to feel radical. She sincerely believed that new music should make a new sound, otherwise it had little point. After the discoveries made by Schoenberg, Stravinsky, Bartók and Webern, to use the harmonies, gestures and rhythms of the nineteenth century would be, she claimed, like a modern poet using the diction of Shelley, and she was more interested in experimenting with a new language, even at the risk of being misunderstood.

She was not afraid of working in isolation – almost preferred it, as she did not enjoy competing – and she had a positive relish for some types of adversity. This was no masochistic desire to be reviled and ostracised; again, she was struggling to mark out territory for herself *inside* the family of music by evolving a distinctive identity. But she did like a fight; Ursula observed shrewdly, 'She has to have the antagonism which justifies her inability to conform.'[11] And by moving up into the vanguard of contemporary music at that moment, Betty could be sure of encountering as much antagonism as anyone could want.

There are logical reasons why Schoenberg's music, and that of other twelve-tone composers, should have met with incomprehension, impatience and initial dislike. Berg once tried to explain why Schoenberg's work was difficult to appreciate.[12] To 'understand' a piece, one must be able to distinguish the different instrumental voices within it, identify the beginnings and ends of melodies, recognise the simultaneous soundings of notes as harmonies, pick out the various rhythms.

All these functions are more complicated in serial music. The melodies, for example, bear little relation to what has traditionally been understood by the word; they are all different lengths, they stop and start all the time, there is no symmetry in their structure, and they are not framed in regular two- or four-bar phrases. They are stated very quickly and then varied at once, with no literal repetition permitted. Although the order of notes in the series must be strictly observed, the notes may appear in any octave; so the intervals between notes are frequently far more extreme than is common in tonal music, and to follow a series one may have to plunge from one instrumental line to another in quick succession.

But this hardly explains the hysterical hostility which greeted each new work from the Second Viennese School. As Britten pointed out (having been prevented by the Royal College of Music from studying with Berg), the prejudice in England against Schoenberg, Berg and Webern in the 1920s and 1930s seemed almost to be a moral one; serial music was foreign, sinister and subversive. But even on the Continent it was considered to be beyond the pale and regarded not so much with distaste as with anger and fear.

Atonality, it was stated, was unnatural; tonality, like pictorial realism, was the norm, was somehow in man's blood. 'It has been wittily said,' Dallapiccola recorded, 'that God, who gave us the moral law, also took care, in His infinite bounty, to provide us with the tonal system.'[13] Atonality in general had no physical or psychological basis in natural laws; *ergo*, the serialists, practitioners of atonality in its most extreme form, were mad or bad.

'The only person who can help poor Schoenberg now,' wrote Richard Strauss to Mahler's wife Alma, 'is a psychiatrist. . . . I think he'd do better to shovel snow instead of scribbling on music-paper.'[14] At a concert of the music of the Second Viennese School in Vienna in 1913, rioting had broken out by the interval. Testifying in the lawsuit which followed, a Viennese doctor declared that the effect of such music was 'enervating and injurious to the nervous system. . . . Many of the audience showed exterior signs of deep mental depression.' Twelve years later in December 1925, the première of *Wozzeck* in Berlin was described in the press as 'tortured and mistuned cackling . . . bestial outcries'. 'Berg,' the critic spluttered, 'is the poisoner of the fountainhead of German music. . . . Everywhere, plain madmen . . . the shock troops of atonalistis, the dervishes of Arnold Schoenberg. . . . A musical swindler . . . a musical danger to the community. . . . We are confronted here, in the field of music, with a capital offence.'

Twelve years later still, Hindemith was referring to them as 'Dode*caco*phonists', a rather German play on the word 'dodeca-phony'/'twelve-tone'. In 1940, as Betty was finishing her Chamber Concerto, *Time* magazine guffawed, 'The main difficulty is to get all of Schoenberg's wrong notes in the right places.'[15] And as late as 1951, more than twenty-five years after the first explicitly serial piece had been performed, Neville Cardus was describing Dallapiccola's *Il Prigioniero* as 'the familiar unpleasant ejaculatory onomatopoeic sadistic composition presumably in the fashion at the moment. . . . When indeed is the contemporary composer going to grow up and outlive the Meccano set of his orchestra?'

Betty already relished a row, and she was more than willing to take up arms. She first set foot on the field of battle, with Edward at her side, at the ISCM Festival of 1939, which was held in Warsaw. She later described this expedition as 'the halcyon period of my whole life'. It was her first professional trip, her String Quartet II having been selected for performance by the international jury. It was the first time she had travelled with Edward, who was attending the Festival in his capacity as Honorary Secretary. There was a heat-wave, Warsaw was *en fleur*, and, to Betty and Edward at least, the clouds gathering over Germany as yet cast no shadow on Poland.

To linger in Eastern Europe in the summer of 1939 was to tempt fate, especially with Edward's past record of being in the wrong place at key moments in history. Nevertheless, as the British Legation in Warsaw began to evacuate its nationals, Betty and Edward pressed on to Moscow, where Edward had ISCM business to attend to and a cache of back fees in roubles which he was obliged to spend in Russia. All Betty's dreams of a cosmopolitan and cultured existence were being realised. She went to rehearsals at the Bolshoi; she met Prokofiev; she talked modern music incessantly; and in the train on the way home across Russia she wrote her first string trio, Op. 5/6, 'steppe by steppe'.

Inevitably, the return to England was an anti-climax. Although she had been spending less and less time with Ian, she was still living with him and the children, and they had planned to move into a small house of their own in Old Church Street, Chelsea. But by May 1939 he had joined the War Reserve Police and was out much of the day. As the threat of war and the fear of aerial bombing increased, Sebastian, Rose and Tess (now aged five and three) had been sent to live with Lady Emily and their nanny at Barbie's house, Beechwood, in Lavington, Sussex, which had been the Reverend Henry Manning's rectory before he went over to Rome. (Euan Wallace had sold the Scottish estate to be nearer London as his political career flourished.) The basement at Mansfield Street was being packed up and the new house was cold and empty. Memories of Warsaw were too powerful, and Betty seized the opportunity of a trifling argument with Ian to make a break. She turned up on the doorstep of 12 Fitzroy Street at eight o'clock in the morning. 'I did not even know', she wrote later, 'that I would be welcome.'

CHAPTER SEVEN

Just a Bloody Char

BETTY'S FIRST DISCOVERY when she went to live with Edward would not have surprised the BBC, but it surprised her. He had no money; and this cast a rather different complexion on their life together, which was in any case about to be transformed by the war.

Edward's reaction to Betty's arrival, on the other hand, can only be guessed at. In the short term she was able to deduce that he was pleased from the fact that he telephoned a friend to invite him to lunch at Prada's 'in a celebratory tone of voice'. In the longer term he must have seen his past life of late restaurant breakfasts, picturesque Bohemian disorder and European jaunts flashing before his eyes. Betty had no intention of relinquishing her children, and Edward – jobless and living in what were very definitely bachelor apartments – found himself with an instant family in prospect.

In the autumn of 1939, while the children were evacuees with Lady Emily in Sussex, final decisions could be postponed. Betty visited them as often as she could, and was able at the same time to see Edward, who was staying with friends at Ditchling not far from Beechwood. For almost a year Betty and Edward found it possible to maintain some of the glamour of their courtship. A war which was presented as a threat to civilisation encouraged people to place a far higher value on the arts than they had ever done in peacetime. Everywhere groups sprang up to promote concert-giving and protect the welfare of musicians and other artists who in the past had been left to fend for themselves, and for Edward and Betty, responsible for several of these initiatives, life was busy and purposeful in the limbo of the Phoney War.

Provided that he had assistants to deal with the paperwork, Edward enjoyed organising, and he revelled in events for special occasions. His last project in peacetime had been the Festival of Music for the People which, with Alan Bush, he had been planning when Betty first visited Fitzroy Street. The Festival was intended as a celebration of international socialism, and took for its motto 'Art Made By the People and For the People, A Joy to the Maker and the User'.

Its centrepiece was a grand pageant, 'Music and The People', at the Albert Hall, in which Paul Robeson starred, with a hundred dancers and five hundred massed voices drawn from working men's choirs all over the country. Betty's contribution was a brass episode entitled *Feudal England*, with Parry Jones in the role of 'the Reaper'. This was followed on the second night by Schoenberg's *Peace on Earth*, three cantatas by Hanns Eisler, and a medley for balalaika orchestra. The final concert opened with Britten's *Ballad of Heroes*, in memory of the members of the International Brigade killed in the Spanish Civil War, and moved by way of John Ireland's *These Things Shall Be*, which quotes the Internationale, to Alan Bush's Piano Concerto, in which the audience is exhorted to consider the position of the musician in present-day society. The Festival absorbed a great deal of effort and enthusiasm, and Edward must have been disappointed by the uncharitable reaction of Edward Dent, his long-time colleague as President of the ISCM. 'Most of it seemed very amateurish and boring, with the usual graceful young men and lumpy (not very) young women bundling about over the arena in folk dances. . . .' [1]

More strictly functional was 'Corno and Co.', an agency largely operated by Betty, whose object was to find musicians the bread-and-butter work – copying, notating, research – which might help to subsidise their serious composition in the lean years to come. Edward meanwhile was absorbed in a separate organisation entitled the Association of British Musicians, which aimed to support serious music directly by promoting concert-giving, always his favourite occupation. (It ran neck and neck with the Council for Education in Music and the Arts – later to become the Arts Council – which was founded in January 1940.)

The ABM's first venture was a highly ambitious Anglo-French Festival intended to celebrate and cement the alliance and spiritual entente between the two countries. The programmes were a marvellous mélange of French and English music from Boyce and Grétry to Berners, Bizet and Ibert, and Edward made an entirely characteristic foray to France to engage performers to stand alongside the likes of Maggie Teyte, Clifford Curzon and Malcolm Sargent. He arrived in Paris when the French leaders were already discussing terms for surrender, and this time beat a hasty retreat. But nothing could salvage the first concert, which took place, without French artists, on 18 June, three weeks after the evacuation from Dunkirk and two days before the capitulation of the Pétain government. 'The Marseillaise,' Betty recorded, 'sounded like the swan song of Europe'.

The Phoney War and Betty's unquestioning sense of security with Edward came to an end at about the same time. By the middle of 1940 the problem of the children was acute. Ian, still hoping to salvage the marriage, was unwilling to give Betty a divorce; he was anxious to remain close to the children, but on his air force pay could not afford the nanny he would need if he were to take them. Number 12 Fitzroy Street was totally impracticable for children, but Edward had no money to live anywhere else. Lady Emily wanted to leave Sussex and return to London to be with Sir Edwin – who had in any case begun to resent the arrangement whereby his wife looked after the children and he himself effectively paid for their support.

Crippled by supertax for which he had not made provision – 'Tax vobiscum', he wrote – Sir Edwin also objected to the aura of muddle which seemed to surround Betty and Edward. Photographs of Betty from the late 1930s show a slight, taut, angular figure, elegant legs and beautiful, well-displayed hands, aggressive cigarette already firmly in place. The clothes are smart, the hairstyle more sophisticated, but behind the dash the air of doubt and defensiveness is much the same. A valuable violin belonging to Betty, which she had hidden from a prying landlady, had just been burnt as rubbish. 'Slip-slop – O dear,' Sir Edwin lamented to Lady Emily. 'What a mess Betty has made of her first thirty years: what will she do twenty years on?'

When Euan Wallace, now Minister of Transport, warned that in the event of a threatened invasion Lavington would be totally cut off from London, Betty knew they had to find another solution. For a short time she took a bungalow in Ditchling for the children and their nanny and spent every weekend there, returning on Monday mornings to Edward and Fitzroy Street. But in the circumstances she was grateful when Ursula offered to house the children, their nanny and herself at Blagdon, the Ridley family home outside Newcastle. In June 1940 they moved north; and the decision became irrevocable weeks later when in the first phase of the Blitz, Fitzroy Street was bombed.

The rescue seemed providential, but all were soon regretting Ursula's generous gesture. The Ridleys were a long-established family; her husband Matthew or Matt had inherited the title of the third Viscount Ridley as a teenager in 1916, and they were both conscious of their position in the county – though in their neighbours' eyes, they were

considered eccentric and positively avant-garde. Matthew Ridley, though
he had some of the interests of a country squire, also had a passion for
racing cars that he built in his own workshops, and commissioned
William Nicholson, Rodrigo Moynihan and Rex Whistler to paint his
children. He was a highly intelligent man with some extremely conservative ideas and a resistance to the contemporary arts, and he
strongly disapproved of Betty's ramshackle ménage – for Edward soon
followed Betty and returned to his home town of Newcastle. Nor was
Matt overly fond of the company of children, and, coming home
exhausted on leave from the army, was not best pleased to find their
numbers swollen by three.

Betty's relationship with Ursula was very little easier – had, in fact,
hardly altered at all since their childhood. It is hard to change how your
sister sees you. 'All communication', writes Brigid McConville,

> takes place on the current page of a sort of psychic family album which
> stretches as far back as our memories of each other. . . . Beneath a sister's
> surface are layers and layers of herself and we have watched them
> accumulate, never quite forgetting what is underneath. . . . A meeting
> with a sister means coming face to face with the images of your former
> self which still live in her mind's eye.[2]

In Ursula's mind's eye, Betty was eternally the 'problem' sister,
always wanting to be different; and the label applied in youth became
self-fulfilling at Blagdon. The desire to shock, which had carried Betty
far as a social technique in London, had an element of overkill in
Northumberland. She was by now a chain smoker, jerkily talkative, with
a taste for loud jazz records. Her 'colossal belches and uninhibited
language' were a source of wonder to Ursula's weekend guests, and she
persisted in 'twining' herself round Edward in front of Ursula's children
and their French governess, necessitating a good deal of explaining. At
some point, in the early 1940s she joined the Communist Party, an
anti-Fascist demonstration which seemed appropriate to a great many
left-wingers at this time; she did not find the Party congenial, but this
was a gesture which was not well received in a house whose politics
were to be better represented, if in an extreme form, by Matt and
Ursula's second son, Nicholas Ridley.

Edward was better behaved, though Ursula, who had much preferred
Ian, found him irredeemably vulgar, 'with a pink shirt, blue and white
check suit, pink socks and a carnation and monocle – the moustache, the
voice, are all unreal, and I don't want to know him any better, I find'.

Nevertheless he was, as his son James put it, 'entirely house-trained'. It was Betty who was always fighting against that, 'piddling (metaphorically) on the dining-room table'.

In part she was reacting against the Ridleys' money – she always claimed to be the only one of the Lutyens children to have made a 'poor' marriage (though Mary had equally anxious financial battles to fight at this time, required as she was to keep up appearances as a stockbroker's wife and struggling, like her mother, with an oversized house that was a constant drain). The fact that Ursula was generous with help did not lessen Betty's resentment.

She also suspected intellectual pretensions. Ursula, who was widely read, had a flair for interior decoration and did exquisite needlepoint, could have had great success in London cultural life. She had no sympathy at all with Betty's music, but she envied her artistic milieu, just as she envied Mary, who was by now established as a novelist. But Betty saw everywhere the spectre of upper-class dilettantism which had dogged her at the Royal College, and never allowed anyone to forget that Ursula had (purportedly) said, 'If I hear a woman talk about her "work", I feel physically sick.' (Ursula in fact numbered many women doctors among her closest friends, and claimed to have been bitterly disappointed when Sir Edwin dismissed out of hand her hopes of becoming an architect; but it is the kind of remark which, in a particular context and an unguarded moment, she might have made, only to have it pounced upon by Betty.)

Ursula did offer provocation by taking Ian's side in the arguments about divorce and the children. But her prime failing in Betty's eyes was her conviction of superior skills in raising children. When Betty came to Blagdon most of the house had been converted into a babies' hospital and Ursula was deeply involved in the running of it. She was also taking an active part in the pioneering work in Newcastle of James – later Sir James – Spence, the eminent paediatrician. She had read a good deal about the theory of child care – 'It has been to me as music has been to [Betty]', she wrote to Lady Emily – and saw herself as a professional and Betty as an incompetent amateur.

Ursula loved children, would have liked to have had a larger family than her two sons and one adopted daughter, and in inviting Betty to come north had had visions of them sharing 'her children and my comfy house'. In the confidence of her greater knowledge and with the natural patronage of the older sister for the younger, she had no hesitation in informing Betty that she was over-coddling her family with Chilprufe vests and Scott's Emulsion.

She genuinely wanted to act for the best, and there was almost always a sharp edge of truth to her criticisms of Betty, but she must often have seemed insufferable. 'The truth is, of course,' she remarked to her mother, 'that they are all incompetent livers. They none of them know how to *live* – a far more difficult, more necessary art than music! . . . I stand for her sanity and she hates me for it.'

Added to this were the old family jealousies. 'We are a beastly family,' wrote Ursula, 'always imputing the worst motives, always suspicious of selfishness in each other.' With less animosity, Mary's second husband Joe Links (whom she was to marry in 1945, having divorced Anthony Sewell the same year) once said life in the Lutyens family was rather like a country dance – two in, two out, and the pairs constantly changing.

From the centre of the family web, Lady Emily had a good deal to do with this state of affairs; each of the children wrote regularly to her, and without malice, she merrily circulated among them the reports and opinions of their siblings. 'It is rather like being on a seesaw,' she confided to her husband. 'If I have sympathy and understanding for one it tilts the balance against the other – and finally upsets me! However I need never be dull!' Every twist and turn in Betty's wartime saga was reported to her from two sources – Betty herself, and Ursula, to whom Lady Emily turned quite frequently during the war as the only one of her children without pressing personal worries. Barbie in particular was to suffer atrociously during the war; in 1941 Euan Wallace died of cancer, and she was to lose two sons and both stepsons by 1945. (She would later lose her second husband, Herbert Agar.) In comparison Betty's tribulations often seemed insignificant to her mother, whose feelings for her at this time seem to have been a mixture of somewhat detached compassion and exasperation.

Before long, patience was wearing thin all round at Blagdon. Ursula was now inclined to feel it might be easier to help Betty's family if they were to move right away. (Barbie and Robert were in full agreement, provided she did not come and live near them: both heartily disapproved of Betty's flouting of the conventions in setting up house with Edward.) But when Betty and Edward decamped, it was only a matter of six or seven miles, to the nearby village of High Callerton and what Betty described disdainfully as a 'modern villa . . . built as a suburban sun-trap' with badly fitting plate-glass windows. In the terminology of the Mitford family, hovering on Matt and Ursula's doorstep in this way would have constituted a 'tease'.

But Betty had more to worry about than aggravating her sister. She was now confronting a totally new way of life. Before her marriage she had led a sheltered existence centred on her parents' house. The violinist Jessie Hinchliffe, who later married Alan Rawsthorne, was a friend from those early days and remembered Mansfield Street as being Betty's only point of reference;[3] if she wanted to travel anywhere, she always had to set off from Mansfield Street, or she would become hopelessly lost. Life in the basement with Ian and the domestic staff had likewise been cushioned.

In Newcastle, however, money was short. Until the beginning of the war she had been entirely dependent on the allowance she received from her father. But by 1940 Sir Edwin's supply of commissions had virtually petered out because of the war, and he was owed a great deal of money which he was never to receive. He moved the office out of Mansfield Street, kept the top floor open as a *pied-à-terre* for himself and Lady Emily, and closed the rest. The circles in which he moved, as Britain's senior architect and President of the Royal Academy, had never been more elevated – his letters to Emily are full of Their Majesties, Winston, Augustus John and H. G. Wells. But for years he had been badly advised on his financial affairs, and he and Lady Emily were faced with the relatively impoverished old age he had worked all his life to avoid. Betty's allowance was cut from £600 to £100, and even this it shamed her to accept. 'It hurts me so terribly,' she told her mother, 'not being in a position to help and support you and Father, which I feel I should be doing, instead of being a heavy burden on you all.' Though Ian, himself struggling on his air force pay, was always far more generous in his support for the children than she ever publicly acknowledged, she found herself selling off the music box which Lady Cunard had once given her, in order to make ends meet.

Many wartime housewives wrestling unaided with rationing, fuel shortages and the Blitz in the bitterly cold autumn and winter of 1940 might have smiled a little sourly at Ursula's description of Betty's trials. 'She is finding the food problem very difficult as the kitchen maid burnt her foot and had to go home.' But hardship is largely relative, and to Betty learning to cook was a major effort. Her cuisine at Mansfield Street had been of the duck-in-red-wine variety (vegetarianism having been abandoned with Theosophy), and her mother kindly sent her a cookery book in which every recipe seemed to start, 'Take six eggs and four gills of cream.' But now she experimented with vegetable fricassees and sardine kedgeree, and sent the children picking nettles and dandelions – a favourite reminiscence of hers in later life – to put in stews as a prophylactic against scurvy.

An agonising abscess on a tooth, and whooping-cough which afflicted all the children in turn until the house smelt permanently of sick, further drained her energy. Winter in Newcastle in wartime was not the easiest moment to learn for the first time how to run a house without a housemaid and look after the children without a nanny. Betty was no craven – 'I will work for them to the death,' she declared dramatically – and she took a certain pride in mastering skills to which she had not been bred. 'I've polished all the brass, polished the parquet floor, stained the stairs and washed fifty garments, cleaned the lavatory, brought in the coal,' she boasted in one letter. But tidiness did not come naturally; her cleaning had more vigour than system, and she ended most days exhausted, feeling as if she had been beaten black and blue. 'I did so want to be everything to and with Edward,' she wrote, 'but now I'm just a bloody char from morning till night.'

'How far away the days seem,' she wrote, 'when my nightdress was laid out and bottles put in my bed and breakfast brought in in the morning.' One can only hope that her mother did not regale her with Ursula's summary of the situation. 'It is a rich and satisfying life she is living, near the soil, and in many ways healthier and more content than composing, parties, drink and all she has had to forego.'

Music had indeed largely faded into the background; she wrote tiredly of 'the agonising noise of the children and the strain of never getting free of them night or day.' There had been one landmark that year, soon after the move to Newcastle, when Betty received her first Prom performance. Three Pieces for Orchestra, Op. 7, was her first full-scale purely orchestral work, which she had begun in 1939. Side by side with Delibes' 'Bell Song' from *Lakmé*, it formed part of a huge mixed programme for the opening night of the season, the last of the old-style Henry Wood farragos; and, as it happened, the last Prom for four years, for the first night of the 1940 Proms was also the first night of the Blitz.

It was fairly typical of Betty's luck. The circumstances surrounding her concert were memorable – on their way to the Queen's Hall she and Edward saw the first bombers coming over, and on their way out they were halted by the sight of a blood-red sky to the east, where the docks were burning – but they decimated the audience.

This, her first major work, had been announced in the London press as being by, variously, Sir Edwin Lutyens's daughter or Mrs Euan Wallace's sister. In Newcastle it was credited on the women's page to Lady Ridley's sister, and featured in between items on the imminent rationing of bread, the 'sandal scandal', the colour in fashion for woollens ('the shade you called gamboge in your nursery paint box'), and a newsflash from the local council chamber – 'Without hats at the last meeting were progressive councillors Mrs A and Miss B.' Now its performance passed almost completely unremarked.

Since the Three Pieces she had composed almost nothing. And music seemed further away than ever before when at the end of 1940 she discovered she was pregnant. Predictably, the news caused dismay at Blagdon; and Betty was incensed by what she perceived as Ursula's reluctance to send the chauffeur over to the house of shame with much-needed coal and eggs. By this time she and Edward had moved to a smaller house – 'Duncairn' in the village of Ponteland, a two-storeyed, semi-detached villa with stained glass over the front door and 'modern' fireplaces in sky-blue marble on the skew. 'Most refained,' commented Betty in disgust. 'The curate was the late inhabitant and therefore the scullery is full of empty lemonade bottles.'

It was to the horrors of Duncairn's architecture she attributed the fact that when her father came on a rare visit to Blagdon, he did not make the ten-mile journey to see her or the new baby, Conrad, born in August 1941. She did her best to rationalise his behaviour, even take pride in it as evidence of his good taste, but she was dreadfully disappointed. He wrote humbly to her, 'I was sorry and somewhat ashamed of missing the chance of seeing you. . . . Ursy offered me a car, but I funked my emotions. . . . If I didn't love you I could have done it. But I love you. Please forgive your – Everloving father, Father.' The affection was warming; but his staying away only underlined the feeling that she was gradually sliding into squalor.

'Money seems to be the only thing that counts and oils the wheels of all conduct or behaviour,' she wrote bitterly.

> One's work, talents, achievements, honesty or integrity apparently are not only valueless in this chaotic social system but on the contrary one must suffer for them as if they were crimes. Be rich, cheat one's husband and lie to one's children is apparently the true council [sic], and then one's respectable and no one is ashamed to come to one's house.

As long as Betty and Edward were not married, Ursula was reluctant for them to come to Blagdon. And even when the wedding did take place (in May 1942, after Ian had finally agreed to a divorce), it was a day of the greatest mortification for her. She had done her best to make it an occasion, arranging for the children to be looked after and providing Betty with pink carnations and a wedding outfit (though the ring was bought for ninepence at Marks and Spencer). Betty's only headgear was a beret of Sebastian's, and 'I took her that blue hat I wore in London,' Ursula told Lady Emily, 'which she tried to put on back to front so that the snood covered her face like a veil!'

Ursula was rewarded by a prolonged encounter with the friends Betty had asked to be witnesses, who might have been specially selected to annoy. One, she explained to her mother, was 'this Jewish gentleman . . . most effusive and kind, but terribly vulgar. "Mind the step, Mrs Ridley, dear," and later on enquiring if I wanted another drink, "How's your bin, dear?"' The other, at a ceremony which she had hoped would be as unobtrusive as possible, was the gossip columnist on the local newspaper.

Embarrassment made Betty 'more ribald', Ursula reported. When the Registrar said, 'Make yourselves comfortable', Betty, her mind running on children, 'couldn't resist the obvious retort'. At the reception in the Jewish gentleman's flat, during which she drank rather too much, she grumbled incessantly to Ursula about her life, 'harping on the theme of her recent marriage. "When you are just married, you do want to go about together, and it is hard to be held by a baby." It is awfully funny really!'

Though Betty was delighted to be married to Edward, she greatly regretted having changed her name to the undistinguished 'Betty Clark'. She was still a member of the Communist Party, but her democratisation was never as convincing as she perhaps hoped. For the first time she saw the conditions in which working people lived, and she genuinely raged at the injustices and suffered in sympathy. But her manner when she met the working classes was invariably *de haut en bas*.

She was lonely in Newcastle, and a further move was no help. This time it was to 26 Westfield Road, Gosforth, yet more genteel – 'exactly the place one could imagine "the funeral cortege will leave from"'.[4] And still there was not enough time for composing. Late at night when the children had gone to bed she would force herself to write a few bars simply to keep her hand in; but it seemed that just as she had seen the true path opening before her, barriers had sprung up across it which she was too busy and too tired to scale. 'Oh God! the agonising ache to do music all the time.'

In 1941, in the interstices of pregnancy and children's illnesses, she had finished the second of her set of Chamber Concertos, for clarinet, tenor saxophone, piano and strings. She had also completed Five Intermezzi for solo piano, tiny pieces which were all that time would allow, but even these meagre achievements were a lifeline to which she clung desperately. 'My contact with music,' she told Lady Emily somewhat defiantly, 'gives me an invulnerability against the "slings and arrows of outrageous fortune" and the fear that that touchstone was for ever out of reach [is] removed.' Her mother's sympathy was limited; Lady Emily (with a convenient amnesia of her own priorities twenty years before) felt that the children must come first and if necessary the music (which she never really accepted as anything more than an abstruse pastime) should be shelved, and she did not refrain from saying so.

In 1942 Betty wrote more small-scale music – the Nine Bagatelles, Op. 10, for cello and piano. She set two poems by W. H. Auden – 'As I walked out one morning' and 'Refugee Blues' – creating songs that were pleasing in themselves, purely tonal, but too direct and unambiguous to reflect Auden's tone of voice and release the multiple meanings implicit in the words. As she might herself have said, there was too little of the Deep South in her blues, and too much suburban Gosforth.

She also devoted a good deal of her limited time and energy to a medley for Tommy Handley and ITMA, which would have fused the National Anthem with the Marseillaise, the *Meistersinger* overture, the March of the Toreadors from *Carmen*, the opening bars of Beethoven's Fifth Symphony, and the march from *Colonel Bogey*, had not Bogey's composer refused copyright permission and rendered the whole exercise a waste of time. All this fell into the category of experiment rather than achievement, taking her new-found techniques little further. One work, however, she was prepared to acknowledge later – Three Symphonic Preludes, roughly expressive, with a remarkable impetus considering the circumstances in which they were composed.

Frustration, fatigue and constant anxiety about money are destructive enough, but had Betty felt emotionally secure she might have weathered them easily if not uncomplainingly. Her real problem during the years in Newcastle was Edward, whose world was disintegrating with extraordinary speed. Very much in love with him when they first moved north, the glamour of the relationship heightened by the struggle to find a home together, after three years in Newcastle Betty discovered not only her romance but also her respect for her husband disappearing.

Well over military age at the start of the war, Edward tried with increasing anxiety to get a job – first a musical job, then a war-related job, then *any* job – but he was handicapped in the music field perhaps by his reputation as an erratic administrator, and in all other fields by his lack of practical training or academic qualifications and his inability to drive.

He had had high hopes of becoming adviser to the Sadlers Wells opera and ballet company, a position for which he *was* eminently well suited, but the job went to Humphrey Searle, in his twenties. In CEMA, too, and ENSA and the BBC, a pattern formed of younger men being given the jobs he wanted and then ringing him for advice. He lectured sporadically for the Workers' Educational Association, and laboured for the Society for Cultural Relations with the USSR. (He was also temporarily to have a job with Novello's, cataloguing their Russian music.)

One afternoon or so a week, according to Betty, he helped her with the children; to Sebastian, Rose and Tess he was as kind and solicitous as to Conrad, and they loved him. Sebastian still remembers his laugh –

> very loud, from the depths of the belly, his body shook. . . . To me he was a great teacher. He never talked down and would answer my questions with the same serious attention that would be given to the most erudite musician. During these years the Allied advance was followed with the red crayon on newspaper maps – the room looked like Ike's strategic planning HQ – and very interesting free lessons on geography, history and language resulted. Pity the radio announcer who mispronounced people or places. . . .

But most of Edward's energies were poured desperately into the last long-term project he was ever to organise. 'NERO', the North East Regional Orchestra, was largely reconstituted from his old BBC Newcastle station orchestra. He planned to use it not only to maintain musical activity in the area, but also to boost morale, and its programmes were as unashamedly and unremittingly popular as most of the concerts mounted in Britain during the war. In deference to patriotic feeling Edward included Walton's Prelude and Fugue: *Spitfire*, and Lambert's *Merchant Seamen*, which were also the nearest he approached to modern music, but in general he relied on the well-loved and familiar nineteenth-century overtures, concertos and operatic arias. What lent the concerts distinction was the roster of soloists on whom he was still able to call – Solomon, Ida Haendel, Moura Lympany, Clifford Curzon, Isobel Baillie, Eileen Joyce, Heddle Nash: all the names which had been lined up for the abandoned Prom season.

With dedication Edward did his best to reconstruct his pre-war routine of concerts and dinners, leaving Betty feeling envious and left out at home. But in truth NERO was small beer compared with the days when every post brought letters from the likes of Webern, Stravinsky and Bartók and every concert was a blow struck for the music of the future. When he was not in full fig for a concert, Edward now began to let himself go. Betty grew used to his sullen silences, punctuated by outbursts of anger and disappointment; by mid-1942 he was having constant nosebleeds. She was a little like her mother in her capacity for hero-worship, had perhaps been drawn to Edward largely by his authority and what she perceived as his superiority to her, and this new face was not just a worrying inconvenience but a profound disillusionment.

'I thought when I married Edward,' she wrote to Lady Emily, 'it was an escape from the gloom of domesticity, that I would share his musical life in Paris, Vienna, Budapest, New York, BBC. Did I foresee cook-general-cum-char-cum-mother in a suburb of Newcastle – oh boy!' In some ways her attitude to him was irrevocably damaged in these years. She never stopped loving him, but she began to question his feelings for her: Ursula quoted her as saying he looked after his suits better than he did her. And now she could no longer restrain herself from nagging, at home and in public. She harped on his age – 'always asking him how they did things in the Eighties!', according to Ursula – and criticised the mannerisms she had once admired. 'Every time he uses a foreign word when an English one would have done, she hauls him over the coals.'

Long before the war, Betty had been accustomed to drink more than was ladylike; a friend referred admiringly in 1939 to 'the sharp edge of your sherry-besozzled mind'.[5] As life grew harder in Newcastle, so did the drinking. In *A Goldfish Bowl* Betty admits to having had a serious drink problem by 1946; but in 1942 Ursula was already complaining of her 'pub-crawling' while Conrad was left with a baby-sitter. George Braithwaite, a lawyer and amateur oboist whom Edward encouraged to play with NERO when his minesweeper was in port, remembers quite often meeting Betty with Edward in the Eldon Grill in Newcastle. 'I can picture her now, with a pint in each hand, holding forth vigorously on any (usually musical) subject. Her phraseology was manly, to say the least!'[6]

After she had visited her parents in London in July 1942, Lady Emily had the same story to tell. 'One side of her is very maternal and I think she has been wonderful with the children. . . . But she has a very masculine side, which longs for a bachelor life – pub-crawling, talking endlessly. She is not satisfied with producing children, but feels her musical talents are being stifled. She managed to get to a pub every morning at twelve and was out every evening from 7–10.30.' As the pressures increased, she began to dispense with the baby-sitter and simply waited until Conrad was asleep before going to the pub.

She did not need the reproaches of her mother and sister to persuade her that she was not caring for the children as she should, torn as she was between their needs, Edward's, and her own. 'You say I don't appreciate the children enough,' she wrote angrily to her mother, 'but I never seem to have time to watch them, talk to them, fondle them. It's just rush, rush, rush to get through the chores, to keep them fed and warmed and more or less clean.' At the end of 1942 she had a breakdown, slipping into 'a nightmare world, when sound is a torture, especially children's noise, and the nervous panicky beating of my own heart in some unknown dread sounds like A.A. guns night and day.'

In a long and anguished letter to her mother she listed the causes. She had been worn down by the strain of leaving Ian and the worry that he would take the children (at the time of the divorce he had been awarded custody, though he could hardly claim it while he was in the air force). And then Conrad, the one child she could keep safe, had been the source of months of embarrassment, her ostracism from Blagdon and her father's apparent rejection of her. Perpetual anxiety about money, an endless succession of illnesses, scanty sleep broken by bombing – and now Lady Emily had suggested a solution which was the final insult: abandoning 'serious' music for the duration.

'With regard to letting the "composer sleep",' Betty wrote, 'if artists could let their art rest and didn't suffer from the divine discontent which demands expression like labour demands a confinement, there would never have been any art at all. . . . It is an urge as strong as the urge to love, labour, and have children, which has and will always surmount all vissisitudes [sic]. It is therefore an act of faith, of faith in life, which I have and which Father has. . . . Nothing could have prevented Father having children and producing works. He is ill when he cannot work. . . . Do not judge me because Father's earned thousands of pounds and I only a few pennies. . . . I should be a better, less irritable wife and mother if I could compose more. . . . I lost all confidence as a child and girl – the bed-wetting, the plainness, the social failure. . . . Edward has given me a confidence by his love which has made me feel reborn. He had confidence in me as a composer, as a woman, as a wife, as a mother. We were to work together at music.'

But now their lives were drawing apart, and 'in this process of being mangled by exhaustion, of being always tired and dirty . . . this love for which I've suffered so much is being spoilt. It isn't easy for two jumpy people, apart from the noisy children, to live without solitude or privacy. And solitude and privacy, I now realise, are the prerogatives of private incomes. . . . The other day, coming home from the dentist I saw in a window a woman reading the paper, with the sun streaming and flowers in the room, and I started weeping. I'd forgotten a time where one could sit down quietly, watch the clouds move, have time to walk instead of run – a world of flowers in the room, books to finger, people to talk with.'

Her resistance lowered, she was now persuaded without much difficulty to send the three older children away to schools paid for by Ian, and a pattern was set which was to dominate the rest of their childhood. She had seen in the meantime a cheaper house – 14 Leazes Terrace, nearer to the centre of Newcastle (and, Ursula noted, to the pubs), and architecturally more acceptable than any of its predecessors, rather similar to Fitzroy Street. Ursula was initially impressed by the cornices, grates and generous windows, the 'refreshing and enviable' ambience; Betty,yshe felt, visualised it becoming 'a Quartier Latin under her aegis'.

But the day the Clarks moved in, in the summer of 1943, Ursula noticed only the footprints they left in the dust on the bedroom floors (the glass in the generous windows having been out for two years), the water flooding the kitchen from a leak in the scullery roof, and the indescribable single lavatory. 'And the men were toiling back and forth with Edward's gramophone records and dress suits. *He* had decamped for the day and left Betty to cope alone – so she was roundly abusing him to all and sundry.'

The area (which Ursula had now been informed was a red-light district) was not as safe as it had seemed, as there was a barrage balloon in the park opposite, and a constant stream of lorries up and down the road. Traffic notwithstanding, the children were all in the gutter, Conrad (aged two) sitting in the road alone. 'Betty quite calmly said he must get used to it and learn not to get run over – she is wonderful!' Edward was out at a meeting and dinner, and Betty was preparing 'tea and bread and cheese for all the furniture men who were all sitting round her. . . . Her chief concern was what to do with Edward's suits.'

The family had not been in Leazes Terrace for more than a few weeks before Ursula became really alarmed at what she described as Betty's 'complete moral degeneration' and 'protracted suicide'. Like Betty, she had a penchant for the dramatic, but even allowing for exaggeration she had cause for concern. Betty was not eating properly, was smoking far too much, going every night to the pub, and squabbling constantly with Edward.

He was little better, and soon had a collapse of his own. One morning Ursula was summoned by a panic-stricken Betty, who told her, 'sobbing into the soup', that Edward had not spoken for forty-eight hours, had merely made idiot noises and tried to throttle her; she for her part had attempted to commit suicide but 'from force of habit' had lit the gas. Ursula went in search of Edward and, deeply unsympathetic, found him lying unshaven on two chairs, the floor round him littered with cigarette ends and cups of tea, crying and giggling, complaining of a headache and an unendurable life. Informed that a trumpeter from his orchestra had come to see him, he brightened up considerably, while Betty battled through her tears and a haze of cigarette smoke to look after Conrad and cook the lunch.

For Betty to try to combine music and domesticity any longer, Ursula realised, was pointless. She could not face the prospect of another failed marriage, and the only way to build a relationship with Edward was through music. In addition, her financial dependence on her family (who all helped her, now and later, with money) was 'gnawing into her soul. . . . She can't bear to feel,' Ursula told her mother, 'that . . . you have to deny yourself comforts to keep her.' (At one point the seventy-year-old Lady Emily had made elaborate plans for moving herself and Sir Edwin into a caravan.) Betty was convinced that if she could work uninterrupted, she could keep herself and her family with her music, and Ursula felt there was no point in any of them swimming against the tide any longer.

In *A Goldfish Bowl* Betty is understandably vague about this time, and how she came to leave Newcastle. ('My sense of chronology over the next few months seems as blacked out as London was.') Initially Ursula proposed finding and paying for someone locally to clean the house and look after the children in the school holidays while Betty worked. But then, quite unexpectedly, Edward was offered a job in the south by concert agent Harold Fielding, organising tours for the National Philharmonic Orchestra. Ursula had always liked Fitzroy Street, and before the war had taken a lease on a flat at number 6. This she now offered to Betty. By the middle of November, 1943, Betty was installed and Edward was with her. Sebastian, Rose and Tess were away at school, and Conrad temporarily with Ursula at Blagdon. Edward's job soon fell through, and he went back to Newcastle and NERO. But Betty had issued a challenge to herself and a boast to her family, and with the Blitz entering its second phase, she decided to stay in London and earn her living as a composer.

CHAPTER EIGHT

The Fitzrovian Years

'Do You Want It Good or Do You Want It Thursday?'

'ANCHOR YOUR HEART in kindness,' Betty had written in her scraps of emotional autobiography. But somehow kindness had not been enough, and she had voyaged on without Ian. Now at the beginning of 1944 she was to all intents and purposes without Edward; and except for the two-year-old Conrad, whom she brought down from Blagdon and kept with her in London until the threat from the V1s and V2s became too severe, she saw the children only spasmodically for visits and school holidays. 'At last, and so long last, and on the bridge,' she wrote, 'we can captain our own ship.'

Her freedom, however, was nothing like as absolute as in Mansfield Street days. Then she had been able simply to pass the children to a nanny – something she regretted, perhaps, but the usual arrangement in her social milieu and hardly culpable. Now, for a period of eight years during and after the war, Sebastian, Rose, Tess and Conrad moved between a succession of relatives, foster homes and schools, from Northumberland to Dorset.

In one sense Betty had little choice. Clearly she could not both write music and look after all four children – she had tried and failed in Newcastle – and she could not afford, in either emotional or financial terms, to stop writing music. It would have meant abandoning a thirty-year struggle to define her identity in her own and her parents' eyes – and her ambitions had been sharpened by Mary's successes as a writer and Robert's recent rapprochement with Sir Edwin. (In 1942 he produced a monograph entitled *Sir Edwin Lutyens: An Appreciation in Perspective*, published by *Country Life*.) It would also, in practical terms, have meant financial disaster; because precarious as the proceeds from composing might be, they were the only income in prospect in 1944, with Edward wholly preoccupied with NERO.

Nevertheless, Betty was perfectly aware of the risks she was taking with their security and happiness in allowing the children to be bundled from one temporary home to another, and then and ever afterwards she felt guilty. She missed them, and she felt obscurely humiliated: had she failed, so soon, to make a success of motherhood? As often as she felt she could (and she had the demands of Edward as well as her work to contend with), she went to see them – visits that they both longed for and dreaded, for in her battered fur jacket, wide-bottomed trousers and aura of cigarettes, she was not as other mothers. As for Betty, 'I loved every minute with them,' she wrote with pardonable exaggeration twenty-five years later, 'and it broke my heart (and sent me to booze) when I had to be in London during the week to earn for them.' [1]

In the basement at Mansfield Street in the 1930s, Betty had had unlimited time, but scanty musical material on which to work. Now ideas were pressing and her technique flexing itself, but she had to make a living for six people, and from now on her musical attention was to be divided between her 'own' and her commercial work. It would be unfair to equate this simply with the distinction between 'serious' and 'hack' work, though she sometimes did; one of her virtues was to take *all* her composing seriously, and she never consciously offered less than her best effort. She enjoyed the sensation of meeting a challenge and living on her wits when she was writing for film, radio or theatre – though always at the back of her mind was the awareness of her own individual music unwritten, new territories unexplored.

Her first money-earning occupation was straightforward drudgery – copying 'Limehouse Blues' for a Wardour Street music publisher at tenpence a page, the first of many similar chores. Copying frayed her temper – Conrad remembered from those days the ashtrays heaped with lipsticked cigarette ends amidst the stone jars of very black ink – and left her with a permanently bruised index finger; but it was a regular wage. The serious money, however, was in films (as it is today) and the radio. She knew that these were the bastions which she had to storm, and both were heavily fortified against women. There were no female film producers, virtually no female directors or music directors, few women radio producers, and Betty quite often encountered the belief that she was trying to enter the business purely for pin money. 'A misinformed producer once announced to me that he had turned me down for four films as I had "solved my economic problems by marriage"' – her smile must have been a little sour. But this was the world she had to penetrate; and the most promising point of entry, it appeared, was through the remains of what has since been labelled Fitzrovia.

'Fitzrovia' is the name which for thirty years or so has been used as shorthand, like 'Bloomsbury', to refer both to an area and a society. Towards the end of the nineteenth century and during the first four decades of the twentieth, a small patch of central London attracted to itself the reputation of being a scruffy equivalent of the Latin Quarter in Paris. Defined roughly by the Euston Road and Oxford Street, Charlotte Street and Tottenham Court Road, it was an area of small businesses and workshops – cabinet-makers, French-polishers, upholsterers, tailors, picture-framers and innumerable Italian, Greek and Middle European food shops. Cosmopolitan, dirty and noisy, it was a cheap and interesting place for artists, writers and students of all kinds to live, with dozens of small restaurants, cafés and pubs, stiff with 'atmosphere'. The name 'Fitzrovia' – applied only in retrospect and not by the inhabitants themselves – was derived from the Fitzroy Tavern halfway down Charlotte Street, and denotes a diffuse, subdivided community of Bohemians and would-be Bohemians, whose composition and character changed all the time as members elected themselves or were extruded.

The area had already seen several generations of Bohemian life by the turn of the century – writers both on the way up and the way down, painters, critics, booksellers, exiled Russian princes, 'Communists, socialists and Utopians of every hue'. In the years immediately before the First World War, artists predominated, in the public eye at least – the 'Fitzroy Street Group', later to become the 'Camden Town Group', the Omega Workshop, Augustus John and Nina Hamnett. In the 1920s and 1930s, by which time London's 'Bohemia' was more aware of its own identity, writers gravitated again to the area to live, eat, drink, discuss their work and each other – Evelyn Waugh, Anthony Powell, V. S. Pritchett, Constantine Fitzgibbon, Thomas Earp – and the occasional composer like Peter Warlock, Cecil Gray and Constant Lambert joined them. Often, however, the label 'Fitzrovian' is now applied loosely to anyone literary, artistic or aspiring who drank in any of a number of pubs in the area, at any time between the 1920s and the late 1940s.

The Fitzroy Tavern on the corner of Windmill Street, the Wheatsheaf in Rathbone Place, the Bricklayers' Arms or Burglar's Rest in Gresse Street, were at various times the most popular. For afternoon and after-midnight drinking, there were the Caves de France, the Mandrake and the Gargoyle, all slightly south of the heartland, off Dean Street. The risk at the Gargoyle, as it became more fashionable, was that on a Saturday night it would be packed, according to Constant Lambert, 'with the two hundred nastiest people in Chiswick',[2] and to a limited extent that was true of Fitzrovia as a whole by the late 1930s; but during the week the ambience was that of the less inhibited intelligentsia, a self-consciously eccentric 'alternative' world.

'Fitzrovia' still existed in the 1940s, its vague feeling of community heightened by wartime conditions. (Cyril Connolly described the war for those left in London as 'five years in gregarious confinement'.[3]) But in practice it was a very different world from that in which Sickert, John and the young Nina Hamnett had lived. Nina was in some ways the epitome of all that was theatrical, outrageous and traditionally Bohemian in the old Fitzrovia. She took pleasure in fancy dress, in undress, in working-class 'characters', embarrassing scenes, unusual pets and getting drunk. She still haunted the same pubs in the 1940s, but she was a pitiful figure, almost a historical curiosity amidst the new Fitzrovians, whose world had a new hub – the British Broadcasting Corporation.

Radio was the medium which cemented the new society; the pubs, clubs and restaurants were now places where contacts could be made, contracts secured and programmes discussed. Poets, writers and musicians still foregathered – Dylan Thomas, Roy Campbell, Louis MacNeice, Stevie Smith, Tambimuttu, John Lehmann, Alan Ross, William Empson, George Barker, Julian Maclaren-Ross, Henry Reed, Terence Tiller, Rose Macaulay, Muriel Spark, William Walton, Alan Rawsthorne, Constant Lambert, Humphrey Searle, William Alwyn, Antony Hopkins. But, as Hugh David makes clear in his recent study of *The Fitzrovians*, it is wishful thinking to imagine 'an easy-going, harmonious confraternity . . . cosily clustered at one end of the bar'. These new Fitzrovians drank in small groups, and they were drawn to the same pubs mostly by their employment, actual or potential, in or by the Drama and Features Departments of the BBC.

The geographical boundaries of 'Fitzrovia' had been extended to take in both Broadcasting House in Portland Place and the Ministry of Information in Bloomsbury, the other great wartime employer of artists and writers; and different pubs were favoured. The Stag's Head on the corner of New Cavendish Street was, broadly speaking, the Features pub, the George in Great Portland Street heavily patronised by musicians. (For the tendency of orchestral players to stick there between sessions, it was known intermittently as the 'Gluepot'.) Further south in

Dean Street, the Highlander and the York Minster were the focus for the film business.

Times were bleaker than in John's and Hamnett's heyday. Blitz and black-out were followed by austerity – much the same conditions without the adrenalin that had made them endurable – and this was altogether a dourer, more businesslike community. In April 1940 the *New Statesman* had predicted glumly, 'When the freelance is finally liquidated, our art and literature will be produced by little men in striped trousers, Anthony Eden hats and rolled umbrellas, who are punctual at their offices and incapable of dangerous thoughts.' This grim epoch had not yet arrived – no one could have accused Dylan Thomas of being punctual at his office – but the old irresponsible camaraderie was being diluted all the time as the freelances found regular jobs or 'succumbed to drink and despair'.

Nevertheless, into what was left of Fitzrovia Betty waded, diffidently at first but with increasing relish. She was always to claim that it was the quest for work which took her, in the end disastrously, to the pubs, and certainly that was where most potential employers were to be found. But without doubt her own instincts would have drawn her there anyway. 'That was the kind of anarchic, radical, boozy world that she really enjoyed,' James Clark remembered. 'Standing at the bar (she wasn't very tall but she was very upright), a glass of whisky in front of her, or beer if times were hard, shouting away, cigarette in hand – there she was really being herself.' Betty first entered the George for company, as a break from the lonely drudgery of copying. 'After a few years of the sole companionship of small children who, though adored, invariably limited conversation, I was hungry, with my gregarious temperament, for people with interests in common.' During 1944 Edward paid occasional visits, but in between were long stretches of solitary tedium, and she turned to the pubs for instant friendship. It was a time, according to Caitlin Thomas, when 'to be drunkenly funny was everything and to be serious was a sin of dullness'.[4]

In the writing of her music Betty guarded her independence jealously, but socially she rather regretted the fact that musicians generally tend not to flock. She loved to think of herself as part of an 'inner circle' of artistic life in London, relishing the unfamiliar sensation of belonging, and her particular friends at this time offered a neat cross-section of latter-day Fitzrovia.

William Walton was the most successful composer she could ever tolerate, though she once told him he had taken as much time and trouble getting into the upper class as she had taken getting out. (For

his part, he once told a mutual friend that he enjoyed her very much –
in retrospect.'[5]) Alan Rawsthorne had been a confidant and drinking
companion since the days of the Macnaghten–Lemare Concerts. He and
Betty argued furiously about music, and never had a serious quarrel
about anything else. His first wife Jessie Hinchliffe vividly remembers
those intense and disordered years around the end of the war, when the
Clarks and the Rawsthornes lived within walking distance in Fitzrovia
and intermittently lodged with each other. She recalls a lunchtime when
she and Rawsthorne dropped in at 6 Fitzroy Street on their way to the
Carpenter's Arms, to find Betty and Edward in bed. Edward was not a
pub-crawler, preferring an urbane bottle of claret over a restaurant meal,
but Betty, nothing loth, pulled her trousers on over her pyjamas and
went with them.

Constant Lambert, though she had reservations about his music and
had suffered from his reviews of her own, Betty loved perhaps next
after Edward. He had the apparently effortless talent she most envied;
a dazzling combination of composer, conductor, authority on ballet,
writer, critic and talker, he was one of the few people who never bored
her. For his part, he enjoyed her quickness of wit and sharpness of
tongue; and his second wife Isabel remembered them pelting each other
affectionately with cloves of garlic in Pagani's restaurant near the BBC,
and holding long and hilarious midnight telephone conversations even
on days when they had already met for lunch. Like Edward, Betty
received a specimen of his verse – for her a reminiscence of Coleridge:

> Tongue-tied on Koka-Kola,
> Britannic-born liberal female
> composer Betty Lutyens can now
> lecture thousands on slugs of rye.
> On either side the river lie
> Slugs of rye and slugs of rye.

Isabel Lambert (who subsequently married Alan Rawsthorne) was
herself to become one of Betty's closest friends. This was despite her
remarkable beauty which depressed Betty, still plagued by physical
insecurity. In low moments she would animadvert on her looks to an
embarrassing degree, complaining, according to Francis Bacon, who knew
both women and painted Isabel, that everything was made for the
beautiful. Bacon's amiable acquaintance with Betty was, he felt, founded in
the fact that he knew so little about music. This made him more receptive to
its extremes and made her, perversely, more willing to talk to him about it.

Her relationship with Dylan Thomas was more complicated. She sensed genius, which always brought out a tendency to hero-worship, and loved him for a few unforgettably funny and touching evenings in the pub. For a brief period he was her lodger. Abetted by Louis MacNeice, Betty was giving parties almost weekly 'to cheer up some of those black-out evenings'. These gatherings, 'which involved lugging barrels of draught Guinness up the stairs for the Irish contingent and cheap wine (Algerian or poison) for the rest', are still remembered by some of the guests as the best entertainment of the war years. Betty herself was more nostalgic about the aftermath. 'When I lay a-bed of a morning, being by nature a noctambulant, Dylan would pop down, bright as a cricket at an ungodly early hour, sit on my bed with a "Give me a cigarette, love", and then proceed unfastidiously to lap up the dregs from the glasses of the night-before party and bounce off cheerful as a cherub.' Her affection for him survived unpaid rent and a cycle of drunken rows and rapprochments between him and Caitlin, culminating in the occasion when Caitlin roused the house in the small hours to borrow matches with which to burn his handkerchiefs – 'so bourgeois'.

The picture of Dylan as a maudlin, bloated drunk Betty always rejected angrily, maintaining that his undoing was his weak head and careless eating habits. But his firm belief that the world owed the artist a living went against her work ethic, which came from her father and verged on the Puritan. She belaboured him about it – and lent him money just the same.

Thomas's poetry seems peculiarly difficult to set to music; his friend the composer Daniel Jones believed him to be musically illiterate,[6] incapable of relating word stress to musical accent, and this perhaps made his rhythms unruly, impossible to ignore but hard to reproduce. The density and individuality of his imagery virtually defies translation into anyone else's personal language, so insistent is his own voice. Betty was to make several attempts at illuminating his writing, but with the exception of three songs, including 'Do not go gentle into that good night', which she set for his memorial concert at the beginning of 1954, and which grew unaffectedly out of grief, the pieces are not among her most convincing.

She struggled, too, with the poetry, as with the personality, of Stevie Smith. 'A good acquaintance,' Betty once said, 'but a bad friend,' capable always of making one laugh, but when it came to cadging lifts to and from Palmer's Green, 'the most frightful bully'.[7]

Stevie's self-image, revealed in the blurb she wrote for her *Selected Poems*, was utterly unlike Betty's. 'Her thoughts may also seem deceitful,' she wrote of herself, 'at first simple, almost childlike, then cutting at depth with a sharp edge to the main business of her life – death, loneliness, God and the Devil. . . . She is certainly funny. But it is not a humour one would care to meet on a dark night.'[8] She was not, perhaps, as ingenuous as she liked to appear.

Betty's conception of herself (exposed in exactly the same way, in the blurb for *A Goldfish Bowl*) in contrast puts a heavy emphasis on honesty. It is not surprising, then, that her treatment of Stevie's poems – a set of songs written in 1948 and performed by *diseuse* Hedli Anderson, wife of Louis MacNeice – lacks the requisite subtlety. She mirrors well enough the macaronic technique on which the poems rely heavily, slipping easily from one musical language to another (though all tonal), with competent pastiches of café music, *chanson*, plainsong and ballad. But Stevie's slyness, morbidity and *faux-naïveté*, all alien to Betty's nature, are lost.

Surrounded by her friends, acquaintances and business contacts, Betty had largely left her family behind – or perhaps one should say *Liz* had left them, for this was the name by which almost everybody now knew her. She had never liked 'Betty', and when meeting new people she took the chance to present a different persona. It may well have been Alan Rawsthorne who originated 'Liz'; to Edward she was always 'Lizzie'.

Her family found the transmogrification hard to accept and never learned to call her 'Liz'. Robert in particular took exception to the new Bohemian persona. He was in practice as an architect now, had a smart clientele and a hankering for the *politesse* of a past era; Liz took a delight – fiendish, in his view – in outraging his sensibilities. But after her return to London she saw little of any of the family.

Lady Emily, hardly in a position to know how business was transacted in the worlds of film and radio, intensely disapproved of the pub cruising. 'I was condemned out of hand,' complained Betty, 'as being more addicted to my pub friends than concerned for the children, whereas it was the welfare of my children that had sent me into the marketplace in the first instance.' Over the next five years, when she needed sympathy and approval more than at any other point in her life, her mother, now in her seventies and beset by her own griefs and worries, was least able to offer either. 'To this day,' Betty wrote, perhaps unfairly but with feeling, 'she has not the faintest idea of my work, or mental attitude, ideas or life.'[9]

And the idealised, fragmentary, unfilfilled relationship with her father was over, for on 31 December 1943 he had died of lung cancer. In his last weeks, when Betty had just come down from Newcastle, she visited him often. During the war years his hatred of mess and confusion and his resentment of her contribution to his money worries had distanced him from her. But like her reign as his hostess in 1927, these last meetings brought them briefly together and were crucial in shaping her memories of him.

In those few hours she was able in a sense to start again, to show him the person she would have liked to be – composed, efficient, professional, successful. She clung to the thought of their last meeting, when at last, sitting on the edge of his bed with two bottles of whisky she had ingeniously procured for him with money she could not afford, she had felt she could talk to him as an equal, a creator. They talked about professional ethics and the Musicians' Union and she sensed him looking at, not through her. 'His whole attitude to his work and life was something I received as a blessing, to carry with me down the years to come.' Justified or not – and temperamentally father and daughter were entirely different – this was a belief she desperately wanted to be true.

Ironically, when she had this conversation with Sir Edwin, her own composing, as opposed to her incidental music, was virtually at a halt. The handful of 'serious' pieces she did manage to write were themselves influenced by external circumstances more obviously than she permitted at any other time in her life. It is possible that in wartime she was more anxious for her music to be understood at a first hearing, feeling people would have less patience than usual with the obscure; she may even have been influenced by her political beliefs in the direction of 'people's music'. Either way she seems to have regressed for a year or so in 1943 and 1944 to music that was almost exclusively tonal and deliberately accessible, even overtly patriotic. Three *Salutes to the United Nations*, 'moved by the emotions of the great anti-Hitler struggle', and a suite *Proud City*, in honour of the London which had survived the Blitz, betray a deep vein of 'We Can Take It' sentiment.

En voyage (1944), originally a light orchestral suite, was to crop up again twenty years later in the guise of a Divertissement for double wind quintet, which might suggest that Liz was pleased with it, or at least felt it to be serviceable. The suite is divided into four sections – 'Golden Arrow', 'Channel Crossing', 'Yvette: la Dieppoise' and 'Paris Soir: City Lights'. (She proposed a further 'sentimental' section – her word – entitled 'Flanders Fields', but it would have implied a devious route between London and Paris and seems never to have been written.) It is characteristic of her lighter compositions, perhaps best described as red-herring music – traditional pictorial music slightly on the skew, constantly missing beats or allowing the bottom to drop out of the harmony. It is both poignant and unsatisfactory, building towards grand climaxes which never arrive, always hitting the nail slightly off centre and driving it in at an angle. Later she was to insist on the importance, for setting a scene in films, of being able to distinguish between the French and German accordion; but here 'Paris Soir' constantly threatens to become Vienna or, even worse, wonderful Copenhagen.

Serious music was not extinct, however. In 1943, with the help of Arthur Bliss, the first Chamber Concerto had been given its première at a Boosey and Hawkes concert conducted by Constant Lambert. The second was performed at the end of the war at a concert put on by the Committee (later the Society) for the Promotion of New Music, conducted by Walter Goehr. In 1945 she wrote the third in the set, for bassoon, strings and percussion, a work in classical concerto form but based throughout on a single series, which was performed in 1946 – at an Edward Clark concert which was both a pleasure and an irritation.

By the spring of 1945 Edward had become a permanent fixture in Fitzroy Street, and the uneasy blend of rows and reassurance, dependence and aggravation, was re-established. Frequently intolerant and unfriendly to each other, they could be extraordinarily generous to third parties who broke the tension between them, releasing the reservoirs of affection, warmth and kindness which both possessed and yet expended so rarely on each other. At the end of the war, Edward's first wife Dolly and his twenty-year-old son James came out of the ruined Reich where they had spent the war years, and returned to England to face charges under the Defence Regulations. Far from certain of his welcome, James went to stay temporarily in Fitzroy Street, having heard of Liz's existence only the week before. 'I meet this lank-haired, bony, black-and-grey coloured person, lip trembling, smoking, saying those off-hand, biting, oblique things I was used to hearing in my mother's martini circles before the war. But her eyes are smiling while I come into their home like a black mark and they do not make me feel it. . . . I stay on with them week after week . . . hating their silly rows, but never made to feel out of place. . . . It's pretty amazing how they let me make my soft landing among them.'[10] Liz in particular, all her life, was capable of combining generalised rancour and suspicion with dazzling and spontaneous warmth and kindness to the individual friend or acquaintance.

Shortly after his return to London, Edward had been left £5000 by his brother. Liz badly wanted to use it to hire domestic help and bring the children back home, but Edward was adamant. After four years of

Fingal's Cave and the *Nutcracker Suite* in Newcastle, he could hardly wait to conduct contemporary music again. In January 1946 he mounted three concerts which included Berg's Adagio for violin and thirteen wind instruments, Hindemith's *Cardillac* suite, Rawsthorne's First Piano Concerto, and Milhaud's *La Création du Monde* – and the legacy was gone.

It was as if he felt this was to be his final flourish – though in fact his life promised to fill up again, with the resumption in earnest of the activities of the ISCM, which had gone into retreat in America during the war. In general, music looked like becoming a boom industry in the afterglow of the efforts of CEMA and ENSA, and the prospects for modern music in particular seemed to expand visibly when the Third Programme was launched in 1946. Its aim was Reithian and lofty – to raise rather than reflect public taste – and it became synonymous with intellectualism; the definition of a highbrow, according to Tommy Handley, was someone who 'listens to the Third Programme with the window open'. Since she had been dubbed a 'cerebral' as long ago as 1935, Liz might have expected great things from the Third as a patron of her kind of music.

Doors seemed to be opening. In 1946 Liz was approached by Lengnicks, the music publishers, with a contract. She met Dallapiccola, with whom she perceived so much in common as an independent serialist. She went to Paris for a concert of her works arranged by the British Council representative, Rollo Myers, and there she not only felt in touch with a cultural past once more, but also with allies for the present and future, as twelve-tone music was already accepted among younger composers (such as the young Pierre Boulez, whom she met for the first time). 'It was a rare moment of complete happiness,' she wrote, 'and satisfaction with my re-found and undivided identity.'

But back in England her mood of happy optimism did not survive for long. The Three Symphonic Preludes which in 1942 had pleased her and drawn rare words of praise from Edward were conducted by him at the ISCM Festival, held that year in London. The reviews were respectful rather than affectionate; but more damaging, she felt, than any slight from the critics was the programme note which Edward himself had written for her, in which he described the piece as composed 'in the twelve-tone technique of Schoenberg'. 'This premature phrase,' she wrote, 'was to be my death knell musically in England.' It was not considered unpatriotic to study Palestrina or Bach, apparently, nor even to be influenced by Hindemith or Bartók, but this particular foreigner, it seemed, was *mittel*-European and subversive. 'I was soon made to feel,' she complained, 'like a Communist before the Committee for Un-American Activities,' just getting into its stride in Washington.

She had, in any case, no illusions about earning a living from her concert music alone, and, optimistic or not, had never relaxed her efforts to drum up commercial work as an insurance policy – a task made no easier by the widespread but unfounded assumption that she must have inherited a fortune from a rich father. The film world caved in first under her assault, and the first man to give her work there was Muir Mathieson, then the supremo of British film music. She was commissioned in 1944 to write an item for inclusion in the RAF newsreel *The Gen*; and was inspired by what she described as 'protruding uniformed bums' to compose a march entitled 'Bustle for WAAFs'. This now savours strongly of the music which accompanies many 1950s British film comedies of the St Trinian's variety, but at the time would have been a pleasant surprise to those who had been offended by the first Chamber Concerto.

In the same year, this time through her connection with the producer Basil Wright, present at that first lunch in Prada's with Edward, she wrote the score for a short propaganda film made by the Crown Film Unit entitled *Jungle Mariners*, about the life of a jungle patrol somewhere in the South East Asia Command. A nasty little essay on the theme 'How evil can be beaten in its own surroundings by men who kept [sic] calm and kept together', its dominant motif was the march, but it also required her to evoke leeches, life among the 'natives', the brutal beating of a captured scout – 'We had to get a Jap' – and the construction of a 'Jap trap' out of sharpened bamboo stakes.

This was the first occasion on which she worked with pioneer sound engineer Ken Cameron, who was responsible for coining the epithet 'Twelve-tone Lizzie'. He always researched the composers whose scores he recorded, and from Liz was expecting the tuneless worst; but her 'Jungle' score was if anything over-expressive, worthy of a nobler vehicle on the epic scale, and he came to admire some of her work very much.

Over the next three years *Jungle Mariners* was followed by four more short documentaries on subjects ranging from the repatriation of eighteen million prisoners liberated at the fall of Germany to life on a tea plantation in Assam. The government, in order to conserve foreign exchange, had imposed a quota on foreign and particularly American films, ruling that every foot of film imported must be matched by a certain number made in Britain. 'Quota quickies' began to pour out of British studios, a large proportion of them second features and documentary shorts, and this was where Liz's film future lay.

They were perhaps her forte, because they were shorter-winded than features, and they almost always had to be written quickly – 'Do you want it good or do you want it Thursday?',[11] as she once quoted André Previn. This was the way she preferred to compose; and she enjoyed much about working in films – the company, the opportunity to hear what she had written almost at once, the generous praise of her colleagues, and, she claimed, the common ground it gave her with the milkman, who thought nothing at all of classical music.

She had no illusions that what she was doing was great art – she was never to be given the kind of film that might have encouraged pretensions. But it was a skill worth having, to be able to divine the kind of music that would suit a film, identify the precise moments at which it would be required – to evoke a locale or a mood, introduce a character, underline the action, paper over a hiatus or enliven a longueur – and then write the music required for each cue, stop-watch in hand, timed to the nearest third of a second.

Some composers resented being treated as appendges to the film, on a par with the technicians who provided the echoing footsteps, falling rain and distant cockcrow; but though she may have complained for form's sake, at heart she was not one of them. H. G. Wells, during the shooting of *The Shape of Things to Come*, wrote sympathetically to Arthur Bliss: 'I am at issue with Korda and one or two others of one group on the question of where you come in . . .' I say, "A film is a composition, and the musical composer is an integral part of the design."'[12] But Liz was in fact not unhappy to come in at the end when many of the decisions had already been made, the 'Innitiatives' taken. To her, writing for the films was a giant musical crossword puzzle on the Ximenes level, having no serious purpose but incidentally improving her musical spelling, vocabulary and dexterity with the language.

Liz used sometimes to say that if the audience found itself consciously listening to film music, then the composer had failed; the visual image should predominate and the music achieve its effects almost subliminally. Music for the radio, on the other hand, should expect to be heard, and could afford in some ways to be more ambitious.

Much of the BBC's most original work in the 1940s and early 1950s was done in the Features Department, under its head Laurence Gilliam. The 'feature' was most typically a hybrid of drama and documentary. In the typical example, whether it was of the highly imaginative or homespun 'look-at-life' variety, music had a structural and not a merely ornamental role. The composer shared the responsibility for the programme's coherence and pace, for maintaining the appropriate emotional level, varying the tempo and generating enough suspense to keep the attention of an audience listening in ones and twos. In these circumstances close co-operation with the producer was more important than in the cinema, and in her radio work Liz formed some of the most significant working relationships in an essentially solitary career.

Her first BBC commission was for music to Louis MacNeice's play *Enter Caesar* – a study of power, executed in the form of newsflashes from Ancient Rome, and rejoicing in a Triumphal Marching Song whose first line ran, 'Lock your wives up, gentlemen, here comes Baldy'. 'Being intelligent enough to know what Caesar is about,' wrote MacNeice to the Director of Features, proposing Liz's appointment, 'she would go out of her way to produce the effects I want. This programme will require rather peculiar, but also (paradoxically) rather virile music, which I think she is capable of producing.'[13]

Liz was proud of collaborating with a poet as distinguished as MacNeice, and grateful for a producer eloquent in explaining exactly what he wanted, an attribute rarer in the film world. But by far the greatest proportion of her radio work was given to her by Reggie (R.D.) Smith, the husband of her friend Olivia Manning.

Several of Reggie Smith's productions in the years immediately after the war were for the BBC's American Exchange – slices of English life, in return for which the BBC would receive little gobbets of Americana. In 1946, for instance, American sent Britain *Coney Island*, and were repaid handsomely with *Margate*, as conjured up by Liz and Dylan Thomas.

Thomas cast his evocation in the form of a short play[14] about a GI's return to England at the end of the war to be inspected by his English fiancée's parents, who run a seaside boarding house for theatricals. The lovers nervously put off the moment of truth, and their dawdle along the promenade, past the winkle stall, in and out of the Hall of Mirrors, is an excuse to string together impressions of the English seaside in the off-season of 1946. The dating is precise: the stationary roundabout is furnished with tanks and planes instead of horses and swans and the girl asks sharply, 'Where's the little atom bombs?', a crack which may or may not have been well received across the Atlantic a year after Hiroshima. The cellophane hats read not 'Kiss me quick' but 'Can I do you now, sir?', in homage to ITMA, and the best seller everywhere in evidence is *Forever Wind*. But the scene is peopled by the stock characters of any era – the fat lady paddling, the stand-up comic with his repertoire of jokes about pots and bottoms, the old man with the stomach like a bass drum digging a sandcastle in braces and bowler.

Incidental music required Liz to illustrate only fragments of a documentary or drama, and it is possible she found this frustrating, for by 1947 she had made her first attempt at a theatre work on her own account. To some extent, *The Pit* was as much a political as an artistic statement. A 'dramatic scena' for tenor, bass, women's chorus and orchestra, with words by W. R. Rodgers, it is set below ground, where a rock fall has trapped a boy, his father, and a third miner. Against a background of picks 'pecking and pricking and pocking and poking the rock . . . chirping and chipping', the younger miner (bass) cries and calls in delirium and eventually falls ominously silent. As the father and son await their own deaths, and above ground a chorus of women waits and chants psalms at the pithead, the old man (tenor) recalls scenes from his past and laments the boy's lost future.

Liz's sense of outrage at the appalling conditions of the miner's life was quite genuine and lasted all her life. (She was to be the only person she knew who sympathised with the miners in 1973 in their battle against the Heath government.) In 1946, with Edward, she was invited to sit on the Coal Board's music committee for the *Daily Herald* Brass Band Competition, and her sense of solidarity with the miners was sincere, although her contact with them was limited to conversations with her Newcastle charlady, whose husband worked down the mines.

'Although you have no knowledge of mining,' she wrote, 'although you know none of the miners, although you dislike the district, or the house you live in, or the town, you will be drawn into the community by this powerful spirit and will eventually find yourself at the pithead – waiting.' (She did not, of course; the vigil in *The Pit* was her substitute for any real involvement.) This outburst was incorporated in an article she submitted to the magazine *COAL*, published by the Central Office of Information; and it drew the stateliest of refusals from the editor. 'As *COAL* circulates almost exclusively among the mining community, it would, I am afraid, tend to emphasise the attitude of some miners who see themselves as the inevitable victims of disaster. Though there is something to be said for this attitude it is not altogether justified by the facts.'[15]

The Pit was written to a commission from William Walton, whom she always called 'my favourite diatonic composer'. In 1944, encountering Walton en route from the George to Pagani's, she had asked him for an introduction to Muir Mathieson. He supplied it, and 'Bustle for WAAFs' was the outcome, but he also divined the motive behind the request and immediately offered her £100, a typically generous amount, for anything she cared to compose – an effort at 'playing Paganini to your Berlioz',[16] as he described it.

The fee represented Liz's first earnings from serious music – a useful weapon against her mother, who continued to regard her composing as an indulgence – though hardly a frivolity. 'I really don't know how people get away with things today,' she wrote to Ursula after the first (unstaged) performance of *The Pit*. 'I thought Betty's music much better than the words – and some parts almost harmonious. But the screaming tenor drowned the instruments and the choir of women which might have been beautiful could one have heard it! But Betty's composition was old-fashioned and melodious compared to a French composer who followed [Serge Nigg]. . . . Are they all mad? I wonder – and found it terrifying.'[17]

The Pit is indeed, in a different sense, terrifying – eerie and claustrophobic, with a shrill edge of hysteria. But the music, darkly and even romantically expressive, is hardly radical. Its compositional nucleus is a series – but it is the series used already in the first Chamber Concerto, and Liz may have been conscious that she had made little genuine progress since her first venture into twelve-tone composing. The war years had starved her of information and contact with other composers working along the same lines, and since then she had been preoccupied with the new media of film and radio. She had seen Britten and Tippett, both younger, score major successes with *Peter Grimes* and *A Child of our Time*, and it might have been frustration which provoked her to exclaim petulantly and publicly, 'It's a snub,'[18] when the BBC chose not a chamber concerto nor the Three Symphonic Preludes but her *Petite Suite* for the Proms in 1947. Her embarrassment was understandable; the suite was made over from *Jungle Mariners*, and was crushed between the twin masses of *Belshazzar's Feast* and Ravel's *Daphnis and Chloe*. For the first time a familiar refrain was heard – 'The musical world is a jungle.'

With one piece, however, she soared above the doldrums of these early post-war years. In 1946 she was commissioned by impresario Gerald Cooper to write a work for one of a series of chamber concerts he was mounting at the Wigmore Hall. Music was already running in her head – a lyrical, keening voice supported by a sound like an unusually vibrant guitar – and it was almost complete by the time she found the words which corresponded to what she had heard.

Over and over again in her vocal writing she would compose in this way, working from music to words rather than vice versa. In this situation the words can sometimes be reduced to little more than a footnote to music which is already a self-sufficient entity, and which itself fails to penetrate the text. And at first Rimbaud's poem 'O

Saisons! O Châteaux!' does seem to be at odds with her conception of a voice raised in lament, for he is expressing ecstasy in the visionary power springing from his debauched life. But somehow the sensuality and expressive urgency of the two voices are the same; and Rimbaud did later add a couplet expressing disillusionment with the visionary ideal, so perhaps Liz had picked up undertones of melancholy not far beneath the surface.

The solo voice required a range which was then considered unusually wide, from top B flat to low G, making it virtually unperformable in the eyes of the BBC; and the 'vibrant guitar' had become guitar, mandolin, harp, violin and string orchestra, as lush and colourful a texture as she was ever to use. On its first performance in February 1947 – by Margaret Field-Hyde, negotiating the 'unperformable' vocal line with ease – *O Saisons! O Châteaux!* was encored; even more important to Liz, Edward was full of admiration – '*That* is a *work*.'

'Each separate piece,' she wrote later, 'is a journey of reconnaissance – a discovery, by exploration, of a new way to live a fresh experience.'[19] Musically speaking, *O Saisons!* was the first indication of a new way to live. And yet she was unconvinced that she had the strength to put her discovery into practice. 'At last ... we can captain our own ship,' she had written; but the autobiography continued – 'still it may be rocks or treacherous seas, the ship not sound enough, but now too late to mend.'

CHAPTER NINE

'Too Late To Mend'

IN 1946 LIZ WAS forty. A photograph taken by Bill Brandt for *Vanity Fair* shows her a thin and elegant figure, in an expensive woollen twin-set fastened at the collar with a brooch, leaning with one elbow on the piano behind her. The legs are excellent (a fact she always mentioned), the hair cut *à la* Richard III, and the expression challenging. 'Very much alive,' the caption runs, 'she loves clothes, cosmetics and good food.' The fact that she could now afford none of these things was skilfully concealed.

Technically Liz may have felt she had advanced little in the past six years; but as far as the other face of the music business was concerned, the promotion and publicity which all through her career she despised and yet demanded, she had taken several strides into the public eye. In all lists of 'promising young composers' she was included as a matter of course. At the start of 1947 *Les Temps Modernes* went so far as to see in her work and that of Humphrey Searle the dawn of *real* modern music in England. Searle, who was consistently generous to Liz with small reward, used his position in the Music Department of the BBC to arrange in November 1947 an entire concert of her works, including the first Chamber Concerto, the Partita for two violins and the four songs for tenor and quartet which she had written for Ian in 1937.

But she found it hard to enjoy her success; for as her life was opening out, Edward's continued to contract. In practical terms this meant there was to be no solution to the problem of money; in emotional terms it meant the loss of a companion, in her life and in her work. The years from 1948 to 1952 saw the erosion of her second marriage; the thwarting of her longing to be financially independent; her enforced abdication as a mother, and thus the failure – so long anticipated by Ursula and Lady

Emily – of her attempts to combine composing and child care. 'I could help myself,' she wrote despairingly to her mother, 'earn and work, but preoccupations with Edward and the children are at the moment more than a full-time job – and my work and life must wait.'

It had become clear by now that Edward's lack of employment was not just due to wartime conditions. His position with the BBC could no longer even be described as ambiguous. Not long after his resignation in 1936, with a certain insensitivity to atmosphere, he had asked for a series of concerts, but had been told that the use of staff conductors was still under review.[1] In 1942 three categories of conductors had been drawn up: those worthy of a week's engagement by the BBC (who included Sargent, Wood and Boult); specialists, or those with something unusual to offer (like Boyd Neel, with his own orchestra); and those who might be given token dates occasionally 'as a compliment to their services to music generally'. This last category included Muir Mathieson, musicologist Mosco Carner, and Edward's erstwhile assistant Maurice Johnstone, and might surely have been deemed to encompass Edward himself; but he was not on any of the lists.[2]

In 1944 when the BBC Northern Orchestra visited Newcastle he had asked for a single concert with them, which would immeasurably have boosted his stock and that of NERO. Kenneth Wright, always his principal ally in the BBC, recommended giving him something on account of his 'creative enthusiasm'; but others, including Maurice Johnstone, had heard that NERO's artistic standards were 'falling down', and vetoed the idea. After very careful enquiries into his 'outside activities', the BBC told Edward, they regretted that they 'could not recommend' offering him conducting dates.[3]

Between 1945 and 1948 there were scattered jobs, but nothing which drew extensively on his knowledge, and certainly nothing capable of providing a living. He was an adviser to the newly founded Cheltenham and Eastbourne festivals; and organised the May Day Festival for the Coal Board in 1948. Through Arthur Bliss, Head of Music from 1942–45, who shared his belief that the BBC was not there to pander to the lowest common denominator, Edward gave a series of radio talks on 'Turning Points of Contemporary Music' (two on Stravinsky, two on Bartók and three on Schoenberg). He even did a little conducting. After two harrowing experiences with inexperienced radio musicians, Liz asked if Edward might conduct the scores she was writing for the Features Department. There was a list of conductors recommended for this work, many of them rejects from the other three categories, and Edward was not even on this;[4] but a ferocious telephone call from

Reggie Smith to the Music Department ensured that in the future Edward conducted every radio score she wrote, and a few by other people.

But 'The Eileen Joyce Story' and 'Little Pig Robinson' were hardly substitutes for *The Soldier's Tale* and Schoenberg; and the concerts he had put on in 1946 now began to assume the aspect of a last wave before drowning. Miron Grindea, editor of the arts magazine *ADAM*, met Edward around this time at a party given by the composer Shula Doniach, who owed to him her first BBC performances. The two men had many friends and enthusiasms in common, and Grindea remembers Edward, transported by nostalgia for pre-war Europe, talking for five hours with tears in his eyes, of Cocteau, Enescu, Milhaud.

His only real outlet was the ISCM, and he clutched desperately at this straw. Otherwise, he seemed incapable of doing anything to save himself. He could not face the problem, could not contemplate any other kind of work, merely turned further and further in on himself, and away from Liz. To her the oppressive silence was worse than any abuse, and she could not stop herself attacking him, if only to get a reaction of some sort. 'It was her nature to maul,' James Clark has remarked, 'maul and hug.' And the attacks were now public. John Amis remembers noticing them coming down Goodge Street on the other side of the road, arguing noisily. Suddenly Edward stopped dead, snatched off his panama hat, threw it furiously to the pavement, attempted to jump on it in his rage, and missed – a symbol, comic and pathetic, of his general state.

Edward's position did much to confirm Liz's feelings of being a musical outsider. She was tied to his standard, with all that entailed, but she could no longer be sure of him as an ally. 'I always felt,' she wrote, 'that if an opportunity arose for musical work that might involve separation, for years or for ever . . . with his priorities he would not hesitate to follow the work. . . . It gave me a permanent sense of insecurity, as of trying to build a house and home on quicksand.'

She might have added 'and a career', for her confidence was beginning to be eaten away by criticism which intensified all the time. At about the same period Schoenberg was writing of his critics, 'I never understand what I had done to them to make them as malicious, as furious, as cursing, as aggressive';[5] and Liz may well have been taken aback by the virulence of some of hers.

In July 1946 an article entitled 'Stray Puffs' by 'Flute', in the magazine *Musical Opinion*, had savagely attacked the selection of Liz and Alan Rawsthorne to represent England at the ISCM Festival in preference to Vaughan Williams, Ireland or Bax. 'Who are these doughty champions of English art? Have they any stature? Only, I think, among their own branch members.' The only point in their favour, in the anonymous author's opinion, was that they were not Jews. 'In these days of the infiltration of "bergs" and "steins" into our concert programmes it would not have been at all surprising to find us represented by a Finkelberg (Eng. – Golders Green).'

Less venomous but perhaps more lowering, the *Monthly Musical Record* had likewise queried the committee's choice of the Three Symphonic Preludes. 'Miss Lutyens is in the front rank of our women-composers, but not in the first rank of our composers.' (*The Lancet* was soon to assert that no woman had ever been, or by implication ever could be, a composer of genius.) Two years later her fourth Chamber Concerto for horn and small orchestra was selected for performance at the 1948 ISCM Festival in Amsterdam, and the nudges and whispers of nepotism began. The following year in Sicily, when *The Pit* was given its first full staging at the Teatro Massimo, Palermo, the rumours would come out into the open.

Growing sensitivity, defensiveness and anger did nothing to improve her already poor state of health. In 1946 Liz had become pregnant for the fourth time, to the unconcealed dismay of both husband and mother. 'Surely you don't need more children to prove yourself a mother,' Edward is claimed to have remarked. Liz's concept of motherhood and the maternal instinct was an idealised one. Devoted to babies and the very young, she could not always live up to her ideals as her children grew older. But there is no question that she was one of those many women for whom the act of conceiving, carrying and bearing a child has a profound significance in itself. She found the notion of destroying life abhorrent, but with four children already effectively being looked after by other people, she had no answer to the arguments of Edward and Lady Emily, and she let her mother pay for an abortion.

Rose, Tess and the five-year-old Conrad were all at boarding school in Dorset, but Sebastian (almost thirteen, and preferring to be called 'Bill') had just endured an unhappy term at the Lycée Français in London, his third school in as many years. Liz had looked after him as far as work and the search for work allowed, but Ursula and Lady Emily now decided – taking advantage of Liz's weakened state, she felt – that he would be better off at Blagdon, where Ursula would educate him up to the age of seventeen and then start him in a profession, provided that Liz did not interfere. In her version of events, he had gone by the time she came out of hospital – only to be returned, miserable, a year later, when the arrangement failed to suit anyone.

Sebastian went from pheasant shooting and dressing for dinner to a foster home and a secondary modern in Seaford, Sussex, and Liz was torn by guilt and anger. 'I have had *NO* encouragement in anything I have undertaken,' she wrote bitterly to her mother, 'and all my life been made to feel I was a useless liability and that the family are ashamed of me – that I am irresponsible. Then, please, let me be and stop hurting. . . . For years you've all given me the pit and the pendulum, your children *or* your music. . . . You've taught me that money is all that counts and God knows, therefore, why we wasted so much of Father's hard earnings learning "truth and beauty" in India. . . . One day you may be proud, not ashamed of me, and one day I will *buy* the children back with the filthy god of money. I'm very busy and quite alone. One day – I'll show you all.'

Liz was busy, certainly, but achieving very little in her own music. The contrast with the poised and apparently confident subject of the Brandt photograph was striking. Constantly depressed and exhausted, the abortion having precipitated the menopause at forty, she found Fitzroy Street no place either to work or to relax. Because of its proximity to three main-line railway termini, it had been particularly badly bombed, and Number 6 was shored up by girders on one side, while behind it the bomb sites stretched to Tottenham Court Road. Builders were gradually demolishing and replacing every house in the northern end of the street and Liz, who found the slightest noise disturbing while she worked, was surrounded by perpetual blasting and hammering. Dust coated everything and further complicated life in a flat whose kitchen was also its bathroom, the top of the dining table lifting to reveal the bath underneath.

Early in 1948 she wrote two sets of violin duets for children, and a set of portraits of friends for violin solo, under the nonsense title of *Aptote*, suggested to her by Constant Lambert. Its literal meaning is 'a noun that does not decline'; it is also an anagram of 'teapot', and Lambert combined the two derivations in his suggested sub-title – 'on refusing to become a teapot'. (He had another title ready for her – 'Zeugma: drawing nudes, corks and conclusions' – but she resisted the temptation.) Lambert was one of the friends pictured, as a bat; Dylan Thomas was a tiger, Humphrey Searle a cat, Alan Rawsthorne a moth and his sister Barbara a glow-worm. Edward was a snail; he had turned sixty that year, and his slowness often irritated her.

Hammering or no, the film work had to go on, though it was at about this time that she jeopardised her prospects by taking issue with J. Arthur Rank, the biggest English studio of the day. She not unreasonably refused to grant the studio publishing rights in the music she wrote for them – that is to say, fifty per cent of all her royalties – and her first feature for Rank, *Penny and the Pownall Case* (1948), was also her last.

The drinking also continued, as she haunted the George, the Stag and the Highlander in search of work; and she could no longer avoid admitting she was an alcoholic. Watching over Edward in Fitzroy Street meant neglecting the children, now all in a foster home in Seaford; visiting the children meant deserting Edward. Working hard enough to support all five of them meant seeing too little of any of them, or drinking too much to enjoy it. In the autumn of 1948, unable to juggle her conflicting anxieties any longer, she retreated at Lady Emily's expense for what was described as a 'rest cure' by the sea.

She was dismayed to discover that her refuge was not so much a convalescent as a mental home; its architecture was enough, she claimed, to bring on a breakdown at sight, and like Fitzroy Street it was overrun by builders and filled with hammering. But again, as in Newcastle, these were annoyances she could have overcome had Edward not been too overwhelmed by his own misery to support her in hers. 'He has put his pain and frustration so heavily onto me, whether he means to or not,' she told Lady Emily, 'that coupled with anxiety for the children and my own work, I have felt like Atlas.'

He hated her being ill, had told her 'For God's sake, don't become a clinging ivy,' and now insisted he was 'too busy' even to write with news of himself and the children. Mary, who had been Liz's confidante and closest ally in the family throughout her marital upheavals, tried again and again to persuade him to visit her, only to be informed, 'She should know from what I've told her of my mother that I won't be possessed or bullied.'[6] Whatever Liz believed (and she was never confident of other people's affection), Mary would never waver in her devotion to the sister who had been her nursery friend and heroine, and she never genuinely forgave Edward. 'His impersonal attitude,' wrote Liz, 'was a rock of stability when I was fit. . . . But in time of trouble or sickness it was a rock that crushed all confidence, making me uncertain of his love.'

As she tells the story – and in the description of that essentially subjective experience, a mental collapse, what is 'true' to the sufferer cannot be denied, only supplemented with objective fact – Edward's neglect converted physical and emotional exhaustion into a full-scale nervous breakdown, the worst of her life. She was removed to what ever afterwards she called a 'lunatic asylum', a mental hospital in the south of England, and subjected to what was then a fashionable treatment for depression – narcosis, or drug-induced sleep.

In 1950 Liz was asked to write the music for *Out of True*, a dramatised public-information film (what would now be called a docudrama) on the treatment of depression. Filmed on location in a mental hospital, it featured interviews with psychoanalysts, Rorschach tests, and a grisly sequence on electric shock treatment as it was carried out in 1950, with enveloping headphones and a rubber plug for the patient to bite. It is not improbable that memories of *Out of True*, coming so soon after her own breakdown, coloured Liz's later accounts of her treatment. But even allowing for the widest margin of elaboration, the stories were horrifying.

The pills she was given to induce the therapeutic sleep combined sudden obliteration, which left a frightening collection of cigarette burns on the quilt, with equally abrupt awakening in the small hours. Wakefulness became a nightmare of banging in her head, screams and cries she thought she heard coming from other wards, and horrible delusions. 'It was the time of the Committee of Un-American Activities, and somehow, mixed with the other nightmares, I felt I was imprisoned by its order and the only person who could help me was Charlie Chaplin.' Liz smuggled messages out to 'Charlie' by way of Lady Emily – 'Help ... come quickly ... rescue me', in huge staggering letters, sometimes scrambled to anagrams. At other times she believed she was the Duke of Wellington, shouting and issuing peremptory instructions to the nurses.[7]

This time Mary impelled Edward to come and see her. 'His familiar presence, complete with carnation, was like a mirage in a desert,' Liz recalled. Mary and her husband Joe Links then took them both away for a weekend in the country, an interlude in which Edward did his best to comfort Liz and they seem to have been at least partly reconciled. But in retrospect Liz blotted the episode from her mind. Describing Edward's visit to the hospital she wrote, 'With his usual embarrassment and suspicion of illness or irrational behaviour, I don't remember him even approaching my bed.'

This was, perhaps, more than simple literary licence or her temperamental inclination to look on the dark side – 'to bad to say eny more'. In the end, while the 'lunatic asylum' relieved the symptoms of her breakdown (though she claimed the drug treatment had lasting and unpleasant effects), it could do nothing about the underlying causes.

Her stay had, in fact, simply underlined her insecurity with Edward, and one happy weekend could do nothing to remedy it. 'I had begun to doubt how much he really wanted me or needed me in his all-absorbing life, as a person rather than a money-provider.' And she came out to confront money worries as acute as ever.

Her own music at that time could not fail to reflect her mood. *Requiem for the Living* (1948) was slightly similar in conception and scale to Tippett's *A Child of our Time*, and started as a post-war hymn to peace, on the theme of pain, effort and hatred resolved in faith for the future. But optimism that year was a little forced, and the effect left by the piece, for which she wrote her own libretto, is of a refrain of pain and fear, uncertainty and self-hurt. 'Prometheus,' she wrote, 'in his chain of toil/With poverty and pain like birds of prey./The distant ranges of his thought unscaled,/The uncharted wave of discontent and doubt he flounders in.' She dedicated the Requiem to her mother – a symptom, perhaps, of her tendency to turn to Lady Emily in times of greatest stress. But the gesture went unremarked. 'She did not even postpone her dinner by a quarter of an hour to listen to it,' wrote Liz bitterly in *A Goldfish Bowl*, 'so I removed the dedication.'

A ballet *Rhadamanthus* (1948), based (like *Requiem for the Living*) on the same tone-row as *The Pit* and the first Chamber Concerto, explored the theme of the voluntary victim, in whom it is hard not to see at least the outline of Edward. A man 'in a state between waking and sleeping, life or death' finds himself in the dock before the judgement of his own mind, his accusers the shades of all that could have been, 'the women he had not loved, the children he did not have, the friends or workmates whose laughter he was too timid to accept.'[8]

In a sense Edward was in the dock throughout these post-war years, but the judge was Liz, who found in him perhaps too easy a scapegoat for her own disappointment, her failure to fulfil her own inordinate expectations of herself. As an adolescent her spiritual yearnings had pulled her further towards the mystic, the metaphysical and the occult than anyone of her temperament could safely go. Now her musical aspirations were far weightier than her technical resources could support; and to frustration was added the constant distraction of anxiety for her children, and constant worry about money – for which Edward could legitimately be blamed.

Over the next few years Liz wrote a succession of pieces which made no advances or were so feeble she instantly scrapped them; of three more string quartets, a form with which she was to experiment all her life, one (III) was backward-looking and two (IV and V) discarded.

There were disappointments. A second attempt at a dramatic work, the radio opera *Penelope* on the theme of Odysseus's return, was a resounding flop; and amidst the confetti of grants and commissions which marked the Festival of Britain in 1951, she was given only one for a four-minute carol. Perhaps not surprisingly, her choice of text was a somewhat sour poem by W. R. Rodgers beginning, 'Hark! the Herod angels sing tonight'.

There were further contretemps too with the critics. In 1947 she had written a viola concerto which adhered to the principles of the traditional concerto form but was serial in idiom. In *Music Survey*, Harold Truscott adopted the critic's not uncommon expedient of reviewing the programme note, with a ferocity that may help to explain her later reluctance to write about her work (and prompted editors Donald Mitchell and Hans Keller to print a disclaimer). She had suggested, for example, that the second movement of the concerto was like a song in three stanzas. 'A song without a melody,' wrote Truscott, 'is not a new experience, unfortunately, but it is an illiteracy which should be fiercely repressed.' 'I will take the composer's word for it,' he added, 'that the last movement is a Passacaglia, and merely recommend her to do a little research on the exact connotation of "concerto". . . . I think it is time Miss Lutyens and others of her ilk ceased to hide behind the cover of "twelve-note" or any other technique, and came out into the open with some music or "forever hold their peace" – and ours.'[9]

Liz might well have recalled Virginia Woolf's remarks about the experience of the woman novelist. 'The indifference of the world which Keats and Flaubert and other men of genius have found so hard to bear was in her case not indifference but hostility. The world did not say to her as it said to them, "Write if you choose; it makes no difference to me". The world said with a guffaw, "Write? What's the good of you writing?"'[10]

The 'hack' work at least had an obvious point; and during what were perhaps the unhappiest years of her life Liz distracted and at the same time burdened herself with a flood of commissions for radio and films. 'Oh! if you knew the nightmare of these last years,' she would write to her mother in the early 1950s. 'Knowing Edward and I dependent on the quality and speed of my brain work and the brain toppling with the strain which never lets up.' She tackled a catholic selection of plays from Ben Jonson's *Bartholomew Fair* to Randall Swingler's *The Devil's Horse*, but only seems to have found a theme to which she could wholeheartedly respond when she was asked to write the music for MacNeice's *The Queen of Air and Darkness*.

In this most characteristic of MacNeice's modern morality plays, he explores the theme of the young man possessed by a false ideal, personified by the Queen of Air and Darkness. In each generation the Queen marks down one man for evil; each starts as a sensitive, creative, caring ruler and ends as an inhuman dictator. At last one of the Queen's victims descends to the Catacombs to find her where she sits blind before a mirror with two maids to tell her what is happening in the world she influences from below. He cracks the mirror, redeeming himself and humanity.

MacNeice wanted the music to have an 'organic continuity', to be more than 'incidental'. The longest passage came at the end when the hero/victim descends to the Catacombs, 'where there is never a draught, where no fly buzzes,/Where no dust settles, where the light never changes'. Here, Liz remembered with admiration, he wanted 'music like blue velvet, dripping'. Unfortunately, in the live broadcast when the hero came to smash the mirror the music was allowed to drown the words – a fact commented on by almost all the listeners canvassed by Listener Research (fifty per cent of whom found the music too dissonant for comfort).[11]

The short features were more prosaic – *Canada, Britain and Trade, The Otter, Canterbury Cathedral*. But as she became more expert, she took great pride in sliding from one genre to another, identifying the style required and supplying it, be it to express swimming under water or the soaring arches of a Perpendicular nave. Another series for Reggie Smith and the American Exchange programme, unenticingly entitled *Export Jigsaw*, required versatility. For *Motor Cars* she was able to indulge in cod Futurist music, a reminiscence of Milhaud and the Paris of the 1920s, replete with klaxons and heavy metal crashes to evoke panel beating, the clattering of conveyor belts and the winking of indicator lights. *Jewellery* was more constricting, producing little more than jingles and a plethora of harp glissandi expressive of glittering.

The best of her short features was *The English Seaside* (1949), a suite in eight sections which passes from the 'Regency' of Brighton, along a 'Victorian Parade', into 'Sea Mist', and to 'Pierrot' at the end of the pier; then 'Brass Band' leads back into 'Busy Blackpool', and the 'Palm Court' of a 1930s hotel, ending, in contrast, in a 'Cornwall' enveloped in tantalising wafts of Debussy and even *Peter Grimes*. It is a highly entertaining piece, from which the BBC got good mileage, as snippets from it kept turning up in programmes over the years – 'Cornwall' in a television film on John Piper, and again in a feature called *The Mayflower Sails Again*; 'Regency' in *Emma*; and, more mysteriously, 'Victorian

Parade' in a programme on Christopher Wren. (Liz's music may not always have been quite as specific as she hoped, or the BBC not quite as fussy, as they felt able to use part of her suite for 'Henry VIII' to accompany *Epic Battles – Stalingrad.*)

Some of her incidental music is very touching; and it is possible that it offered her a more direct channel for emotions which lay behind all her music but were sometimes concealed by the infinitely more complex and opaque medium of her 'serious' work. There are signs of the different composer she might conceivably have been had she not followed the twelve-tone path; she was patently capable of writing 'English Renaissance' music. And there is evidence of the person she always was underneath – sensitive, even sentimental, and never cynical – even when in her concert music she was abrasive and uncompromising.

Pressure of work, however, took its toll; for if she is to be believed, it was the task of drumming up trade in the pubs of Fitzrovia which brought her drinking to crisis level. The British system of buying drinks in rounds, apart from being expensive, ensures that all keep pace with the fastest drinker; and she was constantly exposed to the social pressure often applied by other heavy drinkers.

By 1951 her condition was pitiable. It was recorded for posterity, unwittingly, by Jill Craigie in a film on which they worked together – *To Be A Woman* (1951). Craigie was at that time the only female director in the British film industry, and *To Be A Woman* was a plea for equal opportunities for women in every field. She recorded interviews with a variety of prominent women and, anxious to include a female composer, asked Arthur Bliss for his advice. Without hesitation he recommended Liz as the best of the moment – 'Amazing sounds, amazing sounds'.[12]

Her music for the film was neat, appropriate and effective. For the main titles, she made a minor key version, for percussion, of Ethel Smyth's 'March of the Women', the piece which Dame Ethel had conducted in Holloway, leaning through the bars and beating time with a toothbrush for a chorus of her fellow prisoners. But where Liz is concerned, *To Be A Woman* is most remarkable for the brief sequence in which she herself appears. Long, lank hair is parted far back on a domed forehead, and falls down each side of a thin face with set jaw and dull eyes. She is looking up slightly at the camera, swallowing nervously but with a defiant expression that momentarily softens into pathos with the faintest suggestion of a smile. It is a mesmerising face, which gives the impression of utter despair.

She was chain-smoking now, seventy cigarettes a day, constantly throwing back her hair from her face, with her nervous intensity at its height. 'She needed someone to act as a whipping post and sounding board for her ideas about her works,' remembered Denis ApIvor. 'She held forth at considerable length, whenever she was able to find a moment, stubbing at a bit of manuscript with a pencil, pointing out the twelve-tone rows and emphasising the subtlety of her inversions and augmentations, in a rush of syllables, punctuated by snorts and oronasal projections of tobacco smoke. . . . As soon as she had finished one cigarette she grubbed at another with ringed fingers.' She was drinking a bottle of brandy a day; many lunchtimes would find her at the French Club in St James's, already drunk and picking fights.

Glib rationales of alcoholism are futile and even dangerous. Some of the textbook phrases seem to illuminate Liz's drinking briefly, but none is the only light in which to view it. They speak of a 'script' of self-destruction, adopted in childhood in response to conflicts and tensions within the family; of a 'game' designed to show 'I'm no good – and it's your fault';[13] a bid to attract attention from an unloving partner by hurting oneself; insecurity stemming from parental deprivation or feelings of inadequacy as a woman. She herself had an exaggerated horror of psychoanalysis, which she may have brought away with her from the 'lunatic asylum', and would undoubtedly have rejected these explanations out of hand. Drink, she claimed, was first and foremost a means of overcoming shyness, and bolstering the nerve she needed if she was to make her way in the profession.

It is safest and simplest to say that, possibly from the beginning and certainly after the war, Liz drank to escape from unhappiness. Her friends could understand it, but it was becoming hard to handle let alone ignore, and the stories were multiplying. Liz at a concert at the London Contemporary Music Centre, noisy and staggering and having to be carried out. Liz at a public discussion of serialism – 'She emerged from the back of the room,' according to Denis ApIvor, 'blowing smoke from nose and mouth and proceeded, much to the consternation of those present, to draw six lines of music stave upon the board instead of five. . . . Undeterred she growled on, slamming notes on to the board in a cloud of smoke.'

One of the most successful radio plays of 1954 was Henry Reed's *The Private Life of Hilda Tablet*, whose central figure was a twelve-tone woman composer, heavy-drinking and gravel-voiced, given to such expressions as 'Look, old cock' delivered in patrician tones, and possessed of irresistible energy powered by monomania. Within weeks of its broadcast both Liz and Edward were talking of suing Reed, poet, playwright and Fitzrovian, with whom Liz had worked in 1950 on *Canterbury Cathedral*. (They had been on reasonably good terms; at some point Liz offered him a script idea entitled 'Balls: the notion of circumference'.)[14]

The Clarks had good reason to suppose that Liz – and particularly the Liz of 1951 – had been the model for Hilda Tablet. In general outline Hilda might have more obviously resembled Ethyl Smyth – in her homosexuality, her bluff rural heartiness, and the endlessness of her projected biography. (Dame Ethel's autobiography ran into many volumes.) And the Tablet opera *Emily Butter* (whose music was actually written by Donald Swann) drew shamelessly and at length on classical models; if any contemporary target was intended, it was the recently premiered *Billy Budd*.

But the details of her characterisation were absolutely unmistakable. Hilda had a father named Sir Eric and a mother who was campaigning forcefully for proportional representation. In youth she had played the organ in a country church (whose vicar's wife planned eventually to embalm her feet as a relic). She hailed Frescobaldi as a great musical innovator. She had set Schopenhauer (as opposed to Liz, who in 1953 had set Wittgenstein). She talked inexorably of twelve-tone music; Reed, doubtless out of long and painful experience, makes his narrator remark, deadpan, 'Musicians, as the world well knows, are of all artists the most reluctant to discuss their own lovely art.'

Hilda believed in the 'architectonic' in music – 'I have always been *mad* about architecture. . . . I learned it years ago, y'know . . . the first time I ever realised Purcell[15] – and the *Daily Telegraph* was held to have described her music as 'thawed architecture'. This was almost certainly a reference to a running joke Liz had with Constant Lambert, who had once said that if, as Goethe maintained, architecture was frozen music, it might be a good idea to melt down one or two of Edwin's banks. Reed could perhaps have picked this up in the pub, along with the other fragments of Liz's distinctive and oft-repeated stories.

It is important to know that in Reed's play Hilda is, despite everything, ultimately an endearing figure, even a vulnerable one. 'I sometimes begin to think,' she remarks plaintively, 'that the sort of things some people sometimes say to me are the sort of things you'd hardly think anybody would ever say to anybody.' But she is undoubtedly ridiculous, and Liz would have minded the ridicule the more for recognising that the play, and the series in which it appeared, was extremely funny – as indeed the court case would surely have been had she been rash enough to pursue the notion of suing Reed.

Far more deadly, though fortunately she never knew of it, was the portrait which Dylan Thomas drew after her visit to Laugharne in 1951. The visit was recorded by all three participants in the drama, Liz, Dylan and Caitlin, who was alone at the Boat House when Liz arrived, Dylan having stamped off to Swansea after a furious row. The two women went to retrieve him, and Liz in *A Goldfish Bowl* gives a vivid picture of the alcoholic reconciliation: 'Dylan was on his knees snivelling, they were both crying. They were having a whale of a time.' For her part, Caitlin claimed that once peace had been restored, it was Liz who wanted to stay drinking, though they had left the Thomases' small son alone in the house.[16] In the event all three hired a car, on Liz's money, and returned slowly to the Boat House where Dylan drank the contents of Liz's sponge bag, including her shampoo, and retired to bed for days.

Liz's picture of Dylan has an element of farce but is fundamentally affectionate. His of her is not. 'Weasel-eared Lizzie,' he dubbed her in a letter to Margaret Taylor, 'lying in bed reading a book on Erasmus Darwin upside down.' From his room over the pub he could hear her 'hissing and gushing and drooling and bubbling about Edward, money, the BBC, twelve tones, Constant and babies, men, men, men, all the way from her bed in the Boat House where she lies all day monologuing herself to death.'[17]

By the end of 1951 Liz's life had flown apart. She could no longer achieve any kind of equilibrium between the conflicting pressures of Edward, the children, her work and the procuring of it; and at a time when, as she wrote to Lady Emily, she felt she could write better than ever before, she was compelled to waste her energies in 'musical journalism', haunted by the thought of the years rushing past.

The American composer Ned Rorem once wrote, 'We endow those we love with imagined timeless qualities which they neither possess nor (usually) want us to think they possess. When, then, our disillusion of necessity arrives as we witness the collapse we've forced upon them (but for which we take no responsibility), we hate them; and . . . they can only stare back with that blank surprised dismay of corpses.'[18] To some extent Edward had been Liz's victim in this way. His life had been radically and permanently altered when she arrived on his doorstep in 1939; the changes she wrought coincided with others over which she had no control and became inextricably entangled with them, so that in one sense it is understandable that his cry should have been, 'Get on with your life and work and leave me to get on with mine.'

But by now his 'work' amounted to spending most of the day in his dressing gown, sleeping with the wireless on, uttering not a word for days on end. In despair Liz wrote to Emily: 'He cannot keep a date, his word, or do anything but let me down utterly. . . . It is like living with a ghost in the hope that life will come back. . . . I've only got myself unpopular trying to help him when he won't help himself. . . . He should have tackled the BBC and stopped them bullying him years ago and then I would have been well away. But with all his genious [sic] and charm he is no fighter. . . . I should, I suppose, have picked a nice, kind, responsible husband for my work and brood, but I found my "dangerously attractive" E. irresistible! Alas, he's been happy about five times in ten years and when not, makes life hell. . . . I know I still love him and always shall – but sadly it's a love with no future or fruition, nor comfort or comradeship, but it will always stop one from wanting second-best whilst he lives.'

One day when drunk she was persuaded by friends to leave him. She rang him up to tell him, hoping he would say 'Stay,' and was answered only with silence. The next day she was having a drink in a pub with Alan Rawsthorne when Sebastian arrived, white-faced, to say that Edward had had a coronary. For days he was not expected to live.

In fact he made a remarkable recovery, but his convalescence was protracted (curiously enough, in a Musicians' Benevolent Fund convalescent home in Westgate on Sea, only minutes from the school where the young Betty had struggled with 'dulcrows', Microbes and 'Farm Scenes' on the piano). In the meantime, she was lodging with friends in London. The three eldest children were living with Ian, who had remarried very happily and had undertaken to pay for their education, while Conrad was boarding at Christ's Hospital School. Liz was facing a complete disintegration of her health, mental and physical; and when in August 1951 Constant Lambert died, horribly and hallucinating, of diabetes severely aggravated by alcoholism, she was frightened into halting the decline.

Liz chose to see her drinking as a physical ailment, the only kind to which no stigma, 'no smell of psychiatry' attaches, and she sought a physiological cure, from the then fashionable Dr Yerbury Dent. (The cure was possibly recommended to her by her brother Robert, who had had his own battles with drink, and certainly paid for by his second wife Phyllis Warburg.)

Dr Dent believed in a mechanistic explanation of the universe and the denial of free will, arguing that human behaviour, like all physical behaviour, was explicable in terms of the movement of matter and not mind. Alcoholism was accordingly neither a sin nor a weakness of character but a chemical disease, an imbalance between the back brain, which initiates action, and the front brain, which inhibits it. In the alcoholic the front brain becomes over-active, Dent argued, causing a state of permanent anxiety. Because alcohol is a depressant and anaesthetic, rather than a stimulant, it drugs the front brain, temporarily alleviating the anxiety.[19]

Dent's remedy was to stimulate the back brain instead, using apomorphine – a derivative of morphine, but one which has the opposite effect (morphine being, like alcohol, anaesthetic). The treatment also had an important secondary aspect as an aversion therapy, because in combination with alcohol apomorphine provokes vomiting.

From 6.30 p.m. on 17 May 1952 until 10.30 p.m. on 20 May Liz was injected every two hours with apomorphine, and given gin and water, with nothing at all to eat.[20] For a further two days the dose was administered every three hours, in decreasing quantities until 'the desired effect' was achieved with the smallest trace of apomorphine. The desired effect was vomiting. At first, according to the nurse's records, which Liz kept until she died, she was sick every time, then she was merely shaken with violent retching. Once she became cyanosed; at other times the nurse noted hiccoughs, dizziness and hot flushes. At 4.15 a.m. during the last night of the treatment Liz woke sobbing and repeating, 'I am going mad,' and in the morning was seized with panic at the thought of going home and facing up to life. But from then on she became calmer, and after five days of starvation, her appetite began to return.

Dent claimed both to alter the personality and to change the body chemistry with apomorphine. He preferred to lay emphasis on the personality change, as reaching to the underlying causes of the problem, instead of merely obliterating the symptoms with aversion therapy. Beyond question, however, the aversion treatment worked for Liz. For twenty years she enjoyed the total freedom from addiction he had promised she could achieve provided she avoided alcohol completely; friends remembered her anxious queries in restaurants about wine in sauces and the ban on consommé or sherry trifle, where the alcohol would not have been boiled away. But there is little evidence that Dent had in any way altered her personality; Liz remained very much herself, only now she was not drinking and she was alone.

CHAPTER TEN

'Drawing Breath'

GIVING UP DRINKING changed Liz's working life far more dramatically than the long process of becoming an alcoholic had ever done. Overnight, she became the skeleton at the feast in Fitzrovia – in her own eyes at least, a reproach and an irritation to drinking friends. Better, she felt, to remove herself out of range and out of temptation; she left the room at the edge of Regent's Park, within walking distance of the George, which she had been renting from William and Helen McAlpine after she left Edward, and moved to a flat she had seen while visiting other friends, Bonamy and Valentine Dobree, in Pond Road, Blackheath.

On her own again, this time Liz was better equipped to steer her individual course. She was in control of herself, victor in a heroic struggle not just against alcohol but against self-consciousness, self-doubt, disillusionment, frustration, loneliness, and all the other spectres which had impelled her towards the bottle. And she was removed from the ambit of Edward. Much as she continued to love him, his insularity had reached a pitch where there was almost no contact at all between them, nothing he could offer her, and he told her so – 'I am not giving to anyone else that which should be yours; but I have nothing left to give anyone.' Better to be removed, at least temporarily, from the aura of his suffering, if she was to mend her own life.

'I was a composer again,' she wrote, 'and to that identity I would cling, as there was no other in my life at that time,' wife and mother having temporarily retired. In the respite after the storms of 1951 and 1952, she was at last able to hear her own musical voice, and use the practical skills she had acquired over the last ten years to formulate a distinctive language of her own, a blend of serial technique and sensuous feeling. So when in the late 1950s all the elements in her disintegrated life finally came together again, she was in a position to take stock, and to start off in a new direction. The 1950s were a watershed in her career, the moment at which she began to suspect that the years of effort and neglect had not been wasted – that no one would ever again dismiss her as a rich man's dilettante daughter.

In the years following her cure, Liz began to cut a figure on the British musical scene – but this time somewhere near its centre, instead of as an unhappy gargoyle at the periphery. The facet of her new image which she perhaps prized most was that of the working professional, as least resembling the guise in which she had entered the music world.

The professionalism was not a pose, as some suspected; she needed the money now as badly as ever. The tendency was to assume that she had been provided for by the men in her life – by Edward, with his legacy, and by her father, who had been famous for the wealth of his clients as well as for the houses he built for them. But Sir Edwin, for all his efforts, had in the end left his children little. The bulk of the £42,000 estate consisted of the house in Mansfield Street, and Lady Emily felt, as she had been brought up to feel, that property should go to the son of the family.

The furniture – much of it designed by Sir Edwin, and of considerable commercial as well as sentimental value – was originally to be divided among the girls, as compensation. But Robert objected, and on the understanding that he would keep it all together as a collection, he got the furniture as well. He promptly sold a good deal of it, some to Barbie and Ursula, but none to Liz, who could not afford it.

Lady Emily was no longer well off herself, and was forced to stop the allowance which Liz had been receiving from her parents for over thirty years. Over the years she was given a good deal of help by her sisters, particularly in covenants for the children, and Ian paid all his children's school fees, but to meet the expenses of day-to-day living she had to find her own devices.

'All Lyttons write,' Liz once said, and she did not see why she should be any exception. Her autobiography apart, the surviving samples of her writing are not particularly polished, but her personal accents are unmistakable. In 'How to achieve privacy in family life', an article she wrote for the woman's magazine market, reminiscences of her first refuge in the cistern cupboard are strong as the secret of privacy, and arguably of all human happiness, is revealed as being a second lavatory – 'large, comfortable and warm . . . with good books and pot-pourri and a lovely view'.

Taking the precaution of adopting the pseudonym 'Josephine Grey' she tried her hand at romantic fiction. She all too palpably followed advice to write about a world she knew – heroine Joanna, a continuity girl spurned by faithless Elstree film director Ted, meets cartoonist Jeremy, and love blossoms in the restaurant of the Royal Festival Hall – only to fall head first into the common trap of despising and writing down to her imagined readers.[1]

She wrote far better when she was not aiming at any particular audience, and when she had something she actually wanted to say. Her obituary for Dylan Thomas, written for Miron Grindea and *ADAM*, shows her at her best. There are traces of the self-consciously poetic, but her piece holds up well beside those of Roy Campbell, Stephen Spender and John Lehmann. It is about Dylan alone, not 'Dylan and me'; there is nothing in it to his discredit, and by quoting a letter where he is at his funniest and most sympathetic, she evokes a person to be remembered with affection and admiration. It is the kind of memorial that everyone would wish to have, and a good illustration of what she could be like as a friend – loyal, perceptive and forgiving.[2]

Liz would increasingly create her own libretti for stage works; but she could not look to her writing to pay the bills, for which her mainstay was still radio and film music. Her philosophy in the 1950s was to make the most of so-called 'hack' work while it lasted; for there were signs that the boom years were coming to an end in both industries.

The days of specially commissioned incidental music as a regular feature of radio programmes were certainly numbered, but before time ran out Liz produced some of her best 'light' work. At first, as she had feared, when she could no longer keep pace in the BBC pubs she fell behind in the race for radio work. Dr Dent had assured her jovially that he was treating so many of the BBC's producers as well that work should be unaffected; but correspondence with the sober did not produce such instant results as social encounters with the drunk.

In 1952 there were no BBC commissions at all, and in 1953 a single feature on *Westminster Abbey* which bore a certain similarity to her *Canterbury Cathedral*. The score has attractive moments nevertheless – a recurring theme used, on the model of Mussorgsky's *Pictures from an Exhibition*, to convey the impression of someone walking slowly and reflectively round the building; an exciting and expressive use of brass fanfares which make one wish she had written more for the brass bands which Edward so loved; and a haunting 'Soliloquy' for violin and organ, shamelessly reminiscent of Vaughan Williams's *Dives and Lazarus*.

1954 was far more productive. Two years before, when she had forced herself to write to her contacts asking for work, she had had a courteous reply from the poet, playwright and producer Terence Tiller.

'I try on the whole to ask composers to write for my programmes the music they would in any case write if left to themselves; and it has just happened that none of my productions hitherto has in my opinion quite called for your own or "instinctive" music.'[3] Now he felt he had one which did call for it – his own 'radio concerto for solo actor', entitled *Final Meeting*.

With the best will in the world, he could not have spelled out more clearly how Liz's music, and twelve-tone music in general, was popularly regarded, for *Final Meeting* (1954) was in effect a horror story of the highest class. A superb exploitation of radio's powers of suggestion rather than statement, it explores the effects of guilt on a man who, it is hinted, has killed an idiot child and cut the throat of his wife or lover, and must now re-enact their deaths over and over again as he progresses towards madness.

The distinction of scores like this earned her a rich variety of radio work in the next two years, from the classics – Ben Jonson and Calderon (translated by Roy Campbell) – to the contemporary – Jon Silkin's *The Quality of Desert*.

For the eunuch in William Golding's *Envoy Extraordinary* (1956) she found a harp sound which Golding himself called 'quite enchanting'; but she was obliged to concentrate on more mundane noises for two plays by Willis Hall in the same year. Both now, like so many radio plays of the 1950s (and beyond), sound heavily influenced by *Under Milk Wood* (1954) – poetic evocations of small but richly varied communities during the course of a single day.

Any Dark Morning (1956) evokes the pre-dawn awakening of a mining village, accompanying the miners from bedroom to kitchen sink to pigeon coop to bus queue to canteen to showers at shift change and into the cage which will take them to the coal face, as up on the surface the first milk bottles are put out, cats are called in, and lace curtains begin to twitch. *Harvest the Sea* (1956), set on a trawler off Lowestoft, uses the crew's dreams of shore life to highlight both the rigours and the dignity of their existence on board – the wheelhouse full of tobacco smoke, lit by the glow of the overhead compass; the cabin full of snores and the throbbing of engines, the smell of diesel, drying oilskins and hard-worked men; the galley thick with the steam of tea and the rattle of cutlery shifting with the roll of the ship; and, at the play's climax, the 'expectant dripping' as the trawl is raised, followed by the abrupt cascade of fish.

The miner was far closer to Liz's heart than the trawlerman, and her music for *Harvest the Sea* now sounds a little predictable. In fact the feature itself had dated as a form, and as a market for music it was contracting. *Musique concrète*, music in which natural sounds were recorded on tape and then combined and distorted in various ways, was becoming ever more popular with producers as the assertiveness of the Musicians' Union made the live performance of original scores uneconomic. Then in 1957 came the severe cutback of the Third Programme. Bureaucracy finally infiltrated the Features Department, with efficiency studies and work sheets; the drinking continued, but the creativity did not, and the kind of Bohemia which Liz had moved to Blackheath to escape was virtually extinct.

Fortunately, the documentary film business still had a few years to run – and in the early 1950s it was at its height. 'Join Liz and see the world,' Ken Cameron once remarked, and in eight years she touched most continents without ever leaving Britain. In 1952 it was the Gold Coast, for *The Boy Kumasenu*, her much-praised evocation of the African atmosphere explained by an expenses chit for fifteen shillings for a visit to the Caribbean Club. This was followed by *Tyrolean Harvest* (1954), *Little Aden* (1955), the Gold Coast again in *Theresa*, 1955 (this time it was the African Club off St James's, recommended by the painter John Craxton who knew where to find the best bands in London), *The Weald of Kent* (1959) with commentary by John Betjeman, *Morning on Mount Kenya* (1960), and life on an Israeli kibbutz, in *Challenge of the Desert* (1960).

Liz wrote jingles for Be-Ro flour and Cusson's Imperial Leather; the money was comforting, but she found it profoundly irritating, while her most important serious works consistently suffered from under-rehearsal, to be allocated three hours in which to perfect thirty seconds of music whose cues read 'tablet of soap', 'mother and child lathering' and 'petal soft – it laaasts and laaasts'.

Among her other employers were Unilever, Bowater Scott, British Transport, the Gas Council, a variety of oil companies and, more troubling to her conscience, the US Mutual Security Agency, the United Kingdom Atomic Energy Commission, and NATO. *This Little Ship*, which she wrote for the UKAEC in 1952, remained under embargo for twenty-five years,[4] dealing as it did with the fate of HMS *Plymouth*, which exploded while carrying nuclear weapons during Operation Hurricane off the Montebello Islands in 1951. This seems to have worried her less than *The Atlantic Decade* (1959), made for NATO at the height of the Cold War, with a belligerent commentary intoned by Ed Murrow. She ridiculed the 'Boy Scout behaviour' she encountered when she visited NATO Headquarters, muttering darkly about needing her passport to go for a pee, and claimed to have used part of the fee to buy Conrad new shoes for the Aldermaston march.

By 1960 she had broken into feature films in a modest way. The cue sheet for *Don't Bother To Knock* (1960)[5] gives a vivid idea of the demands that might be made of the film composer, passing in rapid succession from 3 minutes and 11 seconds of Austrian night club to 35 secs. Venice, 57 secs. mountain mist, 3 mins. 8 secs. Spanish folk club, 15 secs. in the bath, 29 secs. of an Edinburgh pipe band marching to 'Cock o' the North', 53 secs. of a contemporary concert, 1 min. 37 secs. of car chase and 1 min. 2 secs. on a raft.

The rewards of film writing were considerable, and not all material. Liz was never ashamed of her film work, and felt that writing at such speed and in such a hotch-potch of styles increased her technical facility. But in truth her achievement was simply to have made a career in a highly competitive and male-dominated business, for at heart she was not a natural film composer. In her feature films at least, she consistently fell between the two stools of the art film and the popular success.

Hanns Eisler, whom she knew and liked, had recently predicted a great future for contemporary music in films.[6] Unencumbered by the rules governing repetition and development in classical forms, the new music was flexible, working in shorter and self-contained lengths, and could readily be tailored to fit the most rapidly changing action. It could also express, he felt, the extremes of emotion, free of the hackneyed associations which by now dominated conventional film music.

In the kind of film Eisler was talking about, the kind for which he wrote music himself, where moral and aesthetic quality took precedence over the box office and the composer worked on an equal footing with the director, Liz might have been able to serve the action well by writing her 'own' music. But for the B films and documentaries that she was actually given, some compromise was necessary, and it was to Liz's cost that she was never really able to achieve it.

Philip Martell, who acted as Music Director for most of Liz's films and was a great friend and admirer, nevertheless doubted whether she had a natural instinct for the cinema. Instead of calculating how best to steer an audience's response to a scene, she tended to offer her own emotions directly, in music that was often too difficult to absorb without effort. Traditional film-makers expected music to dissolve into the background, merge with the images and the characterisation; and though in theory she agreed, in practice her music too often had an imaginative life of its own.

Martell often found it necessary to take decisions for her. He did not read music, but from a long career, first as a violinist in cinema orchestras in the silent era and then as a theatre conductor, he knew what films needed. He showed her where the cues should come in a film, and then, when she had written them, told her which truly served the film and which had gone 'over the top' and above the head of the man in the front row.

Liz tended to blame her lack of opportunity in the world of feature films on her dispute with Rank, and on the attitude of influential figures like Muir Mathieson, whom she felt was an irredeemable misogynist. Mathieson would seem to have made an unguarded remark to her about the incapacity of women to express passion in music. But he also gave her her first cinema job and several subsequent films; he worked quite often with female performers, and as a determined campaigner for British composers at a time when the film industry appeared to be dominated by Hungarians, he did not deserve to be so persistently reviled.

If he did not give Liz features, according to Ken Cameron, it was because he thought she did not always do them very well, and already feature films were so expensive to make that there was no room for experiment. Given that she could only partially curb her musical instincts when writing for films, the only features she was likely to get were ones which in the opinion of the film industry spoke naturally with her characteristic voice – and these all had 'skulls', 'death', 'paranoia' and 'screaming' in their titles.

CHAPTER ELEVEN

Bloody Well Compose

'TWELVE-TONE LIZZIE', 'Horror Queen' – the side of Liz that enjoyed the *outré* and outrageous quite relished the labels her film work brought. They were all of a piece with the green or terracotta nails she occasionally affected, the gruff voice, the chain-smoking. But in fact, as she settled alone in Blackheath and drew breath after the years of drink, wrangling and misery, her serious music in the 1950s was moving away from the *angst* of *The Pit* and *Requiem for the Living* towards a greater serenity.

At first, now that she finally had the peace and quiet she had craved, she found it disconcerting. She felt something of the embarrassment of hearing one's words fall into a sudden silence at a party; and without the background noise of teenage children to force her to concentrate – Sebastian was a jazz enthusiast, the twins avid film fans, and Conrad learning to play the horn – she was unable to settle down to work. She walked on the heath, gardened, read, and still the music was frozen; until, by her own account, she found the energy to say fiercely to herself, 'If you're a composer, bloody well sit down and compose.'

The piece that thawed the ice was her Sixth String Quartet, written between 1952 and 1953 – and once she had found a way to begin, she wrote it in one sitting with an urgency she had never experienced before, confronting the blank page after tea and hardly rising from the desk until the small hours of the morning. As she wrote, she remembered Francis Bacon once saying that when he wanted to make a particular impact on the senses, he painted as quickly and instinctively as he could. She wanted this piece to affect the nerves and she plunged into a first movement that was all heat and passion. The second, in contrast, was cold and deliberately 'expressionless'. Then, instead of the two further movements she had planned, she found 'ear, mind and logic' all dictating a reprise of the first movement – but a reprise which sounded quite different, altered by having passed through the quiet chill of the Adagio.

'If you're a composer, bloody well compose.' One of Liz's favourite refrains was that composing was simply the activity by which one qualified for the title 'composer', no sacred charge but a *job*. 'A dog barks, a composer composes.' She would run into trouble repeatedly for seeming to belittle the art of music by reducing it to a craft, or simply a trade, and minimising the role of inspiration. 'If a composer really provides music as an upholsterer provides chair-covers,' wrote Martin Cooper irritably, 'a great many of us are indeed making a lot of fuss about nothing.' [1] He was in fact misrepresenting Liz's true attitude, and the Sixth Quartet proves it.

'The composer's workshop is his Holy of Holies, the temple of his mind, that has to be kept so quiet that he can listen to the faintest sound invoked by his imagination.' [2] Her words are not the words of someone who believed composition should be as standardised, mechanical or insignificant as the act of covering a chair. What offended Liz was the affected picture of the composer as a being apart, the 'pen in the hand of God'. This implied that he or she was essentially passive, a receptacle for inspiration from outside – whereas for her, control was all-important.

'Sanity lies in applying the *conscious* mind objectively and allowing the "unconscious" – "inspiration", "soul", "spirit" – to look after itself,' the young Betty had written with determination in the aftermath of the Theosophical adventure. The adult Liz was never to exclude 'soul' from her writing as rigorously as she perhaps intended. But in theory at least, composition was for her essentially a process of making choices with the conscious mind and arranging the chosen sounds, not an eternal waiting for a bolt from the blue, for messages to come through on 'the divine ticker-tape', as she had been taught to expect all those years before in Sydney. Inspiration, when it came, came from inside, generated by this process of making choices.

In this way the Sixth Quartet, initiated by will-power alone, caught fire as she wrote – and on one listener at least it had the impact she had been aiming for. 'Every note is in place,' wrote Dallapiccola, 'and every note sounds. It is all we can demand of contemporary music. It is beautiful, it is honest, it is sincere.' [3]

But the spectre of intellectualism, the charge that she put head before heart in her music, if not her life, was to haunt Liz for thirty years. For this her next work was largely to blame – more specifically, her choice of text for her next work. For Ludwig Wittgenstein was then taken as a synonym for the abstruse, and his *Tractatus Logico-Philosophicus* had been called the most misunderstood work in twentieth-century philosophy; yet an extract from this was what she chose to set as a motet for unaccompanied chorus. But what might appear to be a piece of highbrow one-upmanship looks rather different in the knowledge that, as with *O Saisons! O Châteaux!*, the music came first. The Wittgenstein Motet (Op. 27) started as a piece of pure musical thought, to which she sought to add a text which would correspond to the music not only in its atmosphere, but also in its grammar and syntax.

Liz was looking for a text that would be impersonal and 'otherworldly' without being religious – something which would have religion's generality and exaltation without its dogma. She was seriously considering Euclid when Terence Tiller, with whom she was to work on *Final Meeting*, suggested Wittgenstein, then much in the news. (He had even appeared recently on 'Desert Island Discs').

The *Tractatus* is a set of statements about what the world *is*, analysed in abstract terms, and how it works. It concerns the relationship between physical reality and language, physical laws and the laws of logic. It also explores the relationship between life and death.

The world, Wittgenstein declares, is 'all that is the case' – a myriad 'states of affairs' or combinations of objects, fitting into one another like the links of a chain; in physical terms, it is composed of endlessly interrelated objects. This physical reality is grasped by means of propositions, which reveal its logical structure. Logic pervades the whole world; everything that exists has a logic expressible in propositions. If something cannot be so expressed, it does not exist. One's life *is* one's world: so the world cannot include death. Death is outside life – at death the world comes to an end.

What really stimulated Liz was the essence of the *Tractatus*, in the sense that her notion of its general meaning and atmosphere governed the way in which she developed the music that was running in her head, before she attempted to combine specific words with specific notes. She had decided to set the series of propositions given prominence in Wittgenstein's own numbering, which effectively constituted a summary of the thought of the book. First Edward read out the German words; then he and Terence Tiller made a literal translation for her guidance – and all this time the music was growing and changing. Then the composer Shula Doniach wrote the German words down in musical notation, giving each syllable its correct quantity, and rehearsed Liz in them until she knew the meaning of every sound.[4] Only then, when the music was virtually completed, were the words finally married to it syllable by syllable.

Wittgenstein had told a non-philosopher friend that he would find the meaning of the *Tractatus* in its 'mystical' sections. Hard to comprehend rationally, it was perhaps best grasped through intuition – and this, many felt, was precisely what Liz had done, seizing the work intuitively herself and offering other people a means of approaching it more familiarly. In the view of one critic, she had created 'a kind of musical geometry answering to Wittgenstein's philosophical thought'. Her music had its logic, with ideas 'hanging one in another, like the members of a chain', as they do in the world itself. Rather than simply illustrating the text, it exemplified it.

The Motet was commissioned by William Glock – pianist, critic and organiser of concerts, married to Anne Geoffroy-Dechaume, sister of Antoine and a friend of Liz's since her teens. Glock greatly admired Liz's work, and was to become her most influential champion. This piece was for performance at the Summer School of Music which he had founded at Bryanston in 1948 and transferred five years later to Dartington in Devon.

Liz had just finished with Wittgenstein when she was offered a commission by clarinettist Georgina Dobree, the daughter of friends and Blackheath neighbours Valentine and Bonamy Dobree. In response, Liz was to write her *Valediction* for clarinet and piano (Op. 28, 1954). This was one of the few pieces whose evolution she ever explained at length, in a lecture she gave in the 1950s which survives as one of the best descriptions of how she worked when she was fully in control of her musical thought and composing could be what she wanted it to be.[5]

She was in condition, as it were, after writing the Motet, her mind and creative instinct still at their peak, without having had time to descend into the trough which often followed her bursts of activity – a cycle which puzzled and annoyed her. She had also just been working on three poems by Dylan Thomas, for an evening in his memory, and it was from this experience that there came what she called the *donnée* for *Valediction* (again, proof that she did not deny the validity of inspiration, just the idea that the composer was given *everything*, in a kind of musical dictation). As she was thinking of Dylan's poetry and of his death, a musical line came into her head, a twelve-tone row expressed as a reiterated six-part brass chord with a rising vocal melody, and with it came the poetic image of a woman's voice raised in lamentation – 'Aie!'

The next step was to examine the material she had been 'given'; could it be developed any further? And with this material as its basis, what would the piece be about? What words would the woman be singing? And who would the singer be? Liz had half-formed ideas on the text and the casting – Shelley's 'Fragment of an Elegy on the death of Bion', and the soprano Oda Slobodskaya – but neither was precisely what she was seeking, and she postponed making her decisions while she let the music germinate, always a crucial period in the evolution of her works. 'I'm tasting, smelling, feeling, hearing, seeing (to mix all metaphors) *what* I *want* to write,'[6] she explained, describing a process which continued night and day without a note necessarily being written.

It was at this germination stage that the commission arrived, and Liz faced the composer's perennial problem of how to combine spontaneity and integrity with working to order. She wanted to write for Georgina Dobree, and she could not afford to turn down the commission, but she was equally anxious not to relinquish the *donnée*; so she decided somehow to combine the two. Because the *donnée* was short and constructed on a small scale, it was relatively malleable; and to her ears the clarinet sounded near enough to the human voice to be able to take up the lament. The melodic line could now cover a wider compass, given the clarinet's greater range; and the brass accompaniment became a piano, less swamping for the soloist. The problematic words disappeared altogether, except for two couplets printed as headpieces to the two movements, reminders of the piece's origins.

Two years later Liz would salute another friend and hero, in her Chorale for Orchestra: *Hommage à Igor Stravinsky* (1956). She liked to recall Stravinsky's picture hanging over her bed in Paris; it is not clear whether she remembered describing him as looking like a dachshund with glasses. She had first actually met him when he came to England in 1954 to conduct his *Orphée* for the BBC, and she went with Edward to rehearsals.

Liz had wanted to return to Edward almost as soon as she had left him, partly to look after him during his illness, and partly because he was inextricably woven into the texture of her life. It was a cruel blow to be told that he did not want her back at Fitzroy Street. 'Until he made an absolute recovery,' she explained in *A Goldfish Bowl*, 'I don't think he could bear anything personal, anything that might be emotional near him. I understand now, but then it was just another painful rebuff to be borne as well as possible.'

When he returned to London after his convalescence, however, they were back in touch almost at once. He lived in Fitzroy Street by himself – reverting to some extent to his Fitzrovian life of the 1930s – but visited Blackheath often, particularly in the school holidays. He usually accompanied Liz when she gave lectures, and from time to time she went with him to parties, concerts and rehearsals, as on this occasion to *Orphée*.

Stravinsky's reunion with Edward was touching – Edward did not exaggerate his friendships, and this was one which endured for over fifty years from the Paris of 1908 to the Hampstead of the 1960s. There followed an evening at the Savoy which Liz never forgot. Waiters shifted chairs, switched lights off, and finally drooped yawning and defeated as Stravinsky, in rapid Russian-American-French, described the recently completed *Agon*, humming, dancing, drumming his fingers and illustrating its choreography with knives and forks.[7]

Liz was ambiguous about Stravinsky's adoption of serial methods, of which *Agon* was one of the first examples. She appreciated that his endorsement, so to speak, of twelve-tone techniques helped to bring them back within the pale for many critics, and speed the acceptance of other serial composers; at the same time she resented the suggestion that what was essentially a compromise with tonal music, 'serialism without tears', represented a happy ending to the sad story of twelve-tone experiments, a last-minute rescue from the atonal abyss.

In every other way, however, Stravinsky had all the qualities she most enjoyed and admired: passionate energy, a quick mind, natural wit, and personal warmth – 'Russian hand-holding' – which she needed but found in very few other people. He was without the good looks which made her nervous in men, but he treated her as if she were beautiful; when she was on his arm people treated her with a new respect, and she loved him for it. In a music world where she found much that was drab and disappointing, Stravinsky represented glamour and genius, the real thing.

In 1956, when she put her feelings into music, he had been ill, and was now recovered. Liz took over Beethoven's heading to his A minor quartet, Op. 132 – 'a Hymn of Thanksgiving to the divinity for the recovery of the revered master' – and used three fragments of the quartet in composing her tiny three-minute chorale of thirty bars, for three violins, three cellos, wind, brass and harp.

The piece had echoes of Stravinskian ritual in its alternation of chorales and canons, culminating in a final tutti chorale, and it was a sign of confidence to send it to him as a musical Christmas card that year. 'If you're a composer, bloody well compose' – in the three years since the Sixth Quartet and her return from the musical underworld, Liz had established her claim to the title beyond question. The bony skeleton of the serial technique was now amply padded with the flesh and muscle of an individual harmony and melody, and illumined from within by the young Betty's expressive passion brought under the control of an incisive adult mind.

Another sign of maturity was the variety of genres in which she was now working. In past years she had tended to experiment with one genre at a time – with songs and small-scale string music in the 1930s, say, and light music in the war. But between 1953 and 1957 her Ops. 27 to 37 encompassed (beside the Wittgenstein Motet for unaccompanied chorus) a baritone song cycle, chamber works for a heterogeneous assortment of instruments, one of her most important orchestral works, and the stage work which some people regard as her best.

The song cycle was *In the Temple of a Bird's Wing*, a setting of poems by her daughter Tess. By the end of 1954 she and Rose had left school and moved back to live in the flat across the corridor from Liz. Tess had had some poems published in *Bottegha Oscura*, and both twins were talented artists; in the autumn of 1954 they went to the Camberwell School of Art. 'I'm so adoring having my daughters back again,' Liz told her mother. 'It's simply heaven to be together again and they are blossoming day by day and are very happy. Edward has been here and they adore him, call him "Eddie", and think him a great "card", and he responds with gallantry and gaiety.'

Valediction for clarinet and piano was followed in 1954 by Nocturnes for guitar, violin and cello, commissioned by Joyce Rathbone for Julian Bream, Emmanuel Hurwitz and Terence Weil. Sinfonia (1955) was her second work for solo organ, interesting more for its reminiscences of the evenings in Woolpit church than as an addition to the repertoire. The original soloist, Ralph Downes, felt that in adhering strictly to the laws of serial technique and prohibiting octave doublings as repetitious, she had forfeited the chance to exploit the unique character of the organ, and made it sound like a woodwind quartet.[8]

The orchestral composition was Music for Orchestra I (1953–5). Anthony Payne has argued that this was a title Liz reserved for particularly important large-scale statements, and the four pieces to which she gave the name (Ops. 31, 48, 56, and 152) occupy the same place in her output as symphonies in the corpus of the more conventional composer.[9] The first *Music* was her last attempt to work within the format of the traditional symphony orchestra; after this she felt that new music needed a new layout, and used ensembles in which every player was a soloist. Accordingly, she tended in later years rather to dismiss Music for Orchestra I as insufficiently radical, and over-emotional – 'occuous', as opposed to 'innocuous'.[10]

Infidelio (1954) was radical enough in conception – an early experiment in music-theatre for small forces, commissioned by the ICA with the intent (never realised) of making up an evening with *The Open Window*, a one-act comedy by Malcolm Arnold on a short story by Saki.[11] But in stagecraft at least, Liz had progressed little beyond *The Pit*. Here too there is virtually no action, nor even a chorus to extend the scope of what is essentially a cantata with a strong plot.

The theme of *Infidelio* is the responsibility lovers owe to one another, which cannot be evaded without disaster. The Woman, seduced and deserted by the Man, kills herself. Their love story is told as a variant of the seasonal cycle – but running backwards, from desolate and despairing winter to hopeful spring. Thus the curtain rises on the figure of the Woman hanging from a leafless branch – 'The heavy bitter fruit droops from a barren tree', runs the text, in a line resonant of Billie Holiday's ballad of a lynching, 'Strange Fruit'. As the story unfolds, in response to the Man's anguished question 'Why?', the Woman is identified with the tree itself – blasted and broken-branched now, but once fresh and tender before her green leaves were scorched by the Man's summer breath, to dangle brittle and yellow in the autumn breeze of memory.

This was one of Liz's few direct approaches to the traditional subject of song and opera. She found the convention of singing loudly and publicly about the most private emotions of all ridiculous on the whole, but there was something she wanted to say about love – about the irresponsibility of insisting on being free without offering any kind of freedom in return. So she not only tackled the subject of love but wrote her own libretto – only to lose her nerve and have it printed under the pseudonym of 'T. E. Ranselm'. (In case anyone should ask inconvenient questions, she endowed Ranselm with a nasty case of tuberculosis and sent him to live abroad; but the piece was not to be performed for nineteen years, and then no one showed any desire to interview him.)

She was right to have misgivings about 'taking the rap' for both music and words. Musically *Infidelio* is strong – though a wintry bleakness tinges all the seasons of their love, which never sounds rhapsodical even in its beginnings. Dramatically, the device of running the plot backwards – influenced perhaps by Schoenberg's *Hin und Zurück*, which goes into reverse halfway through – tends to work *against* the feeling of inevitable decline which the seasonal cycle is often used to convey. And as literature, *Infidelio* veers between extremes of pathos and bathos.

In writing her own text – which she described as 'cod Yeats' – Liz was violating her own code of professional seriousness. Anguish, as ever in her work, rings true and moving, and there is some agile juggling with words; but when she attempts eroticism, the results teeter on the edge of 'stuffed owl'. In later life she took some pleasure in being embarrassing about sex;[12] the foundations are laid here. 'He was the huntsman/Of my moon white nights', sings the Woman nostalgically and with overtones of Osbert Sitwell's 'Winter the Huntsman', one of the first texts the young Betty ever set. 'On his horn' (and here, unhappily, the sexual connotations seem to be deliberately invoked), 'he blew our love's fanfare/As he rode me down/The alleys of the wood.'

The Man's metaphors for their love are equally perilous. 'My summer seas have/Whispered round her shores/Tenderly exploring each rock and cave . . . and as the/Lovetides yielded/To the harvest moon, hightidings of great joy/Broke on her lonely beach.' Liz did say she thought she would not be using Mr Ranselm again, and she was wise. But *Infidelio* should go a long way towards countering any charges of arid intellectualism; Liz's vice in her writing was not obscurity but sentimentality.

It is surprising in a way that her sense of theatre was not more acute, because in perceiving and illustrating other people's dramatic intentions her instincts were sound. She loved the theatre world – funnier, less dour, more broad-minded than the goldfish bowl of contemporary music, with an educated interest in all the arts and not just one – and she was welcomed into it.

There were preliminary flourishes. In 1956 the Berliner Ensemble was brought to England by Bertolt Brecht's wife and daughter, and Liz, through Edward (who had known Brecht in Berlin), was asked to supply a version of the national anthem for their tour, for flute, trumpet, accordion, drums and 'prepared' piano; to her glee, this was hailed by Kenneth Tynan as quintessentially Brechtian, an obvious example of the alienation effect.

In 1958, more oddly still, she was embroiled by Louis MacNeice in a *son et lumière* at Cardiff Castle, for which he had written the text. 'As Welsh history does not appear too gay,' wrote Liz, 'Louis had wanted to end the show with the Welsh scoring a try at rugby, but neither the City Fathers nor the *Daily Telegraph* backing the show would play ball, and insisted on singing "Land of our Fathers" (almost the only bad Welsh tune) as a finale to a pageant mostly consisting of Roman conquerage and Cromwell's army's devastation.'

The following year her theatre career began in earnest when she was invited by Frank Hauser, director of the Oxford Playhouse, to supply

the music for Euripides's *The Bacchae*, translated and produced by
Minos Volanakis. Both Hauser and Volanakis were informed and enthusiastic about contemporary music. Hauser had consistently involved
serious composers in the Playhouse seasons – not to produce music-
theatre ('That's when actors who can't sing are asked to dance as well'),
but to supply incidental music which would contribute more to a
production than acoustic wallpaper. Volanakis too had already employed
South African composer Priaulx Rainier for one of his productions and
at first wanted to use her again.

Fortunately for Liz, Rainier was not available to do *The Bacchae*.
Frank Hauser was to become a loyal and prized friend, and Minos
Volanakis more than that. And with Euripides she was given an opportunity to write for a different medium but largely in her own
unadulterated idiom. The most purely horrifying of all Greek tragedies,
The Bacchae was strong enough to absorb her musical language at its
most violent. Stevie Smith, who drove up to Oxford with Liz for the
first night, thought the score exciting and apt – though she fell out with
its author over two pounds of sausages which she had left in the car and
felt should have been returned instanter to Palmers Green.[13]

Working with Volanakis became one of Liz's great pleasures. She was
involved from the beginning of each production, as she could never be
in her film work. Volanakis was perpetually experimenting; Liz loved
anything she thought brave, and she responded instinctively to his
romantic attitude to art, revelling in the extravagance. 'Rather the tail of
a lion than the head of a jackal,' designer Yolanda Sonnabend remembers
him saying. She worked with him, and with Liz, on his 1961 production
of *The Oresteia* at the Oxford Playhouse and the Old Vic, all three plays
on a single evening, and has vivid memories of a kaleidoscopic setting
for the drama – a Bronze Age basic set, and yet at one point African
overtones requiring tribal music, and a court scene in the last play for
which all the characters wore Dag Hammarskjöld masks.

Her memories of Liz too are vivid – mostly visual, as one might
expect of a painter. The first impression was of paleness, fineness,
translucence; a delicate complexion; long, elegant hands; dead straight
hair, tidy rather than luxuriant. Her clothes were unconventional –
Yolanda Sonnabend recalled one outfit which suggested a plumber at
Versailles – but never artsy, and there was nothing in her manner of the
selfconsciously Bohemian. She sat hunched in her chair but never
gnomish, merely looking rather as if she were defending herself against
a blow. She was at once a temptation to paint and, in Sonnabend's view,
a danger, because as her face grew thinner with age, the nose appeared

more prominent, and lineaments which were near-beautiful when animated could look almost grotesque in repose.

Liz worked for Volanakis at the Old Vic again in 1962, on *Julius Caesar*, and later on *Volpone* (starring Leo McKern and Leonard Rossiter, in 1966), and *The Madwoman of Chaillot* (1967). For another friend, Harold Lang, she braved the rigours of *As You Like It* at the Open Air Theatre in Regent's Park. This was a production almost doomed at the outset by the non-cooperation of the Musicians' Union, which forbade the use of professional musicians, requiring Lang to use only such musical talent as the company themselves possessed. The restriction was overcome by employing a Musical Director with a flair for improvisation.

Kenneth Waller, an actor with long experience in musicals, was appearing at the time with Margaret Rutherford and Sid James in *The Solid Gold Cadillac* in the West End; but in the afternoons he concentrated on rescuing the stricken *As You Like It*. Touchstone turned out to play the guitar creditably, and one of the pages could pass muster on percussion, so the songs were rapidly arranged for guitar and tabor. Waller filled in the requisite fanfares on the trumpet stop of the organ, and the rest of the score was delivered by the cast singing wordlessly in four-part harmony.

Liz revelled in these narrow escapes; and for their part theatre people took her easily in their stride as just another actor. She was in these years laying the foundations of a long career as a Grand Old Woman of music. In the 1960s and 1970s she was rather tiresomely to reiterate that 'the young' were first and foremost self-seekers – that no one worked disinterestedly for the cause of music. Whether or not this was true she herself certainly invested a great deal of effort in musical good works in the 1950s, and by the end of the decade cut an unmistakable figure on the music scene.

She was most proud of the Composers' Concourse, which met between 1953 and 1957. Open to those in or intending to join the profession, it was a forum for discussion of composers' problems, aesthetic, theoretical and practical. Arnold Cooke and Alan Bush were the other prime movers in its foundation, and the executive included, from time to time, John Amis, Lennox Berkeley, William Glock, Shula Doniach and Joyce Rathbone.

In April 1954 *The Times Educational Supplement*, under the heading 'Schoenbergians in Grosvenor Square: a Critical Debate', described the proceedings in a tone that was only slightly condescending. 'Mr Erwin Stein was present to hand on the tablets of the law and to deny Mr Alan

Bush's assertion that Schoenberg had only turned to the twelve-note row to escape from the devastating implications of atonality. Mr Arnold Cooke was inquiring, Miss Elisabeth Lutyens loomed menacingly at Mr Eric Blom, Mr Tippett remained schoolmasterly and Mr Hans Keller was, as usual, maintaining a barrage of semi-public comment in the back row.'

Liz was on the Council of the reconstituted Macnaghten Concerts. Anne Macnaghten remembered her with affection from these years as alternately an asset in meetings – very funny, with shrewd ideas on the length and balance of concerts – and a liability; she would insist on playing the *enfant terrible*, and would follow hares she had started herself with unswerving tenacity.

She was also on the committee of the ICA's music section under the chairmanship of William Glock, with whom she worked very happily for several years. 'You, with your enthusiasm, work and plans are the best news for contemporary music that we have had in a long while,'[14] she told him. The Glocks visited Blackheath for a mixture of good food and cricket, and Liz went on holiday with them more than once. William Glock found her one of her first publishers and arranged most of the scattered performances her work did receive. 'Life would be very grim without your help and good will,' she wrote to him in 1957.

Besides the committees there was teaching. After a shaky start – a one-hour talk which in her nervous eagerness she delivered in twenty minutes – Liz turned herself into a competent and entertaining lecturer, leaping from one topic or topical reference to another with the agility of a grasshopper and the brilliance of a catherine wheel. 'Not one to take a generalisation and hammer it home,' commented William Glock. Her principal concern in her lectures to non-professionals was to stimulate a climate of goodwill towards contemporary music by educating the audience in ways of listening. To understand the new language of music, she argued expansively, it was only necessary to know the alphabet up to G and be able to count to twelve.[15]

She always had to steel herself to perform in public. William Glock invited her to give composition classes at Dartington Summer School, and composer Brian Elias, attending the first series, remembers a dashing figure in shocking pink trouser suit and white knee-length boots, glasses on the top of her head aviator-style in imitation of Stravinsky – with hands that shook so much she could barely read her notes.[16] She had feared that her audience at Dartington would be composed of young people who knew everything and elderly ladies who simply wanted to be near a live composer. In the event, the ladies were sometimes the most imaginative pupils; but it was the young whose

(LEFT) Betty sitting on cushion, front right, with (clockwise) Ursula, Robert, Lady Emily with Mary on her knee, Barbie, c.1908.
(BELOW) Sir Edwin Lutyens, 1925.
(BOTTOM) Betty, Lady Emily and Mary, c.1922.

(ABOVE) Betty on her return from Paris, 1923.

(RIGHT) Krishna, Pergine 1924.

(BELOW) The gopis in Ehrwald, 1923, *left to right –*
Back row: Isabelle Mallet, Mary, Marcelle de
Manziarly, Betty, Ruth Roberts, Lady Emily
Seated: Helen Knothe, Malati Patwardhan.

(LEFT) C. W. Leadbeater, Sydney, 1925. (In the background, Edith Kollerstrom and Harold Morton.)

(ABOVE) Betty c.1926/7.

(BELOW) Betty in Braughles, her Suffolk cottage, c.1930.

(ABOVE) Betty at her desk in 6, Fitzroy Street, with Conrad (on her knee) and the twins, c.1946/7.

(LEFT) Betty with Rose at Blagdon, 1940.

(OPPOSITE PAGE) (ABOVE) With Ian Glennie, Sebastian, and the twins Rose and Tess, 1936.

(INSET) Edward Clark, c.1909/10.

(BELOW) Edward Clark with Arnold Schoenberg, Leipzig 1914. (*Left to right* – Paul Koniger, Edward Clark, Erwin Stein, Edward Steuermann, Arnold Schoenberg, ?, Heinrich Jalowetz, Anton Webern, Josef Polnauer.)

(LEFT) With Stravinsky and Edward at Dartington, 1957.

(BELOW) Liz, c.1966.

(OPPOSITE PAGE)
(LEFT) *To Be A Woman*, 1951.

(RIGHT) Edward and Liz, 1952.

(BELOW) Lady Emily with her children on her eightieth birthday, 1955. *Back row* – Ursula, Barbie, Liz. *Front* – Robert, Mary.

(TOP) Liz with a granddaughter in King Henry's Road.

(ABOVE) Liz in the 1970s, upstairs in 13, King Henry's Road.

approval she sought – emerging figures like Brian Elias, Peter Maxwell Davies and David Bedford. She loved sitting over coffee on the lawn for hours with them, being fêted, and alternately mothering and shocking them.

From the 1950s onwards Liz had been claiming affinity with the young, rejecting in the process not only her contemporaries but also the unfortunate middle generation of composers born in the late 1910s and 1920s, whose careers had been most seriously disrupted by the Second World War. 'The Wenceslas generation,' she called them, perpetually treading in the steps of others; and she denounced them as perpetrators of what she (and other radical musicians) called 'the Cheltenham Symphony'. The Cheltenham Festival, today a major promoter of contemporary music in Britain, was timid in its first ten years to 1955, and sponsored, Liz felt, a particularly unadventurous brand of British music, locked within the cage of the traditional symphonic format and tonal for lack of a better idea.

Liz's first pupil and protégé was Malcolm Williamson (now Master of the Queen's Musick), who went to her as a teenager in the early 1950s, attracted, in his words, by 'the one composer who, as the smoke of Dunkirk cleared away, was thinking in world terms: she had mentally crossed the Channel'.[17] He discovered later that the prospect of teaching – which she had undertaken solely because she needed the money – terrified her, and before his first lesson she had sat up all night with the harmony primer of Hindemith. This was a measure of her unease, because Hindemith was among the musicians she found least congenial – 'the supreme middlebrow of our times . . . most efficient and determined of mechanics',[18] according to Constant Lambert, whose views she often quoted (with and without acknowledgement). Her idea of hell, as reported by another pupil, Janet Graham, was being forced to listen to Hindemith's *Ludus Tonalis* on a full bladder.[19]

In any event, she could make little of his teachings on harmony, nor those of Schoenberg, and rang Arnold Bax to ask him, 'What *is* a major third?' 'Damned if I know, Betty,' Bax replied, and it was the first question she put to Malcolm Williamson. In that first lesson, very smart in a blue denim suit, she showed him the Chamber Concerto I and explained how it had been written. To him, her teaching was concerned primarily with different instrumental sounds and the harmonic sensuousness one could achieve with them, with very little emphasis on theory. She sharpened up his understanding of complex textures, and his sense of flowing contrapuntal lines; years later he wrote affectionately to her, 'If you were to undress my musical personality, you would find the fingerprints of your own still there.'[20]

A little later Richard Rodney Bennett became (his phrase) 'one of her first "groupies". As a schoolboy of ten, on a routine diet of Debussy and Vaughan Williams, he was intrigued by a magazine review of *O Saisons, O Chateaux!*, which made it sound a highly exciting kind of music, and he too became a protégé, though not formally a pupil. He still has vivid memories of coming up to London, full of anticipation, to spend his days out from school with her – visits which acted as 'a shot in the arm' in his progress towards becoming a composer.

She was motherly, he remembered, but treated him as an adult, showing him pieces, giving him practical hints on notation and orchestration, introducing him to Rawsthorne and Marcelle de Manziarly, and, later, finding him work copying – and above all, conveying the glamour of being a composer. 'That was her genius,' he once said, 'that's why young people have always been enchanted with her.'

Then, in one of the saddest rows of her long fighting career, they broke completely. Bennett freely admits that, having met her at an extremely impressionable age, he was much influenced by her; but she now claimed to others that he consciously used her ideas, copying them down from memory – a quite different charge, which he categorically denies, 'although I know some pretty startling things came up'.

Liz's resentment was certainly magnified by Bennett's meteoric early success, in such painful contrast with her own struggles, and by his apparently effortless talent, which she both suspected and envied as something she had never had. She claimed Bennett now intrigued against her, he felt she deliberately blocked his way, and the connection was severed for ten years.

Then he heard from one of his pupils that in a lecture at Dartington on originality, she had cited him in order to make a distinction between using other people's technical methods, which she considered fair game, and copying their personal mannerisms, which she did not.[21] He was incensed at the public re-emergence of the feud, and tackled her, hard. 'She had a sadistic streak,' he remembered, 'and if you cowered, she got worse.' If you fought back, on the other hand, she enjoyed it and was impressed, and the friendship with Bennett, though battered, was restored.

Liz also saw a good deal of the Manchester Group – Harrison Birtwistle, Alexander Goehr and Peter Maxwell Davies – when they first came to London. Though never her pupils, they were attracted to her as a senior composer of avant-garde leanings. She was drawn to them because they took serialism for granted as a touchstone, and because they had the passionate enthusiasm for music which she felt was its due.

She gave excellent parties, at which she took care that they met people who could help them, and she helped them to find a platform at the ICA. Alexander Goehr – who was perhaps the most interested of the Group in the Second Viennese School – recalls performing her *Valediction* there with Harrison Birtwistle in 1955. He found her consistently entertaining, with a ruthless eye for the phony and an insistence on the unorthodox. He once attempted to reconcile her with his father, Walter Goehr, after they had had a quarrel; her opening gambit was a disquisition on the recent invention of tights illustrated by direct visual reference to her own, and Goehr senior fled.

To Alexander Goehr she was endlessly hospitable and generous. Coming to the end of a series of lectures in Brighton, she decided to turn the last one into a 'Brains Trust' with a panel of three – herself, Edward and Goehr, the latter to receive the entire fee of £5 on the grounds that his need was the greatest. She paid for the Pullman going down to Brighton, for drinks on the train, for dinner at English's with a bottle of good Chablis, and for drinks in the Pullman on the way home. She, of course, stuck to ginger ale all evening; she preferred it to tonic water because, she explained, a brown drink was less conspicuously non-alcoholic, and had a less lowering effect on one's friends.

Throughout the lecture, Goehr remembered, Edward dozed peacefully. A question was asked on harmony, and Liz said loudly, 'I think that's one for you, Edward,' whereupon he woke with a start and began, 'In 1912, Schoenberg. . . .' After several minutes of reminiscence, she hissed in a penetrating stage whisper, 'That'll do, Edward,' and he subsided into sleep.

Liz found Harrison Birtwistle intriguing, and looked at all his scores as they came out, particularly impressed by his range of reference and interests outside music. Peter Maxwell Davies she knew from Dartington. They were temperamentally quite different, and their relationship was never to be easy. He once told her, as a very young man, that he felt he had not suffered enough to be a good composer, a remark she greeted with derision. It was, in fact, a view with which she had much sympathy; she was to write of herself, 'I know my early troubles made me want to create something for myself to give me independence, and I feel if I had ever been happier or more popular as a child I would never have become a musician.' But she preferred the sentiment expressed with a little irony.

The composer Iain Hamilton was a close friend during the 1950s, and he paints a vivid picture of her during this time – full of nervous energy, restless, highly intelligent, 'interested in things that people of her class don't often bother with', like socialist politics. 'She had such strong opinions on everything, she could hardly have been apolitical – but I can't imagine her getting on with the general Labour Party caucus.' At concerts, which they sometimes attended together, her strong opinions could be highly embarrassing, taking the form of a perfectly audible and invariably critical running commentary.

She loved the show tunes of Gershwin and Richard Rogers, and she and Hamilton would play them loudly on the piano together. She also regaled him with her favourite passages from Monteverdi, rendered with great fervour and inaccuracy. '"This bit is wonderful," she said, "look – it finishes in E major and goes straight to B flat!" Of course, she'd turned over two pages at once; I told her I'd dine out on it – but she just swep' on. . . .'

She was plagued by discontent and uncertainty, Hamilton remembers. He would tell her that, as chairman of the ICA music section (in succession to William Glock), he was putting on a work of hers – and it would always be in the wrong place on the programme for her, or on a bad night. 'Insuring against success', he called it, guarding against disappointment by expecting the worst and finding reasons for failure. But when others were disappointed, or in any kind of trouble, her response was instant and overwhelmingly generous. 'She gave one the kind of evening one never forgot.' Liz never counted the cost of friendships, nor calculated the potential risks or advantages inherent in them.

She was always a better hostess than guest. She revelled in bringing people together, and provided food for them on a lavish scale – 'very Alice B. Toklas', according to Iain Hamilton, with whole York hams, pheasants, and raw garlic in the salad. In Blackheath she evolved a social circle which, with a little more money and a lot more self-consciousness, she might have called a salon.[22]

Its survivors remember her with great affection as she was then. Her sins were all sins of excess rather than deficiency – extravagance not meanness, jealousy not indifference, tyranny not neglect – and her virtues correspondingly ample. She was instinctively kind – and at the same time appallingly funny at other people's expense; she never seemed to see any contradiction in this. Her wit is difficult to reproduce, depending as it did on expression, tone of voice and the particular situation; it was also usually actionable.

It is possible that in the first years after leaving Edward she had lovers. Some people were firmly persuaded that she did – and this was without doubt what she wanted them to believe. She enjoyed talking about sex, had her own 'catalogue aria' of past encounters, the more spectacular of them featuring the armed forces on trains – and the less sympathetic the audience, the more lurid the stories would become. One line she loved to produce has proved immortal among her contemporaries – 'I've had a hundred lovers, ninety-nine men and one woman – and the woman was by far the best.' It would have carried more conviction had the numbers not altered, sometimes up and sometimes down, every time she said it.

She would perhaps have liked to have been rampant because it would have signified, to others and almost more importantly to herself, that she was desirable, something she never really believed. Alexander Goehr remembers her often repeating the story of her encounter in a restaurant with a small child who, to the mortification of his parents, said loudly, 'That lady looks like a monkey.' Pressed to recant, he refused and Liz leant over to them and said, 'He's right: I *do* look rather like a monkey.'

There is no evidence for hectic sexual activity, every suggestion that the emotional dimension of love was more important to her – and by 1956 Edward, who had been visiting Blackheath with increasing regularity, was staying there on a more or less permanent basis, though he kept the flat in Fitzroy Street. The next two or three years were the first really happy ones she could remember since before the war, the years in the basement at Mansfield Street and the brief, blissfully ignorant premarital honeymoon at 12 Fitzroy Street. Now all the children were home again, Edward was with her, and she had won from Lady Emily and Ursula, her sternest critics, some of the understanding and support she craved. Neither would ever like or comprehend her music, but at last they were prepared to respect the efforts she had made for it, her professionalism, and the courage that had gone into starting a new life.

By 1957 Liz had the confidence to take stock. 'I wanted to discover,' she wrote, 'to what extent I was living, acting, working and loving in genuine faith, fervour and belief, and whether one, some or all of these elements had solidified into habits, turning the ever-changing creativeness of life into mechanical existence.' Did she still love Edward? – there was no question. Did she still want to be a composer, find it a convincing identity for herself? Yes – but she needed to be a different kind of composer, less timid and laborious and tied to pre-compositional planning. The technique, she felt, should be there by now (she was fifty, and had been composing for over thirty years); from now on, her motto was to be 'Just live and write.'

The result was a rapidly swelling output. In her first thirty working years she wrote some forty pieces to which she was prepared to give opus numbers; in her last twenty-five she wrote almost 120. Her work was also to become more uneven, distressingly so to some of her critics. There is a temperamental divide between perfectionist composers, for whom each work must be without blemish before it can be uttered, and those who will use four flawed pieces as stepping stones to a fifth which goes straight to the heart of the matter. Composer Nigel Osborne has described a particular kind of composition as appropriate to our age, and it seems to sum up what Liz was aiming for at the end of the 1950s – 'the uninhibited, intellectually generous, vulnerable utterance. . . . A temporary utterance, a kind of exploration'.[23]

Six Tempi (1957) was the first piece she wrote in this new frame of mind. It is, in fact, still tightly and carefully written, but there are signs of experiment. In her early years, her originality had shown itself, broadly speaking, far more clearly in her harmonies than in her rhythms. Then in her Sixth Quartet (1952–3), amidst the other omens for the future, there appeared signs of a new rhythmic freedom. And now *Six Tempi*, which started as an atmospheric homage to Baudelaire with snippets of his poetry attached to each fragment of music, ended as an overt experiment in six different types of rhythm.

Her real strides, however, were taken in two large-scale works for voices and orchestra, her most complex writing so far. *De Amore* (1957), or 'Pleasaunce of Love', was written round extracts from Chaucer on the nature of love.

> The lyf so short, the craft so long to lerne,
> Th'assay so hard, so sharp the conquering,
> The dredful joye, that alwey sut so yerne [passes so soon]:
> All this mene I by love.

To judge from this music, for Liz love was not tender or sweet, but exciting, difficult and dangerous. There are moments of gentle poignancy, but the effect is mostly of a glowing orchestral sound, brass-heavy, which surges into the foreground when the voices die down and shrinks to a skeleton to accompany the soloists.

There are problems in *De Amore*. Liz's vocal writing still taxed non-specialists, and the chorus at the première needed discreet prompting from the organ to hold them in tune. Required to lapse into speech at one point, they sounded British and embarrassed, like a church congregation with an unfamiliar psalm or a class of schoolchildren repeating its twelve times table in *Sprechstimme*. But throughout the work Liz was audibly relaxing away from the strictest twelve-tone system and from the purist influence of Webern.

De Amore was not to be performed until 1970, so the critics made these discoveries in hindsight. It was *Quincunx* (1959–60) which at the time signalled to them what had happened to Liz's work (though even this had to wait two years for performance). A quincunx is an arrangement of five objects – four occupying the corners of a square or other rectangle and a fifth the centre. The centre of Liz's design was a passage by Sir Thomas Browne from 'The Garden of Cyrus' – 'But the Quincunx of Heaven runs low, and 'tis time to close the five ports of knowledge; we are unwilling to spin out our waking thoughts into the phantasms of sleep; which often continueth precogitations, making Cables of Cobwebbes and Wildernesses of handsome Groves.'

This she set for baritone, wordless soprano and full orchestra, and surrounded it by four other sections for orchestra. The five tutti sections enclose four sections for single instrumental groups – wind, strings, percussion and brass in turn. To complete the complexity of the structure, each of these instrumental movements is itself a quincunx; five tutti passages are separated by four solos. Her ambition was to have the quincunx pattern mirrored in the placing of the performers on stage, but the resulting instrumental balance was too eccentric and the plan was modified.

Edward loved this piece, and boasted to other people of the chamber-music clarity which Liz had managed to extract from her huge orchestra. The tone was rich, the texture varied, and the melody passed easily from one group of instruments to another, picking up new resonances and a different character on the way, constantly evolving. It was a voice in which she could say what she meant, almost without thinking; when the piece was recorded, Anthony Payne was to write, 'Lutyens's language now becomes a perfect analogy of her stream of musical consciousness . . . capable of instant response to the promptings of her nervous vision.'[24] At the same time, *Quincunx* has a structural elegance and strength which she did not often attempt, let alone achieve; it is the one work where claims of an 'architectural' quality undeniably apply. When it was first performed in 1962, Liz felt herself to have reached a new level of achievement, and for once the critics agreed.

CHAPTER TWELVE

The Rock and the Vultures: Edward and the Frankel Affair

THOUGH LIZ AND Edward spent most of the early 1950s living apart, they did not succeed in genuinely disentangling their lives; in Liz's 1957 'stock-taking', emotional and professional, Edward was once again a central figure; and in a sense she was never to be free of him. In 1955, while he was still alone at Fitzroy Street, his affairs had come finally to a crisis, when he sued a former friend and colleague, the Jewish composer Benjamin Frankel, for slander in a case which opened ugly rifts in the music world and from which everyone emerged the loser. Liz, notionally independent, without hesitating entered the fray at his side.

Romantic as she was, she would always have said that her relationship with Edward was worth the anguish, anxiety and irritation it caused her. 'I suppose love,' she wrote, 'the "falling in love" sort, has caused more pain to people than any other emotion. Yet for all that – for its moments, hours, days, months, possibly years of MAGIC I would suffer *any* pain.'[1] Fighting for him in 1955, she displayed her most admirable qualities – a loving nature, courage and loyalty. They came out of the Frankel affair reunited and stayed together until Edward's death. But Liz also emerged tainted with a bitterness which twisted the frame in which she saw the rest of her life.

Edward had long been a source of rancour in himself – his insularity, his inertia, his failure to give her the cosmopolitan, cultured existence for which she had once hoped. From the late 1950s she was also to be possessed by fury at his fate, the total eclipse of what had once been rare, attractive and important gifts. Her wrath was concentrated on a few specific targets – the BBC, as arid, vengeful bureaucrats; the young, supplanters of maturity and experience; the Jews. But it spilled over to corrode her outlook on life in general, and at times came near to obliterating the affectionate, idealistic, aspiring personality underneath.

Benjamin Frankel was Liz's exact contemporary, born in London in January 1906, of a Polish father and Austrian mother. He began his working life as a watchmaker's assistant, but soon moved into the music business through his skill as a jazz violinist. He conducted revues for Cochran and Coward, and served for years as Geraldo's right-hand man. In the 1930s he wrote a good deal of film music, and was to have several extremely successful features to his credit, including *The Seventh Veil*.

By the 1940s he was composing serious music, in a relatively conservative style although he had a thorough knowledge of serial techniques. He worked a good deal in the traditional symphonic form – in all he wrote seven symphonies – and Liz would doubtless have labelled him a 'Cheltenham symphonist'. She was certainly to call him 'a musical Chiang Kai-shek',[2] (perhaps seeing herself as a musical Mao).

For years Frankel was a good friend of the Clarks. He gave Liz one of her first copying jobs, a Coward score; and he and Edward were close colleagues in the British Section of the International Society for Contemporary Music, where, as President, Edward did much to promote his music. Before it was even finished, Edward was petitioning the BBC to programme the Frankel Violin Concerto.[3] He may even have briefly sublet the Fitzroy Street flat to Frankel in 1948.[4]

But at the 1951 ISCM Festival in Frankfurt, which Edward's heart condition prevented him from attending, there was a revolt against the old regime, of which Edward was very much a part; and as battle lines were drawn, Frankel was increasingly to be found on the opposing side. It was decided in Frankfurt that henceforth the selection of works for the Festival should be made not by open competition, but on a geographical basis; each country should automatically have the right to field one work – an idea Edward much disliked, as a threat to absolute standards. In his absence a caretaker committee of much younger men was appointed, and it was suggested that, in order to break British domination of the Society, its central office should be moved from London – or in other words, out of Fitzroy Street.

Edward in fact agreed that the central office should move, and had already proposed that when he retired as President he should be succeeded by Pierre Capdevieille, head of the French Section. But he was understandably anxious not to be excluded from the British Section (the London Contemporary Music Centre) as well; and there, by October 1951, a nucleus of opposition to him had formed, consisting of composer Matyas Seiber, musicologist Mosco Carner, music publisher Dennis Dobson – and Benjamin Frankel. It was partly to keep the British Section within his grasp that Edward negotiated its amalgamation with the Institute of Contemporary Arts (whose Music Section it eventually became in April 1953). He tried at the same time to shake off opposition by changing the composition of the committee, but he failed, and found himself still President of the British Section but outnumbered on the committee by those who were now his enemies.[5]

The 1952 ISCM Festival in Salzburg was the first at which the principle of geographical representation came into action – having the effect of demonstrating, in Hans Keller's words, 'that there is no difference between the rubbish of twenty-four different countries'.[6] Keller's ire was at least partly aroused by his regard for Frankel, whose Violin Concerto was one of the first casualties of the quota system. Only two British pieces were selected for performance, and Frankel's was not one of them.

Liz was not to mince her words about the Frankel Violin Concerto, dedicated to the survivors of the Holocaust. 'Six million Jews murdered for the second time,' she remarked, 'a chipolata off the old Bloch.'[7] Edward was more temperate, but he too had cooled, and was presumably at least partly responsible for the work's omission. In his own extremely partisan account – and from now on, tempers were to be high and bitter on both sides – 'Frankel was so terribly upset by this event that his consequent behaviour was as frightening as it was pitiable.'[8]

Edward came to believe that Frankel was angling for the presidency of the ISCM. In the summer of 1952 he retired from the position as planned; but at the last minute Pierre Capdevieille declined to become his successor. Alarmed at the prospect of the presidency falling into unfriendly hands, Edward considered standing again. When Frankel suggested that he would be embarrassingly defeated, Edward put the worst possible interpretation on his motives, and did his best to sabotage what he saw as an independent bid for power, though hampered by his still precarious health. In the event, against Edward's will a five-man executive committee was again appointed, this time including Frankel and his pupil Stanley Glasser.

Events in Salzburg after the appointment of the executive committee are both crucial and hopelessly confused. Edward later maintained that the delegates had agreed there would be a short interim period before the committee took over, during which he would continue his duties. Frankel maintained that control had passed instantaneously to the committee, and, putting the point directly, that Edward was no longer entitled to draw cheques on the ISCM account or perform any other official functions, although for a couple of weeks the office was still in Fitzroy Street.

From this moment on, there was a sharp split between the British Section at the ICA, with which Edward was still associated, and the Frankel faction, which now set up the ISCM Central Office in London once more. Edward was convinced that his opponents were attempting to merge the ISCM with the Society for the Promotion of New Music; to his cost, he refused to open correspondence from Central Office. It was at this time that he was first warned that Frankel was making accusations about him to mutual friends; but he chose to discount the stories.

1953 opened well for Edward, with the award of a Civil List pension, procured for him by William Walton. But at the ISCM Festival, held in Oslo, disaster struck again. At a critical meeting, to which he claimed he was not invited, the minutes describing the previous year's events were presented along with accounts of the ISCM's financial standing prepared by Stanley Glasser. It would seem that there were hints of irregularities; and at a subsequent committee meeting Frankel publicly accused Edward of 'underhand crookery'.

He may have been referring instead, or as well, to the methods which Edward had used to amalgamate the British Section with the ICA. Either way, in Edward's rather pompous report of the occasion, 'Clark, not unjustly incensed by the language, upped and clocked Frankel a straight left to the jaw: this, I regret to say, in disregardance of his doctor's orders concerning reasonable behaviour in a post-thrombosis condition.' [9] At the end of the year, Edward was notified that, after almost thirty years of membership, his name had been erased from the list of the ISCM's honorary presidents; no explanation was offered.

During 1954 the rumours that Frankel was spreading slander could no longer be ignored. The previous year Edward had invited Christian Darnton, the first person to warn him of what Frankel was saying, to see his solicitor, with a view to taking legal action. Now Liz advised taking the step of consulting counsel. Her loyalty and his need combined to draw her ever deeper into the feud, and she feared for his health if the strain and suspense continued.

Meanwhile, back at the ISCM Festival, the battles continued. The international jury was meeting in Rome; there was a postal dispute, and by the time of the first jury session the eight works nominated by the British section had not arrived. A week later they had still not reached the jury, who felt obliged to consider such of the eight works as were already available in Rome. The only two to hand, which were duly 'selected', were a string quartet by Matyas Seiber – and the Frankel Violin Concerto. The air was thick with accusation and counter-accusation; and in high dudgeon Frankel withdrew the piece.[10]

This was the background to the case for slander which Edward, after much procrastination, eventually brought against Frankel in June 1955 – an affair which became a *cause célèbre* in the music world. The protagonists were both well known, and to some extent they represented groups beyond themselves – radical versus middle-ground music, British Section against Central Office, ISCM against SPNM, and, if some observers are to be believed, Gentile against Jewish musicians. Less predictably, the case also made the front pages of the popular press, which seized upon another apparent antithesis – Communist stalwart against Communist apostate.

The case was heard in the High Court, before Sir Malcolm Hilbery; appearing for Edward were Leslie Scarman (now Lord Scarman) and A. Melford Stevenson QC. Edward's plaint was that in July 1952, shortly after the executive committee had been created in Salzburg and the books handed over to it, Frankel had told Christian Darnton that Edward had been embezzling ISCM funds; and that later that year, he repeated the slander to composer Bernard Stevens.

More specifically, Frankel was alleged to have said that Edward, having been given expenses by the ISCM to go to the Festival in Salzburg in 1952, had also accepted expenses from UNESCO's International Music Council to visit Paris on separate business – but had combined the two expeditions into one round trip and pocketed the money he had saved. In addition, Edward was accused of having drawn three cheques on the ISCM account, totalling about £7, *after* the executive committee had been designated. (The pathetic amounts involved only added to the indignity of the charge, and the resulting bitterness.)

Frankel's primary defence was a flat denial that he had ever uttered such slanders – which amounted to the charge that Edward's witnesses, Darnton and Stevens, were lying. This he elaborated by pointing out that they were both members of the Communist Party – Stevens had caused a sensation by refusing to take the oath on the Bible – and that all Party members were willing to lie at its behest. The Communist Party was anxious to harm him, he explained, because he had left it, with maximum publicity, at the time of the Prague trials and executions in 1952. Frankel implied that the Party had played on Edward's personal grudge to persuade him to bring the action, which they might also have financed, and may even have volunteered the witnesses.

Frankel was quite blatantly taking advantage of the anti-Communist feeling which was discernible in Britain in the early 1950s, though it could not be compared in severity with American McCarthyism. In 1952 Thomas Russell, Managing Director of the London Philharmonic Orchestra, went on holiday to China. It was a personal visit, but Russell did have Communist sympathies, and when the *Daily Worker*, in its notice of the visit, identified him as the representative of the LPO, the board sacked him *in absentia*. The climate was hostile, and at last Edward's political pigeons, puny as they were, were coming home to roost.

Frankel's defence in the alternate – usual in slander cases – was that if he *had* made such statements, they would have been true. He was to suggest outside court[11] (though not inside it) that other accusations could have been made against Edward which would have more than justified any rumours. In mid-1952, he claimed, the ISCM's balance of funds had amounted before the Salzburg Festival to £186; when Edward handed over the books, there was an overdraft of £11. Edward was short of money at this time (and this Frankel did mention in court); after the official close of the Festival he had asked Glasser for £5 from petty cash to cover his expenses in Salzburg. The implication was that he had taken some £200 from the ISCM account and destroyed the evidence, merely leaving traces (from carelessness) of his double expenses and the three small cheques. This may have been the accusation Frankel made in Oslo which prompted Edward to hit him. Had the minutes of the Oslo meeting been available in court, Frankel felt he would have had evidence to support any statements he might have made about Edward's malpractice; but Edward's counsel argued successfully that they were not admissible.

Ultimately, at least in the public perception of the affair, the Clark Frankel case had more to do with Edward's alleged embezzlement than Frankel's alleged slanders.

The question of slander was dealt with relatively quickly. Darnton testified that he had met Frankel at the time alleged, but he was vague as to what had been said. Stevens was more definite: he had been asked by Harry Pollitt, head of the British Communist Party, to visit Frankel and discuss his 'hasty' action in leaving the Party,[12] but on the same occasion they had also talked about ISCM business, which included the allegations concerning Edward. The following year, Darnton said, he saw Edward's solicitor, learned that Stevens could testify to similar slanders, and wrote to him.

Frankel denied discussing Edward with either of them, and portrayed their exchange of correspondence in 1953 as a conspiracy of Communist Party members. Darnton's evidence was inconclusive and needed little rebuttal; Stevens did not equivocate, and Frankel had nothing to adduce against him except his political sympathies. He made it his word against Stevens's, and relied on the effectiveness of the anti-Communist gambit.

As to the charges of embezzlement, Edward had an explanation. He readily admitted that he had accepted both sets of expenses, having every intention of accounting for them; on his return, he had informed the British Section's auditor, Sydney Giebel, of all his transactions, pointing out that his stay in Paris had been useful to the ISCM as well, as he had been able to hold discussions with Capdevieille. As for the cheques, he had believed it had been agreed that there should be an interim period before the changeover, during which he was still entitled to draw money (which had been used to pay the office cleaner and take a visiting composer out to lunch at Prada's). If the minutes showed otherwise, then they were wrong.

From the general tenor of Mr Justice Hilbery's summing-up, it would seem he considered Edward's delay in taking action after learning of the slanders to be at best foolish and at worse suspicious; he appears to be hinting that Edward might never have acted at all had he not been prompted to do so by Darnton. Lord Scarman remembers, 'Hilbery was a good judge, but never concealed his feelings. We all appreciated that he did not like Clark, his friends or their politics.' The judge said of the ISCM, 'This is obviously very much a Communist society', (echoing its first President, Edward Dent, who once remarked, 'Our detractors from the first went about saying . . . that we were all of us Bolshevists and Jews').[13] And Hilbery said of Darnton, 'I have omitted his name of "Christian", a name which it is perhaps a little odd that he should carry.'

Lord Scarman is categorical: '[McCarthyism] never percolated into British society, let alone the judiciary. It was treated with contempt and horror' – and he points out that in his summing-up the judge warned the jury against being swayed by politics. But by that time it was perhaps too late. The jury decided that Frankel had not uttered the slanders, by implication rejecting the testimony of Stevens and Darnton. Edward had lost his case.

But the jury added a rider – 'Mr Clark's reputation is not in doubt' – effectively rejecting Frankel's attempts to prove embezzlement – and

Edward's counsel were able to argue that since most of the court's time had been spent on these futile attempts, the financial burden of the case should be shared. Frankel's counsel concurred, and no specific order was made as to costs. Both men were saved from financial ruin, but the bill was heavy nonetheless; it is not clear that Edward ever managed to pay his share. As for Frankel, a fund was set up by his friends; the founders were Leonard Woolf, Anthony Asquith, Cecil Day Lewis and Gerald Finzi, and among the contributors were Terence Rattigan, Kingsley Martin, Arthur Benjamin, Lennox Berkeley, Francis Chagrin, Howard Ferguson, Peter Racine Fricker, Gordon Jacob, Goffredo Petrassi, Edmund Rubbra, John Amis, Felix Aprahamian, Mosco Carner, Myra Hess, Hans Keller, Lawrence Leonard, William Mann and Donald Mitchell.[14]

Leslie Scarman was to say after the case, 'We have never been particularly proud of the architecture of our building, but we have been proud of our English justice – and today for the first time I feel ashamed of this.' In 1988 he was still prepared to describe the jury's decision as 'strange and unjust'. 'Clark ought to have recovered substantial damages but was denied by failing on what at the trial was the less hotly debated issue.'

It may be, however, that the result was unjust in a different way. The jury concluded that Frankel did not accuse Edward of financial mismanagement, but that if he had, the accusation would have been untrue. There is every reason to believe that he *did*, in fact, accuse him – if not to Darnton and Stevens at those precise times, certainly to other people at other times – and that it *was* true.

Edward was not deliberately dishonest – both Lord Scarman and Sydney Giebel remain convinced of this. Rose remembers harrowing bus journeys when Edward would avoid paying the fares, relying on the conductor's reluctance to doubt the integrity of a man with monocle, Homburg, carnation and a child in tow;[15] but at any level above the trivial he was simply not interested enough in money to play games with it – 'lordly' is perhaps the best word for his attitude. Nevertheless he was uninterested to the point of being insufficiently scrupulous with it to defend himself against people who were looking for ammunition against him. It was imprudent to take both sets of expenses, even if he did intend to account for them; well before the trial, Steuart Wilson, who served on the UNESCO International Music Council with him, had written to Liz warning her that there existed damaging evidence of Edward's malpractice.[16]

Whatever the truth behind the case – and virtually all the protagonists are now dead – everyone involved in it suffered as a result. Bernard Stevens was to refer to a 'witch-hunt' conducted against himself and Alan Bush by 'opportunist colleagues, particularly those in the film industry'.[17] (William Alwyn, himself in films, suspected that Frankel had emphasised the Communist angle largely to impress Hollywood with his anti-Communist fervour.)[18] Benjamin Frankel's wife Xenia (who married him only in 1972, but attended every session of the trial as a young family friend), had to live with the repercussions seventeen years after the case was concluded, and can testify to the damage he felt it had done to him. It was surely no coincidence that in 1956 he suffered a serious heart attack from which he never entirely recovered. As for Edward, the case made him yet more unemployable. Lord Scarman recalls, 'One had to read the small print to appreciate that . . . he had cleared his name of serious charges of dishonesty.' In 1956, through the efforts of William Glock, Luigi Dallapiccola and Gian Francesco Malipiero, he was reinstated as an honorary member of the ISCM, but he was never a significant force again.

In Liz, the trial and its outcome exacerbated above all the anti-semitism which until then had been perceptible but not significant. Edward's sufferings in court and outside it, attributable in her view largely to Frankel, helped to turn what may originally have been little more than a social posture into disfiguring bigotry.

Anti-semitism was not untypical of the class into which Liz had been born, a prejudice which had as much to do with snobbery as racism. Lady Emily was unusually unprejudiced, given her background; during the Second World War she took in and virtually adopted two young Jewish refugees[19] (which may of course have been another source of bitterness to Liz, always jealous of her mother's affections). Ursula was positively pro-Jewish – again, not a recommendation in Liz's eyes – and Mary's second husband Joe is Jewish. But Sir Edwin was not at all averse to jokes about business acumen, lisps, and what he called 'jewboy' astrakhan collars.

Liz, generally quite imaginative in her dealings with friends, had a curious blind spot about the effects her anti-semitic remarks might have. At lunch with Adolph Hallis on the day of the Munich Agreement, he had been deploring it for some time and holding forth about 'perfidious Albion' when she lost patience and pushed the menu towards him, saying 'You Jews!/You choose'. 'My bad pun,' she explained ingenuously, 'was not adjectival, still less derogatory; he had been abusing my race for some hours, yet his must not be mentioned lightly.'[20] Her race, of course, was not under a comparable threat; but all her life she was to see Jewish sensitivity as 'touchy and boring'.

Liz was not above using her own (very real) tribulations as an emotional bargaining tool and a social weapon, and she did not like competition; she later deplored what she depicted as Jewish self-pity, 'the whine, acting as if they had the sole prerogative of suffering'.[21] There are echoes here of Constant Lambert, who had gravely offended Jewish musicians by writing in *Music Ho!* of the 'curiously sagging quality so typical of Jewish art – the almost masochistic melancholy'. Tin Pan Alley, he said, had become a 'commercialised Wailing Wall'.[22] She may also have unconsciously been aping Edward; as his son James has pointed out, 'that generation of old-fashioned Bolsheviks was very anti-semitic, historically it's lodged in the Soviet system.' For Edward, like many people, Jewishness was a quality to be held against an enemy, overlooked in a friend.

Within the music profession as a whole, long before the war there was widespread nervousness at the outstanding success of Jewish musicians, and an equally widespread belief that they would automatically operate as a clique. These fears were aggravated by the influx of refugees throughout the 1930s, resulting in the paranoia which could produce the 'Stray Puffs' article in which Liz's selection for the 1946 ISCM Festival had been savaged. English musicians returning from the war, wrote the anonymous author, might find themselves squeezed out of their jobs by foreign 'cuckoos'. 'I am so afraid the music profession will in time adopt as its signature tune the last lines of Blake's "Jerusalem" – "Till we have built Jerusalem/In England's green and pleasant land". But I do not think Blake meant it the way I do.'

Liz increasingly tended to see Jews in music as yet another group who might close ranks and exclude her; she suspected connivance between Jewish conductors, composers, publishers, agents, promoters and BBC producers. The Jews were a convenient symbol for all the cliques and cabals she saw ranged against her. As the years went by, she tried to clothe these feelings in respectability by presenting them as detestation of Frankel; and gradually vague fears and antipathies, focused fiercely on a single figure, coalesced into a crude and unmistakable racial prejudice.

More generally, the Frankel affair confirmed for good Liz's suspicions that she and Edward had enemies everywhere. Paranoiacs are not always entirely mistaken, and certainly the case left a legacy of ill-feeling in some quarters which did the Clarks no good at all. Liz felt it helped to explain her relative neglect by the BBC in the 1950s. Frankel for his part suspected that he paid the price of the trial in the 1960s, when Liz's 'side' in its turn might be said to have been in the ascendant.

CHAPTER THIRTEEN

The 'Musico-Marital Association' and the BBC

LIZ'S RELATIONS WITH the BBC had in fact been strained and tortuous well before the Frankel affair. There was to be a long time-lag between her musical achievements in the 1950s – the nerve-affecting vitality of the Sixth Quartet, the Wittgenstein Motet's inspired amalgam of thought and feeling, the emotional openness of *De Amore*, the expressive flexibility of *Quincunx* – and any true critical recognition of them. Liz was inclined to attribute this entirely to the lack of interest in her work, or worse, the positive prejudice against it at the BBC.

In the 1950s the cultural climate generally was not favourable to the radical or the pioneer. After the war the arts seemed to have entered a Cold War era, 'an atmosphere of self-conscious nationalism, easy sentiment and deep conservatism'.[1] The high Reithian ideals, the desire to challenge and educate, had apparently been submerged during the war by the need to calm and cheer. A large proportion of administrators seemed timid, complacent, backward-looking, suspicious not just of Communism – though anything which smacked of it was treated with hostility – but of all that seemed to question the cultural status quo. Cyril Connolly's 'Mandarin' class still occupied the majority of influential positions – upper-middle-class Oxbridge graduates, with their roots in the English country house and pastoral tradition, their nostalgia for 'more leisurely epochs', and their tastes for verse plays, craftsman-like novels, foreign holidays, good food and fine wine.

The Mandarins controlled the institutions which little by little were sucking in all cultural life. In the dour economic climate of post-war Britain, and especially after the austerity measures of 1947, it was increasingly difficult for the freelance to live by art alone, and one by one intellectuals were absorbed into the arts bureaucracy. Outside the large organisations opportunities became progressively rarer, jobs fewer, activity more limited. Liz was not alone in decrying restrictive monopolies in the arts world – though the BBC was a particularly conspicuous example, with its monopoly of broadcasting and an outlook on the arts which, in comparison with the 1930s, at least, had become distinctly constricted.

Robert Hewison, who in his cultural history of Britain is particularly illuminating about the ethos of the 1950s, has written of this period,

> The most directly influential cultural institution for an Oxbridge graduate to enter was the BBC. The BBC had the greatest potential for producing a homogeneous middlebrow society, and in the middle Fifties seemed to have turned the social solidarity of wartime into a respectful deference for authority and tradition. . . . Just as only 'acceptable' speakers were allowed to take part in current affairs programmes, only artists and critics who had already succeeded contributed on the arts [2]

– or, one might say, in the arts.

Writing at that time, in the *New Statesman* of 14 February 1959, Malcolm Muggeridge spoke in less measured tones about the BBC. 'The party line does not have to be formulated; it beats naturally in their hearts, it speaks in their mouths, and wanly illumines their eyes.' The party line within the Music Department, broadly speaking, was nationalistic and conventional, the current of opinion positively anti-Reithian. The Corporation, it was felt, should attempt not to mould popular taste in music but to reflect it, and popular taste was conservative – partly, to complete the circle, because it had been exploited by the BBC during the war at the level of the lowest common denominator.

Structurally, the specialists were now weaker within the BBC, the administrators stronger, with their overriding interest in budgets, personnel management, and public relations. The Music Department was a good deal less independent than it had been in Edward's day in the 1930s – though its members perhaps minded less than they would have done had they been more radical. [3]

The Music Department in the 1950s was not a setting congenial to Liz or Edward, nor tolerant of them. The general consensus was antiserial, the tone having been set to some degree by Steuart Wilson (already Sir Steuart), who was Head of Music from 1948 to 1950. Far from wholly opposed to the new, he was nevertheless condescending about serial music. 'Twelve-tone writing is all right,' he wrote, 'but don't take twelve tones to be ten commandments.' [4]

Wilson's successor, Herbert Murrill, was in very poor health, and Liz and Edward had more to do with his juniors in the Department. Leonard Isaacs, who from 1950 to 1954 was Third Programme Music Organiser, had been Liz's contemporary at the Royal College of Music, an outstanding pianist and a successful composer. Again, he held no torch for the Second Viennese School, calling Schoenberg's *A Survivor from Warsaw* 'a pernicious piece of horror'. [5]

When Herbert Murrill died in 1952, he was succeeded (as the first Controller, Music in the new Music Division) by Richard Howgill. Howgill had known Edward for years and Liz counted him a friend, but his tastes were mainstream and his policy that of promoting the new music of established composers, principally British – Walton, Tippett, Britten, Rubbra, Alwyn, Bliss and others. Unlike Boult twenty years before him, he had little interest in developments on the Continent; his tastes may have stretched as far as Poulenc, but there was to be no Boulez, Nono, Stockhausen, Messiaen or Henze. [6]

Another influential figure was Maurice Johnstone, Head of Music Programmes (Radio), who in 1935–6 had been Edward's assistant in programme planning – and had been far from impressed by him. ('I wondered why the BBC allowed him to conduct,' he wrote later.) [7] Nor did Johnstone share Edward's tastes in new music; he had initially been a protégé of Malcolm Sargent, the most reactionary chief conductor the BBC Symphony Orchestra was ever to have, and though he later became impatient of Sargent, he was himself musically conservative.

Most outspoken of all was the composer Robert Simpson, then one of Maurice Johnstone's assistants. In 1956, in language that had been used in Vienna thirty years before, he described twelve-tone music as 'abnormal and psychotic in origin'. Those who wrote it did so, he felt, 'because they have long ago given up all hope of spontaneous composition. . . . They have become capable of expressing only hysteria, claustrophobia, manic depression, and all the other cognate states of mind, some of them nameless. Many of them have no intention of expressing such things, which makes the helpless result of their cerebral pattern-making all the more pathetic.' Arguing against the spread of twelve-tone music on the Third Programme, he claimed, 'The real trouble starts when, in preserving desperately our famous impartiality, we stultify ourselves by saying, in all sincerity, "no nonsense is too absurd, no destructiveness too violent to be, perhaps, something too profound or original for our comprehension".' [8]

Several of these men were lukewarm about Liz's work in particular; and she was probably right in thinking that she was damned further by her relationship with Edward – as Maurice Johnstone put it, 'this exceptional but unfortunately not illicit musico-marital association'.[9]

Seemingly they liked Liz's husband no better than they liked her music. By the mid-1950s Edward's contact with the BBC depended entirely on Liz. In August 1950, dismayed by his state of mind, Constant Lambert had co-ordinated an appeal to the BBC on Edward's behalf. Signed by Berkeley, Bliss, Boult, Britten, Harriet Cohen, Walton and Vaughan Williams among others, the appeal asked for help in finding him work, pointing out that it was deplorable that anybody 'of such talent, artistic integrity and disinterestedness' should be reduced to the dole.[10]

Unfortunately, the letter landed on the desk of the departing Steuart Wilson. Wilson could in some respects have been a kindred spirit; he had, for example, himself successfully sued the BBC for libel. But as head of the Arts Council, he had had recent dealings with Edward over the ISCM Festival in London, and again at UNESCO's International Council of Music, and he cared neither for his style of office management nor his politics. 'It is unfortunate,' he wrote, 'that Edward Clark's organising ability in connection with the ISCM has apparently been so tinged with political colour as to have done considerable harm to the Society itself.'[11]

Looking at the appeal, he could not see that Edward had anything unique to offer the BBC. He was not a good conductor, he did not write particularly distinguished programme notes, and he appeared to resent it if the BBC used other commentators for concerts of contemporary music. 'The man who seeks for employment in music,' wrote Wilson, 'who is neither performer nor teacher nor recognised journalist is certain to find difficulties.' Richard Howgill added, 'I am sorry for Clark but he is of limited value to us,'[12] and the appeal was ignored.

Edward's conducting continued to raise blood pressures amongst the staff of the Music Department. He now fell, in their view, into the category of 'people we cannot possibly regard as qualified musicians',[13] and they deplored the fact that Features and Drama regularly invited him to conduct Liz's scores. One of Maurice Johnstone's assistants 'dropped in' to a rehearsal of *Mother Courage and her Children*, produced by Reggie Smith, and was appalled by what he perceived as 'sheer concentrated incompetence, utter waste of time and the abuse of music's fair name . . . a cosy *gemütlich* atmosphere of small talk which went on indefinitely while precious money was being ticked away'.[14]

Why Features and Drama persisted in using Edward for Liz's music was a mystery, he informed his superiors, since a studio manager had told him that she frequently abused Edward in front of the orchestra – 'snatches the stick out of his hand, saying, "What an old fool this is".' Reggie Smith replied furiously that in more than twenty productions together he had never known her behave like that; and that, on the contrary, Edward's tact, knowledge of German, understanding of Paul Dessau's music, and sympathy with a difficult performer had been invaluable.[15] But the damage was done.

Edward's vicissitudes indelibly coloured Liz's own relations with the Corporation. She became obsessed by the idea of a man of first-rate gifts mouldering in unemployment while lesser men prospered, and her tone, never ingratiating or even conciliatory, became ever more belligerent. 'I'm damned if I'll be pushed around by a lot of third-rate mediocrities,' she stormed later. 'This makes me obstinate and to many aggressive and has, apparently, resulted in everyone wanting to take me "down a peg" (when I was never "up").'[16]

Between 1952 and 1956 she conducted a running battle with the renamed Music Division. She protested at the terms in which her compositions were rejected (with an undeniably terse standard letter declaring them simply 'unacceptable for broadcasting'). She deplored the BBC's penchant for playing music which was thoroughly untypical of her output; *En Voyage* was featured in a Festival of Light Music 'with Max Jaffa and The Lot', while the Music Division busied itself rejecting her chamber concertos. She criticised the standard of the performances she did get. And finally she complained that her bad relationship with the Corporation was affecting her employment prospects elsewhere, as performers were reluctant to learn works they were confident would not be broadcast.

On the BBC's side too the resentment escalated. 'Most of her concert music strikes everybody as ugly and overblown,'[17] wrote Frank Wade, Richard Howgill's assistant, in 1953. The following year he was goaded to remark, 'She should know by now there is no living in composing for her.'[18] 'I do not think we are neglecting a musical Chatterton,'[19] sagely concluded Lionel Salter, Maurice Johnstone's senior assistant.

When it became necessary for Richard Howgill, as Controller, Music, to reply to her charges, the letter was drafted for him by Leonard Isaacs. Howgill altered the draft considerably, but unfortunately chose to retain a sentence which compared her incidental work favourably with her serious music, as 'far more the real Elisabeth Lutyens than those of your works which show you as the disciple of Schoenberg'.[20]

He would have been hard put to express himself less felicitously. Liz hated to be considered anyone's 'disciple', had not cared greatly for Schoenberg's music, and was deeply offended by the implication that the 'real' Lutyens wrote pastiche.

She wrote in return a seven-page letter,[21] bristling with references to 'party lines', 'cow-pat music', the 'Cheltenham school' and discrimination, which prompted Leonard Isaacs to summarise the Music Division's attitude to her.

> She is, as always, bitter, virulent and dissatisfied – but we must also be allowed our collective opinion that she is a poor composer. She may despize [sic] the 'Cheltenham' School but that makes no difference to our attitude to *her* music. . . . She is not discriminated against except in so far as any individual among us may recoil from her vitriolic and tendencious [sic] tongue.[22]

Liz's problem was that by the late 1950s the Music Division were recoiling to a man. 'Am I on the black list of the BBC, and if so why?' she queried. Her position had certainly not been improved by the Frankel affair; Frankel was on the reading panel which assessed many of the scores sent to the BBC for consideration,[23] and Steuart Wilson, Maurice Johnstone and Leonard Isaacs all subscribed to the Benjamin Frankel Fund.

As for the BBC 'black list', it remains a mystery. There are those who have worked for the Corporation in the past who claim to have seen actual lists in circulation; those who work there now deny their existence – and point out quite cogently that there is no need for them. The BBC remains in some of its crannies personal and pluralist; individual producers have considerable scope to exercise their own tastes and take evasive action on their own behalf without central direction. To be 'blacklisted', or branded as a potential trouble-maker, all that is necessary is to fall out with every producer individually, and this Liz had contrived to do in the 1950s – greatly helped, it should be said in her defence, by their uniform conservatism.

To some extent, then – though there were scattered broadcasts and of course Liz's work for the Features Department was at its height – she and Edward were marooned together in limbo. Liz would refer dramatically to her 'twenty years in the wilderness'; the mid-1950s was the period when she had most cause to feel an outcast.

Her relationship (a word Liz abominated) with Edward was, of course, as tortuous as ever. Mary was later to write, 'I believe that one pays for all one's happiness in life . . . and that the love affair you had with Edward at the beginning was like Prometheus stealing fire from heaven. You certainly had years afterwards chained to your rock with vultures eating out your guts.'[24]

Edward was no more capable of earning now, nor inclined to try. He spent much of his time in his room conducting to the radio, or sleeping with the periodicals scattered round him and *The Times* over his face. In accordance with his preferred monetary system, Liz gave him £3 pocket money per week which, added to his Civil List pension, kept him in scores, books, theatre tickets and carnations. (He changed later to passion flowers, which they grew themselves.)

In the circumstances it incensed her that he was frequently 'too busy' to collect the dole; and despite his socialist principles, he saw National Insurance as a government plot and stopped paying contributions as soon as they became voluntary. Because he had not contributed enough over the years, and because, as a married woman, she was not permitted to make contributions on her own behalf, when Edward died Liz was to receive neither a widow's pension nor an old age pension. Perhaps rightly, he would never consider selling any of the valuable musical memorabilia he had amassed – 'selling my friends', he called it. But his integrity, which was completely unforced, was also completely financed by Liz's commercial work. His principles consumed much of the time when she could have been developing her music, and most of her emotional capital.

He was still prone to devastating explosions of rage, usually about trivia, like buttons torn off his shirts by the laundry. The genuine disasters in his life he greeted with long desolate silences; John Amis once said of Edward, 'He didn't let himself know what he was thinking very often', and he certainly did not let Liz know.

She could not help herself nagging him relentlessly – Alan Raws-thorne, stricken by the expression on Edward's face, would try to stop her.[25] But all her life Liz could never endure silence, and this was the worst kind of all, an apparently deliberate withholding of communication – though Conrad remembers him as being virtually *unable* to speak in these moods, just as he was unable to write. It made her chronically uncertain of his feelings, haunted by the suspicion that he had come to Blackheath only because he had no money and nowhere else to go, and at times she felt her hard-won confidence seeping away.

To those who had not known Edward before the war, Liz's passion for him – and nobody really doubted it, whatever she said about him – was hard to understand. His former authority was gone, and much of his reputation. His years at the BBC were almost as if they had never been, partly because he had had no readily recognisable title as a peg on which to hang his achievements; even critics as well informed as Peter Heyworth, then beginning his career, were uncertain where to place him in the music world.[26] The poise and fire and lightly worn erudition had evaporated, though a gentle courtliness to young women remained, an infinite kindness to the children, an amusing tongue when his interest could be roused, and an endless capacity for taking pains with his reply if one asked a question about music.

To Liz he often seemed to offer nothing. In the face of her need, so aggressively displayed, he was tired and passive. Richard Rodney Bennett remembered him simply letting her rant, 'fuelling her misery'; Alexander Goehr witnessed an occasion when Liz was talking to him about her music, pouring out her ideas and ambitions to an elderly man who quietly went to sleep.

Though her music was developing crucially in the late 1950s, few realised it, and she depended once again on Edward's approval, as she had done before they separated, bitterly resenting his enthusiasm for the work of other, younger composers. Denis ApIvor, for example, remains deeply grateful for Edward's efforts to get his opera *Yerma* performed; but Liz, he feels, held it against them both.[27]

More than his support, she needed Edward's affection and his company; but where she was demonstrative, he was not.

> I once wrote what I thought a beautiful poem for Edward regarding our love [she remembered]. 'Very serious. He ignored it as a bad joke and was 'not amused'. When I first went to live with him I gave him 'Wuthering Heights' (he was *not* a novel reader) for I think it contains a marvellous definition of love. . . . I came home to find Edward rocking with laughter and still caught up in the ghosts and Nellie Dean beginning. Years later, at one lunchtime at Pagani's Dylan . . . read out loud and from memory that last magical page. . . . Perhaps Edward did not think me *quite* so foolish.[28]

Whatever Edward felt, he could or would not express it; and Liz's nagging was perhaps less to punish him than to provoke him into a reaction, any reaction. Malcolm Williamson remembers one archetypal row from the Blackheath days. After a sustained bout of recriminations, Edward abruptly leapt to his feet, overturning Williamson, the rocking chair and a bottle of red wine, and slammed out of the room. During the pause while Williamson repaired the ravages, Liz went in silence to find Edward's diary; opening it to the page for the following day, she wrote simply, 'Love Lizzie more.'[29]

In 1959 they planned finally to merge their two households, and Liz made Edward clear out the flat at 6 Fitzroy Street. Now that the district had been reclassified as light industrial, the textile sweatshops had moved in, rents were rising, and Edward had been under an eviction order for some time. At the French Club one day Liz virtually ordered composer Hugh Wood to help him pack. It was an extraordinary week of smog, and the flat was gritty, damp and dark, stuffed with a chaos of books and papers and great sacks in the middle of the room waiting for the rubbish.

All Edward's life the printed word had been sacrosanct to him. Liz used to claim that when he had gone to visit Bartók he had kept the bus ticket from Buda to Pest; and before newspapers could be thrown away, they had to be arranged in chronological order and carefully tied with string. Now there were dozens of bundles of newspapers, unordered, in the flat, muddled with scores, manuscripts, both sets of Edward's marriage documents littered around, and letters from Webern, Schoenberg, Bartók and Berg stuffed in a bottom drawer. For several days the two men were grimly absorbed in the documents of a past era in music. Every time Hugh Wood found something which interested him he would pass it over. '"Oh, my dear chap," Edward would say, and he'd be off. It was lovely – he knew all these people, and he loved talking about it. And he didn't really want to clear out his flat.'[30] It is perhaps worth mentioning that Edward and Liz took thirty-two tea-chests of papers with them when they moved.

They went first to 13 King Henry's Road, Chalk Farm, a medium-sized Victorian terraced house which they bought with money from Mary and her husband Joe Links. It was the first house since Newcastle which they had bought with a view to living together as a family. Professionally too it seemed that at last doors might be opening to them.

In 1959 – interestingly, at Richard Howgill's instigation – William Glock was appointed his successor as Controller, Music. At the time of his appointment, Glock was as little a part of the British music establishment as Edward had been in the 1930s, though unlike Edward, he had undergone formal music training, as organ scholar at Gonville and Caius College, Cambridge, and a pupil of Artur Schnabel in Berlin. Since the war (which he spent as the *Observer*'s music critic), he had been vigorously promoting the music of the continental avant-garde which the BBC would not touch, through his summer school at Dartington, his chairmanship of the ICA Music Committee, and his editor-

ship of *The Score*. During these years he attended one meeting of
the BBC's Music Advisory Committee, stayed long enough to hear a
variety of derogatory remarks about the music of Webern, and then, like
Edward, never went back.

William Glock's appointment raised Liz and Edward's hopes very
high – he had been an admirer of Liz's work since *O Saisons! O
Châteaux!* over ten years before, and a friend of them both – and this in
its turn precipitated a misunderstanding which indelibly coloured Liz's
attitude to Glock and in later years prevented her from acknowledging
sufficiently generously the transformation of her reputation which he
had achieved.

For some time before Glock officially took up his appointment,
Edward had made it clear that he would love some form of consultative
role. Glock frequently discussed BBC policy with him in general terms,
and suggested they might perhaps do a little work together in the
future. This was never, in Glock's view, intended as a formal arrangement, as Edward was over seventy, well past BBC retiring age. But the
Clarks could see no reason why Edward should not be an 'official'
freelance adviser, and he took the venture desperately seriously. He set
up a trestle table in the sitting room, furnished it with graph paper,
coloured pencils and lists of the composers and performers available,
and set to work. 'His years dropped away,' recalled Liz, 'and he was like
an enthusiastic, happy young man again. . . . "It is Dr Glock who has
cured me!" . . . Our hearts became lighter than at any time in our lives
together since those first days of 1938.'

Glock knew nothing of all this activity. Then came the moment when
Edward, having completed his provisional plans, needed information
from the BBC in order to finalise his programmes. He asked for Glock's
authorisation to use BBC resources – and Glock construed this as a
request for a job, which he could not grant.

Liz referred to the episode in *A Goldfish Bowl* as Edward's 'last
musical death'. His subsequent reaction to Glock's appointment of
young and relatively inexperienced men as planners was reminiscent of
the breakdown he had suffered during the war. He 'shook and complained of feeling icy cold. . . . He then started muttering, "I can't see, I
can't see, put on the light" (which was blazing). I really feared he was
dying and that the strain had affected his already damaged heart.'

From then on she was never able to assess Glock's achievements
impartially, without the spectre of Edward coming between them. The
contrast between Edward, working in comparative obscurity and leaving
in disgrace, and Glock, honoured as the architect of a revolution in the

BBC's tastes, was more than she could bear. In her mind, and often her conversation as well, 'Glock getting credit that Edward too should have had' became 'Glock taking credit for Edward's ideas'.

By 1961 Liz felt that the children needed the house in King Henry's Road, and she and Edward needed solitude, for the first time in their married lives. She found a large basement flat at 76 Belsize Park Gardens, and they eventually moved there at the beginning of 1962.

She took trouble preparing Edward's room, just as Edwin had painstakingly planned the 'little white house' for Emily almost seventy years before. Shelves went up ready for him to reorganise his books, his favourite pursuit, and an intercom was installed between their two studies.[31]

There was a little more money: Liz had recently been told by William Alwyn (who was largely responsible for it) that she would be receiving a major award from the Phoenix Trust for her achievements in music – a gratifying professional compliment, and a large sum of money. Instead of family stews, she felt they could afford the odd sole or steak, and the occasional dinner party.

It was at a Saturday dinner at the end of April that Edward was irritated by being unable to remember his French. The following morning, reading the Sunday papers, he was distraught to learn of the death of the soldier who had accidentally killed Webern in 1945. He was so agitated that Liz promised she would take him to the doctor for an overhaul the next day. She was herself feeling ill that Sunday, and retired to bed early, leaving him sorting his books.

On the intercom she told him not to stay up too late. Then, according to her description in *A Goldfish Bowl*, she felt unaccountably impelled to go to him, and burst out,

> 'I do love our new life together. Promise you'll never leave me.' Quickly realising his dislike of all sentimentality I changed my mood. 'I'd have no one to sharpen my wits on.' 'Or argue with,' he said – the last words he ever spoke.
>
> I was woken in the night by a fearful noise beside me. Edward was panting and gasping stertorously, his face red with congestion. . . . My first thought was that something had stuck in his throat. . . . I tried to remove the non-existent obstruction, even attempting an inopportune and pointless kiss of life in a desperate effort to do *something* – at once.

During the last weeks Edward had several times remarked how pleased he was to have renewed contact with a young doctor friend; this had stuck in Liz's mind, and now she telephoned him. (He lived in Victoria, with further to come, and the delay later haunted Liz.)

The ghastly noise seemed to continue for ever.... I had to make frequent dashes to our front door lest the doctor made for the main door upstairs instead of our side entrance. I also tried to keep the four cats out of the bedroom and away from the bed, but did not want to shut the door on Edward or let him feel deserted. After years seemed to have passed, Edward's body suddenly gave a violent jerk and stayed twisted at a contorted angle; one bright blue vacant eye fixed blankly on nothing and that fearful noise stopped. (His eyes were dark brown, I know, but I shall never forget this peculiar blue eye glaring.)

Though Edward had clearly had a coronary, the doctor, not having attended him recently, was unable to sign the death certificate, and there was talk of an autopsy, because his sleeping pills were spilt by the bed. For the rest of the night, as Liz passed in and out of sleep, a single refrain ran inexorably through her mind – '"It's all too late, too late, too late . . .".'

Chapter Fourteen

Driving Out the Death

'Edward's death seemed to blot me out,' Liz wrote ten years afterwards. She was desperate for work as a lifeline, but out of sympathy and respect people left her to herself, with too much time to reflect. To outsiders she seemed to behave strangely. Not least, she sold, in great haste, most of Edward's possessions – many of the books, records, gramophones, scores, and the most valuable of the letters from composers – for a fraction of their potential value.

Her excuse, valid enough, was that she needed the money for the funeral expenses. Edward left £927 net and no pension; and it was a large funeral. 'Wasn't it Sydney Smith,' wrote John Davenport, 'who said that his idea of heaven was "eating *pâté de foie gras* to the sound of trumpets"? I like to think that that is what Edward is doing. He may, of course, be eating ambrosia to the sound of *O Saisons! O Châteaux!*; or caviare with Schoenberg. Something agreeable, anyway. Bad luck, though, for the rest of us.' [1]

Liz received hundreds of letters and flowers from 'the rest of us' – ApIvor, Arnold, Bliss, Bush, Cooke, Dallapiccola, Eisler, Gerhard, Goehr, Hamilton, Ireland, Josephs, Maconchy, Rawsthorne, Rubbra, Searle, Stravinsky, Thomson, Wood, and Williamson, to name only the composers – and a great many came to the service at Golders Green Crematorium in the pouring rain. Her flowers, lily-of-the-valley, freesia and iris, were labelled 'To you from me', as if nobody else existed.

Liz was the life and soul of the funeral. In her own words, 'I fastened my safety belt and floated high and punchdrunk on a strange, unreal plain.' Conrad remembers her acting 'very violently as if everything were normal', organising her life with even greater obsessiveness than usual, caught up in a baffling tangle of feelings. First, the shock.

Edward had said only the week before, 'I don't want to die, but I am not afraid of death.' Liz, however, had been present at the moment when Nannie Sleath died in 1938 after a desperate struggle with liver cancer,[2] and she was afraid of death; the manner of Edward's dying only confirmed her fears.

For years afterwards, perhaps until her own death, Liz was also to be made very unhappy by guilt. She may well have described her last exchange with Edward – 'Oh, I do love our new life together' – as she wanted it to have been, but not as it was. Several people remember her revealing that she and Edward had had a row over nothing – both trivial and, as a symptom of underlying tension, deadly – and had gone to bed that night without bothering to make it up. As Liz revolved the events of his death in her mind, she was to be tormented by the fear that he had not woken her because he was afraid she would be bad-tempered with him; instead he had struggled with the sleeping pills which the doctor had found spilt on the floor by the bed. She was sorry that she had not understood the irritations and indignities of being seventy, and had too often been impatient with him; and she was filled with regret for all the time together that they had wasted.

Her immediate emotion though, mercifully, was the anger which the one who is left very often feels for the one who has left them. It was this, perhaps, she was venting when she sold his possessions. With one part of her, she had always felt suffocated by his books. They represented a past which she had not shared – his life in Europe, his knowledge of pre-war culture, his huge circle of friends – and to which it sometimes seemed he was reluctant to admit her. If she ventured an opinion on a subject within his particular preserve, as often as not he would snub her; and when she took down a Webern score to study and wrote in it, he was furious.[3] Disposing of his library was a part of the process of reconstructing his image which she completed in *A Goldfish Bowl*.

The irony was that at the time of Edward's death, Liz's life had at last seemed to be taking the shape she wanted. In her work she had developed technical virtuosity which excited her, and she had time in which to experiment with it. (The children were all living elsewhere: Sebastian, now a qualified electrical engineer, had married Gloria Brand early in 1952; Rose and Tess were living in King Henry's Road; Conrad was finishing three years as an art student at the Slade and planning to travel in India.) There was even the promise of a degree of critical recognition. Then suddenly the fabric had collapsed; even the resentments, grievances and frustrations of her marriage had occupied space, and now she was left with 'a large dark cavity inside, which Edward used to fill with his undying passion and enthusiasm'.[4]

From now on the vacuum was to be filled largely by her obsession with his professional neglect, her determination to make something out of his flawed life and the ruined career which had so damaged their lives together. The legacy of Edward was to affect the whole of the rest of her life, her relations with the music business, and her attitude to herself.

Her first effort to come to terms with his memory was by completing Music for Orchestra II, half-finished when he died. But this was not the outpouring of emotion that one might have expected, for Liz did not believe in musical catharsis – or indeed, in 'self-expression' of any sort. In this she followed Stravinsky, who had once written, 'I consider my music, in essence, incapable of expressing a feeling, an attitude, a psychological state, a natural phenomenon or whatever, Expression has never been the immanent property of music.' [5]

In particular Liz did not want to express *herself*; the last thing she enjoyed doing was exposing her personality to criticism. '[Writing music] is the opposite of self-expression,' she insisted. 'On the contrary, one loses consciousness of oneself in the concentration, and all one is – has felt or been – is harnessed and at the service of the idea.' Edward's death had changed her life, but no one should be able to tell that from Music for Orchestra II. 'There must be no break in continuity.'

Continuity had always been, in fact, the guiding idea of the piece. When she started it, she had had no particular form in mind, just a musical line which she drew out like a spider's thread, not knowing where it led. Then the idea of a fountain possessed her; she heard/saw the music in her mind's ear and eye as progressing not left to right but vertically, each cell or phrase caught up by the next, coiling upwards in a spiral. Edward's reaction to the first page had been, 'Bloody marvellous! but it mustn't let up' [6] – and she was determined now that the impetus should not slacken. Thus she let the piece shape itself into a series of 'fountains' of differing heights and pressures, its line like a ping-pong ball suspended on jets of water. The 'jets' form a single fast movement ending on a surprise chord. This dies away to leave only a G; then on that single note is built a coda in the form of a very slow chorale, each 'line' of which ends again in a G, but scored for different instruments each time, with an extraordinarily poignant effect. 'To say that G is given varying colours and dynamics,' wrote one critic, 'is like saying sunset is varying colours in the sky.' [7]

Music for Orchestra II incorporated a huge range of sounds, from the alto saxophone to the sarrusophone – so huge as to be a deterrent to would-be performers, and the piece was not performed live in Britain for thirteen years. But then, despite all her protestations of objectivity and abstraction, the critics saw at once what she had been doing. The fountain conception, impressive on paper, was hard to grasp in performance – not so the chorale. The work, wrote Joan Chissell, 'comes from an intellectual rather than a hedonist. But suddenly, near the end, calculation dissolves into humanity: the brief, fragile, touching coda seems to speak from the heart'[8] – speaking directly to Edward.

Edward had said repeatedly to Liz, 'You'll never get the breakthrough you deserve while I'm alive.' She was perhaps too easily tempted to accept his offer of himself as scapegoat, and to ignore the other reasons for her lack of recognition. But it is a fact that within months of his death she had achieved unprecedented success, and that the years 1962 to 1971 were the period of her greatest critical approval and acceptance as part of the British music scene.

This was largely due to William Glock. Glock always maintained that as Controller, Music at the BBC he did not programme *more* contemporary music, but he placed it with a view to making more impact, in the Proms and in high-profile Invitation Concerts, and he made no compromises in his choices. 'If you are prepared to put a foot anywhere,' he said, 'then you must be prepared to put it wrong.' He revived the Reithian ideal of leading public taste from well in the vanguard. The 1950s, in his view, had seen the Second Viennese School and related composers like Liz disgracefully neglected, and he proposed to correct this with a policy of 'creative unbalance', giving serial music, especially that of Schoenberg, an 'unnatural prominence' in its turn. His reading panel was more 'advanced', including Humphrey Searle, David Drew and Iain Hamilton, and he dropped what he described as 'Spa repertory' – the dread spectre of 'Cheltenham music' raising its head again only to have it lopped off. He deflected the BBC's gaze from Honegger, Rubbra and Frank Martin, and directed it towards Schoenberg, Webern, Stravinsky and Gerhard.[9]

He also transformed the BBC into a full-scale commissioning body.[10] In the seventeen years of its existence before the war, the Corporation had issued a mere fourteen commissions (three of them initiated by Edward, including *Belshazzar's Feast*). Between 1946 and 1959 there were forty-three, but most were in honour of the Coronation in 1953 and the tenth anniversary of the Third Programme in 1956, leaving no more than one major 'ordinary' commission in each remaining year. Of these, Lennox Berkeley received four, Alun Hoddinott three, and Michael Tippett, William Alwyn, Herbert Howells, Kenneth Leighton, Daniel Jones and Malcolm Arnold two each.

In Glock's era, 1959–72, commissions shot up to 124, an average of nine a year. He contrived to have the commissioning fund multiplied by seven, and insinuated the notion of stockpiling new pieces against a shortage.[11] Among the composers who benefited were Harrison Birtwistle with five commissions, Richard Rodney Bennett, Malcolm Williamson, Hugh Wood, Alan Rawsthorne, Peter Maxwell Davies, Gordon Crosse and Malcolm Arnold with four. Liz was given her first BBC commissions, eight of them during this period – almost twice as many as any other composer. This, in the words of one of her best works of the new era, was 'driving out the death' of the 1950s with a vengeance.

The early 1960s marked a watershed in Liz's reputation. In 1962 *Quincunx* was given the best reviews of her career so far – ironically enough, for a première which took place in Cheltenham. (*Quincunx* has never had a London performance.) J. F. Waterhouse wrote, 'Never before, not from Schoenberg, not even from Berg, have I heard twelve-note music embody such glowing luxuriance of full orchestral sound.'

Almost more important, in the following year the Wittgenstein Motet at last got the performance it deserved, when it was given at a BBC Invitation Concert by the John Alldis Choir, newly formed with a specialisation in serial music.[12] That same week, in a public lecture, Ernest Ansermet had launched a sweeping attack on serial music. A mathematician and a student of physiology, Ansermet claimed that while tonal music is based on 'a series of logorhythmically related sound vibrations which correspond to and thus awaken precise psychological experiences', serial music is not so based; it is not a language and can have no meaning. Warming to his theme, he concluded that those who claim it is music have never had a real musical experience.[13]

The piece to which the critics pointed in their eagerness to rebut him was the Wittgenstein Motet – indisputably a musical experience of the highest order, according to Peter Heyworth. And in the process, they woke up to a realisation of the changes that had taken place in Liz's music during the 1950s – changes which to some extent had been concealed from them by the reticence of the BBC. Anthony Payne contributed to the *Listener* of 5 December 1963 the kind of evaluation by which reputations are made. In an article entitled 'Lutyens's Solution to Serial Problems', he wrote,

Ten years ago, already in her middle forties, the composer appeared committed to a narrow if individual range of feeling, but now, quite suddenly it seems, she has become a considerable artistic force. In this late flowering she has doubled her potential, and the appearance of any new work by her in the future must be considered an important event.

Unfortunately, this pronouncement came too late to save her first BBC commission from oblivion. Liz had already been invited to write a piece for the Proms when she went to hear a young pianist, Katharina Wolpe, play at the Wigmore Hall. She was deeply impressed, in particular by Wolpe's interpretation of Beethoven, and decided on the spur of the moment to make the Prom piece a piano concerto for her. It was a typical gesture; where many composers select a soloist whose reputation will enhance the piece and improve its prospects of perform-ance, Liz chose a young and unknown performer whose cause she had to plead with the BBC, simply because her playing corresponded with a sound Liz had in her head.

She started work on the new piece with two preconditions: it must be for piano, and it must take into account the sound the piano would make in the hollow and resonant Royal Albert Hall – the only place, according to Sir Thomas Beecham, where a composer can hear his new work played twice in one evening. For Liz, the choice of the piano determined the rest of the instrumentation; for its sonorities to sound unhindered, there must be no strings, but instead twenty-two wind and brass, with a large percussion section. She wanted her players to perform as thirty-two soloists, so she gave instructions that they were to sit not in traditional formation, but in four lines with the players in Indian file one behind the other, arranged fanwise around the piano.

This fan shape, inside a circular hall, initially suggested to Liz that the form of the piece might be an arc – the first half rising gracefully to the summit of the semicircle, and then descending backwards to a close. A week or so later, however, she saw a television programme about the potter John Leach, and was struck by one particular pot with a lid like a Japanese temple roof, whose gently curved inverted V-shape prompted a more obvious palindrome. Symphonies for Solo Piano, Wind, Harps and Percussion (1961) opens with an exhilarating crash on the tam-tam, rises to a sharp peak in the middle as it gains its maximum speed, and declines in reverse until it reaches the tam-tam again.[14]

Liz was sadly disappointed by her first commissioned Prom per-formance – not by the playing of Katharina Wolpe, who remained a favourite artist and a close friend, but by inadequate rehearsal time and the piece's failure to 'sound' in the hall. Despite the fan arrangement of the players, much of her carefully balanced sound disappeared into the vast dome; and few appreciated the work's elegant symmetry. When listeners are familiar with a piece, they will recognise an indifferent performance for what it is; in a new work they have no touchstone and will often simply dismiss the piece along with the performance.

Symphonies, like so many of Liz's works, has never been given a second chance; as one artist remarked unkindly, 'I seem to spend my life doing Lutyens *dernières*.'

Few people consider Liz's piano works to be among her best; she herself felt she did not really understand the instrument. Her piano playing certainly remained makeshift all her life. 'She would hold down an open fifth in the left hand as a kind of drone rhythm,' remembered Malcolm Williamson, 'and pick out the rest as best she could with the right.'[15] When she was in more romantic mood, according to Joyce Rathbone, 'down went the damper pedal and out came these wistful, watery sounds . . . rather like marbling, only in wishy-washy colours. . . . Like somebody who didn't know how to play the piano pretending to play Debussy . . . very lovely, and evocative of *something*. . . .'[16]

Liz generally failed to exploit the full potential of the piano. She distrusted people who wrote with what she described as 'a lot of notes' – but one of the piano's principal strengths is the torrent of sound of which it is capable; as a pianist Katharina Wolpe regretted Liz's reluctance to 'proliferate' in her keyboard works, and her consequent inability to write piano music that moves really fast.

Liz herself focused attention on her difficulties, in the programme note she wrote for *Helix* (1967), a short work for two players and one piano.

> Faced with the endless (too many!) possibilities and multiplicity of notes playable with four hands at a piano, I decided to choose one note; to emphasise this and let the sounds radiate, 'coil' out from this one note: as one might throw a stone in the water and ripples radiate from the impact.

As a solution to the surfeit of choice, this was rather too drastic. The sounds she created are not flowing enough to suggest the 'coiling' which is implied in the title, and the line too choppy to evoke the idea of ripples; the effect is more like sparks thrown off from a cogwheel slowly grinding.

One of the techniques employed in *Helix* in the attempt to make the music 'coil' was simply to strike a single key hard and let the harmonics sound and resound. Liz once said that being at heart a string player, she did not have a sufficiently well-tempered ear fully to appreciate the tone of the piano, and preferred to use it as a percussion instrument. This she did most unusually in *Scroll for Li Ho* (1967), a sonata for violin and piano.

Once again, as in the case of the Wittgenstein Motet, she found that the music was virtually complete at the back of her mind before she tried to bring the sonata into sharp focus with a title and detailed interpretation. She had been reading about a poet whose habit was to conceive and complete a poem before understanding its meaning, and this she felt was what happened with *Li Ho*. Writing the music was a process of exploration rather than navigation; only afterwards could she locate where she had been.

The voyage, of course, was not completely directionless. 'I made sure,' she explained, 'before exploring my musical landscape, that I started with a compass'[17] – in the form of a basic idea for the work, and an absolute confidence in her technique.

Her basic idea was this notion of using the piano as if it were a pitched percussion instrument, in this case a Balinese gamelan. Through what she described as aural 'tasting', she identified a corresponding character for the violin, another for the sound of the two instruments combined, and she attached to each sound a 'germ' or 'embryo' of notes or chords. Then holding these three strands – piano/gamelan, violin, and piano/violin – 'I aurally followed, so it seemed, where they led me, knowing there would be a strong, logical structure to my musical thinking, recognised or not – doesn't matter.'

She had recently been given the work of the poet Li Ho. She felt as she worked on the sonata as if she were unrolling a Chinese scroll depicting the kind of scene Li Ho described – as if she were discovering a musical landscape bit by bit as it appeared, deciphering broad outlines behind a mass of detail. She now imported this idea into the piece, inscribing snippets of the poetry above each instrumental line.

Not all Liz's critics shared her confidence in the 'strong, logical structure' of her music; some felt that it mattered very much that the structure was recognisable. Certainly the procedure she employed in *Li Ho*, following a hidden trail rather than leading from the front with a map, is conducive to rambling, and of this she was sometimes guilty. She occasionally described herself as using the 'stream of consciousness' method, which again can be antipathetic to form, or an excuse for the lack of it.

Like most other composers, when it came to commissions offered by smaller organisations than the BBC or by individual performers, Liz benefited enormously in the 1960s and early 1970s from the Labour government's increase in subsidy to the Arts Council. Of her other commissioned instrumental works, several of the most successful were written for the oboe. She liked its plangent timbre, and tended to write for it in melancholy mood, finding the 'busy' writing so common in contemporary woodwind compositions both monotonous and irritating.

Driving Out The Death (1971) for oboe and string trio is the most frequently performed of all Liz's works. The *donnée*, she explained when the piece was first performed,[18] was an oboe phrase which came to her as solid as a sculptural object and as hard to change. In consequence, the piece is essentially a ritual reiteration of it, punctuated by the three strings' response which colours the phrase and alters its significance.

The domination of the work by a single phrase gives it an obvious unity, but Liz was anxious to achieve variety as well. To her, the most obvious manifestation of variety within unity was the cycle of the seasons – the inevitable alternation of cold and hot, dark and light, barren and fertile, within the confines of a single year – and she found the context within which to develop her *donnée* in a Thuringian ritual celebrating the coming of spring: the straw figure of Death, dressed in old winter clothes, is carried out of the village and thrown into the river.

The death and rebirth of the year was a profoundly important source of material for Liz, and the motif of the seasons runs through her long list of works from beginning to end. As she got older, the emphasis shifted inexorably towards winter; but at the same time she remained fascinated by man's belief in the unfailing regeneration of Nature. She had her own practical demonstration of it in the late 1960s when she became a grandmother twice over. Tess had been married in 1963 to writer Patrick Fetherstonhaugh, and Rose the following year to Mohammed Abdalla, a Sudanese potter. Rose and Mo had their first daughter, Amna, in 1967, the same year that Sebastian and Gloria's Susan was born.

Liz's writing in *Driving Out The Death* shows far less restraint than other works from the same period, and is more openly emotional, more highly dramatic than any of her stage works. 'All Miss Lutyens' virtues are here concentrate,' wrote Andrew Porter, 'the creation of a musical line so vivid and definite that it seems like a visible gesture traced in space before us ... the sureness of aim in its continuation ... the supple athleticism of musical mind and musical muscles, and the romantic imagination.'[19]

Liz liked to feel that the qualities which distinguished her best chamber work could be exhibited on a larger scale; but she wrote few orchestral works during the 1960s. The difficulty she experienced in getting Music for Orchestra II performed deterred her from writing on this scale without a commission, and she was only ever to do so once more. (She wrote *Tides* in 1978 simply because she wanted to; it has never been performed.)

What was new in the 1960s was the outpouring of vocal works – twenty-four between 1960 and 1971 (not counting stage works), as opposed to seven in the 1950s – and the development of her expressive range in writing for the voice. She set a truly extraordinary mixture of texts from Sophocles to Gertrude Stein by way of Edward Lear, the burial chants of the pygmies of Gabon, Rabelais, Eskimo poetry and the *Oxford English Dictionary* – the fruits of her constant trawling through the literature of every era and virtually every culture.

'I find it almost impossible to read anything that's more than two pages,'[20] she once declared, explaining her preference for poetry. If a text was interesting, she wanted to write music for it at once, and if it was boring. . . . She read incessantly, almost obsessively, without ever managing to be well read in the conventional sense because of the high preponderance of the obscure in what she consumed, but certain major figures she loved and knew well – Byron, Yeats and Shelley.

From time to time she was tempted to set anthologies of short snatches from different poets – not often among her best works, as they encouraged a certain tendency towards scrappiness. The first 'portmanteau' piece was *Catena* (1961), which set Chaucer's young Alysoun side by side with James Joyce's ageing beauty, Dylan Thomas's *Winter's Tale* next to Shakespeare's, and managed to incorporate snippets of both Dryden and Japanese Noh, as well as another of Tess's poems. 'Catena' means 'chain' in Latin, and the final motif of the cadence of each section was taken up as the start of the following section – a neat link, but not strong enough to bind her miscellaneous texts into a unity, especially since she used different instrumental combinations for each passage.

She prefaced *Catena* with a tag from T. S. Eliot – 'These fragments have I shored against my ruins.' But she may have sensed that the bulwark was itself precarious, because she proposed as well a highly elaborate disposition of instruments on the platform – forming circles, triangles, kites, stars, diagonals – in what appears to be an attempt to superimpose pattern and an artificial order on a work that has no organic unity.

More convincing were the works in which she concentrated on the verse of a single poet. She particularly enjoyed Chaucer, whose language reminded her happily of the Suffolk dialect spoken around Braughles, and she set his version of Boethius's cosmogony in *Country of the Stars* (1963), a motet for unaccompanied chorus. *Encomion* (1963) had other resonances of the past, because this piece for chorus, brass and percussion was to be performed in the crypt that was all that Sir Edwin had built of Liverpool Cathedral by the time he died. She took as its centrepiece part of the school song from Kipling's *Stalky and Co.* and paid her father and his unfinished cathedral her own tribute of affection and admiration –

> 'Let us now praise famous men' –
> Men of little showing –
> For their work continueth,
> And their work continueth,
> Broad and deep continueth,
> Greater than their knowing!

For her mother there was to be no special memorial. In her eighties Lady Emily's extraordinary energies had at last failed her. In Liz's words, 'her memory and many faculties had gone and from being a tall, large woman she had shrunk to a small frail skeleton.' In 1962 Liz took her on holiday for a fortnight in Surrey, visiting the houses Sir Edwin had built as a young man and returning to Thursley and the Lutyens family home. In *A Goldfish Bowl* Liz reports in some detail her mother's bewilderment. It is as though she almost felt relief at the dwindling of the personality which for so long had dominated her emotions.

But now, when there was no longer the pressing need to seek her mother's approval, the compulsion for Liz to distinguish herself, she found herself able to see more clearly what was truly admirable about Lady Emily. Rose and Mo wanted to visit her in her highly conventional Haslemere hotel, and Liz, in the racially sensitive 1960s, dreaded the possibility of a snub for Mo. She mentioned her fears to Lady Emily, who remarked 'with a firm, unusually resonant determination and a glint in her eye, "If he is not welcomed I shall get up and walk out!" It was touching, as she needed an arm to walk on – and where to? But it showed that the strong spirit of love and tolerance still burned in that dear, worn body.'

Two years later in 1964 Lady Emily died in her sleep at the age of 89. For some years Liz had felt confident that her mother appreciated what she had achieved, but she never deceived herself that Lady Emily liked her music. She wrote no specific work, but Music for Orchestra III, on which Liz was working when her mother died, is dedicated to her, as Music for Orchestra II commemorates Edward.

In 1965 Liz set her first and last Christian texts – a Magnificat and Nunc Dimittis commissioned by Coventry Cathedral. Whether these were ever used is unclear, and it would be fascinating to know whether they were rejected. But it is probably safe to say that a motet written the same year offers a truer guide to her thoughts on metaphysical subjects.

The Hymn of Man (1965) is a setting for male chorus of a long passage of Swinburne. Uninvitingly subtitled 'During the session in Rome of the Oecumenical Council', the poem is an attack on the established church; but more significantly, it is also a humanist paean to the spirit of man. Liz was uncompromising in her dismissal of organised religion – partly perhaps in deference to her short-lived membership of the Communist Party, but more probably as a consequence of her rejection of the Masters, Leadbeater, the Manor and the taking-over of her imaginative and emotional life.

She was painfully aware of the power of the non-rational, which had threatened her adolescence, and sentiments like Swinburne's – 'Lo, saith man, this is my spirit; how *shall* not the world's make way?' – appealed to her conviction of the importance of self-control and the opposing power of the will. But something in her responded instinctively to the broadly 'religious': conventional piety disgusted her, but she studied other faiths as philosophies, and even looked to them as possible sources of comfort in a loneliness that grew no less acute with time.

After Edward's death, she explored as many different theories of the afterlife as she could find, searching vainly for one in which she might believe. But even as she searched she knew she was clutching at straws. Lines she set in 1965 seem to give a glimpse of the desolation she still felt, and the fear she preferred to conceal in anger –

> It was hard enough for two
> of us to cross the autumn
> mountain. How could you cross
> by yourself alone?
>
> In this cold night when the
> light snow falls over the
> garden, am I to sleep all
> alone without any hand to
> cradle my head?

The words come from a collection of Japanese verse,[21] which she set under the title of one of the individual poems – *The Valley of Hatsu-Se* (1965), commissioned by William Glock for Dartington, and performed

there in the summer of 1965 by the Vesuvius Ensemble. The soloist was
Jane Manning, a singer Liz greatly admired, for whom she was to write
several of her best vocal pieces. The following year, the same artists
performed *Akapotik Rose* (1966), a musical experiment in the collage
techniques that were so fashionable in the 1960s. Eduardo Paolozzi, one
of the pioneeers of Pop Art, supplied Liz with a quantity of verse
composed by free association and gave her *carte blanche* to use it as she
wished. Thus the words of *Akapotik Rose* are his, but the order and
overall sense, such as it is, are hers, and the choice of section titles such
as 'Blue print for a clock of straw' and 'Kakafon Kakoon'.

As long ago as 1922 Arthur Bliss had experimented (in his Concerto
for piano, tenor, strings and percussion) with words chosen purely for
their sound and rhythm, of 'so abstract a character as not to interpose a
logical meaning'.[22] More than likely he had in his mind the 'chance'
poetry of the Dadaists working in Zurich some five years before. Liz
was loudly contemptuous of neo-Dadaism wherever she detected it in
the work of younger musicians in the 1960s, and it is possible that
Akapotik Rose was intended as a send-up. The use of a loud-hailer, for
instance, so soon after Peter Maxwell Davies had employed one in his
Revelation and Fall (1966), can hardly have been coincidental. But
parody would have been less than polite to Paolozzi, whom she liked
and admired as an artist, and it is more probable that she simply could
not resist having a go herself. Unfortunately she was never at her best
when 'unbuttoned'; discipline suited her, as it had done when she was a
child, in a way that Californian-style 'self-expression' did not, and
Akapotik Rose comes across now as a slice of 1960s silliness.

Hugo Cole was to say of Liz, 'If she is a disconcerting composer, it is
partly because she sometimes seems to treat her best and her most
prosaic ideas with equal favour and at equal length.'[23] Within months,
even weeks of writing one of her weakest vocal pieces, she had written
perhaps her best.

And Suddenly It's Evening (1966) was composed for the concert
which christened the Queen Elizabeth Hall – a well-publicised occasion
and the most prestigious commission she had ever been offered. It came
at a busy time, when she needed every spare moment for composition;
Antony Hopkins, discussing the piece in his series 'Talking About
Music'[24] (and his choice of the work says as much about her new-found
prominence as about his courage), made much of the fact that it had its
genesis under the hair-dryer.

The commission was for a choral piece, and Liz's first idea was a
work with overtones of the madrigal, specifically the madrigals of

Monteverdi. She then seems to have made a side-step in her thought, as Antony Hopkins points out, to the canzonas of Gabrieli, and the alternation of voices with brass; she punctuated her evolving vocal line with contrasting blocks of sound for four brass intruments and a double bass. To this pattern, for further contrast, she added two more instrumental groups – one of harp, celeste and percussion, the other of horn, violin, and cello. Having established her accompaniment, she decided she needed to re-think the vocal line, which she now gave to a single tenor instead of a chorus. But she had not departed too far from her original conception, in Antony Hopkins's view, for this is a conspicuously Monteverdian tenor, his line, complete with trills, clearly reminiscent of some of the writing in *Orfeo*. (Here, perhaps, the 'realisations' Liz had done in the 1930s, even the bizarre *Lamento d'Arianna*, stood her in good stead.)

When madrigals had been uppermost in Liz's mind, she had considered using Elizabethan words as her text, but as the music developed, what she described as their 'Hey-nonny-nonny' associations became ever more inappropriate. Coincidentally, she had just been reading the poetry of the Sicilian poet Salvatore Quasimodo. He bore, of course, little resemblance to the madrigalists, but she was strongly attracted by his tone of voice, hearing in it a kind of dissonance which was akin to her own.

Her task now was to make a unity out of the poems she had selected. She was prepared to admit that her music, even if it was not designed to express or describe states or objects extrnal to it, was frequently influenced by the circumstances in which it was composed; and in the case of *And Suddenly*, the environment was one of severe overwork. Exhaustion, she claimed, dictated the work's structure, inclining her to lean on the device of repetition. But it was repetition of the Monteverdian sort; the piece was woven together by constant ritornelli, 'returnings' of the various instrumental groups, with the brass/double bass group taking the additional role of a Greek chorus, commenting on the action and interaction of the other performers. Thus each of the four Quasimodo poems she chose is 'enclosed' – ushered in and out – by instrumental ritornelli. And in the last section, 'Everyone is alone on the heart of the earth', both ritornelli groups together introduce and bid farewell to the unaccompanied tenor, and the brass chorus alone has the final comment.

In the unaccustomed glare of public attention, it was crucial that Liz write the best work of which she was capable, and she anxiously canvassed the opinions of her friends. Cross-questioned on her first impression of the pencil score, Katharina Wolpe found herself full of doubts. On the page, she remembered, the work seemed thin, insubstantial, rhythmically loose; because the occasion was so important, and there was still time to make changes, she spoke honestly – and instantly regretted it. Liz, alarmed, looked hard at what she had written, and found she could not alter a note.

In the event, Wolpe realised after hearing the first bars of the piece in performance that she had misread it. She had looked at it with the eye of a pianist rather than a conductor or composer, had taken in the placing of notes, their movement and rhythm – but not their timbre. Looking back, it seemed to her that she had totally underestimated the effect the percussion would have, wrapping the piece in 'a sort of glow' and creating the distinctive, dreamlike atmosphere in which all four poems live. This shared sound-world made a single song of the piece, which has a focus and impact missing from some of the more disparate vocal works. *And Suddenly It's Evening* has an elegance of structure, beauty of sound and directness of appeal which earned her an ovation at that celebration concert and is remembered today by people who have not heard it for twenty years. It marks a very high point in her work – and the point at which many would like to stop the clock.

CHAPTER FIFTEEN

Avant-garde to Old Hat: 1967–71

LIZ USED TO joke about *And Suddenly It's Evening* and the aptness of certain friends to refer to it as *Suddenly Last Summer*; had she chosen to set Tennessee Williams's musings on homosexuality, incest and cannibalism, she suggested, she might have drawn bigger audiences. Nevertheless, *And Suddenly* was important to her, and had about it an aura of emotion expressed with an unusual directness. Anthony Payne has detected as well a corresponding unbending in technique which continued in much of her later work – simpler gestures, less complex harmonies, a tendency to structure works in larger blocks, as her writing became less austerely Webernian.[1]

Much of her remaining work – and Liz was to write almost a hundred more numbered pieces – adhered in fact less rigidly to the twelve-tone method. As early as 1960 she had been evasive about her use of serial techniques. When a researcher asked in puzzlement precisely how the last movement of her Wind Quintet, Op. 45 (1960) grew out of the series she had originally chosen, she replied, 'When a sculptor casts a plaster work in bronze he forgets the armature although it existed. This is as I do in my music.'[2]

Even by the start of the 1960s she seemed to be saying that the twelve-tone technique took her only part of the way towards her goals; as Schoenberg himself had recommended, she used the method as a starting-point but felt free to use the products exactly as she wanted. In 'forgetting the armature', ignoring the theoretical constraints of the tone-row, she risked formlessness, for serial techniques had after all been adopted in the first place to restore order amidst the wreckage of traditional structures of key and tempo. But she was able to achieve originality, which the opponents of serialism have often claimed to be incompatible with a purely 'mechanical' technique.

By 1967 Liz could claim, 'A series is hardly necessary now';[3] the lessons the technique had to offer were already an integral part of the contemporary composer's aural experience. For herself, she had taken from the twelve-tone system what was of use to her, and her musical thought had been permanently conditioned by it as a result. But now her intention was to use more freely the techniques she had developed with its help.

She was prepared to allow her music greater emotional liberty. The passion and sensitivity were not new, obviously; friends and pupils had long been aware of a profound vein of romantic feeling underlying and sometimes undermining her taste for style and ease and wit. (Her family too, of course, knew a person of moods and tempers, enthusiasms and hatreds, whom they could never recognise in what she wrote – hence perhaps their general disappointment and perplexity in the face of her music.) But the directness with which she now felt willing to express emotion was a departure; and it was this directness, perhaps, which was to be heard in *And Suddenly It's Evening*.

Liz would have denied categorically the suggestion that the piece had any specific autobiographical reference. Feeling was patently an integral component of music – neither she nor any other serial composer ever denied that, whatever their critics tried to claim. But story-telling, and in particular the telling of one's own intimate story, was not. She seemed to see personal reference in music as a sign of intellectual, even moral weakness.

This mistrust of 'self-expression' ('King Kong breast-beating'[4] she called it) was partly temperamental, partly a direct legacy of the days when her music had been invaded and all but stifled by the spiritual and emotional conflicts of her adolescence. The triumph of sensibility over sense had made her deeply unhappy then, and ever after she was to resist letting the emotions generated by specific happenings or people enter her music directly.

Extremes of grief or (less frequently) joy sometimes forced her to make deliberate exceptions. In 1977 Barbie would lose her third and last son, Billy Wallace, to cancer. The sisters had never been close; Barbie disliked Edward and what she saw as Liz's rackety life style. (Liz would expatiate on the blessings of the dole in front of Barbie's butler, implying, quite unfairly, that Barbie was prepared to let her struggle unaided.) But the scale of Barbie's personal tragedy shocked Liz; and she wrote *O Absalom!* (1977) in memory of the five dead sons and step-sons.

This almost amounted, however, to a formal, ritual tribute for a special occasion, in the same genre as *Valediction* or her *Requiescat* for Stravinsky. From day to day Liz preferred to keep personal emotions running in their own distinct channel. But control was no more absolute in her music than in her life. 'I *don't* like those works of mine that are too allied with events of my private life,'[5] she once wrote – by implication admitting that such works existed, and that in many places her life had forced its way through the barriers she had erected around her art. It is almost irresistible to read in the title poem of *And Suddenly It's Evening* the prospect she saw herself facing in a future without Edward. 'Everyone is alone on the heart of the earth pierced by a ray of sun: and suddenly it's evening.'[6] She still had faith in life and in composing, where tranquillity was to be found; but darkness was surely coming.

Overt emotion and the new musical openness are both conspicuous in her next large vocal work. Asked if she was interested only in music written *now*, Liz was reminded of John Donne's remark that 'now' is a word that is out of date as soon as it is uttered; and rereading Donne she was led to more general reflections on time and the passing of time, and thence to the suspension of time and timelessness.

Essence of Our Happinesses (1968) is a setting for tenor, chorus and orchestra of three diverse meditations on the ecstatic sense of eternity – the lines of the ninth-century Arab mystic Abu Yasid[7] starting 'I saw the tree of eternity without beginning' (which Conrad suggested to her); an extract from one of Donne's sermons hinging on the statement 'Time is but a short parenthesis in a longe period';[8] and Rimbaud's verses beginning, 'Elle est retrouvée./Quoi? L'éternité.' The Donne movement sets out the argument of the piece, and on either side of it the other two passages illustrate the ecstasy.

Donne observes that the passage of time seems to carry happiness out of the reach of men. 'Honours, Pleasures, Possessions, presented to us, out of time, in our decrepit and distasted and unapprehensive Age, loose their office, and loose their Name. Youth is their Criticall Day. . . . If this Imaginary halfe-nothing, Tyme, be of the Essence of our Happinesses, how can they be thought durable?' His answer is, of course, that they can not. Human, material happinesses are insignificant in the perspective of eternity, the 'longe period' in which time is but a parenthesis; and it is this perspective which the other two sections describe. The three choral sections of the piece are separated by three orchestral dances, corresponding broadly with the three texts – 'Mystikos', the mystic Abu Yasid; 'Chronikos', the Donne with its reflections on time; and 'Manikos', the frenetic exaltation of Rimbaud.[9]

Essence of Our Happinesses was, despite its abstract themes, a personal work; age and the transience of happiness had somehow become constant preoccupations for Liz since Edward's death and her own sixtieth birthday. The piece was also conceived on a very large scale, with a great deal of effort and emotional energy invested in it. 'Everything seemed at stake,'[10] she later wrote of it, and she was sick with nerves before its première, which formed part of the 1970 Prom season at the Royal Albert Hall.

All seemed to go well; the response from the Promenaders was warming, and several of the critics selected *Essence* as the most distinguished of the season's new works. They commented in particular on the strong, even compelling rhythmical energy of the dances – a feature some had felt to be too often lacking in Liz's earlier writing. She had a penchant for constantly changing time signatures, feeling rhythm should be more akin to breathing and spontaneous movement than to the military march, destroyer of freedom. While giving performers more scope to mould individual phrases, this fluidity often made it difficult for either players or listeners to feel changes in the pace and overall direction of pieces which could seem shapeless and meandering as a result.[11] William Alwyn once took her up on her vigorously expressed distaste for 'the tyranny of the bar line': 'It is like saying that by abandoning the tyranny of the picture frame we have freed painting from unnecessary confines; or by abandoning the chessboard we have left the chessmen free to move as we choose.'[12]

The bounding rhythms of the instrumental dances helped to fuse the three texts in *Essence* into a unified whole. But for Liz it was not enough that reviewers should praise the cogency of her design, the elegance of her logic, the clarity of her language. She was writing about mystical inspiration, and would have loved to have been told she had succeeded in exemplifying it. But if she had reached a state of exaltation in her writing, the critics could not follow her there.

Her choral writing, they complained, was not lyrical enough. Some felt this to be a general defect of twelve-tone vocal writing, others saw it as a particular weakness of Liz's music – and a weakness thrown into sharp relief by her persistent choice of markedly lyrical texts. Commenting on her setting of Pablo Neruda's 'Oda à la Tormenta' (1970), Gillian Widdicombe spoke of 'the Lutyens paradox – a spartan composer with a taste for heavily sensual, frantic romantic poetry.'[13] Too often, it was suggested, Liz's commitment to her texts remained an intellectual one, an involvement which she could not translate in musical terms, with the result that she offered to florid texts an accompaniment which barely rose above the recitative in expressivity.

To Liz it seemed that her critics were either obtuse or inconsistent. She could feel her musical personality becoming wider and freer all the time, and could not understand why they perceived no change and persisted in labelling her an austere, desiccated serialist. At the end of the 1960s she was to speak of 'a violent reassessment' of her attitudes. Music, she declared, was 'more allied to religion and magic . . . than [to] elementary arithmetic or science. . . . I for one refuse to compete with computers.'

'Architect's daughter writes blueprint music': she neither forgot nor forgave the old taunt. But the picture this and other critics seemed to have in mind – the bony, eccentric female hunched over metronome, graph paper and slide rule – could hardly have been more ludicrously misleading. Liz lacked almost all the qualities of the genuine intellectual – objectivity, rigorous logic, the capacity for tranquil reflection. At the lowest level, she lacked even the requisite facility with numbers. The point is perhaps best made by comparing the structure of her pieces and the explanations she offered for them with the music and musicology of, say, Pierre Boulez, whom one might call an eminently intellectual composer.

And when Liz did try to speak in a softer voice and a more easily intelligible language, there were those who were still not satisfied. Her music now occasionally opened to admit tonal chords, pulsed rhythms, even what might be described as programme music of a type she had hitherto tended to confine to her film scores.

Anerca (1970) was written for the extraordinary combination of ten guitars (in an ensemble led by her pupil Gilbert Biberian) and the speaking voice of Freda Dowie, an actress Liz particularly admired. The title was derived from the Eskimo word 'anernerk' meaning breath, spirit or ghost. The words were fragments of Eskimo poetry designed to evoke 'the mysterious moment of apprehensive silence before disaster strikes', in a setting of moonlight on wastes of unmarked snow where the dog team is led by the hound of death. Throughout the piece a beautiful, swooning instrumental motif returns again and again, used like a pop melody whose effect is intensified by repetition.

More ingratiating still was the anthology piece *Islands* (1971). Of the four texts on the subject of islands, two are straightforward descriptions of particular scenes, with no hidden subtexts or wider application, leaving the music little function beyond simple illustration. The work opens challengingly enough with an extract from Sophocles's *Philoctetes* in the Volanakis translation, on the island where Philoctetes has been left to die with his gangrenous wound and festering hatreds. But his soliloquy of revenge is followed by Shelley's 'little lawny islet/like mosaic paven by anemone and violet', and Robert Louis Stevenson's contrasting but equally pictorial evocation of the isle of Aros, where great granite boulders step down like cattle to the sea rushing in to meet them.

Even the extract from Rabelais' 'Pantagruel' which ends *Islands* operates in Liz's hands on the level of simple description rather than as the satire Rabelais intended. His aim was to savage the Church; his 'Ringing Island' echoes with the calls of priest-fowls – birds, once priests, who live, fat and idle, in over-magnificent cages. Liz's score is as heavily decorated as any piece of pastoral programme music with bird calls, bees buzzing, bells and 'alleluias'; and her admirers were disappointed. To Andrew Porter, who considered her special contribution to have been 'romanticism tempered by a toughness of mind, and by an intransigence . . . of structural logic',[14] the piece seemed altogether too easy, almost lazy; somehow, obscurely, it was a surrender.

In the early 1970s Liz repeatedly sensed the suggestion that her time might have passed; 'from avant-garde to old hat overnight,' she complained. Certainly she was no longer regarded as a pioneer. Serialism had finally been accepted in Britain in the early 1960s, some forty years after Schoenberg had written the first classifiable twelve-tone work, and a significant number of middle-aged composers had boarded the bandwagon, just as Liz had said they would, making the technique almost a commonplace of 'contemporary' composition. Younger musicians not only took it for granted, they took it to ever greater extremes, at which Liz herself balked. Of the serialisation of dynamics and rhythm, she remarked, with an attempt at bravado, 'I let the young go down the cul-de-sac. They came back with some interesting things which I could take advantage of.'

Alexander Goehr has suggested that at this time Liz was more tempted to be a follower than a leader[15] – that her enthusiasm for the young led her to adopt their ideas and wear some fashions that did not best become her. Certainly there were some superficial borrowings: the loud-hailer from *Revelation and Fall*; tentative experiments with the block forms being explored by Birtwistle and Maxwell Davies. Brian Elias[16] remembers as a student taking her what he considered his first original work, a piece for solo voice on three staves; full of excitement and pride, he was bitterly disappointed by her scathing reaction – she maintained he had mangled his chosen text – and incensed when within a fortnight she came out with *Tre* (1973). A virtuoso display piece written for clarinettist Alan Hacker, *Tre* treats the solo instrument as if it were three, exploiting the three registers and three tone colours – and at one point spreading over three staves.

These, however, were not attempts to imitate the personal styles or mannerisms of other, younger composers, but straightforward appropriations of technical devices, less significant in musical terms than for what they said about her attitudes to those from whom she borrowed. More remarkable, if Liz's independence is in question, is the fact that she chose to keep well clear of the two most conspicuous and fashionable avant-garde movements of the period – the schools of aleatoric and electronic music.

She once wrote aleatoric music, containing random elements, when she obliged a jazz band in one of her operas to ad lib briefly; but since improvisation is of the very nature of jazz in any event, this could hardly be called a wholehearted espousal of the doctrine of chance. In fact, she doubly disapproved of 'chance' music – firstly on the trivial grounds that it was dated, 'dear dead Dada'. 'To hand players a ham sandwich and say interpret it,' she remarked with withering scorn, 'you don't really need to go for four years to any school of music or know the compass of the bassoon, you just need to know where to be able to buy ham.'[17] More seriously, she could not see music as anything but a matter of purposeful choice. Composing, for her, was in its essence about choosing between notes and chords, rhythms and dynamics, with courage and clearheadedness.

Electronic music too was alien to her sense of the dignity of composition. She would offer a variety of facetious excuses for the fact that she was not drawn to it: she could not even change a plug, so could not be expected to feel at home with synthesisers; her one and only rehearsal for *The Pit* on a Sunday in 1947 had been ruined when Edward had been obliged to go in search of a mechanic to repair a defective ondes martenot needed for one of the other pieces in the programme.[18] . . . and so on. But at heart her objection was that the ethos of electronic music-making was uncongenial, the nature of the creative act involved was different and by implication inferior. 'I visited one composer's "laboratory",' she wrote, 'where differing lengths of brown tape hung like the stoats and weasels near the gamekeeper's hut in the Knebworth woods . . . producing the same revulsion in my vegetarian stomach now.'

After *Akapotik Rose* in 1966 the only piece in Liz's output which one might fairly accuse of being 'modish' was one of her most successful – *Time Off? Not A Ghost Of A Chance!* (1967–8), a 'charade in four scenes with three interruptions', which the uncharitable might portray as an attempt to cash in on the 1960s vogue for music-theatre.

Time Off certainly has some of the hallmarks of what would then have been called trendiness. It is peppered with topical references – to Edward Heath, to a 'great leader' whom she identified in different drafts as John F. Kennedy, Stalin, Churchill and Mao Tse-tung, and to the vagaries of the GPO. It employs the collage effect then fashionable in all branches of the arts,[19] piling together masque, masks, mime, tapes, film and a whiff of Noh, and forcibly mixing 'high' and 'low' culture – music-hall routines and a pop song within the irredeemably exclusive medium of serial music. It betrays at every turn her irresistible urge to provoke – as one authority on censorship puts it, the 'desire to spit in Nanny's eye'.[20] (In Liz's case, it was perhaps the family's eye she was aiming for; the Lord Chamberlain privileged to read her verses about farting and her rendition of homosexual banter was Lord Cobbold, husband of her cousin Hermione Lytton.)

But *Time Off* must be seen in context. In Liz's defence, she had been intrigued since the early 1950s by the possibilities of an alternative to traditional opera, well before the 'music-theatre' vogue was in full swing. And *Time Off* evolved not out of a vacuum, but in reaction to the fate of a much-cherished project which was anything but modish, and it should perhaps not be judged on its own, but more as a work written on the rebound. In the knowledge that she could not find a stage or an audience for the serious messages she wanted to convey, she contented herself with a joke.

The serious project for which she cared so deeply was an opera she made from Elias Canetti's play *The Numbered*, a parable on the de-structive implications of knowing the future. For Canetti, preoccupied with the behaviour of the individual within the crowd, this meant not future history but the future of the individual man. He described a society where each knows how long he will live, is in fact named according to his lifespan – the hero's name is Fifty – but is ignorant of when he was born and thus of when precisely he will die.

The Numbered explores the effects of this knowledge on personal and communal morality; the child whose name is Ten is indulged and excused any fault, and women select husbands for their potential longevity. Liz was mesmerised by the idea, and dismissed all objections to the notion of turning play into opera. 'Deep down,' remembers

Canetti, 'I am afraid I was never quite convinced that it could be done. But I had a very high opinion of her, it was very much her wish, and Mr Volanakis promised to help her with the libretto.'[21]

In her excitement, and working under the unfamiliar constraint of having a libretto which she could cut or vary only very little if at all, Liz disregarded all her own practical precepts. She set *The Numbered* for eighteen soloists, chorus, three actors, and a symphony orchestra which included a huge percussion section, two mandolins and two electric guitars; it lasted over two hours not including intervals, and had twenty scenes, all similar in construction. With part of her mind she must have known that its chances of being staged were slim; she could not even afford to have the score duplicated, at £20 a copy, to send round for promotional purposes. 'It may be the greatest white elephant,' she wrote to a pupil only days after finishing it, 'but I had to do it.'[22] For the rest, she hoped against hope; and the total neglect of *The Numbered*, which remains unperformed, was one of the severest disappointments of her life.

Her next stage work, therefore, was specifically designed to be cheap and easy to mount, *Time Off* (or *Time Orf*, as Liz herself pronounced it) was scored for far smaller forces – one baritone, one actor, a vocal quartet, a chorus of sixteen, and a small instrumental group consisting of an alto flute, two keyboard players doubling harpsichord, piano, celeste and electric organ, two electric guitars and four percussion players. A black-and-white drawing in comparison with the rich oils of *The Numbered*, Liz called it; and the tone too was lighter. The themes, as one would expect from her, were serious, but they were presented almost in cabaret style.

In calling *Time Off* a 'charade', Liz was hinting that she intended it to be an elaborate musical guessing game for the audience. There were elements in it, she claimed, of both the riddle and the crossword puzzle. But both of these have predetermined answers, and this is not something one could say with confidence about *Time Off*.

When the piece was accepted by the New Opera Company for production in 1972, the producer Anthony Besch visited Liz to discuss its interpretation. As he remembers the occasion, in the course of a three-hour encounter he spoke not one single word beyond noises of assent, as Liz poured out 'a wonderful Joyceian monologue'. A small proportion of the flow had to do with *Time Off*, but she came nowhere near explaining what she thought the piece was about; and when, later, he asked for further illumination, she replied that it meant whatever people wanted it to mean. Guess. . . . *Time Off* 'meant' no more than the sum of its words and its music, she concluded glibly; the problem is that sometimes this amounted to a good deal, sometimes to nothing at all.

There were four word-syllables to be 'guessed' in Liz's charade – time, chance, age, and ghosts/spirit, set out in four scenes disjoined by 'interruptions'. Two characters move through every episode. The singer is Harold – serious, idealistic, introspective, chronically uncertain; Liz had John Shirley-Quirk in mind as his physical type while she was writing.[23] The actor is Stooge – frivolous, cynical, sardonic, camp, a Feste figure whose function is to deflate pretension and lower the *angst* level. The face Liz fitted to this character was that of Buster Keaton or at other times, bizarrely, Tom Jones, and she was not pleased by an initial casting suggestion of Harry H. Corbett.[24] In the event the part was taken successfully by Barry Foster; fortuitously, Foster bore quite a marked physical resemblance to the baritone cast as Harold, John Gibbs – a bonus for Anthony Besch, whose conception of the piece hinged on presenting the two figures as complementary aspects of a single personality.

Two of the sources of inspiration discernible in the libretto of *Time Off* are threads to be followed through its maze of ideas. Liz was interested in the theories of Jacques Monod. All forms of life, he argues, are the products of chance (through unpredictable mutation) and necessity (by Darwinian selection). 'Man knows at last that he is alone in the indifferent immensity of the universe, whence he has emerged by chance';[25] no values are implicit in the order of the universe, and man must choose his own.

Choice is one of the themes of Stevie Smith's poem 'Harold's Leap', the last lines of which Liz used to conclude *Time Off*. 'Harold was always afraid to climb high,/But something urged him on,/ He felt he should try.'[26] Stevie's Harold has the wit to know there are decisions to be made, but not how he should make them. He has the courage to make his leap between two rocks – but is killed trying.

Time Off? Not A Ghost Of A Chance! is an account of the progress of Liz's Harold/Stooge through life. It is not impossible that, consciously or unconsciously, Liz had been influenced by Louis MacNeice's modern moralities, which Reggie Smith described as 'follow[ing] a kind of contemporary Everyman through the snares and temptations that modern civilisation sets for intellectual and professional people'.[27] We observe Harold's efforts to identify the choices he must make and values he should adopt, his struggle to come to grips with the most profound questions and find some answers before meeting the same fate as Stevie's Harold. What is the nature of time? What becomes of the past? (and here Liz quotes Villon's lines 'Where are the snows of yesteryear?')

Where does the future spring from? Is anything preordained? (Her references here include the Jehovah's Witnesses and the prophecies of Nostradamus.) Where does man come from? Has he appeared by chance? (It was during this section that she introduced the jazz band with its 'chance' music.) Where does the young person disappear to as age approaches? Where is happiness to be found? What is the spirit or ghost of man?

In *Time Off*, Liz had given herself the opportunity to offer a medley of opinions on subjects which intrigued her. The making of choices was a principal preoccupation of hers; at moments the dual figure of Harold-Stooge can be heard to speak with her voice and the piece becomes a personal testament, working by free association.

One of the wittier passages in *Time Off* is a diatribe against the type of bureaucrat-administrator she saw as her natural enemy and Edward's destroyer: 'Inner Circle – Underground; little cliques go chattering round. . . . Musicmakers/Music-breakers/Messianic, preying pundits, mantra-murmurs/Indecisive, catching credit, sudden fervours. . . . Deaf and diddle, peacock vain, "Admins" wander in their train.' In other scenes she delivers herself of snipes against homosexuals, political *bêtes noires*, 'the bloody young'. And occasionally, amongst the badinage, the *cris de coeur* are heard: 'What are the advantages of youth if it is infected by the black vein of melancholy?' 'Can one love someone when one hates oneself?'

For much of the piece, however, Liz chose to deck herself in other men's flowers, making her points with a mishmash of quotations from Sappho, Eliot, Baudelaire, Jonson, Japanese lyrics, and (liberally) Yeats. She felt these greater writers lent authority to her work, but frequently she seems to lose more than she gains by her imports; an elegant, alien phrase is introduced and the tension at once slackens. (She may herself dimly have sensed this; in an early draft of the libretto she made Stooge complain, 'No dead geography AND no more quotes.')[28]

Speaking through the mouths of others was partly the product of a form of cowardice, which she had betrayed once before when inventing a librettist to 'take the rap' for the words of *Infidelio*. Now in *Time Off* she used Stooge as her shield against ridicule. She informed John Amis in 1970 that she had derived some of Stooge's characteristics from him; in particular, his reaction to serious emotions – a very English embarrassment covered by facetiousness.[29] One might say that in using Stooge to provide a deflationary running commentary on Harold's earnest heart-searchings, she was manifesting exactly the same reaction herself. Every time she/Harold expresses a deeply felt sentiment, she/Stooge hastily cracks a joke or changes the subject, lest she be accused of taking herself too seriously and so look foolish.

Time Off contains some passages of beautiful music, some athletic word-play, and a few good jokes; it was in its way a type of music-theatre which had not been seen before, and has not really been attempted again since. But as compared with *The Numbered* it represents a failure of nerve. Liz had gone from full-scale opera most of the way towards revue. She had conceived the elegant and impressive idea of an intellectual charade whose solution would offer insights into some of the profoundest mysteries of existence – and achieved, in the end, little more than what one of her pupils described as musical 'pinches on the behind of society'.[30]

CHAPTER SIXTEEN

A Woman's Work

THE PUBLICITY which was to accompany the first production of *Time Off* would set the seal on Liz's image as a 'personality' in the world of British music. Since reputation almost always trails achievement, the media were in essence celebrating what Liz had been over the last twenty years – a pioneer and leading protagonist of a once-revolutionary musical technique now accepted as an essential resource of the contemporary composer. Occasionally they went as far as to depict her as mother to a younger generation of serialists, with Dallapiccola perhaps as the father.

Liz herself would not have claimed to have procreated any direct musical descendants, and it is too early to look for signs of her lasting influence in the music of pupils some of whom are still in their thirties. But in the sense that she was an affectionate, authoritative and inspiring teacher, the matriarch image is not completely inappropriate.

Liz's teaching was remarkable not so much for the doctrines she expounded or the technical information she handed on as for the attitude she encouraged. As she frequently remarked, she had no intention of proselytising – she could not even spell it – and as often as not pupils had to ask for instruction in serial technique if they wanted it. She would recommend mastering the use of twelve-tone methods as an invaluable aid to aural awareness, but did not teach it systematically. (One or two of her pupils have doubted whether she would in fact have been capable of teaching it, so vague and idiosyncratic was her own use of serial technique by the time they went to her.)

Far from feeling obliged to pass on the dodecaphonic message, Liz much preferred helping younger musicians to discover the resources they had within themselves – with the single proviso that what they were looking for was *new* music. She was deeply suspicious and resentful of what she perceived as musical time-serving, hard on those who liked to 'slip into something a little more comfortable' for the sake of an easy life. From time to time this insistence on breaking new ground was counterproductive; at least one pupil, Carol Barratt, felt she had been pushed further towards the avant-garde than really suited her own musical personality.

And occasionally Liz allowed other prejudices to impinge. Robert Saxton, who went to study with her in 1970, once showed her a threnody he had written for children killed in the Holocaust (he is himself Jewish), to be told that it looked like nothing more than a bid for sympathetic reviews. During the five years he was her pupil, Saxton was inclined to treat her anti-semitism as a joke in poor taste; she was patently very fond of him and his family, and they of her. But in retrospect the prejudice seems darker to him and more significant, and he much regrets having allowed her to dissuade him from at least experimenting then with music of a specifically Jewish character.

Nor was the teaching of theory ever Liz's forte; she had not changed in this respect since the hasty telephone call to Bax in the 1950s on the subject of the major third. (Almost twenty years later she could write to Brian Elias, 'I suppose I once knew what the Neopolitan [sic] sixth was and my ear surely knows the bugger, but I've managed quite well for fifty years without recognising it by name and have felt no want.') She was not the person you would go to, one pupil has remarked, for detailed analysis of a score; she herself studied scores only sporadically, and listened to music less and less as time went on.[1]

But her practical knowledge of the craft of composition was an unfailing and invaluable source to be tapped. She trained her pupils to write legibly and lay out a score correctly; as Edward had taught her, she taught them the range of every instrument, and insisted that 'inspiration' should not lead them beyond the bounds of the playable – all this came under the heading of the 'professionalism' on which she had placed so high a premium all her working life. More important, she knew and could explain how to make a part 'sound' for an instrument – how to display the instrument at its strongest and most characteristic, or exploit its oddities to advantage.

She had what Alison Bauld calls 'a hearing eye'; she could look at the music pupils brought her and pinpoint precisely what would be wrong when the notes were sounded. More than one student has observed that while she only rarely offered useful suggestions as to the form of a piece, her ear for texture was almost faultless.

After years of sitting through over-stuffed contemporary concert programmes, she spoke feelingly of the need to keep compositions within a manageable length. Of one piece by a young composer (not a pupil), she remarked that it should be shortened by twenty-five minutes – *any* twenty-five minutes. And without trying to influence her pupils' individual styles, she urged consistency above all things. She once rebuked Robert Saxton for offering her a piece which hovered uncertainly between tonality and thoroughgoing serialism: 'I don't mind if you write in D minor, but do it *properly*. I don't like going into a good restaurant and wasting my money on a meal which is roast beef with a Chinese meal on top and a curry on top of that. One thing at a time, please.'

Above all, Liz had a genius for conveying the feeling of why it was exciting to compose. She could remember how she had felt when it first dawned on her that she wanted to write music. She felt about music the way Dylan Thomas had told her he felt about poetry – 'I love the bloody stuff'; [2] and the commitment which kept her composing until she died was something she found it easy, even necessary, to share.

The impression she made on her young students when they first met her was usually unforgettable, and at least partly calculated to shock the offspring of conventional middle-class homes. Robert Saxton remembers his first arrival at King Henry's Road in 1970.

> She was sitting there in a green corduroy trouser suit with flared bottoms, bent over the phone, having a row with the answering service. 'The day staff tell me it's the night staff, the night staff tell me it's the fucking day staff, I'm fed up with all of you, you can all go to hell, bugger ORF!', and she slammed down the phone. She turned round, Conrad said, 'This is your student,' she said, 'You're *early*,' and I nearly left. . . . She said, 'Now – tell me about yourself. You haven't got much talent, have you, but we'll have to find some.' I said, 'I've been helped by Britten,' and she said, 'You can wipe that smile off your face for a start'. . . .

From then on her pupils knew to expect an overheated room, a pot of appallingly stewed tea constantly topped up with hot water, and chocolate cake which had to be Fuller's. Those who went to Belsize Park Gardens in the 1960s would usually find a notice pinned to the front door, with an arrow pointing to a prefabricated hut in the garden, which was her refuge from extraneous noise. (To Liz all other sounds were unwanted when she was composing, because every noise – traffic, distant conversation, running water – had pitch and competed with the notes in her head. To whistle in the house was a cardinal sin, Conrad remembered; the notion that all musicians' houses are full of music could not have been further from the truth in her case.) Later, after Liz had moved back to King Henry's Road in 1969, they would make their way past Mo's pots, the materials for Rose's dressmaking, the children's tricycles, up the stairs to the top floor. 'She'd be waiting for me at the top of the stairs,' recalls Carol Barratt. 'I can see her now, leaning on the banister. . . . Such an affectionate person.'

As the lessons wore on, tea would merge into drinks – Coca-Cola for Liz in the 1960s and early 1970s, wine for her pupils, or whisky served in wine glasses. And the lessons always did wear on, far beyond the regulation hour for which the students actually paid and late into the evenings. To some extent Liz modelled herself as a teacher on Polyxena Fletcher, the heroine of her youth, of whom she had written, 'Music, life and people were inseparable to her, and our lessons, which lasted hours and seemed timeless, were occupied as much with talk and discussion as piano playing.'

Liz's pupils were more sophisticated than she had been at their age, and she did not become the yardstick for all their experiences as Polyxena Fletcher had been for hers. But she played an extremely important part in the lives of the half-dozen of so to whom she was closest, involving herself far more deeply in their lives than the average teacher, trying to meet emotional as well as musical needs.

Many of her pupils came to her very young, and she felt strongly maternal towards them. Conscious of her failures with her own children and husbands, she had a great deal of emotional energy to expend, and she poured it into her pupils' lives. Alison Bauld had lost her own mother shortly before becoming Liz's pupil, and remembers

the generosity of spirit which made her accept a phone call from a totally unknown Australian girl wanting help. . . . I had a lesson for an hour, which was more like two, handed over the statutory £5 – which she then gave to Conrad to take me to the theatre. From that moment on she regarded herself as a substitute mother. . . . I can remember her tucking me into bed as if I were a child. When she met somebody with whom she need feel no embarrassment in her displays of affection, they were real and very attractive. . . . I think she was an impulsive and a romantic person, with a sense of occasion, and if she had a responsibility to you at that moment, she gave you her all.

To Michael Blake Watkins (who with Brian Elias and Alison Bauld formed the 'inner circle' of pupils in the mid-1960s) she wrote on his twenty-first birthday,

> If I were a fairy godmother (and I'm neither 'fairy' nor 'god' nor 'mother'), I would wish you
>   (a) successful and fruitful relationship with EXCELLENT PUB-LISHER
>   (b) several performances a week
>   (c) lots of filthy lucre
>   (d) AND – more important than ALL
>   that you keep for ever your sweet nature and kindness and do not become swollen-headed – a pundit – a bore – WHEN YOU ARE RICH AND FAMOUS – SOON.

But she also made these pupils forty years her junior feel that they were colleagues in the practice of a vocation which she took deeply seriously. Being a composer was, she said, like being a priest administering a religion; you do your best to serve music, it is not a commodity for your use. You are engaged in the same activity as Monteverdi and Mozart; think of their achievement and you look to the hills. But reverence did not keep her from getting caught up in the sheer thrill of the chase after a new idea. Brian Elias had a vivid memory of her reaction when he took her some piano pieces that she considered original – 'wildly excited, hopping round', putting her cigarette in her mouth the wrong way round and burning her lip.

And her enthusiasm was highly contagious; when he was twenty Robert Saxton wrote to her, 'Mozart once said he only had to go into an opera house and hear the orchestra tuning up before the curtain rose, and he immediately wanted to rush home and write an opera himself, and I feel much the same way coming to see you.' He remembered later,

> Whenever I went into Liz's sitting-room I had a smell of an artist's room.... A wonderful lamp which was an upturned French horn with a little lavatory chain to switch it on. Things on the wall that had been given to her or Edward by people like Cocteau. This great big table, with a sloping architect's board, just made out of hardboard, and her stop-watches. And her piano, with a writing board specially arranged so you could put lots of manuscript paper right across it. All sorts of African drums and her grotty old settee and her telly and Edward's score of *Pierrot lunaire*, which Schoenberg had signed. ... Just the room of an

artist. You could smell that she had known Constant Lambert and Alan Rawsthorne and William Walton, Everything was real, and for me, coming from a middle-class Jewish family and boarding school, it was *very* exciting.

On Brian Elias's twenty-first birthday she sent him eight telegrams: seven of them reading simply 'BOOM BOOM BOOM' – three rounds each of a twenty-one gun salute – and the eighth bearing her love. 'I can't describe the warmth she emanated, sitting one to one,' he has said of those early lessons, 'the warmth and generosity never faded, every lesson they were there'; he thought of her as his guru, 'a musical mother to me', and he has kept the first manuscript he ever took her, as a talisman.

The public image of a teacher is hard to convey, since her achievements lie in other people's careers, and the press preferred to home in on other angles of Liz's public persona. One well-worn motif was the marked contrast between her 'serious' and her 'hack' careers. Looking at her serious music by itself, the BBC had been correct in observing in the 1950s that there was no living for her in composing. Though she was by no means at or even near the bottom of the earnings table for serious composers, in 1971 all her BBC broadcasts added together earned her less than a single showing of *Dr Terror's House of Horrors* in Spanish cinemas. Her total earnings that year from *O Saisons! O Châteaux!*, one of her more popular works, was £1 3s 10d; and she claimed to have been paid for her Prom commissions in Green Shield stamps.

As ever, the income from films remained crucial, but it was typical of Liz's luck that the male strongholds she had worked so hard to storm should turn out to offer little real security. By the end of the 1960s the British film industry was in decline, and Liz's film career forked in two different directions.

She was able to take a break from the industrial 'shorts' and travelogues when she was offered a retainer by her cousin Anne Balfour-Fraser who, besides having trained as a singer and trekked across the Sahara, ran a film production company called Samaritan Films. Some of Samaritan's output, it is true, was of the most severely practical kind. Liz was asked to illustrate in music a history of housework, made for Bex-Bissell (*A Woman's Work*, 1961); a public information film on child molesting (*Never Talk To Strangers*, 1971); a short documentary for the Post Office on the process of choosing the colour gradations for stamps in the new decimal currency (*Rainbow Verdict*, 1970); a plea to hospital administrators to abandon old-fashioned methods of sterilising utensils and clothing on the wards (*Central Sterile Supply Department*, 1963); a promotion for anti-depressant drugs, at a time when they were not so freely prescribed (*Depression – Diagnosis in General Practice*, 1961). (Liz successfully concealed from her cousin the fact that she was herself taking anti-depressants with increasing regularity.)

But Samaritan also offered a series of art films, which engaged Liz's genuine interest and produced some of her very best film music. In 1963 David Thompson, then *The Times*'s art critic, was asked by Samaritan to make a film about Francis Bacon to accompany his Tate retrospective. He was apprehensive about working with Liz, some of whose music had struck him in the past as 'a little etiolated'; but by good fortune he had recently come to know Webern's Five Pieces for Orchestra, and won Liz's sympathy immediately by suggesting a film with no spoken commentary, only an accompanying musical sequence structured similarly in five movements. The result, inspired by Liz's affection for Bacon, had a heat and strength that considerably surprised Thompson.

The same was true of her music for *Turner*, which they made together in 1966. Full of sweeping, sensual vigour, and incorporating with ease a lavish quotation from *Harold in Italy* to illustrate Turner's travels, the score betrayed a more than sneaking sympathy with some aspects of nineteenth-century culture. The music for *The Pre-Raphaelite Revolt* (1967) required more of an effort of will. Liz succeeded in simulating, with a very small orchestra, an admirable variety of styles – English pastoral, for the creed of fidelity to nature; Victorian parlour ballad, to accompany Ford Madox Brown's *The Last of England*; a pious Hammond organ for what she described as 'that repulsive picture' *The Light of the World*.[3] But she had no real interest in the paintings, and it was not a score of which she was proud.

She took more pleasure in the best of the work she was doing at the same time at the other end of the spectrum of taste. The major part of Liz's income in her last years came from television repeats of films with titles like *The Earth Dies Screaming* (1964), *The Terrornauts* (1967), and *The Skull* (1965).

The skull in the title of what was one of Liz's favourite horror ventures is a relic of the Marquis de Sade. and it spends the film inciting its second owner to crime when the moon is new. Liz's score has all the hallmarks of horror music – a thudding heartbeat in the percussion for the compulsory walks in the dark, seesawing strings and cymbals trembling as cupboards creak open to reveal The Thing in grey moulded plastic, eye sockets glowing green as a sepulchral voice intones 'The Skull is angry . . .' The owner's wife is preserved from its snapping jaws when she rolls over in her sleep to reveal a crucifix in the folds of her nightie, and an organ does battle with the clarinet that represents the bony menace; but the outcome is otherwise a clean sweep for the skull. Liz loved to retail instalments of this deathless work. It also amused her that the audience for horror films accepted without a murmur shrill atonal music which they would have rejected with irritation in the concert hall.

In the eyes of the press, there was an added piquancy in the fact that the composer of these lurid works was not merely a highbrow but also a woman. The issue of the 'female composer' was of course another favourite topic for interviewers in the 1960s, with the explosion of interest in feminism, but it was one on which Liz had in fact changed her views very little since the time of the Macnaghten–Lemare Concerts in the 1930s. She dismissed it as 'the subject which has dogged – or should I say "bitched" – me all my life',[4] found organised feminism tedious and irrelevant, and was only provoked to wrath by a single aspect of male discrimination.

Why, she asked, did people speak of 'women's music' and 'female composers' and yet stop short of implying that male homosexuals wrote 'queer' music? 'If women are to be butts,' she argued, 'let homosexuals be also . . . and impotence or any other private sexual consideration, all of which, no doubt, affects one's work.'[5] In 1973 she would write to *The Times* complaining that William Glock was labelled a supporter of Women's Lib because he had included four pieces by female composers in that season's Proms, and yet no one drew the obvious inference from the fact that he had programmed the work of no less than sixteen male homosexuals. (In 1979, five minutes before appearing live on Radio Four's 'Start the Week' she threatened to address Russell Harty as a 'homosexual interviewer' if he so much as mouthed the phrase 'lady composer'; both followed the path of prudence.)

There were other causes she felt more strongly about – the decline of standards in broadcasting, the invasion of privacy as represented by the census (she refused to fill it in), and the Wilson government's apparent support for American policy in Vietnam. She was no more diffident now about airing her views than she had been when she embarrassed Ursula in front of her weekend guests, and she gave a series of radio talks on subjects ranging from the ISCM to the youth of the day.

The most cogent lecture of all was, perhaps fortunately, never delivered. Liz was wont to refer to critics as 'the second oldest profession'; and her talk on music criticism was scripted to culminate in Reger's riposte to an enemy journalist: 'I am in the smallest room in the house. I have your review before me. In a moment it will be behind me.' In Liz's patrician tones this anecdote would no doubt have had impact, but higher echelons within the BBC disapproved, and the talk was cancelled.[6]

The Liz of the late 1960s and early 1970s is the one most people care to remember. To some extent she had inherited the mantle of Edith Sitwell in the public eye; there were superficial physical resemblances, and both, it seemed, were archetypal English lady eccentrics, odd but grand.

Liz gave every appearance of enjoying a certain level of outrage; she derived much of her energy from experiencing outrage and her pleasure from provoking it in others. This trait was cultivated rather than instinctive, but in combination with the grandeur that did come naturally, it made her formidable. Composer Anthony Gilbert,[7] who was also her principal music editor, remembers her as having limitless concern for people; when she entered any room she would make a point of speaking to everyone and finding out about their lives and preoccupations. But quite often her enquiries took the form of demanding gruffly, 'Who's this, then?' At one point it was rumoured in musical circles that Richard Rodney Bennett's new opera was to be 'Who's Afraid of Elisabeth Lutyens?'[8]

Friends who knew Liz well – and they included Bennett – were aware of depths of insecurity behind the ferocious façade, and when not at odds with her, found her touching. It was while working on *Turner* with David Thompson that Liz first met his wife, the actress Freda Dowie, who spoke the passages of poetry that formed the greater part of the commentary. Inspired by her voice, Liz wrote several pieces for the combination of speaker and instruments. (Besides *Anerca*, 1970, there were *One and the Same*, 1974, and *Like a Window*, 1976). From the years they worked together, Freda was left with an ineradicable image of Liz in the concert hall – 'this little figure, little tiny head and short hair, marching up the hall and on to the platform and bowing absolutely completely, like a Japanese, from the knees, arms straight by her sides – none of the old bob or duck of the head, complete classical bow, just once, and then off, lips compressed to keep back emotion.'[9]

Certainly Liz was anything but stately in her grandeur. She was an exceedingly fast, passionate and argumentative driver, and an erratic housekeeper. Generally as untidy as she had been in the days when the floor of her Paris room was invisible beneath a layer of shoes and manuscript paper, she was also subject to sporadic violent fits of cleanliness. Since she only really approved of two groups in society – the upper and the working classes – on these occasions she was unable simply to pick up the Hoover, but was transmogrified into Mrs Mop, on her knees with a bar of green carbolic. Her dress, too, was hit and miss. She would buy expensive clothes and then immediately get grease or ash on them, or they would fall off their hangers and lie at the bottom of the wardrobe until they were unwearable and she had to buy more.[10]

Liz's attitude to money in general was inconsistent. She had inherited at least some of her father's anxieties about poverty, heightened by her struggle to survive each summer when film and radio work dwindled and the income tax demand invariably arrived before the cheque from the Performing Rights Society on which she largely depended. At the same time she seemed to have imbibed Edwardian notions of style abe hospitality. When making his gloomy prognostications and reproaching his wife for her travelling and her theatre tickets, Sir Edwin always seemed conveniently to ignore his own account at the Garrick. Liz too kept meticulous accounts but seemed to draw no moral from them.

She invariably felt poor in comparison with the Mansfield Street days, and she drove hard bargains with the BBC and other paymasters. But this did not stop her from buying five pairs of boots at a time,[11] offering guests champagne at all hours, smoking over fifty cigarettes a day, persisting in telephone habits developed before calls were costed in time units,[12] and simply giving money away – to her children, her pupils, her friends, or acquaintances she thought needed cheering up.

'She had no idea of how to do things easily, or even reasonably,' remembers Katharina Wolpe. 'She was the most unreasonable person. I rather liked it.' Many other people forgave Liz much for her warmth, and their scattered memories of her in the 1960s are affectionate: Liz helping her granddaughter to dig for worms to be stroked.[13] Liz dancing the *pas-de-deux* from *Swan Lake* with Malcolm Williamson at three in the morning, and breaking two ribs;[14] Liz camping overnight in a car in the middle of Salisbury Plain with Virgil Thomson; Liz passionately arguing the merits of Edward G. Marshall's case in *The Defenders*.[15] 'She had a lovely *basic* quality,' remembers Stephen Plaistow, now in charge of contemporary music at the BBC, then a senior producer and a close friend. 'If you were in a jam, or needed advice, she was certainly someone you'd trust. You could say *anything* to her; it might not be altogether wise, it might reappear in unguarded moments, but you could say it.'[16]

There were a good many friends to cheer when in 1969 she was awarded the CBE. The honour was canvasssed for her by Jane Manning and Anthony Payne, with the support of Bliss, Boult, Bennett and a forgiving Michael Tippett; Liz went perfunctorily through the motions of pouring scorn on the honours system, but was patently delighted. 'I think I will go and take my CBE,' she told Stephen Plaistow. 'I've always wanted to tell the Queen she really ought to wear a higher bra.'

Her other reason for accepting the honour, she claimed, was to annoy her relations. 'I feel I have at best been patronised, at worst snubbed by my family as being the poor relation,' she wrote, 'and this was one in the eye for them.'[17] She told Malcolm Williamson she had decided to take it to give her brother Robert a heart attack.[18] Communication between the two of them had virtually ceased since their father's death, when Liz had been outraged by what she considered the unfairness of the will, and by Robert's subsequent behaviour. He had written to her on Edward's death, though he had had to ask around for her address, but since then they had lost contact. With his far higher regard for family, title and the Lytton heritage, he would have found it galling that, all the Lutyens children having gone out of the peerage at Lady Emily's death, Liz was the only one to re-enter it on her own account.

But otherwise the award did not generate as much chagrin as Liz might have liked. Mary was unaffectedly pleased. And the person whom Liz would perhaps have liked to impress and irritate almost more than anyone else was dead. Since the late 1950s Liz had grown closer to Ursula; once she was widowed and no longer mistress of Blagdon, the contrast between their circumstances was no longer so conspicuous. In 1967 Liz went up to Northumberland for a concert of her settings of Stevie Smith and Shakespeare, which Ursula had arranged for the benefit of the Laing Art Gallery. (The soloists were Ian Glennie, whom Ursula had always liked, and Jane Manning.) Stevie went with her, and a remarkable pair confronted the staid, culture-loving Newcastle audience. Stevie was wearing an imperfectly dyed evening dress with the familiar Peter Pan collar, which had travelled to Newcastle in her handbag; Liz, more dashing, displayed a white Persian lamb coat, butterfly glasses, scarlet nails and green suede boots; and both sported the long, dead-straight hairstyles which, in the opinion of the local paper, were characteristic of the British female highbrow.[19] (Nicholas Ridley, who drove the pair back to London after the concert, remembered them spending the whole journey fighting about who would sit in the front seat.)

Liz had often been disturbed by what she felt was Stevie's excessive insistence on 'gin and tears'; and she became increasingly uncomfortable that afternoon at the way Stevie and Ursula were talking about death. 'She kept saying, "I wish they wouldn't",' remembered Jane Manning.[20] Soon afterwards Ursula, who had been suffering from depression, committed suicide.

By 1969 Liz must have felt that at last she was receiving her due. She had visited the United States for the first time, with successful concerts in New York and Pittsburgh; her friend and sponsor, Benjamin Sonnenberg, had been nervous of trouble with the immigration authorities over her past political affiliations,[21] but once safely in America she was much fêted, with appearances on breakfast television and a smart New York party in her honour, whose guest list included Truman Capote, Anita Loos, Norman Mailer, Edward Albee, Isaac Stern and Leonard Bernstein.

At home that year she received the Lord Mayor's Midsummer Award of £1500, given annually to a figure who had as yet been 'insufficiently rewarded' for an outstanding contribution to the arts; winners in other years included the poet Edmund Blunden and the writer and painter David Jones. She was invited to the first ever Ladies' Night at the Royal Academy of Arts ('the final seal of success' in the view of the *Evening Standard*) in company with Violet Bonham-Carter, Edith Evans, Barbara Hepworth and Rebecca West; and she had her portrait drawn for an anthology on women entitled *Women and Men's Daughters*, this time rubbing shoulders with the racier team of Jean Muir, Cleo Laine and Virginia Wade. From any point of view (other than the financial, as she was always quick to point out), she was collecting the badges of success.

But for Liz, renown had come almost too late. 'Honours, Pleasures, Possession, presented to us, out of time, in our decrepit and distasted and unapprehensive Age, loose their Office.' She was far from decrepit, but her health was indifferent enough to alloy her enjoyment of most things. 'One day I will show you all,' she had written defiantly; but Sir Edwin, Lady Emily, Ursula and Edward had all died before she could prove herself conclusively. And there was a pervasive sense now that, parallel with the passage from the avant-garde to the *déjà vu*, she was crossing the divide into old age. Out of time, out of time. . . . It was as if, one friend observed, she suddenly made the decision to become an old lady.[22]

Chapter Seventeen

Imagination Dead, Imagine

'The bad,' wrote Rebecca West once, 'is more easily perceived than the good. A fresh lobster does not give such pleasure to the consumer as a stale one will give him pain.'[1] Liz would heartily have agreed.

In 1971 she was sixty-five, and it should have been a triumphant, fulfilling year. The BBC's Radio Three celebrated her birthday with a generosity which their predecessors in the Music Department of the 1950s would have found incredible, mounting a retrospective series of six programmes devoted exclusively to her work. The Park Lane Group, leading promoters of new music, made her their featured composer in a further series of six concerts. Her autobiography had been commissioned, and its publication was imminent. *Time Off? Not A Ghost Of A Chance!* was scheduled to be produced in London. She had won some extravagant admirers; the following year Nicolas Nabokov was to describe her as 'one of the best serial composers of all time'.[2]

But for Liz the applause was never enough. After the première of *The Tears of Night* (1971), one of the very few pieces she wrote for the London Sinfonietta, she was given a rapturous reception; but when Robert Saxton congratulated her, she shrugged it off. 'Think of Churchill,' she said, 'and the kind of cheers he got.' Temperamentally she was unsuited to success, could never really believe it was happening. She quoted her friend Roberto Gerhard's description of the experience of success as 'essentially fleeting: it never seems to grow into . . . a sort of permanent, unflappable state of self-assurance'.[3]

1971 was, like many high points, a peak from which the ground sloped away precipitously. 'Being sixty-five did not seem auspicious or much fun,' wrote Liz, and her birthday marked something of a crisis of confidence. She complained that the BBC series, for all its length, had failed to do justice to her work; the pieces could have been better chosen, much more thoroughly rehearsed, and sometimes more sensitively performed. But her dissatisfaction was at least partly directed at herself, reflecting uncertainty in her own mind about what exactly she had achieved.

Liz had not lost faith in her ability, but she could not avoid confronting the fact that few people were apparently willing to listen to what she so urgently wanted to say. The obscurity imposed on her in the 1950s had in one sense been a protection, postponing the moment when she would present herself and her work to the public and discover what they thought of it. Throughout the 1960s there had been more frequent opportunities to hear her music; now with the retrospective came the chance to sum up and pronounce judgement.

At this point she might almost have welcomed a furious frontal attack; it would at least have been a gesture of interest. Instead, for the most part, there were formal and respectful pats from the critics – and elsewhere, the profoundest indifference. In her sixty-fifth birthday year, she said later, she received two letters about her work: one a fan letter from a young American composer, John Patrick Thomas; the other, in the wake of the BBC broadcasts, from a listener who asked simply, 'Why is your music so ugly?' [4]

'Is this it?' she might have felt justified in asking. Was this the sum total of the career for which she had strained two marriages and jeopardised the happiness of her children? 'When physically low, I feel like the Red Queen,' she wrote. 'It seems to have taken all the running I could do to keep in the same place.'

For the first time she faltered in her determination to compose. To be completely content with what one had written was, she thought, a sign of complacency and self-deception; but her fierce self-criticism had always previously acted as a stimulus to try again. Now she not only doubted that she had achieved anything in the past, she lacked confidence that she ever would achieve anything.

'To my deep consternation, as I grow old I find some ambition and its first cousin envy rearing their ugly heads,' she wrote.

> With a reason, however. If I still, nearing seventy, get [*only*] the first under-rehearsed performance before a work is shelved ... with few repeats and nothing played often enough to be known, still less in repertoire, and nothing outside London ... then one's life, one's living and working are rendered null and void. ... I never worried or thought of this till the spate of deaths thrust at me, and my own growing old,

changed *something*. Till then it didn't matter; I was the student; *one* day –
perhaps – I *would* write something. . . . I've generally lived for a future
that never came: the job Edward would get: the holiday we would have
one day together: the money and recognition that would come with this
work or that performance. The past, with its romantic looking to an
imaginary future . . . suddenly went – poof!

Even if hope and energy were to return, Liz was no longer absolutely
certain of the direction she would take. Towards the start of the 1970s,
as new composers came to the fore, she had felt her musical *raison
d'être* undermined. Gradually it came to seem as if Webernian serialism might not be the way forward for music. Almost all her working life she had regarded Webern's compositions both as an excellence
in themselves and as a beacon for the future; she had seen Webern
in the vanguard and herself not at his shoulder but in his ambit,
pushing back the boundaries of music for herself and for those who
came after. But if, as some were starting to claim, serialism had been
exhausted as a source of fresh material, where did that leave her?
Not as part of a living, creative tradition, but a a small subsidiary
branch on a dying tree.

Liz had been leapfrogged by younger composers with their eyes on a
different horizon, and the sense of being left behind was now as
irritating and desolating for her as, in the past, the sense of being ahead
had been crucial. In order to have any real feeling of achievement, she
needed to be an acknowledged member of the avant-garde – to be
making something *new*. She thrived, too, on the friction generated by
radicalism, needing a certain degree of antagonism as an oyster needs
grit to produce a pearl. The persona of the rebel was one she found it
impossible to abandon. 'She has to create an outcast environment for
herself,'[5] remarked Ursula shrewdly during the war; and thirty years
later Liz found intolerable the suspicion that she might suddenly find
herself inside the fold with the other sheep.

Her work, she always claimed, had grown out of adversity. Friends
pointed out that, complain as she might about the lack of time to write,
she never took herself out of reach of the telephone, discouraged visitors
or turned down invitations.[6] Often she seemed positively to prefer
working in a hectic, crowded environment, with deadlines to meet and
crises to surmount. 'Your request for a reference,' she once announced
to Brian Elias, 'has hit me on a week when I barely have time to fart.'[7]
She wrote the reference anyway, and forged on to the next drama.

But the adversity of the early 1970s seemed all to be unconstructive: a faulty damp course which allowed black slime to appear in the cracks of the parquet floor; perpetual noise from trains at the front of the house and a print factory at the back; dustmen throwing bins around at dawn, and paving so uneven that, in her phrase, it 'practically constitutes steps'; applications to add extensions to what seemed like every house at that end of King Henry's Road; a threat of prosecution for rates allegedly unpaid, and the bank's humiliating refusal to give her a credit card. Liz's combative nature could let nothing pass, and over the years trivial battles with the council, the builders, the neighbours, consumed time and energy she could not spare,[8] reminding her occasionally of the state in which Bartók had ended his life, 'ill, exiled, isolated, in poverty, trying to write his last works in the bathroom with taps running to drown the sound of the next-door radio'.[9]

Worst of all, she too was ill. The ear and chest infections of her youth had been followed by a severe and debilitating attack of shingles just after the war, and a patch of tuberculosis on one lung in the late 1950s. She had been a very heavy smoker for forty years, and her drinking had undoubtedly damaged her general health. Now in the last fifteen years of her life she was attacked by arthritis – 'one of the horrors of getting old,' she remarked, 'along with meals on wheels.'[10]

'Old age is a bugger.'[11] Liz was distressed by growing old – not simply as a painful physical reality but also as an idea, hating the implications it carried for her status and value. One particular article about ageing, by Susan Sontag, she cannot have failed to read, as it formed part of a feature in *Nova* magazine to which she herself had contributed:

> The emotional privileges this society confers upon youth stir up some anxiety about getting older in everybody. All modern urbanised societies – unlike tribal, rural societies – condescend to the values of maturity and heap honours on the joys of youth. . . . The most popular metaphor for happiness is 'youth'. . . . What now amounts to the latter two-thirds of everyone's life is shadowed by apprehension of unremitting loss.[12]

Apprehension and frustration played their part in Liz's wide range of 'chronic and emotionally expressive illnesses'[13] in her later years. All were quite real, but perceptibly related to her state of mind. (Even arthritis, it has been suggested, may be connected with stress.) From time to time she complained of aches and shakes, pins and needles and shooting pains in her legs and arms, giddiness, hot and cold flushes, gout, tinnitus, and chronic insomnia which magnified the effects of the other ailments.

Her address book included, besides doctor, dentist, chiropodist and ear specialist, the names of an acupuncturist, meditation centre, hypnotist, 'organic vitamin' supplier and the London Ionizer Centre.[14] (Astonishingly, she also paid £50 to the Maharishi favoured by John Lennon for a secret word of great power upon which to meditate – a revealing gesture of vulnerability, which sat oddly with her retrospective contempt, proclaimed ever more loudly, for the 'mumbo jumbo' of her Theosophical years.[15]) But Liz's primary resource was a cornucopia of pills, prescribed at different times by different doctors – literally dozens of tranquillisers, barbiturates, anti-allergy tablets, steroids, anti-inflammatory drugs and, most essential of all, anti-depressants.

Weaving in and out of the Lytton family history is a clear thread of chronic depression. Bulwer Lytton's temperament was, to say the least, uncertain; and Lady Emily's father Robert was afflicted, in his own words, with 'periods of almost intolerable hysterical depression'.[16] Lady Emily herself had had bouts in her youth,[17] and her brother Victor may also have been depressive. In his memoirs Liz's brother Robert wrote, 'About the time of adolescence when I was thirteen, I suddenly became melancholy; and since then my mental processes have been directed to a sort of perpetual valediction.'[18] Ursula too had bouts of depression all through her life.

For years Liz had had several of the symptoms of the manic depressive. The malaise stirred up by Theosophy, culminating in nervous collapse at the age of seventeen, had, she believed, been confirmed twenty-five years later by the treatment she had been given after the bad nervous breakdown of 1948. In the first draft of her autobiography she hinted that she had become addicted to the drugs prescribed for her then, and that this had left her depressed.[19] (Certainly sodium amytal, for which she had a prescription in the 1950s, is now rarely prescribed, as being overly addictive.)

She never wavered from her belief that her condition had physiological rather than psychological roots, but she recognised that her 'patches' of depression could be triggered by events. She saw the patches as episodes in a single protracted nervous breakdown from which she was perpetually at risk; fighting the threat without the resilience of youth was, she wrote, like 'being in the arms of an octopus'.

Hers was not the total annihilating depression which leaves the victim unable to eat or speak. (It is not inconceivable, from descriptions of his behaviour in his later years, that Edward may occasionally have been prone to such blacknesses.) Liz, in Frank Hauser's opinion, was more of a 'Bombay beggar – in a state of extreme dereliction, but bouncing like crazy, able to pursue you from one end of the town to the other on one leg.'[20]

But Hauser knew her best, perhaps, in the 1950s and 1960s, and as Liz got older, her depression could reach troughs which frightened her. She wrote of 'the sick-making abyss-like fear'; and a scrap of poetry among her papers looks like an effort to explore its depths, certainly written under its influence:

> me – that is I and you and all of them
> who've pained and been hurt,
> that's laughed and laughed and laughed till I cried and cried –
> wish to bear testament
> First to the sky – that
> Wraps my insomnia in a velvet leaden gown –
> so grey – so green –
> so here – so now – Nightmares
> keep quiet; loneliness
> steal silently. The curving bat
> circles my grey fears for shyness is at foot
> Myself – the victim of a nameless fear
> THROTTLE FEAR.[21]

Liz spoke of experiencing 'cyclical dooms'; and she observed similar cycles recurring in her composing. A period 'in spate', when she felt as though she were being eaten by crabs and could think of nothing but the work, would be followed by a spell of intense fatigue, boredom, illness, lethargy. 'During these low times I cannot even read – I seem to take nothing in. . . . Stupidly, I just do crossword puzzles to the "Telly".' But she flatly denied that the two cycles ran together. Throughout her life she had maintained that her music was not to be explained in terms of her personal life and her subjective emotions, and she was not prepared now to use physical depression as an excuse for dearth of musical inspiration, though undoubtedly it would have sapped her energy and weakened her concentration.

Whatever the causes, in the early 1970s she noted that the price of her creative 'spates' was getting higher; the doldrums of ennui and exhaustion lasted longer, and from time to time she was subject to attacks of what she described as 'musical death of the soul'. When she listened to the music of others it evoked no response; and sometimes she could no longer hear her own creative voice.

Already in 1970, when the first draft of *A Goldfish Bowl* was leaving her little time to compose, she had told Brian Elias, 'My imagination has gone dry. . . . My confidence has temporarily seeped away and left an arid uncertainty.'[22] In June 1971 she was still 'idea-less, stale, flat and unprofitable' – but only weeks later she wrote *Driving Out The Death*. Early in 1972 she announced resolutely that it was time for a change – 'away from dirges and laments to something that feels like Hallelujah!'; and this time she had neither the strength nor the confidence to carry out the kind of reassessment of her work which had produced the Sixth Quartet and *Six Tempi* twenty years before.

In the spring of 1972 she was in hospital for a rest cure,

> hoping and trusting that life will re-honour me with its presence if I make the habitation less tense. . . . My non-reaction to music – other than the writing of it – is as a 'loss of faith' – a 'crisis of faith' that appears to afflict the religious as the devil, doubt. . . . I presume (*my* faith) that it's all there, that imagination, life, excitement, joy, thrill as a sun behind the clouds. Whether I ever *see* that sun again or feel its warmth is a very moot point. I must just presume it's there and act accordingly.

Two poems by D. H. Lawrence, which she set in 1974, suggest a renewal of sorts: *Shadows* and, perhaps significantly, *The Song of a Man Who Has Come Through* –

> If only I am keen and hard, like the sheer tip
> of a wedge driven by invisible blows,
> The rock will split, we shall come at the wonder.[23]

But by the end of the year the clouds had gathered again. She kept on working in the half-light: 'I . . . write (apparently to commissioners' satisfaction) when kicked in the arse or for necessary money.' But it was without joy; and in January 1976 she concluded grimly, 'I've had almost two years of "musical death of the soul" – or as in the title of Beckett's novel, *Imagination dead, imagine*.'

CHAPTER EIGHTEEN

And Suddenly It's Evening

ENDING *A Goldfish Bowl* in 1970, Liz had hoped for 'some fun around the corner', and the gloom of the early 1970s was not unrelieved. Old friends still figured in her life – Jessie Hinchliffe, Dorothy Gow, and Priaulx Rainier, for whom she contrived to secure a Civil List Pension. A new friendship began when Liz discovered to her surprise, freely expressed, that Ursula Vaughan Williams was a good poet despite being the widow of an eminent man; and it survived Liz's ruthless musical manhandling of several of the poems. As in all Liz's most durable friendships, there was no element of either dependency or competition; 'a great gel'[1] Liz called her (she always wrote the word as she pronounced it), and over lunches at a local Greek restaurant confided many of her anxieties and aspirations.

Her morale was periodically renovated by the visits of a Dutch friend and admirer, radio producer Frans van Rossum. He had been captivated by her response to his request for a series of programmes; after a planning meeting at King Henry's Road which lasted seven hours and incorporated a candlelight supper, she solemnly proposed four programmes which included not a note of her own work, focusing instead on Constant Lambert, Dylan Thomas, Stravinsky and Dallapiccola. 'I loved her noble character,' van Rossum wrote later, 'her fierceness, her undiplomatic and straightforward way of life, her love of life, her love for her husband and family, her intelligence and wit.'[2]

Her sense of occasion was what struck Clayre Percy[3] (then recently separated from Liz's nephew Nicholas Ridley) when she accompanied her to Corfu in 1974. Liz insisted on them both spending the night before the flight at a hotel near Gatwick, at her expense, to put them in the holiday spirit. And once installed in the tourist hotel in Corfu, she rapidly became its life and soul, on first-name terms with all the guests, happily baby-sitting their children in the evenings.

Liz also found a good deal of comfort and pleasure in a renewed friendship with William Alwyn, one of her few surviving musical contemporaries. She had seen little of Alwyn since the Phoenix Trust award which he had largely stage-managed, but they had much of their past in common. Their musical tastes and objectives were very different, but she greatly respected his opinions, invited his comments, and accepted criticism with a humility which might have surprised some music reviewers. 'The friendship you show me by writing in such detail,' she told him after he had criticised her word-setting in *Time Off*, 'I find exceedingly moving.'

They shared the sensation that the musical world of their youth, inhabited by giants, had been somehow overrun by pygmies. Both felt isolated in the uncongenial surroundings of the musical 'goldfish bowl'; and Alwyn was one of the few friends with whom Liz could enjoy the kind of conversation which begins 'in *our* day'. 'I sometimes feel I'm living on a strange moon,' she wrote to him, 'where no one is over forty, and *no one* remembers the last war.'

True enough, the majority of her friends in these years were at least thirty years younger than herself. 'The old are always particularly appreciative of any support from the young,' she wrote, 'for it gives them that degree of extended life.'[4] In her last years she found herself looking to her pupils and young protégés for encouragement just as much as they looked to her for guidance. She had always needed a 'sounding-board' on whom to test her ideas; with Edward dead, she sometimes felt cast adrift. 'It's doleful,' she wrote, 'when you've just finished an op. to have no one to show it to – for *that* moment, for the composer, is the performance.'[5]

One major contribution to her musical survival came from the composer John Patrick Thomas, whose unsolicited letter of admiration was the only cheering feature of the dismal sixty-fifth birthday rites. Her professional life had seemed to her to be closing down when he stuck a foot in the door, and she grabbed at his friendship almost with desperation. Towards the end of 1971 he became her lodger for what he has described as 'six of the most extraordinary months of my life'. In return for his board and lodging, he did her shopping, looked after her post when she was away, and most important of all, was there to talk to, after concerts, over supper, and late at night when she could not sleep.

Thomas had for Liz the great advantage of knowing little of her earlier life. She could present to him the versions of herself and Edward and their life together which she wanted to be true. He for his part offered her fresh stimulus – an open enthusiasm for her work, the different cultural background of America, and regular bulletins from the international music scene, gathered in the course of his other career as a busy counter-tenor. Because he was not a pupil, the relationship was not complicated by any element of obligation, awe or jealousy; he gave her straightforward companionship, and when he left England, maintained a constant correspondence. Her letters to him show her at her best – candid, affectionate, perceptive, unaffected, vulnerable. For him and many others the best Liz was the real Liz; the other face – the aggression and self-pity forced on her by old age, illness and adversity – was the mask.[6]

'Keeping the affection of a younger generation' (Liz's phrase) seemed to her to confirm what she had already achieved and to keep her in the forefront, or at least in contact with it. Liz's inner circle were bound to her in a relationship that was a responsibility as well as a privilege, because she had both a professional and an emotional stake in them.

A visit to Liz at the top of 13 King Henry's Road, amidst her Paolozzi prints, Sudanese pottery and Lutyens chandeliers, offered younger friends a great deal beside a music lesson – artistic stimulus and the sense of being in touch with the aesthetic revolution of the 1920s and 1930s; intuitive understanding of domestic or emotional problems; instantaneous sympathy, and money or presents, to rescue or comfort. What Joyce Rathbone once called Liz's 'creative generosity', her kindness, and what she herself described as her 'unbounded capacity for affection, given or accepted' survived until the end of her life, concealed sometimes by her fears and angers but always waiting beneath the surface to emerge when called upon.

In their turn, her friends helped to fill the vacuum she abhorred. She surrounded herself with books, pictures, casual visitors, interminable telephone calls, in an attempt to stave off the incurable loneliness which had descended when Edward died. She ordered books by the dozen over the phone, a habit left over from the days when tradesmen delivered, and plunged into three or four at a time. One friend of the 1970s, the young contralto Susan Tyrrell, saw her reading as obsessive, designed to occupy the spare waking moments leaving no time for reflection or painful self-assessment. 'These fragments have we shored against our ruin. . . .'

There was a constant ebb and flow of grandchildren, particularly from the lower floors of King Henry's Road, where Rose and her family now lived. Liz faithfully observed the ritual of nursery tea; and at

Christmas it was she who wore the beard and red wellingtons, distributed the presents, and provided the Christmas lunch – far too much of everything, eaten, to everyone's deep satisfaction, on trays in front of the television. For hours at a time she would carry Rose's second daughter Khalda clinging to her front like a little frog, and would sometimes be found working at her desk in this condition.

The affection overflowed to her pupils' children. She once came to show Alison Bauld how to burp her first baby. 'I remember these great arthritic hands flapping – twisted hands, no longer beautiful, but red nails fastidiously painted. She was far too heavy-handed with him – whack, whack, whack – but the *love*. . . . And the belief in her understanding of the maternal carry-on. . . .' [7]

This belief was not as absolute as it may have appeared. Liz enjoyed her grandchildren largely because she had missed so much of her own children's youth. She was troubled both by guilt and by the resentment which often quite unreasonably accompanies it, and they complicated her relationship with her children, now all living away from home except Rose and her family. She both invaded her children's lives to show her concern, and complained of their lack of independence. In 1972 she set another text by Salvatore Quasimodo (in a work for tenor and lute entitled *Dialogo*), of which one line had particular resonance for her – 'Because it is always late to love, forgive me then.' [8] She wrote to John Patrick Thomas, 'I think *much* of my four children. . . . I should have acted, felt, done, helped, loved THEN. Now is always late. . . . I let them down.'

The most painful self-reproaches, however, hovered round the memory of Edward. Liz kept among her papers a quotation from Blake which it seems only too likely that she applied to herself – 'I know/Too late now to repent. Love is chang'd to deadly Hate/A life is blotted out, and I alone remain, posses'd with Fears'.

Left to herself, plagued by insomnia, she revolved over and over again the events of their lives, tormented by old bitterness and fresh regret. 'Alas, Edward and I had our share of fighting,' she wrote to William Alwyn, who had known Edward well, 'and mutual – but very hurting – abuse which haunts me now. The pressures on both of us were almost unbearable – his *forced* unemployment resulting in my overwork. . . . What a horrible waste of a real mutual love.'

And when sleep came it did not heal. As Sir Thomas Browne had written, 'Sleep often continueth precogitations, making Cables of Cobwebbes and Wildernesses of handsome Groves.' For years after Edward's death, Liz dreamed every night of losing him. 'Edward never gave me any cause for jealousy,' she told Alwyn. But in 1973 she was still occasionally dreaming of 'him leaving me for another woman, producing a child by some other etc. I have felt – and do feel still – bereft and the dreams put it in a corny way. It makes it difficult to get over his death. Dreams are so powerful.'

In 1976, fourteen years after his death, she wrote a piece called *Constants* for Joyce Rathbone and the cellist Joan Dickson – the 'constants' being four intervals repeated again and again without transpositions, only inversions. While writing she was troubled by its loose fragmentary quality, afraid it might be 'just a doodle', and certainly the players found it extraordinarily difficult to grasp, until they played it to a third person, the composer Iain Hamilton, and it suddenly came together. Back in rehearsal it disintegrated again; and then at the public performance, Joyce Rathbone remembered, 'it went better than almost any other piece of contemporary music we've ever played.' [9]

Constants was a piece that needed to be *spoken* to someone; it had the same quality of personal, intimate communication as the chorale at the end of *Music for Orchestra II* – and for the same reason. The second section is headed 'Lament'; and the closing notes of the piece sounded as 'a wail of despair', in Joyce Rathbone's ears. Liz herself, most uncharacteristically, revealed that the main element of it was supposed to sound like a cry of 'Edward, Edward, Edward'. 'It had been a long time since he died,' comments Joyce Rathbone, 'but things rear up and hit you. . . .'

'One cannot *rest* one's heart or companionship or a little fun on *people*,' wrote Liz in 1972. 'They die; they go; they are the least firm of anchors.' In 1971 she had lost both Stevie Smith and Alan Rawsthorne; it was their 'night' she was commemorating in *The Tears of Night* (1971). This was an excercise in contrasting timbres, written for a combination of ancient and modern instruments (the Early Music Consort and the London Sinfonietta), on texts which ranged from medieval English poetry to Gertrude Stein and James Joyce, all woven together by the counter-tenor voice, a sound closely associated with the two poles of early and contemporary music.

1971 also saw the death of the figure Liz identified most closely with past happiness – 'Eager' Stravinsky, as she pronounced him, 'a frail, vibrant and never never dull old man whom I had come to love and for whom I felt lonely.' Her memorial to him (*Requiescat*, 1971) is one of the few works where she did not shrink from consciously expressing emotion – or, it might seem, an underlying religious belief.

She was one of several composers invited by the editor of *Tempo*,

David Drew, to write a piece on the model of Stravinsky's own memorials to Raoul Dufy and Egon von Furstenberg. The brief was that it should be in canon form, no more than two pages long, for instruments within a prescribed range. She chose soprano and string trio, and set a particularly moving passage from Blake's 'The Couch of Death' (which typically, she slightly amended to suit her purposes): 'The lofty hill drank in the silent dew, while on his majestic brow the voice of Angels is heard, and stringed sounds ride upon the wings of night. . . . Angels are around him, voices of comfort are heard over the Couch of Death and he breathes out his soul with joy into eternity.' It was as if she did not dare to trust in Christian tenets for herself; but for Stravinsky, whom she knew to believe them, she could hope.

'My world was emptying of familiar faces,' wrote Liz; and as the 1970s progressed, the problems of sustaining friendships across a gulf of forty years became more apparent. Corresponding to her unlimited generosity when people were down was an irresistible urge to kick them when they were up. She found other composers' successes hard to bear – every commission to another was bread snatched from her own mouth – and her pupils' triumphs sometimes worst of all.

Liz believed sincerely that each generation of composers should help the one below to make its way; but seeing her juniors not merely survive but flourish, she felt both proud and at the same time threatened. She suspected that having breathed her air, sucked her lifeblood, as it were, her protégés would no longer need her and would pass on. Her most common complaint against them was that they were getting 'grand' or self-absorbed – both forms of withdrawing from her. So racking were her fears and resentments that often by her behaviour she succeeded in precipitating what she most dreaded, and drove some of them away.

Others were faithful, despite the fearful quarrels which scarred many of her relationships. In the terminology of transactional analysis,[10] any social interaction whatever has a biological advantage over no interaction at all – in other words, better to fight than to be ignored. By treating younger friends as equals, Liz lulled them progressively into a sense of security, ease and then familiarity, until in their confidence they presumed to offer her support and unsolicited advice in their turn – when she turned fiercely on them and denounced their praise as condescension, their criticism as impertinence. To Malcolm Williamson it seemed that 'as soon as she was aware that she had the devotion, she would take a scimitar and try to decapitate the devotee';[11] more often the crime was less the devotion itself than the fact that it had ceased to be uncritical. Her daughter Rose once said Liz was more of a Lytton than a Lutyens, and on these occasions she behaved like it, showing no scruples in pulling rank on the grounds of age or class.

Sixty years before, in the nursery with Mary, each day of quarrels had ended with an unvarying ritual of forgiveness – 'Good night, little Mary darling', 'Good night, little Betty darling'. At nearly seventy Liz appeared to feel that when offended she could say what she liked and then start again in the morning all square, a neat line drawn under the sum of rights and wrongs of preceding days. But adults lose the capacity to forget injuries; and Liz inflicted too much damage as she hacked and slashed. There was provocation, but it was rarely as severe as the punishments she handed out; many of her victims never felt the same about her again, and the circle of her really intimate friends dwindled. With compassion, Frank Hauser applied to Liz a remark once made of Mrs Patrick Campbell – 'She was like a sinking ship firing on rescuers.'

'It was her trial to take her fence without looking to right or to left,' wrote Virginia Woolf in *A Room Of One's Own*, about her protagonist, a woman writer trying desperately to establish herself in a male-dominated world. '"If you stop to curse, you are lost", I said to her.'[12] Increasingly in Liz's conversation the disappointments and resentments swamped the wit and sympathy. In 1925 when 'Brother' had been asked to magnetise the young Betty's ring with the quality she most needed, he had chosen 'balance'. Half a century later she still lacked it; and in the tide of rancour the same motifs bobbed to the surface again and again.

Liz never ceased to deplore the absence of real excitement in the contemporary music scene, the lack of response to Cocteau's command, 'Étonne-moi!' She detected only synthetically generated enthusiasm for cult figures moulded by public relations officers – 'clowns in their own circuses', 'musical Messiahs' dictating musical recipes 'from which the young in their thousands can produce their little snacks. . . . I have tasted many meals from this or that aural Boulestin (or more often, ABC teashops).'[13] They were, she felt, all talk and no music, dedicated to the 'aural programme note'; they offered a prescription for music rather than music itself, the musical equivalent of the conceptual artists of the early 1970s who instead of producing objects were documenting concepts of potential objects.[14]

All too often these stellar figures were very young. Beside her natural envy was the genuine and disinterested fear that early over-exposure had a corrupting effect. Liz heard the media eagerly canvassing the opinions of what seemed to her to be pimply adolescents, and remarked, 'Out of the mouths of babes comes wind.'[15] She saw the contemporary music societies becoming forcing-houses for immature talent, churning out music in indigestible quantities and pushing composers into the limelight of public rehearsals, recordings and television, before they could be called even half-baked, in stark opposition to Schoenberg's Society for Private Musical Performance with its ideal of forty rehearsals and no public performance at all. The contrast with her own obscure early career, when she had had neither the loving rehearsals nor the public attention, would have been laughable had it not been so irritating.

'Missing the giant monolithic integrity of Edward by my side, all around seems a sea of self-interest,' she wrote to John Patrick Thomas, 'businesslike self-promotion and intrigue.' Despite her distaste, Liz could not ignore the importance of promotion. On the one hand she heartily despised the phenomenon of the personal publicity agent. She was induced to use one for the première of *Time Off*, and wrote, 'For a week I was *in* (by exchange of money) and needed a RITUAL BATH afterwards.'[16] (As usual she maligned herself; she was 'in' because *Time Off* had been a considerable success, with some of the best reviews of her life. Anthony Besch's production, mounted in the teeth of the miners' strike and the power cuts which meant rehearsing by candlelight, brilliantly enhanced the strengths of the piece – the novelty of the genre, the flashes of wit, the stretches of beautiful music – and by sheer pace helped to conceal its weaknesses.)

On the other hand, she saw the need to advertise one's wares like any other craftsman, and since she did it very badly herself, out of pride, shyness and abruptness of manner, she required someone to do it for her: in Stevie Smith's phrase, 'a shover, a nice honey-tongued worm to belly around for me'.[17] In Liz's view the 'shover' should be her publisher – and here was another hobbyhorse whose saddle was shiny with wear.

The average music publisher would make more profit by keeping his money on deposit in a bank than by publishing most contemporary music.[18] Liz either did not believe this, or did not care. In her eyes, the publisher's job was to *publish* a work – not merely to make parts so that it might be performed, but to produce a printed score which could be sent around to interest *potential* performers, an indispensable promotional tool. The fact that printing the score cost more than the publisher could hope to recoup from one or even two performances (and lamentably few contemporary works are given more than two)[19] was in her view no excuse for failing to do it.

As Liz herself conceded, her output was almost unmanageable. 'From the publisher's point of view the ideal composer is one who produces two new works a year and has fifty performances of each. I produce fifty new works and have about two performances of each.'[20] (The second figure was as much an exaggeration as the first.) One of her publishers commented glumly, 'By the time you'd focused on Music for Orchestra I, Music for Orchestra II was upon you.'[21]

But she could not forgive successive publishers for what she saw as neglect and indifference bordering on hostility. Sometimes her suspicions were justified; more often she underestimated just how hard they were trying. Bill Colleran of Universal Edition, Sally Groves and Anthony Gilbert of Schotts, were among her most loyal supporters. And when Michael Vyner was put in charge of promotion at Schotts in 1967, at the age of twenty-four, he started out with the best of intentions towards her.

Vyner could, he felt, have been an invaluable ally for Liz at a time when she desperately needed one. He was a passionate enthusiast for contemporary music, he was fascinated by her family (which he visualised in sharp contrast to his own working-class background in Leeds) and by her links with a past he knew only as a historian, and he wanted to be friends. But to her he represented much that she disliked about the music scene; he was very young, apparently very confident, and imbued with a belief in the value of publicity. Their first encounter set the tone for the five years of their professional relationship, and quite possibly influenced the rest of Liz's career.

She invited him, with a flourish, to an expensive Mayfair restaurant without giving him the chance to explain that it was his local eating place. 'So she came down from her North London house,' he remembered, 'and I walked round the corner from my W1 flat. . . . We got inside; I said, "Hello, Miss Lutyens, it's a great delight to be here", and she said, "The reason I've invited you here today is to show you how to hold a knife and fork". And I suppose I disliked her from that moment to today. . . . She insulted my mother and father, everything that I had, and I thought it was pretty dreadful, but unfortunately I didn't tell her that, I was just very wary of her from 1972 till the day she died.' It was absolutely typical of Liz's luck – as it had been typical of Edward's – that with a single ill-judged and wounding remark (which she would certainly have described as a joke, though the undercurrent of ill will was obvious to all but her) she should have alienated a man who was to be one of the most influential promoters of contemporary music in the 1970s and 1980s.

'When she phoned,' Michael Vyner recalled, 'at times my heart leapt, thinking "This is going to be a good conversation". . . . Whilst loathing and dreading the phone call – she talked non-stop for an hour – at the same time there was something so nice and loving and fun. You could imagine having a lovely evening with her and screaming with laughter and kicking your legs up. But for some reason she didn't allow it. . . . This strident upper-class voice going on and on and on saying the same things – I just put the phone down on the desk and continued working. When the noise stopped I picked it up and said "Yes" and put it down again.'

It was after her relationship with Schotts had finally come to an acrimonious end that Liz started her own publishing company, the Olivan Press, with the money that had accompanied the Lord Mayor's Midsummer Prize that year. She took pleasure in informing her previous publishers – who included Chester and Mills Music, besides Schotts – that Olivan had generated more commissions than all of them put together, and had found no difficulty in having printed scores ready for each performance. In five years, however, the operation cost her £1500 and much effort, and it was with relief that she handed it over in 1974 to Universal Edition.

She had known Bill Colleran, one of Universal's directors, for nearly twenty years. In his words, they both moved in the same world of burning enthusiasm and no money, helping young composers working with a new language; and she gradually overcame her instinctive mistrust of publishers to see him as an ally. It was he who persuaded Universal to take on the responsibility for storing, distributing and promoting her existing work, with a vague commitment to produce future works once Olivan stopped operations altogether. 'This has really injected a strong dose of optimism,' Liz told him, 'into a musical life that was appearing to be all failure.' [22]

What she felt to be her failure – though the last five years had contained some remarkable achievements – was rubbed in by the success of others, her particular bugbears in the musical world.

By the 1970s the Manchester Group, and in particular Peter Maxwell Davies, were hailed as having joined the circle of Britian's leading composers. During the period of their rise, twelve-tone music had been completely accepted; and Liz may have been plagued by the humiliating suspicion that, whether or not her generation had blazed a trail for Davies, Birtwistle and Goehr, the progress of these younger composers may have played a large part in making her own passage easier in the 1960s.

But far higher in her personal pan-daemonium came the most successful contemporary composer of all. Liz found Benjamin Britten's triumphs hardest to endure because his fundamental attitudes to music were entirely antipathetic to her own. 'Artists are artists,' Britten once said, 'because they have an extra sensitivity – a skin less, perhaps, than other people. It is a proud privilege to be a creative artist'[23] – precisely the attitude Liz had in mind when she resolutely insisted that the composer's soul was no more elevated than that of the postman.

In return for the privilege of creativity, Britten felt it was the artist's duty to communicate as intelligibly as he could with the less fortunate. 'It is insulting to address anybody in a language that he does not understand'[24] – under which heading he certainly included the more complex serial language. Liz, on the other hand, would have subscribed, *mutatis mutandis*, to Cyril Connolly's dictum: 'The only way to write is to consider the reader to be the author's equal; to treat him otherwise is to set a value on illiteracy.'[25] 'Why shouldn't music be difficult?' she wrote to John Patrick Thomas. 'Everything else in life is.' To her mind, Britten did not aim high enough in the use to which he put a natural facility she would have loved to have had. 'A brilliant journalist,' she called him, 'able to produce an instant effect at first hearing, understandable to all. Each repeated hearing yields less – or so I find.'[26]

But beneath her genuine suspicion of his music, in which she was not alone, simmered persistent resentment of a musician achieving infinitely greater success with far more ease. (She tended to overlook the belabouring which Britten had received at the hands of critics in the 1930s and early 1940s, some of it more vicious than anything she ever had to endure.) Liz both despised and envied the efficiency with which he was promoted by Boosey and Hawkes: 'if Britten can make it, Boosey can hawk it,' in the words of John Ireland.[27] The publishers were backed up by the recording company Decca, who first recorded Britten's work as early as the 1920s and subsequently recorded virtually every piece as soon as it appeared. Liz summarised her own commercial recordings acidly: 'Seven – one for each decade of my life.'[28]

She objected to what she perceived as the cliquishness of the Aldeburgh Festival, with its sprinkling of earls and musical knights, and its resolute resistance to her music; in over thirty years she had one performance there, of her tiny Variations for Flute (1957). 'Holy, holy, holy,' Ursula Vaughan Williams remembers her saying, 'casting down their golden crowns upon the glassy sea.'[29] And as she toiled over *The Earth Dies Screaming* with school fees or income tax in view, or made her increasingly painful way to the chemist or the television rental shop, she may have ground her teeth over reports by Britten's admirers of his ultra-civilised life-style. 'As recreation from intensive work on his next opera,' wrote Basil Coleman, 'he loved to drive his car [an old Rolls

Royce] very fast down small Suffolk lanes, take three or four sea bathes a day, discover new churches, play several sets of tennis or go for long country walks.'[30]

With Michael Tippett she had much more in common, outside music at least – liberal politics, wide cultural interests, sympathy with and attraction for the young, the urge to express ideas in words as well as music – and whenever they met, they got on better than just amicably. But musically he came to represent in her eyes everything she most distrusted – the inspired amateur as opposed to the craftsmanly professional, the mystic, the pundit. Liz insisted that the musician should think *in* music rather than talking *about* it, and took Tippett as the prime example of the vice of extra-musical explanation, much beloved by critics because it gives them something to write about.

She may have found it hard to forgive his remark – made in an entirely non-specific context – that 'Nothing gets unjustly neglected.'[31] And on a strictly practical level, she felt that Schotts devoted far too much of their energies to promoting his music, which did not need it – 'He only has to fart, and the critics applaud'[32] – at the expense of hers, which did need it.

It was Liz's habit to argue from the particular to the general and then, armed with fresh ammunition, back again to the particular; and she tended to distrust her *bêtes noires* not just in themselves but as representatives of larger groups which she saw as conspiring to exclude, frustrate and surge ahead of her.

'When was the word "homintern" invented?' once queried Geoffrey Grigson. 'I won't say that in the late thirties it was intellectually fashionable or acceptable to denigrate a writer or painter because he was homosexual, though the fact might be mentioned in conversation if he was a bad writer or a bad painter, and aggressive and conceited, and in a position to promote other bad writers, or bad painters, for homosexuality's sake.'[33] Liz was certainly not concerned with fashion in her onslaughts on homosexuals, and in some respects they were mystifying, as the larger proportion of her friends, including almost all the most intimate ones, were homosexual. ('Aimer les femmes intelligentes est un plaisir de pédéraste' – Baudelaire.) She took a keen interest in their private lives, and was as ready with advice, encouragement and comfort as with her heterosexual friends.

It would seem that homosexuality was a charge to be levelled in anger only against people with whom she was offended for other reasons – people whose works were played too often, for example. 'I, for one, am tired of queers' quartets and sodomite symphonies,' she declared, 'and their harem of supporters, critics and sycophants (not and never the music itself, if it be good, but the edifice of a mutual admiration society supporting it).'[34]

On the subject of homosexuals Liz could be quite entertaining; about Jews she never was. Charitable friends gave her the benefit of the doubt over her anti-semitism, which became more pronounced with every passing year, though now she often dressed it up as ideological identification with the Palestine Liberation Organisation. On the strength of having a Sudanese son-in-law in Mo she liked to describe 13 King Henry's Road as an Arab household.

Like Lady Emily, Liz was entirely free from colour prejudice. She was very fond of Mo and of Conrad's Japanese wife Hiromi, whom he married in 1975, and she boasted about her multiracial grandchildren. Ever since 1964 when she had visited the Sudan for Rose and Mo's wedding, she had cherished a passionate generalised enthusiasm for Africa and Africans. She expressed some of her feelings in *The Linnet from the Leaf* (1972), a drama of the generation gap between a white mother and her two children, and the role a black couple plays for them all. The blacks, presented as sun and light, are the focus for the desires of the whites, their hopes for freedom and excitement – and also the target for their dark hatreds. Again and again the white son re-enacts the murder of the black husband as he pours out his love for the black wife. *Linnet* shows its age now; the blacks are presented as essentially foreign, associated with sunshine, sex, rhythm, dancing. But it vibrates with energy and sincerity.

Colour prejudice was as much a part of Liz's social background as anti-semitism. Lady Emily was quite remarkable in her love for India and Indians at the start of the century, Sir Edwin far more typical of his breed in frankly considering them an inferior race, and it would not have been surprising had Liz inherited his views. That she patently had the will and the courage to challenge so many of the preconceptions of her class makes all the sadder her prejudice against Jews. She was swayed very easily by the personal factor, and had any of her children married a Jew she would almost certainly have set aside her prejudice in her relationship with the individual, as she did with those of her friends whom Sebastian has described as 'non-combatants'. Whether a Jewish son- or daughter-in-law would have affected her general outlook as strongly as an African son-in-law is more doubtful.

To Katharina Wolpe the anti-Jewish gibes were no more than tantrums – angry, empty talk not reflected in Liz's actions. Malcolm Williamson, whose wife was Jewish, was inclined to discount Liz's anti-semitism simply because she made equally disgraceful remarks about his Catholicism. But there were others who could not endure it, whatever its rationale; and at the time when she most needed friends, she alienated a significant number beyond retrieving.

The threads of disappointment and spleen, regret and envy, anxiety and outrage, were now woven – along with her daily doings, stories of the past, scurrilous and very funny gossip – into a seamless discourse which it became harder and harder to interrupt. Iain Hamilton recalled going to visit her after having been abroad for several months. 'She would say, "Now, tell me all that's been happening to you – let's deal with sex first, money next, and music last" – and before you'd got a word out on any one of them, she'd say, "Now I, on the other hand" – and the gramophone record started.'

Following the refrain could be difficult. 'She had a funny kind of mind', in Anthony Payne's recollection.[35] 'It went off at angles, to the left and right of a question. Within ten seconds she'd be talking about something completely different. . . . It didn't matter what you said, she'd bring it round to her cherished topics . . . nettle soup in the war. . . . You would never hear a reasoned argument, she came out with isolated perceptions and statements. She was a one-line person, and she had a monologue which consisted of these one-liners one after the other. Every now and then she'd come out with something very interesting, and at the same time she'd say things that were absolute nonsense. . . . She wouldn't talk about a composer at length, she'd just say "Varèse? Oh – . . .", and a colourful phrase would come out, and then she'd be talking about nettle soup again.' And if one were rash enough to attempt an interjection she would simply raise her voice and roll on over it, somehow absorbing it on the way and replying several stanzas later.

To the people who knew her well, it was obvious that the monologue was at least partly the social defence mechanism of a shy woman – the adolescent with the blue silk evening dress and red spotted handkerchief struck dumb by the attentions of two young Russians in Paris; the uncomfortable country weekender skulking in the dank corners of the garden at Blagdon; the young Lizzie hovering on Edward's doorstep at 12 Fitzroy Street, daunted by the clatter of typewriters and confident uproar of the preparations for the Festival of Music for the People; the Liz who drank to get herself through the conversational hoops at the George and over the hurdles to employment in Wardour Street and Portland Place.

'She protected herself by talking,' observes John Patrick Thomas, 'and would carry on a quite inventive monologue if she was in any way worried about what the other person might say to her – questions they might ask that she wouldn't want to answer: the fear that they didn't really care for her music, or the horror of discovering that they didn't know it or care enough to have looked into it before they came to see her.' Convinced that people would dislike her if left to themselves to find out the kind of person she was, she would remove the initiative from them by verbal force. The telephone increased the flow, if anything. 'It was like a migraine, you couldn't stop it,'[36] remembered Richard Rodney Bennett; and Liz became the scourge of her friends with calls which only outright rudeness could restrict to half an hour. Brian Elias, who was on her telephone list for almost twenty years, marvelled at her stamina: 'She'd be on for an hour, and then you'd phone friends and they'd say, "Oh God, Lizzie's been on for an hour." . . . And you'd see her that evening and she'd say, "I've written a whole movement for string quartet today."'

In part she talked to fill the silence; she herself acknowledged 'the petty grumbling expressions by which one keeps the world away from the sick-making abyss-like fear . . . that is behind the quibbling surface'.[37] Those who loved her best came to see the monologue as a ritual that must be enacted at every meeting, important less for its actual content than for its symbolic significance and soothing effect. Once it was over, they could go forward together; but not everyone could be bothered to wait.

Out of the monologues came the myth – the authorised version of Liz's life, transcribed in her autobiography, which was published by Cassell's in 1972 after many alarums. For Liz introspection was something to be feared, and this was no Stendhalian self-examination, undertaken 'in order to guess what sort of a man I have been'. Her gaze was directed firmly outwards at the people who had helped to shape her life, and her primary intention was to vindicate Edward. The idea of an autobiography had been put to her in the first place as an alternative to a monograph on him which, to her pain, no one was interested in publishing. Edward's story, it seemed, was acceptable only as part of her own. She saw the book as a means of rehabilitating him, and devoted the middle chapters to a reverent and stilted account of his achievement; but at the same time she could not resist formulating the picture of herself that she wished to be preserved for posterity.

A Goldfish Bowl was very far indeed from being a whitewash. Compared with the majority of 'serious showbusiness' memoirs, complacent anodynes, it was astonishingly candid about the upheavals in her life, her personal and professional failures, her family and her enemies – though not as frank about the latter as Liz would have liked. Cassell &

Co. had recently lost an expensive libel case, and nervous lawyers recommended more than four hundred deletions;[38] in Frank Hauser's phrase, Liz was 'loudly puzzled'.

But nor was the book the fearlessly honest account she claimed it to be. She over-dramatised some of the hardships of her life, exaggerated her isolation from the rest of her family, and underplayed the support they had given her, moral as well as financial. To Mary in particular she had been very close, both before the war, when they were simultaneously experiencing the collapse of first marriages, and after it. Mary was a confidante and ally in the early days of the affair with Edward, and supported Liz through the breakdown of 1948, the cure of 1952, and recurring problems with her children. All three of her sisters, and Mary most conspicuously, helped Liz at one time or another with money. But these facts detracted from the picture of the lone survivor, and Liz chose to leave them out. That she was also, despite her protestations of affection, harsher towards her mother even than she meant to be is suggested by the reviews. The book was widely and generally well reviewed; without exception the reviewers focused on the portrait of her parents' troubled marriage, and also without exception championed her father and pilloried Lady Emily.

A Goldfish Bowl is alternately touching and irritating, sometimes funny and always absorbing, but it is not the book of a natural writer. (There was a strong element of professional jealousy in Liz's later attitude towards Mary, whose writing career was increasingly successful.) Liz had a distinctive writing style which she fought to preserve, resenting every effort by her editors to keep her within the bounds of good taste and legality. 'Words are put into one's mouth in a peculiarly "Woman's Weekly" manner,' she fumed, outraged at what she considered 'appalling lower-middle-class prissy sentiments or expressions . . . attributed to me.' (One such expression was 'upset' – 'an appalling middle-class word. . . . Should *only* refer to stomachs.') When the editor tried vainly to haul her account of one crisis back this side of libel, she exploded, 'I will *not* lie *and* in bad English.'[39]

Her writing has a curious off-centre quality produced by spurious 'poetical' expressions which blur the edges of her thought; pithy phrases effective in themselves but warring with each other; artificial emphases created by superfluous inverted commas; and a maddening indulgence, after the fashion of lady crime writers, in tags from Palgrave's *Golden Treasury* which only half-fit the points they have been imported to illustrate. It sometimes has a tone which she would have been horrified to detect in her music – contentious, subjective and sentimental.

The early 1970s saw the failure of two stage works which finally put paid to Liz's writing ambitions. In *The Waiting Game* (1973), an essay on the women who wait (for lovers, husbands, babies), she wrestled with a dilemma that had interested her since *Time Off* – the problem of finding a convincing musical version of colloquial speech, a language more appropriate to music-theatre as she wanted it to be. She deplored what she called the Britten/Menotti 'have-a-nice-cup-of-tea' school of musical dialogue; but she cannot honestly have believed that in phrases like 'bloody awful traffic' and 'buggered by geography' she had served her singers much better.

A ballad-opera confusingly entitled *The Goldfish Bowl* (1975) Liz dismissed simply as 'awful – falling between all stools'. An exploration of bourgeois values, student protest and the compromise between them, this *Goldfish Bowl* was loosely constructed round three nursery rhymes, exploiting their familiar associations rather as Harrison Birtwistle had exploited folklore in his *Punch and Judy* (1968). Liz lifted directly from *Rhadamanthus* (1948) the figure of the Administrator in the dock – the archetypal bourgeois, Edward's antithesis and adversary, accused by the Humanities and defended by the deadly Safeties. 'I, said the Bureaucrat, I killed my hope.'

Neither *The Waiting Game* nor *The Goldfish Bowl* was ever performed. But these disappointments were as nothing compared with the failure of *Isis and Osiris* (1970), a piece which bound together many of the principal themes of Liz's work.

She had first begun writing it in 1969 by accident, after being asked by Stephen Plaistow to contribute to a programme of settings of Petrarch. Liz always paid inadequate attention to names, though she was infuriated if her own was misspelled, and before she realised her mistake she had read a good deal of Plutarch (for Stephen Plaistow she set Petrarch's version of Ovid, *The Tyme Doth Flete*, 1968). Plutarch's description of the origins of the cult of Osiris, based on the Egyptian Book of the Dead, fired her imagination, and she set to work.

Her plot begins with the illicit union of the Sky with the Earth, wife of the Sun who, when he discovers Earth has conceived, denies her a time to give birth. Thoth, scribe of the gods, plays draughts with the Moon and wins five days, on each of which Earth is delivered of a child. The five include Osiris, deity of the Nile, fresh water, corn and wine; his sister Isis, deity of earth and vegetation and, like him, a fertility god; and Seth, god of sea, salt, drought and death.

Isis and Osiris subsequently marry. Osiris travels the world to introduce the cultivation of grape and grain; he returns home to find that the jealous Seth has offered an ornate coffer to whomever it fits. Tempted, he climbs into it, and Seth promptly has it sealed and thrown into the sea. Isis wanders the earth lamenting, until she finds the coffer and brings it back to Egypt. Seth discovers it, breaks it open and hacks the body into fourteen pieces.

To prevent further desecration, Isis makes clay models of each part and scatters them over Egypt; at the place where each part lands, a temple of Osiris is founded and the cult established. One piece alone, the phallus, is missing, and Isis makes a large replica for Egypt to worship for all time. In a triumphal third act, Osiris rises again as God of the Dead and King of the Underworld; a set of choral dances re-enacts his life through the symbolism of the harvest rites: the corn ripens, is cut down, and springs up again.

The choral dances, written first, include some of Liz's most luxuriant and openly expressive music, a symptom of the emotional capital that she had invested in *Isis*. If one had to select a single theme as characteristic of her work, it would be the continuity of life and death as represented in the seasonal cycle. She also expressed in *Isis* some of her inchoate but powerful feelings about fertility and motherhood as the point and focus of sexuality.

But the strength of her instincts alone could not endow the plot with drama or the libretto with life. Even before the opera was finished, she was writing wearily, 'Isis plods on wailing page after page – but I'm trying to make some "magic" fire by rubbing dry sticks together.'[40] Days before the first performance, she was still apprehensive: 'Audiences are so quick-witted these days. I have this worry: am I going to bore the pants off everybody?'[41]

Her forebodings were fully realised. In the words of one of the more charitable critics, 'Lutyens the librettist presented Lutyens the composer with an almost impossible task.'[42] In writing her own words, Liz had once again transgressed her principle of professionalism, and this time fatally. The libretto is too long, cratered with solemn invocations, and every so often it is slowed to a standstill by repetition – five throws of the dice in the contest with the Moon, five sets of birth pangs, five fittings of the coffer.

For once Liz's sense of irony seems to have deserted her. Lines which would have convulsed her had some other composer written them slipped past somehow. Seth summoning his assistants to seal Osiris in the coffer sounds ominously like the Goon Moriarty – 'Go quick, and get the nails and molten lead I hid behind those screens.' Isis gazing on Osiris's dismembered corpse exclaims, 'Help me, Nepthys, to collect these poor royal bits . . . One precious piece is missing.'

A dazzling production would have helped, though it could not have salvaged, *Crisis and Osiris*, as it came to be known at Morley College, where it was premièred in November 1976. The production might well have benefited from the 'Cubist' approach later employed by Birtwistle in *The Mask of Orpheus*, where events were presented from several different perspectives, simultaneously and in sequence; each singer represented the thought of his character, a mime created his action, and puppets symbolised the underlying myth. Again in hindsight, the techniques now used regularly by producers in staging the minimalist operas of Philip Glass and others would have been invaluable in making a virtue of *Isis*'s repetitions.

What was called for was a thoroughly 'interventionist' approach, it now seems to producer Mike Ashman, who takes upon himself perhaps too much of the blame for the shortcomings of *Isis*. But he had never produced opera before, and Liz did nothing to help him. Having tried vainly to interest Glyndebourne and Covent Garden, she was bitterly disappointed to be given only a semi-professional production of *Isis*, and in her chagrin was ungenerous. She could or would tell her producer nothing about her attitude to the myth or the conclusions she drew from it, she had no idea of how she wished the characters to look, and she refused to come to the first stage rehearsal on the grounds that she did not want to miss the third episode of *I, Claudius* on television.

The Morley College stage was tiny and the budget negligible. Unwisely, as he now believes, Ashman and his designer Ellen Graubart (wife of the conductor, Michael Graubart) were lured into straightforward naturalism on a shoestring – sets composed of multitudinous pillars and flats made of unbleached calico; shadows deployed as props; costumes of tubular lampshade material, spatter-painted and skin-tight; Seth's mane a bush of plumber's hemp, normally used to lag pipes.

In thoroughly atrocious circumstances, the production team achieved miracles. But once performers are past school age, audiences no longer make allowances. Liz had behaved impeccably with her conductor Michael Graubart (who had arranged for the opera to be mounted at Morley College), and the orchestral performance was irreproachable. But neither stage action nor underfunded design had enough variety to relieve what threatened to be a very long evening indeed, and Liz was braced for disaster.

'Artists are funambulists,' she once wrote. 'Accompanied by a side-drum roll, they are aware of the ever-hopeful expectancy of the crowd waiting for the unprofessional fall from grace and height, and the critics looking for a belt to hit beneath.'[43] In *Isis* they had an easy target. 'A pace so funereal as to make *Parsifal* seem like an operatic steeple chase,'[44] quipped one; and another described it cruelly as 'a tomb painting brought to life but only just.'[45]

Liz's behaviour during the writing of *Isis* had been near-compulsive. 'I'd go and see her one day,' remembered Brian Elias, 'and then four days later there'd be another fifty pages of short score. She couldn't stop.' The reception of the piece hurt her very much, and *Isis* was her last full-scale theatre work.

Earlier in 1976, Liz had completed what she regarded as another unsuccessful venture – a year spent as composer-in-residence at York University. She had in fact given a good deal to the students she taught. Wilfrid Mellers, then Professor of Music, had appointed her because he wanted a department staffed not by academics but by practising musicians; he believed she would generate enthusiasm, and she more than fulfilled his expectations. She made close friends of some of her students, among them composer Glyn Perrin, who was to be a staunch and selfless friend for the rest of her life, and her musical executor after her death.

But Liz's role in York seemed to her to be ill-defined. The damp precipitated miseries of arthritis and bronchitis; and she missed London – 'I'm a big-town gel!'[46] she proclaimed with bravado. More truthfully she confessed to John Patrick Thomas before she went north, 'If only I had my Edward ... to be with me. ... Alone, I'm scared, scared of physical exhaustion, loneliness, inadequacy, practical arrangements, and smaller cowardices.'

By the mid-1970s she was drinking again. She blamed the collapse of Dr Dent's cure on an acupuncturist whom she consulted for her arthritis.[47] He was an elderly man, according to her version of the story, who told her a glass of whisky would do her good. She tried to explain her situation, he refused to listen and simply repeated the advice – and she went home and followed it.

To drink again of course required an act of will on her part – or rather an act of resignation. In the summer of 1976, amidst celebrations of her seventieth birthday, she had experienced a burst of success. *And Suddenly It's Evening* and Music for Orchestra II were both revived at the Proms, the production of her treasured *Isis* was promised, a series of six concerts was imminent from the BBC in the autumn, and she had been invited to the Royal Garden Party. 'And do you know,' she wrote to John Patrick Thomas, 'that without Edward – with everything being too late to give me any pride or *fun* – I don't give a damn, and would rather read Beethoven's letters, hear the *Egmont* overture and have better health.'

CHAPTER NINETEEN

Staying With It

'I HAVE PERHAPS only one merit,' wrote Schoenberg in 1947. 'I never gave up.'[1] Liz had given in to the urge to drink, but she had not given up. Drinking was an aid to survival, a means to an end, not an end in itself, not the end of everything. At the age of eighty-one Stravinsky had commented with understandable complacency, 'Anyone who survives a sixty-year span of creative activity in our century must sometimes feel a satisfaction merely in being able to metabolize new experiences, to "stay with it".'[2] Staying with it had long been vital to Liz, and she drank not to opt out, but to be able to carry on.

She was no coward, either in her life or, usually, in her work – on the contrary, written all over *A Goldfish Bowl* is her preoccupation with moral courage. In *The Winter of the World* (1974), which she composed after months of musical desolation, she quoted Camus's description of strength of character as 'one of the conquering virtues of the world. . . . [It] stands up to all the winds from the sea. It is that which, in the winter of the world, will prepare the fruit.' Liz did not suffer her afflictions in silence, but she did have this kind of strength to endure them; and throughout the 1970s, despite the depression, the arthritis, the loneliness, drink and pills, she continued to compose. 'The aether appears to be filled with Lutyens pieces, real and potential,'[3] wrote Paul Griffiths a little wearily in 1981. Between 1976 and 1983 there were almost sixty real pieces – thirteen in 1979 alone, when Liz was near her lowest ebb.

To some extent, prolixity was an inevitable consequence of her technique. For her, she declared, quality was to be achieved through quantity; and she rejected the conventional notion of the creative process – the original intuitive perception followed by the long period of pre-composition, the careful sketches in which every element of the final piece can be detected, and then, after the act of composition, the conscientious revisions, until the work is as near perfect as the author can make it. Liz was temperamentally unsuited to this way of working, and might have been incapable of it, even had she approved, but she also had objective reasons for dismissing it.

Too often, she suggested, laborious pre-composition squeezed the life out of the generative idea. She quoted an observation by Matisse – 'I am driven on by an idea that I really only grasp as it grows. My reaction at each stage is as important as the subject itself'[4] – and took it as a prescription for flexibility.

She far preferred to work quickly and almost, it seemed, without reflection, the basic series providing an ever-unwinding thread of material. 'I *have* to work quickly,' she wrote, 'because my *conscious* mind is so stupid, I can but trust that I have more interesting layers of mind.'[5] In *Scroll for Li-Ho*, she had claimed to be trusting to an innate sense of form to provide the structure of her piece; here she was apparently leaving everything to the subconscious.

This was more than simply an easy way out of the rigours of self-criticism and self-discipline. Liz could also offer a positive rationale for the way she worked. The unstructured approach could lead, she knew, to mistakes, superfluities and vacuities; but she was prepared to accept flaws in individual compositions because she saw them not as would-be masterpieces in themselves but as components in a larger whole. Her music tended to bunch itself into groups of works, each displaying a different aspect of a core idea. 'I personally find a *series* of works "incorporate a mode of thought",' she wrote, 'an *idea* that needs working out in many varied ways; hence a spate from *one* major stimulus, possibly followed by a hiatus.'[6]

In a sense, Liz was writing pieces as other composers made sketches; nine works might be in some way preparation for the tenth. The problem was that where other composers would discard their sketches, Liz offered all her pieces equally for performance and criticism, without indicating that she regarded them as in any way partial or preliminary.

She explained her methods only in private, in a letter to William Alwyn in which she quoted advice the young Dylan Thomas had given to another aspiring writer.

'Your present method . . . the draft after draft, the interminable going-over-again . . . can be compared to the method of the marksman who spends weeks and weeks getting the ammunition . . . weeks and weeks deciding on a target, weeks and weeks weighing his rifle in his hand . . . and, at the end of the year, having a pop at the bull's eye. Why not, for a change, fire off round after round of ammunition from any old gun you can get hold of. You'll miss hundreds, but you're bound to get the bull's eye a lot of times too. You'll find the hit-or-miss, the writing with no plot technique will help you considerably in loosening your mind and getting rid of the old stifling memories.'[7]

This, Liz explained, was how she tended to work, without the deadening rigmarole of formal pre-composition which she saw and suspected in younger composers like Stockhausen. And once a work was written, she almost never revised it. For her a composition was like a long jump – it could be repeated but not amended – or a crossword, which once solved repays no further attention.

There was an emotional reason too, besides the intellectual rationale, for the almost uncontrollable outpouring of music. In these last hard years composing had become a form of therapy, an escape from unacceptable realities.

This was, of course, an attitude to art which she had once despised. In the awful weeks after the outbreak of war in 1939, Lady Emily had encouraged her to submerge herself in work on the first Chamber Concerto; 'music can never be a dummy,' replied Liz loftily. But now she turned avidly to it as a means of absorbing her complete attention. 'Poetry reading, painting, sculpture, conversation with someone sympatico [sic] all help, but MOST of all the DAILY BAR/BARS however bad. . . . You're trying to hear something you can't hear clearly – there isn't room for anything else.'[8]

Writing music was a way of keeping calm, of imposing order on an existence which old age and illness were taking beyond Liz's control. It was the only effective method of staving off loneliness; as she explained to Alwyn, 'It's only in work (wherein one always *was* and *is* alone) that the aching void of where Edward was eases and is forgotten.' For all these reasons, composing had become not so much a pleasure as a necessity. 'Practice is Art,' wrote Blake. 'If you leave off, you are lost.'

The compulsion produced some fine works, among the most significant being Music for Orchestra IV (1981), her last full-scale orchestral piece. *She Tells Her Love While Half Asleep* (1979) was a rhapsody for high soprano to words by Robert Graves, which Liz wrote for Hazel Thomas, wife of her accountant Sydney Giebel, in gratitude for their kindness and support, unfaltering since the days when Sydney Giebel had testified on Edward's behalf during the Frankel case.

Relationships with particular performers weave their way throughout the body of Liz's work – Jane Manning, Janet Craxton, Katharina Wolpe, Ian Caddy, Michael Finnissy – and in her last decade she derived a good deal of pleasure from working with the Medici Quartet, for whom she wrote four pieces – *Mare et Minutiae* (1976), *Doubles* (1978), *Diurnal* (1980) and String Quartet XII (1981).

She had not lost the urge to experiment, nor her professional interest in the expressive possibilities of any and every instrument. She had always used the percussion section extensively in her film music; now she wrote *The Living Night* (1981) for solo percussion, an evocation of the extraordinary multiplicity of the sounds of darkness.

James Wood, who commissioned the piece, described it as 'mildly programmatic'; and in many of the late works there is a degree of pictorialism which would surely have astonished the young Liz, with her Stravinskian insistence on the self-sufficiency of music. *Mare et Minutiae*, for instance, contrasts the vastness of the ocean with the detail of each sea scene – shells, weed, crabs, wood-sculpture, cornelian and amber, harking back to the days when the greatest pleasure of the fat little 'Buddha' had been 'seeking' for such treasures on the cold beaches of the east coast. 'The times when the sea metamorphosed all into beauty,' wrote Liz, 'and was not built on. Now – oil rigs, tar, plastic and French letters . . . Pity.'[9]

Too often, however, Liz betrayed the fact that for her the process of composition was more important than the end result. Occasionally she showed an ominous lack of interest in her work. At a seventieth birthday celebration concert at the end of 1976, *Mare et Minutiae* was given its first London performance. It was the kind of occasion Liz hated: she was not allowed to skulk nervously in the audience, but was obliged to sit on one side of the platform in a miniature Brains Trust with John Amis and Malcolm Williamson, and answer questions between the pieces. She was embarrassed, self-conscious and, as the long evening of tribute wore on, tired and even a little bored: once a piece was composed, after all, she lost interest in it very fast. Some five minutes before the end of *Mare et Minutiae* the audience, fooled by a lacuna in the music, began to applaud – and to the astonishment of the quartet, Liz promptly took her bow. 'It's not the end', hissed the leader as she inclined graciously towards him. 'Oh yes it is,' she muttered, and carried on down.[10]

Liz liked to think of her work as akin to poetry, in its vocabulary, grammar and scale. But in comparison with works like *And Suddenly It's Evening*, much of the vocal writing of the 1970s seems increasingly prosaic. It was not simply that she chose to set more prose; more and more often her vocal writing resembled prose, a long recitative, in its pace and rhythm – 'taking a line for a walk', in Klee's phrase, and sometimes simply for a meander.

Baritone Ian Caddy (who had played Harold in the revival of *Time Off*) commissioned a song cycle in 1979, and was disconcerted by her attitude to it. She had been looking for an opportunity to set another poetic sequence by Tess, entitled *Mine Eyes, My Bread, My Spade*; Ian Caddy had asked for a work twenty minutes long, and the poem was too short – but Liz decided to set it anyway, declaring that this would be a 'minimalist' work and she would make a little go a long way. The device she used was to intersperse the verses with passages for string quartet. This made the piece far less of a practical proposition for touring, and in truth the musical material was not strong enough to survive being extended so far. Liz had once told Ian Caddy that the ideal length for a piece of hers was seven minutes, and in this case he was inclined to agree.

In 1960, commissioned to write a piece for wind quintet, a combination which did not then interest her, Liz had determined 'to achieve a metamorphosis in myself to *want* to do it. . . . The phrase "Ich muss" was in my mind.'[11] Now she seemed sometimes to be unable to make commissions her own in this way. Too often it seemed that the externals of a piece had dictated it – an unusual instrument or combination of instruments trying to build a repertoire, or the need for a work that could be easily toured, and would neither embarrass the performer nor tax the audience.[12] Liz could be relied upon to oblige, but the result risked becoming, in Hugo Cole's phrase, 'atonal Kapellmeister music.'[13] Asking her for a piece, it was a matter of luck whether a performer got authentic Lutyens or one of the pieces in which it sounded a little as if she were imitating herself.[14]

Paradoxically, at a time when it seemed as though she might be losing her ability to respond to a challenge, the opportunities came thick and fast. There were more BBC broadcasts, more commissions from friends and new admirers, and more royalties from past 'hack' work enabling her to concentrate in peace on her own music. (By the end of the 1970s, when her scope for spending money pleasurably had been curtailed, she was earning a good deal of it. One year, she boasted to Barbie, she made £10,000 from *The Skull* and its ilk; and the films continue to make money for her estate.) More honours arrived – in 1979, the American Academy and Institute of Arts and Letters Award 'for lifetime accomplishment' as 'one of the small number of British composers who has

worked successfully in the advanced idioms of the twentieth century'
– and the standard format interviews began in earnest.

The mask of 'Twelve-tone Lizzle' was beginning to set firm, though
some new friends took the trouble to look behind it. Liz had first met
Paul Silverthorne when he was the viola player in the Medici Quartet,
and she first met his wife Mary at the première of *Doubles* in the
Everyman Theatre, Hampstead. Liz, remarkable on this occasion in a
mothy blue fake-fur coat and sandals, detested first performances –
'acute embarrassment, the feeling of having "dropped a brick", hearing
one's voice continue with an inanity in a sudden silence; and being
stripped in public, all rolled into one.'[15] Mary Silverthorne did her best
to reassure, and they became close friends.

The Silverthornes gave Liz treats – more interesting food than she
could now prepare for herself, conversation about music that was
entirely free of 'shop', a Christmas holiday, an outing to Brighton.
While traffic wardens hovered, they helped her to make the long painful
journey to the water's edge so that she could wash her face in the sea.
For her part she always fêted them when they visited her, and she was a
constant source of encouragement and advice to Paul Silverthorne
embarking on a solo career. She wrote *Echo of the Wind* (1982), a
fiendishly difficult short work for solo viola, specifically to stretch him.

Liz's seventieth birthday was much celebrated, with festivities in
York; a South Bank recital, later recorded, in which Richard Deering
played music by Liz, her influences and her pupils; an *Omnibus* film
entitled, in the words with which Liz had ended *A Goldfish Bowl*, 'The
First Seventy Years Are The Worst'. But 1976 was also the year in
which Liz was deeply embroiled in the problems of her children,
practical and emotional. She agonised for them, provided what money
she could, put them up when they needed it, soothed and drew them
closer – and at the same time complained of their lack of independence
and accused them of ingratitude. 'I sometimes feel like King Lear,' she
told Rose. The guilt she had felt for so many years she now did her best
to transfer to them.

The following year she suffered a bad blow when Universal Edition
informed her that they were no longer willing to act as her publishers.
For all his efforts, Bill Colleran could only persuade the firm to house
her material and promote existing works, in return for a fee of £200 per
year, an arrangement that continues to this day. Liz felt humiliated and
discarded; but her worst affliction by far in the late 1970s was her
health. 'The beastly body,' her sister Mary had written when she
learned that Liz could no longer move easily between her study and her

bedroom. 'I remember so well too how Mummy used to dream she was running along the sands and woke to find herself imprisoned in her old body.'[16] Liz had arthritis in her spine, and her hands and feet, once her principal vanities, were swollen and twisted. Her right hand had lost the use of all but the thumb and first finger, and writing was an agony; her pupils took their turns to decipher the pathetic, quavering script and reveal the resilient strength of some of the music that lay beneath it.

The gradual stiffening of her legs stopped her driving and led to bone-breaking falls; after one, an excruciating sprained ankle necessitated an operation or a caliper, and she chose the operation. Waiting on the trolley in cap and gown, she refused to enter the operating theatre unless the surgeon in charge extinguished the soi-disant 'soothing' muzack issuing from it.[17] The operation was only partially successful, and in her last years she could not walk without sticks.

Had she had the option of retreating to a warmer climate, she could have been saved a good deal of pain. 'She was a different person in the heat,' reported Glyn Perrin, who accompanied her to Crete on the last of the sun-worshipping holidays she took whenever she could afford them. Liz suspected that this might be her last encounter with Homer's 'wine-dark sea', as she called it, and she made the most of it. She arrived on Crete in a wheelchair and made Glyn take her right down to the water in it. Swimming had been an abiding passion since the days when the young Betty had found consolation for Krishna's pi-jaws on the beach at Adyar. 'In the sea old age, arthritis, personal pain and other aches evaporate,' she told William Alwyn, 'and one is just part of its impersonal wash and whisper.' Now she swam every day in the Mediterranean, and within four or five days could walk unaided. Back in King Henry's Road she wore her coat indoors and kept her room at a temperature that oppressed visitors.

Her address book, once studded with names like Alfred Burke, Sean Connery, Judi Dench, Marty Feldman, Gabriel Josipovici, Nyree Dawn Porter, Wynford Vaughan Thomas, was now dominated by the Electric Blanket Service Department, the Geriatric Health Visitor, Aidcall, the Musicians' Benevolent Fund and the Crime Prevention Officer.

From time to time she suffered from ulcers, gout and kidney infections. She had perpetual 'figits' in her legs – the twitching, perhaps, which Krishna had noted disapprovingly in 1925. On the night of her Acceptance as a disciple of the Master Kuthumi she had wrapped cold towels around her legs; in her old age she preferred to sit with her calves in tepid water. Liz thought her symptoms might be produced by some sort of electrical discharge; she also turned pearls black, and watches went wrong on her wrist.[18] In fact, the 'figits' are a recognised nervous complaint, a functional disturbance of the physical nervous system, often related to stress and tiredness and hard to alleviate.

Overlaying – perhaps underlying – all her other ailments was depression, and she experimented with a number of anti-depressant drugs before settling most frequently for Marplan. One of its disadvantages (besides the risk, if it was taken inadvertently in combination with certain foods such as cheese, of a sudden leap in blood pressure which could even result in a stroke) was that it encouraged her to put on weight. She developed a remarkable bust, which forced her to buy maternity clothes and men's jumpers, and she complained bitterly, 'I never used to have boobs when I was young, and now I've got them I don't know what to do with them.'[19]

To some observers she appeared a frightening figure of physical decay – her teeth going, her hair thinning, her profile a witchlike caricature of itself. She was smoking furiously again; in the early seventies she had been disturbed to read in the *Guardian* that it was the lower socio-economic classes who found it most difficult to give up smoking, and had resolved to stop straight away, but aristocratic abstinence did not last long.[20]

Her drinking was never as heavy as in the worst period of alcoholism, but it was constant throughout the day. There was usually a bottle of wine under her work table and brandy for the evenings; her drink bills were startling – £750 for December 1982, though this included a good deal of entertaining – and when the demands from the off-licence became pressing, her remedy, quintessentially Edwardian, was quickly to order another case of champagne. 'It gives them confidence,' she explained.[21]

Taken in combination with her multitudinous pills, she needed, in fact, less drink to produce the same sensations; she told Bill Colleran that she hallucinated nearly every night. Her anti-depressants sensitised her to alcohol. They may in their turn have been affected negatively by the sleeping pills. The anti-inflammatory drugs she was using to relieve her arthritis may have caused the ulcers for which she was taking Tagamet, and they may besides have had a depressing effect. Liz was trapped in a vicious cycle which she refused to break.

In the broadest sense, she was perhaps no longer 'in her right mind'. Drinking on the scale of the late 1940s and early 1950s would almost certainly have affected her central nervous system and accelerated the ageing process; at seventy she looked ten years older. 'I've always thought that Lizzie was a little bit like a radio,' John Amis has remarked. 'When it was tuned in, it worked marvellously, excellent reception; but when it was badly tuned, it was as if the brain wasn't quite in synch.'

She seemed to have no emotional thermostat, and her aggression and virulent dislikes were exaggerated. Sensing less and less response from others as she got older, she pushed harder and harder for a reaction, with the outrageousness of a child demanding attention; those friends who were brave enough to interrupt the flow of bile sensed her profound relief at being stopped. 'Her mouth would be pouring out this garbage,' observed Alexander Goehr, 'and you'd look in her eyes – which were beautiful – and the venom simply wasn't there.'

The combination of physical and mental pain was at times almost unbearable, and by 1979 Liz had seriously considered suicide. (There were family precedents. Her grandfather Robert Lytton had attempted to kill himself with heroin at the age of nineteen;[22] Ursula had committed suicide in 1967, her brother Robert had contributed considerably to his own death with drink, and Barbie was to kill herself in 1981.) Liz joined EXIT,[23] and signed a testament expressing her desire for euthanasia should she suffer from illness causing her severe distress or rendering her 'incapable of rational existence'.

She would later ask friends to promise to help her out of life if it became unendurable; but she seems to have left EXIT after only a few months, for reasons which one can only guess at from remarks she had made earlier in her life. 'Life, however hard the living, is my faith – to be respected in all its forms, its denial, or disrespect for its laws, my blasphemy,' she wrote in 1972. 'I would always choose waving not drowning.'[24] As existence became harder, Liz certainly became more pessimistic, but possibly her respect for natural laws survived, and consequently the hope of regeneration.

This was nothing as clear cut as a belief in the afterlife. Among her papers was a cutting from *The Times*, quoting an American sociologist's description of death as 'a nonscheduled status passage. This state implies absolute dysfunction within a zero transitional probability to a higher state.' Liz certainly kept the cutting as a joke, but it coincided with her own beliefs.

Nevertheless, as long as 'absolute dysfunction' could be avoided, there was always the possibility that the present life might improve. In 1973 Liz wrote, in *Laudi*, an extraordinary song of praise out of the cold and dark of her musical death of the soul. 'Dark/and cold/winter/sun gone/wind gone/life gone/days done/Amen./Ah,/men move to make/ Roar and sing/make new/renew. Spring soaring . . . round to the/ ringing/song/life singing/Laudi, Laudi.'

A year later came the two D. H. Lawrence settings which marked a temporary parting of the clouds of musical deadness. One, *Shadows* (1974), spelt out even more clearly what she was going through in the darkness – it verges at moments on a clinical description of depression – and yet was a still more emphatic statement of hope.

And if as weeks go round in the dark of the moon my spirit darkens and goes out and soft strange gloom pervades my movements and my thoughts and words. . . . And if, as autumn deepens and darkens, I feel the pain of falling leaves and stems that break in storms and trouble and dissolution and distress . . . then I shall know that my life is moving still with the dark earth and [drenched] with the deep oblivion of earth's lapse and renewal. . . . And if, in the changing phases of man's life I fall in sickness and in misery, my wrists seem broken and my heart seems dead and strength gone and my life is only the leavings of a life and still among it all snatches of lovely oblivion and snatches of renewal odd wintry flowers upon the withered stem, yet new strange flowers such as my life has not brought forth before, new blossoms of me, then I must know that still I am in the hands of the unknown God, he is breaking me down to his own oblivion to send me forth on a new morning.[25]

It would be unjustifiable and sentimental to argue that Liz had recovered her faith in God, but the identification of human life as an integral part of the cycle of nature, which she shared with Lawrence, seems to imply the constant expectation of renewal. She experienced the 'snatches of lovely oblivion' in her composing, the 'snatches of renewal' in the music that came after periods of blackness, the 'new blossoms of me' in the pieces that particularly pleased and surprised her, and she determined to 'stay with it'.

For her seventy-fifth birthday concert of music by her pupils and friends, Glyn Perrin wrote her a piece entitled simply *keep going*. Liz could no longer make her Japanese bow, but she rose in her seat and swung her stick to acknowledge the applause. In mid-1981 she was the subject of a long feature in the *Observer*. Jane Bown,[26] who was to take the photographs for the article, had been waiting for some time in the flat when Liz finally tottered in, fresh from a family row. Her first act, at ten o'clock in the morning, was to pour the champagne; then she pulled out a cigarette packet covered with musical jottings, lit up, and proceeded to retail every cut and thrust of the argument while Jane Bown helped her to hide the meals-on-wheels she never ate.

The stairs in 13 King Henry's Road were beyond her now, and after a brief but conspicuous stay at the Post House Hotel on Haverstock

Hill, she moved into a ground-floor flat down the road at 17 King Henry's Road. She had been there only a few months when one night, in her own words, 'my electric blanket burst into flames with me in it.'[27] Whatever the cause of the fire – and it is far more likely that she started it herself by falling asleep while smoking in bed – the flat was uninhabitable, and Liz herself was badly burned. Offering to exhibit her back and shoulder to Mary Silverthorne, she remarked, 'My dear, you'll never eat salami again.'[28]

During her months in hospital, she persuaded the nurses (whom she insisted on addressing as 'gels') to chill her white port in the fridge where the specimens were kept.[29] Other bottles accumulated in the locker by her her bed, and whenever her nineteen-year-old niece Candia,[30] Robert's daughter, visited, she brought champagne which fuelled long and involved near-monologues on socialism, sex and, as often as not, Liz's dislike of Candia's father. Amidst the impedimenta of pillows, dressings and bedpans, the noise of hoovers, daytime television and other people's visitors, Liz held court, complained loudly, and somehow managed occasionally to compose.

With the help of Ursula Vaughan Williams, she moved on to convalesce at a Musicians' Benevolent Fund home in Bromley. She lived in considerable comfort, and was treated with tact, humour and consideration – but to Liz it was the outer darkness. 'She would look at a plant and invest it with socio-economic class,' remembered Alison Bauld. 'The very word "Bromley" would have been the equivalent of the variegated evergreen with red berries which she abhorred.' For the duration of her stay, Ifor Newton House, Bromley, was alive with murmurs of 'Did you *hear* what she said . . .' 'Usually "fuck" at breakfast,' commented Ursula Vaughan Williams resignedly.

Liz in her impatience removed herself from Bromley before her flat was ready, and had to return for another sojourn at the Post House. Bel Mooney,[31] who was making a television programme about her in a series on 'Mothers and Daughters' for Channel Four, used to take her over the road for lunch at an Italian restaurant. Liz always put on lipstick for these occasions, in defiance of a hospital matron who had suggested that make-up was unnecessary, even unbecoming in an old lady. She ordered plain pasta, because her digestion could not cope with a sauce, and wrestled to control the fork with twisted fingers, revelling in the treat of being out.

As she slowly recovered from the fire, there were fresh diversions. 'Rather late in the day,' remarked Hugo Cole, 'journalists have discovered that her wit, her shrewdness, her honesty, her carefully modulated indiscretion, make her one of the most rewarding of all interviewees.'[32]

She was invited to the 'Woman of the Year' lunch, and made the *Observer*'s 'Sayings of the Week' column by remarking that she was only accepting because she liked the Savoy. She was asked to read her personal selection of poetry in a late-night series on Channel Four entitled 'Sit Up and Listen', and chose Quasimodo, Donne and other English metaphysical poets.

Her work was fluctuating wildly now. In 1981 she had written and then withdrawn a piece, a string quartet, something she had not done for years. (The following year she successfully completed another quartet, her thirteenth.) At the start of 1983 a score she had written for the television drama series *A Married Man* was rejected as being too obtrusive for incidental music and insufficiently melodious for the titles;[33] it was the kind of commission which in her 'hack' heyday she had always wanted, but apparently it had come too late.

Between these two reverses, however, she had shown signs of new life. In *A Goldfish Bowl* she had asked for three wishes – most importantly, 'to be given time for ... at least *one* more musical renewal – or new beginning'. She had had to wait ten years, but now it seemed that she might get her wish.

For some time the pieces she wrote had been getting shorter. This was the product of physical weakness rather than any intellectual decision, but Liz was able to make a virtue of it. 'With old age people know what to leave out,' she declared. 'There is just the skeleton.'[34] She pointed to Turner, progressively minimalist as he grew older; and Cézanne too, she observed, had learned to build a picture with fewer and fewer tiny strokes. Her admirers would claim that this is how her best music works – like a late Cézanne painting, a Matisse drawing, or, in Mary Silverthorne's analogy, a Rembrandt drawing; when she gets her outline right, it gradually rounds and fills of itself.

Now she wrote the shortest works of all. Visiting her in hospital early in 1982, Brian Elias had found her for once defeated and fretting at the distractions. She described her state of mind as 'butterfly'. This glancingly reminded him of Schumann's *Papillons* – they had been talking about the Schumann *Romanza*, which they both loved – and he urged her to make something positive of her mood, as once she had created *And Suddenly It's Evening* out of exhaustion. Might she perhaps write a work on the same lines as *Papillons* – 'a string of short self-contained pieces, independent but related'?

By July she was writing grudgingly to John Patrick Thomas, 'I have started a series of "short" breaths – being breathless and having to use what I've got.' She added, 'I can't say this is living'; but with these 'short breaths', which eventually became Triolets I and II, her composing had somehow resisted the combined onslaught of the fire and the National Health Service.

Each set of triolets, or 'little trios' – the first for clarinet, mandolin and cello, the second for cello, marimba and harp – contains nine tiny movements. In its other meaning, the 'triolet' is a verse-form, and Liz's music here regained the affinity with poetry which many feared it had lost for ever. 'Everywhere in the Triolets,' in the words of Glyn Perrin, 'one hears not so much instrumental song, as the gestural dynamics, the heightened sensitivity to metre, stress and punctuation that marks intensified speech.'[35]

To the friends who saw the Triolets – Susan Bradshaw transcribed them with the help of a magnifying glass, so tremulous was the writing now – the pieces signalled the return of the old Liz in their clarity, control and inspired exploration of the character of each instrument, her musical ear seemingly uncluttered by the unlovely noises of the hospital ward in which she had begun writing them.

But by the beginning of 1983 Liz was virtually bedridden. Her diet consisted principally of cigarettes, brandy and Brie, large wheels of it which she somehow persuaded the local Pakistani grocer to bring to the door. (She also expected the chemist to deliver.) Her digestion had given up the unequal struggle, and she had perpetual diarrhoea. At the end of March 1983 she told her children she had had what she called a 'presentation' of Edward. She refused to discuss it in detail, inhibited perhaps by the long years of scepticism in the aftermath of her early encounters with the supernatural, and possibly afraid that she would appear to be losing her mind. But in its essence it sounded like a profound religious experience which, if it did not remove physical pain, made (in Sebastian's words) 'a big dent in depression, worry, fear and the feeling of failure', and she chose to take it as a presentiment of her own death within the next two weeks.

Meanwhile life continued as normal. On 16 March she had been taken, in a wheelchair, to the première of her thirteenth string quartet, given by the Edinburgh Quartet at the Wigmore Hall. On the same programme was a work by Peter Maxwell Davies, who had also come to the concert, and in the interval she treated him with her customary abrasiveness. Not long afterwards she had a ferocious quarrel with Brian Elias, who for twenty years had been a long-suffering friend and near-amanuensis. At last her anti-semitism goaded him beyond endurance; he fought back, as he now feels he should have done years before, and when later he tried to heal the breach, she slammed down the telephone.

On the evening of 13 April, exactly a fortnight after the 'presentation', the Silverthornes visited Liz. They found her furious and distraught, obviously regretting the loss of a friend but incapable of relinquishing her grievances. They calmed her, drank brandy with her, urged her – successfully, they felt – to repair her damaged friendships, and talked resolutely of other things. She startled them considerably by suggesting that she had been unfair (a virtually unprecedented admission for Liz) about the Maxwell Davies piece in March, that she now felt it was better than hers; and as they were leaving she called them back to thank them, hug them, and say goodbye again.

Late that night her upstairs neighbours heard her calling for help; she had fallen out of bed, and they settled her in again. Later still her son Sebastian rang, at a time when normally her insomnia made her eager for conversation, but this night she wanted to sleep, and she was brusque. The next morning at about noon she was found by the home help, huddled over the telephone on the floor. It seemed that in the early hours of the morning she had felt ill, and had tried to telephone the doctor, just as she had done twenty-one years before for Edward. She had been dead for five or six hours; her face was congested, much as she had described Edward's, and she had apparently died of a heart attack. Suicide was examined as a possibility, because she was known to have considered it as an option, but the coroner found no suspicious concentration of any one drug.

A dozen years before, Liz had written to Stevie Smith, 'Won't death be a bit of an anti-climax when you come face to face?' – Stevie having had years of contemplation and close encounters with death. She replied, 'You sound rather as if you *had* met him and found him not quite the dish I thought.'[36] 'No,' wrote Liz in *A Goldfish Bowl*, 'I don't find him such a dish as Stevie. We will both soon know.' By the time *A Goldfish Bowl* was published, Stevie already knew. In her last months Liz had told Rose she would like someone to be with her when she died, to hold her hand; in the end she met death alone.

She had given orders that there was to be no funeral, only a cremation which no one should attend, but she had asked that her ashes be scattered in Queen Mary's Rose Garden in Regent's Park. This was impossible, and the children decided on Primrose Hill, her other favourite walking place, as a substitute. Windless days are rare in April, and the result of their efforts was at once comic and horrible – the kind of episode of which people invariably say, when the dead had a sense of

humour, 'How they would have laughed!' Liz might not have found the
fiasco funny, but she would not have been in the least surprised.

For her wake she had made better provision, leaving a large sum in
her will to be spent on champagne and out-of-season strawberries. The
Silverthornes emptied their flat and invited as many people as would fit
into it, asking each to bring flowers. It was a magnificent party with, as
one might have expected, an element of the grotesque. As the champagne
flowed, the home help who had found Liz said to Mary, 'Are you the
boring sister who kept ringing her up?' To which Mary replied, 'As I'm
the only one left, I must be.' 'My last message from her,' she recalled
later. 'And what was so terribly funny was that I used to dread ringing
her up.'

Liz would have been both gratified and irritated by her obituaries,
which were plentiful and mostly generous, yet held faint echoes of the
old accusations of dry intellectualism. 'Crystalline purity of realisation',
'a purity, a kind of intellectual radiance', 'a fierce bright austerity of
spirit',[37] wrote the critics in April 1983. But her output, they concluded
– reasonably enough in the face of 161 numbered works in virtually every
genre and for virtually every instrument, and almost a hundred more
which she did not number – was uneven.

From one perspective, however, unevenness does not matter; as
Malcolm Williamson put it, 'It is *events* that matter.'[38] Better, perhaps,
ninety-five failures and five pieces that are remembered with gratitude
and excitement than a hundred which all pass muster, are accepted
without complaint, and forgotten without regret. Liz would probably
have settled for five 'events'. In her corpus the works that provoke and
tantalise and intrigue far outnumber those that bore or disappoint, and
there is a significant quantity of music that will surely survive.

'Edith Sitwell once said that if you only had the first lines of about a
dozen Donne poems you'd think he was the greatest poet that ever
lived,' remarks Frank Hauser. 'If you could make a selection of Liz's
music, you could make one believe that she was a very great composer.'
The Wittgenstein motet; *And Suddenly It's Evening; Requiescat* for
Stravinsky; *Essence of Our Happinesses; O Saisons! O Châteaux!; Quincunx;* Chamber Concerto 1; *Driving Out the Death* – if Liz had written
nothing else, she would deserve to be remembered for these pieces. And
perhaps she would be remembered with greater enthusiasm if she *had*
written nothing else. In the future, when time has weeded out the
failures, it will be easier to judge the quality of what remains.

Two of the obituaries, by William Glock and Peter Heyworth,

crossed the line separating respect from affection, to commemorate the person rather than just the composer. 'She had to work on equal terms with men,' wrote Virginia Woolf of Aphra Behn. 'She made, by working very hard, enough to live on. The importance of that fact outweighs anything that she actually wrote.'[39] Certainly Liz's survival through sixty years in the goldfish bowl of contemporary music can be taken as a precedent for other women composers, who still have the same battles to fight.[40] But her capacity to inspire was not felt only by women.

Liz was undoubtedly a pioneer, if not quite the lone figure she liked to portray. At the very least, she helped significantly to establish serialism in England. She imported European ideas into a musically protectionist country, offering other young composers an alternative way forward, and so insidiously changed the course of British culture. She would have hated to be called a composers' composer, as Robert Saxton points out, because she did not like other composers. Nevertheless, as she grew older she became something of an icon of modernism to the young, a link with the great European art revolutions. She was important, proposes Hugh Wood,[41] almost as a moral force; at a particularly philistine moment in British cultural history, she suggested to young composers how passionately serious they ought to be about their art.

'It is impossible to compose,' wrote Shelley, 'except under the strong excitement of an assurance of finding sympathy in what you write.' Liz copied out and kept this remark – but in a sense she spent her life disproving it. From her childhood she never felt completely sure of sympathy from anyone, she could confidently anticipate some degree of hostility towards what she wrote, and yet she kept writing. She was aware of what pleased the public, the critics, the BBC, and was quite capable of writing her own version of it – and she refused to countenance it.

Liz feared she had failed in the attempt to be a first-rate composer, though not all would agree – 'but I'd rather fail looking at Mozart,' she wrote proudly, 'than succeed looking at a pile of pound notes.'[42] She memorised a line of Swinburne – 'Save his own soul he hath no star' – and took it as her creed. As an emotional, earnest child the young Betty had conceived an ideal of what music should be, which the adult Liz followed as best she could until she died.

Liz's voice, personal and musical, was neither ingratiating nor always welcome; but when it fell silent, a great many people noticed and regretted the peace. 'Liz?' said one friend. 'She was a person I miss.'[43]

'My own darling Mummy – I am to bad to say eny more. . . . I know that later anyhow I can compose and I'm willing to work oh so hard for it. . . . I feel as a lark singing – up – up – up – nothing to stop. . . . I live in my songs, my songs live through me. . . . Shyness is at foot myself – THROTTLE FEAR. . . . A little love and little pain – anchor your heart in kindness and pay the toll. . . . I still want to write music, fuck you!. . . . Solitude and privacy, I now realise, are the prerogatives of private incomes. . . . The ship not sound enough, but now too late to mend. . . . For years you've all given me the pit and the pendulum, your children *or* your music. . . . One day I'll show you all. . . . Edward, Edward, Edward. . . . It is like living with a ghost in the hope that life will come back. . . . If you're a composer, bloody well sit down and compose. . . . Love Lizzie more. . . . Can one love someone when one hates oneself? . . . They die, they go, they are the least firm of anchors. . . . It seems to have taken all the running I could do to stay in the same place. . . . Love Lizzie more. . . . If women are to be butts, let homosexuals be also. . . . I *will* not lie *and* in bad English. . . . I've always wanted to tell the Queen she really ought to wear a higher bra. . . . I don't give a damn, and would rather read Beethoven's letters and have better health. . . . Edward, Edward, Edward. . . . Love Lizzie more. . . . Love Lizzie more. . . .'

List of Works

Note: Elisabeth Lutyens withdrew, scrapped or renumbered much of her early output; the following opus numbers have no corresponding works – Ops. 1, 2, 3, 4, 5/2, 5/3, 6, 11, 12, 21, 24, 26, 35, 40.

dur. = duration   prem. = première
comm. = commissioned by   * = never performed
ded. = dedicated to

Bold = serious works with and without opus numbers
Italics = radio, theatre or film scores

c. 1927
Job for soloists, chorus and orchestra

String Quartet in One Movement
prem. Macnaghten–Lemare Concerts, ?1931

1929
Sonnet: To Sleep (Keats) for contralto and small orchestra
prem. Royal College of Music, ?1929

1931
Five Songs for soprano
prem. Macnaghten–Lemare Concerts, 1931

1931/2
Frescobaldi – Caprice sur 'La Pastorale' arr. string orchestra
prem. Lemare Orchestra, cond. Iris Lemare, Macnaghten–Lemare Concerts, 28.1.32

Titelouze – Two Organ Fugues arr. string orchestra
prem. Lemare Orchestra, cond. Iris Lemare, Macnaghten–Lemare Concerts, 28.1.32

1932
The Birthday of the Infanta (Wilde)
prem. (orch. suite) Royal College of Music ?1932 (ballet) Camargo Society, cond. Lambert, Adelphi Theatre, 4.12.32

Winter the Huntsman (Osbert Sitwell) for chorus, horn, cello, trumpet and piano prem. Carlyle Singers, E. H. Statham, Peter Beavan, Richard Walton, Grace Williams, Macnaghten–Lemare Concerts, 12.12.32

1933/4
Four Songs for tenor and piano –
Emily Bronte: Stanzas
D. H. Lawrence:
'*Thief in the Night*'
'*Nonentity*'
Shakespeare: Feste's Song
prem. Ian Glennie, Macnaghten–Lemare Concerts, 21.1.35

1934/6
Six Songs for tenor/soprano and piano
A. E. Housman – '*The Deserter*'
prem. Ian Glennie, Laing Art Gallery, Newcastle, 19.9.67
*Emily Bronte –
'*The Night is Darkening*'
'*The Appeal*'
'*Fall, Leaves, Fall*'
Sappho trs. W. S. Landor –
'*Mother, I Cannot Mind My Wheel*'
prem. Sophie Wyss, London Contemporary Music Club, Conway Hall, 8.2.38
Anon. – '*Fara-diddle-dyno*'
prem. Sophie Wyss, LCMC, Conway Hall, 8.2.38

1934
The Dying of Tanneguy de Bois (Austin Dobson) for tenor, four horns and strings
prem. Steuart Wilson, Lemare Orchestra, cond. Iris Lemare, Macnaghten–Lemare Concerts, 4.2.35

1935
Buxtehude – Passacaglia arr. orchestra
prem. Lemare Orchestra, cond. Iris Lemare, Macnaghten–Lemare Concerts, 4.2.35

1936
***'Bring, in this Timeless Grave to Throw'** for voice and piano

1937/8
Op.5/1   **String Quartet I** (scrapped)
comm. Adolph Hallis
prem. Blech Quartet, Aeolian Hall, Feb. 1939

Four Songs for tenor and string quartet –
Rochford: '*O Death, Rock Me Asleep*'
Anon.: '*Die Not, Fond Man*'
Lyly: '*O Cruel Love*'
Quarles: '*A Good Night*'
comm. Adolph Hallis
prem. Ernst Bauer, Joachim Roentgen, Lieselotte Marcus, Oskar Kromer, Antonio Tusa, Braunwald, 21.7.38

***Five-part Fantasia for String Orchestra**

***The Check Book** for piano

1938
Op. 5/4   **Viola Sonata**
dur. 11′
prem. Jean Stewart, Committee for the Promotion of New Music.

Op. 5/5   **String Quartet II**
dur. 18/19′
ded. Aeolian Quartet
prem. Aeolian Quartet –

Alfred Cave, Leonard Dight,
Watson Forbes, John Moore
– ISCM Warsaw/Cracow,
17.4.39

Partita for Two Violins
prem. Jessie Hinchliffe and
Maurice Clark, BBC,
16.11.47

**Lamento e recitativo
d'Arianna** for tenor and
orchestra
prem. Steuart Wilson,
London Symphony
Orchestra, cond. Iris
Lemare, Hallis Concerts,
14.3.39

1938/9
Four French Songs for
soprano/mezzo and
viola/orchestra/instruments
Villon – *'Mort, j'appelle de
ta rigueur'*
A. de Baif – *'Voici le verd et
beau Mai'*
J. du Bellay – *'La nuit froide
et sombre'*
Anon. – *'Quand un cordier
cordant'*
prem. ?Ola Slobodskaya,
Oskar Kromer, Braunwald,
1938

1939
Op. 5/6 **String Trio**
dur. 8′
prem. London String Trio
(Maria Lidka, Watson
Forbes, Vivian Joseph),
Cowdray Hall, 3.5.45 (V.E.
Day)

Op. 7 **Three Pieces for
Orchestra**
dur. 4/5′
prem. BBC Symphony
Orchestra, cond. Sir Henry
Wood, Promenade Concert,
Queen's Hall, 7.9.40 (first
night of the Blitz)

Music for the People
(Randall Swingler) – **Feudal
England**
prem. People's Festival Wind
Band, cond. Alan Bush,
Royal Albert Hall, 1.4.39
(with Parry Jones, Paul
Robeson, 500 singers, 100
dancers)

King Midas (Tony del
Renzio) – ballet
prem. Trois Arts Ballet,
Lyric Theatre,
Hammersmith, ?1939

**Nutcracker, Swan Lake,
Perseus etc.** arr. piano
prem. ?1939

1939/40
Op. 8/1 **Chamber Concerto I** for
oboe, clarinet, bassoon, horn,
trumpet, trombone, violin,
viola and cello
dur. 8/9′
prem. Boosey and Hawkes
concert, cond. C. Lambert,
11.6.43

1940
Op. 8/2 **Chamber Concerto II** for
clarinet, tenor saxophone,
piano and strings
dur. 10′
prem. cond. Walter Goehr,
CPNM, Wigmore Hall, ?1945

?Hommage à la France
(compilation)

1941/2
Op. 9 **Five Intermezzi** for piano
dur. 6′
prem. ?Paris 1946 or Lisa
Fuchsova, BBC, 16.11.47

1941/3
**Three Salutes to the
United Nations**
(i) for brass, strings and
percussion
(ii) for orchestra
(iii) for tenor, chorus and
orchestra (Milton)
prem. (only ii) BBC
Symphony Orchestra, cond.
Clarence Raybould, BBC
15.2.45

Op. 10   *1942*
Nine Bagatelles for cello
and piano
dur. 8′
prem. ?Paris 1946

**Three Symphonic
Preludes** for orchestra
dur. 12′
prem. BBC Symphony
Orchestra, cond. Edward
Clark, ISCM, Royal Opera
House, Covent Garden,
7.7.46

**Two Songs by W. H.
Auden** for voice and piano
'*As I walked out one morning*'
'*Refugee Blues*'
prem. Hedli Anderson,
Norman Franklin, Wigmore
Hall, 17.11.45

Edith Sitwell – '*O yet
forgive*'
Christiane de Pisan –
'*Rondeau*'
J. du Bellay

?La Chambonnières

1944
En Voyage
prem. BBC Concert
Orchestra, cond. Vilem
Tausky, 2.7.60

Suite Gauloise for small
orchestra/violin and

piano/wind octet
dur. 12′
prem. Marie Wilson, Lisa
Fuchsova, Wigmore Hall.

Divertissement for
percussion and
strings/military band
dur. 9′
prem. Bournemouth
Symphony Orchestra, cond.
Rudolf Schwarz

Petite Suite
dur. 9′
prem. BBC Symphony
Orchestra, cond. Boult,
Proms, 26.8.47

?Ouverture** for piano (arr.
of one movement of *Petite
Suite?*)

**?Our Lodger's Such A Nice
Young Man** (?scrapped)

Bustle for WAAFs/ 'Gen' (film)

Jungle Mariners (film)

1945
Op. 8/3   **Chamber Concerto III** for
bassoon, strings and
percussion
dur. 10′
prem. John Alexandra, Boyd
Neel String Orchestra, cond.
Edward Clark, EC Concerts,
18.1.46

Op. 14/1   **Five Little Pieces** for
clarinet and piano
comm. Cyril Clarke for
Frederick Thurston
prem. Thea King and Celia
Arieli, Leighton House,
3.11.62

***Proud City** – overture (but
see 1959 – 'Overture')

1946

Op. 13 **O Saisons! O Châteaux!** (Rimbaud) for soprano, mandolin, guitar, harp and strings
dur. 8/9′
comm. Gerald Cooper
ded. John Davenport
prem. Margaret Field-Hyde, Merritt String Orchestra, cond. Violet Merritt, Wigmore Hall, Gerald Cooper Concerts, 11.2.47

*Purcell: Air, Dance and Ground arr. for viola and piano

Enter Caesar (MacNeice), BBC

Margate (Dylan Thomas), BBC

Oxford (Dylan Thomas), BBC

Greensleeves (?for Harry Locke, 'Variety Bandbox'), BBC

The Way From Germany (film)

1946/7

Op. 8/4 **Chamber Concerto IV** for horn and small orchestra
dur. 12′
ded. Dennis Brain
prem. Brain, Residentie Orchestra of The Hague, cond. Fritz Schurmann, Scheveningen, ISCM Amsterdam, 12.6.48

Op. 8/5 **Chamber Concerto V** for string quartet and chamber orchestra
dur. 12′
prem. BBC London Sinfonia, cond. Kenneth Jones.

1947

Op. 14 **The Pit** (W. R. Rodgers) for tenor, bass, women's chorus and orchestra
dur. 30′
comm. and ded. William Walton
prem. (concert) Parry Jones, Norman Allin, Dorian Singers, cond. Edward Clark, Wigmore Hall/BBC, 18.5.47
    (staged) Wladimiro Lozzi, Mario Tommasini, cond. Ettore Gracis, Teatro Massimo, Palermo, ISCM Sicily, 24.4.49

Op. 15 **Viola Concerto**
dur. 15′
prem. Frederick Riddle, BBC Symphony Orchestra, cond. John Hollingsworth, Proms, 8.9.50

Don Juan, BBC

Port of London, BBC

London Stock Exchange, BBC

Ophelia, BBC

Theatre Workshop, BBC

London Underground, BBC

A String of Beads, BBC

Infinite Variety, BBC

Hyde Park, BBC

Lorna Doone Country, BBC

Sheffield (film)

Voices of Malaya (film)

1948

Op. 8/6 ***Chamber Concerto VI** for oboe, harp and strings (scrapped)
dur. 12′

Op. 16 **Requiem for the Living**
for voices, chorus and
orchestra
dur. 15′
comm. Elspeth Grant
(originally ded. Lady Emily
Lutyens)
prem. Margaret Rees, Maud
Baker, Emlyn Bobb, Stanley
Riley, BBC Chorus, London
Philharmonic Orchestra,
cond. Raymond Agoult,
30.9.52

Op. 17 **Suite** for organ
dur. 5′30″
prem. Arnold Richardson,
All Souls', Langham Place,
16.6.51

Aptote for violin
dur. 9′
prem. Frederick Grinke,
ICA, ?2.3.48

Three Improvisations for
piano ('Adumbration',
'Obfuscation' and
'Peroration')
dur. 6′
ded. Constant Lambert (who
chose the titles)
prem. ?Richard Rodney
Bennett

Nine Stevie Smith Songs –
'The Actress', *'The Film
Star'*, *'Pad-Pad'*,
'Progression', *'The Songster'*,
'The Repentance of Lady T.',
'Ceux qui Luttent', *'Lady
"Rogue" Singleton'*, *'Up and
Down'* (plus *'Be Off'* in
manuscript)
prem. Hedli Anderson,
Norman Franklin, BBC

***Ninepins** for two violins

***Baker's Dozen** for two
violins

***Rhadamanthus** – ballet

?Song (Dylan Thomas) –
'Paper and Sticks' – for voice
and accordion/piano
prem. Hedli Anderson,
Thomas memorial concert,
Globe Theatre, 30.1.54

The Devil's Horse, BBC

Anglo-Colonial Journey, BBC

Children of the Ruins (film)

Penny and the Pownall Case
(film)

1949

Op. 18 **String Quartet III**
dur. 14′
prem. ?Martin Quartet, BBC.
First public performance
Vegh Quartet, LCMC,
23.1.51

Op. 19 ***Ballet for Nine Wind and
Percussion**
dur. 15′

Op. 20 **Prelude and Capriccio** for
cello
dur. 4′
prem. Margaret Moncrieff,
Kew Sunday Concerts, *c.*
8.12.69

***Holiday Diary** for piano
with narrator

Bartholomew Fair, BBC

The Thames, BBC

The English Theatre, BBC

The English Seaside, BBC

The Fisher King, BBC

*The Queen of Air and
Darkness*, BBC

Canada, Britain and Trade,
BBC

Admetus, BBC

1950

Op. 22 **Concertante** for flute, clarinet, violin, cello, piano (Pierrot Lunaire combination) dur. 10′ prem. London Symphony Orchestra Chamber Ensemble/Virtuoso Ensemble with Peter Stadlen, piano, cond. Francis Chagrin, Hampstead Town Hall, 11.2.52

*Penelope (Lutyens) music drama for radio, for voices, chorus and orchestra (unfinished)

Export Jigsaw – Potteries; Motorcars; Jewellery; Wool, BBC

Canterbury Cathedral, BBC

Oil Review No. 7 (film)

Out of True (film)

Waters of Life (film)

1950/1
To Be A Woman (film)

1951
Op. 23 ***Lyric Piece** for violin and orchestra

Nativity (W. R. Rodgers) for soprano, organ/string orchestra comm. Riddick String Orchestra and Arts Council for Festival of Britain prem. Elizabeth Darbishire (?or Audrey Strange), Riddick String Orchestra, cond. Kathleen Riddick, St Bartholomew the Great, 5.6.51

Henry VIII, BBC

The Otter, BBC

Shakespeare's Birthday, BBC

El Dorado (film)

British Guiana (film)

?Anglo-Iranian Oil No. 1 (film)

?Sonnblick Mountain (film)

British Key to Plenty (film)

Persian Story (film)

1952
Op. 25 **String Quartet VI** dur. 8′ ded. Francis Bacon prem. Macnaghten Quartet, Macnaghten–Lemare Concerts, 6.12.54

*String Quartet IV

*String Quartet V

*Bienfaits de la Lune (Baudelaire) for soprano, tenor, chorus, strings and percussion

The Boy Kumasenu (film)

The Third River (film)

Scotland and the New World (film)

Pipeline to the Sea (film)

Wimbledon 52 (film)

Billy Boy (Be-Ro flour advertisement)

This Little Ship (film)

Op. 27

1953
Motet – 'Excerpta Tractatus-logico-philosophicus' (Wittgenstein) for unaccompanied chorus
dur. 10/11′
comm. and ded. William Glock
prem. London Chamber Singers, cond. Anthony Bernard, Dartington Summer School of Music, August 1954

Songs and Incidental Music 'Homage to Dylan Thomas' for soprano and flute + viola or accordion/piano –
'*Do not go gentle into that good night*'
'*It is my craft and sullen art*' (? plus '*Paper and Sticks*')
prem. Hedli Anderson, Globe Theatre, 30.1.54

Westminster Abbey, BBC

We Planted A Stone (film)

On Closer Inspection (film)

School for Colonels (film)

?The Nile (film)

?Ertragreicher Kartoffelbau (film)

?The Forest Is Not A Virgin (film)

?Rievaulx Abbey (film)

Op. 28

1953/4
Valediction for clarinet and piano
dur. 10′
ded. the memory of Dylan Thomas
comm. Georgina Dobree

prem. Georgina Dobree, Iain Kendall, London Music Club, 15.6.54

Op. 29

1954
Infidelio (T. E. Ranselm/Lutyens) – seven scenes for soprano, tenor and instrumental ensemble
dur. *c.* 35′
prem. Alexandra Browning, John Winfield, New Opera Company, cond. Leon Lovett, Sadlers' Wells, 17.4.73

Op. 30

Nocturnes for violin, cello and guitar
comm. Joyce Rathbone
prem. Emmanuel Hurwitz, Terence Weil and Julian Bream, Wigmore Hall, 10.12.54

*** A Rainy Day** for violin and piano

Final Meeting (Tiller), BBC

Death of a Town, BBC

Sir Hallewyn, BBC

Nano's Song from Volpone, BBC

Two songs from Bartholomew Fair, BBC

The Heart of England (film)

Harvest of the Forest (film)

Any Man's Kingdom (film)

?Tyrolean Harvest (film)

?Destination UK (film)

?World Without End (film)

1955

Op. 31 **Music for Orchestra I**
dur. 20′
prem. BBC Symphony
Orchestra, cond. Maderna,
1.6.61

Op. 32 **Sinfonia** for organ
dur. 5′
comm. William Glock for
ICA
prem. Ralph Downes,
ICA/LCC concert, Royal
Festival Hall, 21.4.56

Op. 33 **Capriccii** for two harps and
percussion
dur. 8′
prem. Maria Korchinska and
others, Macnaghten
Concerts 12.12.55

**Diabelleries – Variations
on 'Where's My Little
Basket Gone?'** (one
movement of composite
work)
comm. for 'last'
Macnaghten–Lemare Concert
prem. cond. Iris Lemare,
Arts Council Drawing Room,
16.5.55

The Quality of Desert
(Silkin), BBC

Every Man in His Humour
(Jonson), BBC

The Palm Wine Drinkard,
BBC

Life is a Dream (Calderon tr.
Roy Campbell), BBC

Love After Death (Calderon
tr. Roy Campbell), BBC

The Song of the Grape (film)

We Found A Valley (film)

Theresa (film)

?Intermezzo Antique (film)

?Little Aden (film)

1956

Op. 36 **Chorale for Orchestra:
'Hommage à Igor
Stravinsky'**
dur. 3′
ded. to Stravinsky on his
recovery from a serious
illness
prem. Royal Philharmonic
Orchestra, cond. Elgar
Howarth, 15.8.71

The Zoo (Hooten), BBC

Any Dark Morning (Willis
Hall), BBC

Harvest the Sea (Willis Hall),
BBC

Envoy Extraordinary
(Golding), BBC

*The Trial of Thomas
Cranmer*, BBC

Bussy d'Ambois, BBC

The Bermuda Affair (film)

Pipeline into Persia (film)

The Year of the Princess (film)

?Odd Boy Out (film)

?Simon (film)

?The Oil Rivers film)

?'God Save The Queen' for
the Berliner Ensemble

1956/7

Op. 34 **Three Duos –**
(i) for horn and piano
dur. 10′

prem. Barry Tuckwell,
Margaret Kitchin, 20.5.66
(ii) for cello and piano
dur. 10'
prem. Florence Hooten,
Wilfred Parry, 7.2.60
(iii) for violin and piano
dur. 11'
prem. Hugh Maguire,
Joyce Rathbone, 24.4.58

1957

Op. 37   **In the Temple of a Bird's
Wing** (Tanner) for baritone
and piano (songs 3 and 4
composed in 1957; songs 1,
2, 5, 6 added in 1965)
prem. Benjamin Luxon, Paul
Hamburger, Arts Council
Drawing Room, ?1966

Op. 38   **Variations** for solo flute
dur. 5'
prem. William Bennett,
Macnaghten–Lemare
Concerts, 18.11.60

Op. 39   **De Amore** (Chaucer) for
soprano, tenor, chorus and
orchestra
dur. 40'
prem. Jane Manning, Philip
Langridge, BBC
Singers/London Choral
Society, BBC Symphony
Orchestra cond. Leon
Lovett, Proms, 7.9.70

Op. 41   **Fantasie-Variations** for
violin and piano – see **Three
Duos** iii)

Op. 42   **Six Tempi** for flute, oboe,
clarinet, bassoon,
harpsichord, trumpet, violin,
cello, viola and piano
dur. 12'
prem. Virtuoso Ensemble,
cond. Walter Goehr,
Wigmore Hall, 1959

The Farmstead for two
cellos and speaker prem.
20.2.64

?arrangements for Negro
Ballet Company

The Birth of Ghana (film)

?The Twilight Forest (film)

?One Man's Challenge (film)

1958

Op. 43   **Piano e Forte** for solo
piano
dur. 15'
prem. Wilfred Parry, ICA,
Wigmore Hall, 1960

Carol for a Grandmother,
unaccompanied song for Mary
Links on the birth of her first
grandchild, December 1958

*Son et lumière at Cardiff
Castle*
first of 60 performances
18.7.58; prod. Peter Wood,
cond. Marcus Dods, narrated
by Stanley Baker

Paths of Progress (film)

The Travel Game (film)

?The Iron Mountain (film)

?Moving with the Times
(film)

1959
?**Overture in C** (?re-hash of
Proud City, 1945)
prem. Northumberland
Orchestra, Newcastle,
13.5.59

?**Children's Corner**

The Atlantic Decade (film)

Three Is Company (film)

The Weald of Kent (film)

?Return to Life (film)

?Never Take Sweets From a Stranger (film)

The Bacchae (play – produced by Minos Volanakis)

1959/60

Op. 44 **Quincunx** (Sir Thomas Browne) for soprano, baritone and orchestra
dur. 20′
prem. Josephine Nendick, Joseph Ward, BBC Symphony Orchestra, cond. Norman Del Mar, Cheltenham, 12.7.62

1960

Op. 45 **Wind Quintet**
dur. 12′
comm. BBC
ded. Catherine Lacey
prem. Leonardo Quintet – Douglas Whittaker, Janet Craxton, Colin Bradbury, Geoffrey Gambold, Douglas Moore, BBC Invitation Concert, 26.1.61

?The Kibbutznik's Song for Chorus and Accordion
(from *The Challenge of the Desert*)

Antony and Cleopatra, BBC

Hamlet, BBC

Challenge of the Desert (film)

Morning on Mount Kenya (film)

The Malpas Mystery (film)

Youth Hostels (film)

Off the Beaten Track (film)

?Don't Bother to Knock (film)

?Mikhaili of Skiathos (film)

1961

Op. 46 **Symphonies for Solo Piano, Wind, Harps and Percussion**
dur. *c*.17′
comm. BBC Proms
ded. Katharina Wolpe
prem. Katharina Wolpe, BBC Symphony Orchestra, cond. John Carewe, Proms, 28.7.61

Op. 47 **Catena** (Thomas, Yeats, Tanner, Gregory et al.) for soprano, tenor and 21 instruments
dur. 40′
comm. BBC (with Phoenix Trust Award)
prem. Dorothy Dorow, Gerald English, BBC Symphony Orchestra, cond. Norman Del Mar

∗The Dong with the **Luminous Nose** (Lear) for children's chorus and instrumental ensemble

Cusson's No. 2 'Flower' commercial

The Green Islands (film)

Depression – Diagnosis in General Practice (film)

A Woman's Work (film)

The Oresteia (play – produced by Minos Volanakis)

1962

Op. 48   **Music for Orchestra II**
dur. 11′
ded. Edward Clark
prem. Strasbourg Radio
Orchestra, cond. Charles
Bruch, September 1962

Op. 49   **Five Bagatelles** for piano
dur. 5′
written for Katharina Wolpe
prem. Katharina Wolpe,
Liverpool, 10.10.63

?Ballet for Six Dancers for
vocal quartet, clarinet,
trumpet, piano and two
percussion (scrapped)
comm. Peggy Harper

?fragments of *Lisa of
Lambeth*

Julius Caesar (play)

1963

Op. 50   **Motet – The Country of the
Stars** (Boethius/Chaucer) for
unaccompanied chorus
dur. 10′
prem. Alldis Singers, cond.
John Alldis, Holy Trinity,
20.3.63

Op. 51   **String Quintet**
dur. 21′
comm. Benjamin Sonnenberg
(or ?Manchester New Music
Forum)
prem. Roland Fudge, Peter
Nutting, Avril Schepens,
Elizabeth Brierley, Nigel
Blomley, Royal Northern
College of Music,
Manchester, Seventieth
Birthday Concert, 12.5.76

Op. 52   **Wind Trio**
dur. 10′
comm. BBC
ded. Mona and Aglaya
Mitropoulos

prem. Leonardo Ensemble,
BBC Invitation Concert,
10.12.63

Op. 53   **Présages** for oboe
dur. 9′
written for Janet Craxton
prem. Janet Craxton,
Wigmore Hall, 1965

Op. 54   **Encomion – 'Let Us Now
Praise Famous Men'**
(Kipling) for chorus, brass
and percussion
dur. 17′
comm. Sandon Music
Society
prem. Sandon Music Society
chorus and orchestra, cond.
David Connolly, Lutyens
Crypt, Liverpool
Metropolitan Cathedral,
15.4.64

Op. 55   **Fantasie-Trio** for flute,
clarinet and piano
dur. 10′30″
comm. Chantry Ensemble
prem. Chantry Ensemble –
Patricia Lynden, Georgina
Dobree, Alexander Kelly,
Dublin, December 1963

Cain, BBC

?The Abbot Dies, BBC

?The Uneasy Chair, BBC

Francis Bacon (film)

*Central Sterile Supply
Department* (film)

Angles of the Sun (film)

Kaleidoscope Orissa (film)

The Favourites (film)

1964

Op. 56   **Music For Orchestra III**
dur. 14′

comm. BBC
ded. Lady Emily Lutyens
prem. BBC Symphony
Orchestra, cond. Antal
Dorati, Cheltenham, 17.7.64

Op. 57 **String Trio**
dur. 10′
prem. Oromonte Trio, ICA,
5.12.65

Op. 58 **Scena** for violin, cello and
percussion
dur. 13′30″
comm. David Martin and
Florence Hooten
prem. David Martin,
Florence Hooten, Alan
Cumberland, Macnaghten
Concert, Wigmore Hall,
10.12.65

Op. 59 * **Music for Piano and
Orchestra**
dur. 10′
comm. Katharina Wolpe

Op. 60 **Music for Wind** for double
wind quintet
dur. 11′
prem. Sandon Music Society,
cond. David Connolly,
Liverpool, 24.6.65

Puritan v. Cavalier (film)

The Vital Link (film)

The Earth Dies Screaming
(film)

Troubled Waters (film)

Dr Terror's House of Horrors
(film)

1965
Op.61 **Motet – The Hymn of
Man** (Swinburne) for male
chorus (revised in 1970 for
mixed chorus)
dur. 10′

prem. Alldis Singers, cond.
John Alldis, Commonwealth
Institute.

Op. 62 **The Valley of Hatsu-Se**
(early Japanese poetry tr.
Eiko Nakamura) for soprano,
flute, clarinet, cello and
piano
dur. 10′
comm. William Glock for
Dartington Summer School
of Music
prem. Jane Manning,
Vesuvius Ensemble,
Dartington, 6.8.65

* **Magnificat and Nunc
Dimittis** for unaccompanied
choir
dur. 10′
comm. Coventry Cathedral

?The Dog Beneath the Skin,
BBC

Condor I (film)

Space Flight I.C-1 (film)

As Is When (film)

The Skull (film)

Europe By Train (film)

1965/7
Op. 63 * **The Numbered**
(Canetti/tr. Carol Stewart,
adapted Volanakis) – opera
in a prologue and four acts
dur. *c* 120′

1966
Op. 64 **Akapotik Rose** (Paolozzi)
for soprano, flute, two
clarinets, string trio and
piano
dur. 18′
comm. Arts Council
ded. Virgil Thomson

prem. Jane Manning,
Vesuvius Ensemble,
Dartington, August 1966

Op. 65   **Music for Three** for oboe,
flute and piano
comm. Mabillon Trio
prem. Mabillon Trio, Fenton
House.

Op. 66   **And Suddenly It's Evening**
(Quasimodo tr. Jack Bevan)
for tenor and eleven
instruments
dur. *c.* 24′
comm. BBC for the
inaugural chamber concert at
the Queen Elizabeth Hall,
London
prem. Herbert Handt, BBC
Symphony Orchestra
Chamber Ensemble, Queen
Elizabeth Hall, 3.3.67

          The Fall of the Leafe for
oboe and string quartet
dur. 8′
comm. Exmoor and
Minehead Festival
prem. Leon Goossens,
Dartington Quartet, Exeter
and Minehead Festival,
27.7.67

          Psychopath/?Paranoiac (film)

          The Obi (film)

          Turner (film)

          The Terrornauts (film)

          A Sleep of Prisoners (play –
produced by Harold Lang)

          As You Like It (play –
produced by Harold Lang)

          Volpone (play)

          1967
Op. 67/1 **Novenaria** for orchestra
dur. 12′

          comm. Leicester Arts
Festival
prem. BBC Training
Orchestra, cond. Walter
Susskind, 16.2.69

Op. 67/2 **Helix** for piano duet
dur. 9′
comm. Susan Bradshaw and
Richard Rodney Bennett
prem. Susan Bradshaw and
Richard Rodney Bennett,
Wigmore Hall, 16.2.68

Op. 67/3 **Scroll for Li-Ho** for violin
and piano
dur. 17′
comm. Peter Carter and
Sally Mays
prem. Peter Carter and Sally
Mays, Park Lane Group
concert, Wigmore Hall,
8.4.68

          * **Song – 'From a Prayer
to my Daughter'** (Yeats)
for soprano

          The Pre-Raphaelite Revolt
(film)

          Allegro (film)

          The Mad Woman of Chaillot
(play)

          1967/8
Op. 68   **Time off? Not a Ghost of
a Chance!** (Lutyens *et al.*) –
a Charade in Four Scenes
with Three Interruptions, for
baritone, actor, vocal quartet,
two mixed choruses, alto
flute, harpsichord,
piano/celesta, electric
piano/organ, two electric
guitars and four percussion
dur. *c.* 80′
prem. John Gibbs, Barry
Foster, New Opera Company
chorus and orchestra, cond.
Leon Lovett, prod. Anthony

Besch, des. Peter Rice,
Sadlers' Wells, 1.3.72

1968

Op. 67/4 **Horai** for violin, horn and
piano
dur. 16'
prem. Liverpool Horn Trio,
Stoke-on-Trent, 24.4.69

Op. 69 **Essence of Our
Happinesses** (Abu Yasid,
Donne, Rimbaud) for tenor,
chorus and orchestra
dur. 26'
comm. BBC for the Proms
prem. Richard Lewis, BBC
Chorus and Symphony
Orchestra, cond. Norman
Del Mar, Prom, 8.9.70

Op. 70 **The Tyme Doth Flete**
(Petrarch/Ovid tr. Thomas
Wyatt) for chorus, with
optional prelude and
postlude for two trumpets
and trombones
dur. 10'
comm. BBC
prem. Thames Singers, cond.
Louis Halsey, BBC
Invitation Concert, 11.11.68

Op. 71 **A Phoenix** (Ovid) for
soprano, violin, clarinet and
piano/soprano and piano
dur. 6'
written as a Christmas card
for Miranda Chaplin
prem. Jane Manning, Susan
McGraw, ?BBC, 6.10.69

Epithalamion (Spenser) for
organ with optional soprano
solo
dur. 6'
comm. Hilda Cross
ded. Hilda and Anthony
Gaddum
prem. W. E. Whiteman,
Noelle Barker.

The Egocentric (Oxford
English Dictionary) for
tenor/baritone and piano
written for Dan Klein
prem. Dan Klein, Peter
Alexander, Wigmore Hall.

Tribute to Joe Links for
unaccompanied voice

The Life Class, BBC TV

Theatre of Death (film)

?RAF Recruiting (film)

1969

Op. 72 * **Temenos** for organ
(scrapped)
dur. 9'30"
comm. Dartington Arts
Society

Op. 73 **The Dying of the Sun** for
guitar
dur. 6'
ded. Yolanda Sonnabend
prem. Gilbert Biberian,
Wigmore Hall, 1969

Op. 74 **Isis and Osiris** (Lutyens,
after Plutarch) – lyric drama
for eight voices and small
orchestra
dur. 120'
prem. Anna Bernardin,
Michael Lewis, Omar
Ebrahim *et al.*, Morley
Musica Viva Ensemble,
cond. Michael Graubart,
prod. Mike Ashman, des.
Ellen Graubart, Morley
College, 26.11.76

**Lament of Isis on the
Death of Osiris** for solo
soprano (from *Isis and Osiris*)
dur. 5'
comm. and ded. Jane
Manning
prem. Jane Manning, BBC,
6.10.69

A Pilgrim Soul

The Supplicant for bass
and piano (from *Isis and
Osiris*)
dur. 6′
prem. David Read, Susan
Bradshaw, BBC.

Trois Pièces Brêves for
chamber organ (from *Isis and
Osiris*)
comm. Dartington Arts
Society
prem. Nicholas Danby,
Dartington

Op. 75   **The Tides of Time** for
double bass and piano
dur. 6′
comm. Rodney Slatford
prem. Rodney Slatford,
Clifford Lee, Purcell Room,
22.10.70

A Spanish Tragedy, BBC

Barbican (film)

1970
Op. 76   **In the Direction of the
Beginning** (Dylan Thomas)
for bass and piano
dur. 15′30″
comm. David
Read/Gulbenkian
Foundation
prem. Ian Caddy, Jennifer
Coultas, BBC, 8.9.79

Op. 77   **Anerca** (Eskimo verse, ed.
Carpenter) for
speaker/actress, ten guitars
and percussion
dur. 9′
prem. Freda Dowie, Omega
Ensemble dir. Gilbert
Biberian, Wigmore Hall,
4.5.71

Op. 78   **Oda à la Tormenta**
(Neruda) for mezzo-soprano
and piano
dur. 18′

comm. Park Lane Group
prem. Eiko Nakamura, Roger
Smalley, Park Lane Group
concert, Purcell Room,
15.1.71

Op. 79   **Vision of Youth** (Conrad)
for soprano, three clarinets,
piano and percussion
dur. 23′
comm. Matrix
prem. Matrix, Queen
Elizabeth Hall, 13.11.72

Verses of Love (Jonson) for
unaccompanied chorus
prem. Purcell Consort of
Voices

Rainbow Verdict (film)

1971
Op. 80   **Islands** (Sophocles, Shelley,
R. L. Stevenson, Rabelais)
for soprano, tenor, narrator
and instrumental ensemble
dur. *c*. 25′
comm. British Section
ISCM/ICA and Gulbenkian
Foundation
prem. Jane Manning, Philip
Langridge, Marius Goring,
London Sinfonietta, cond.
David Atherton, ISCM
Festival, St John's Smith
Square, 7.6.71

Op. 81   **Driving Out the Death** for
oboe and string trio
dur. 14′30″
written for Janet Craxton
prem. London Oboe Quartet,
Wigmore Hall, 20.2.72

Op. 82   **The Tears of Night**
(Fourteenth-century verse,
Gertrude Stein, Joyce) for
counter-tenor, six sopranos
and three instrumental
ensembles
dur. 13′

comm. London Sinfonietta/
Arts Council
prem. James Bowman, Early
Music Consort of London
dir. David Munrow,
Sinfonietta Chorus and
Orchestra, cond. David
Atherton, 3.3.72

Op. 83 Dirge for the Proud World
(Thomas Merton) for
soprano, counter-tenor,
harpsichord and cello
dur. 8′30″
comm. The Five Centuries
Ensemble
prem. The Five Centuries
Ensemble, Read Hall, Paris,
13.12.71

Requiescat (Blake) for
soprano and string
trio/mezzo, two clarinets and
two bass clarinets
dur. 5′
written in memory of
Stravinsky, for the memorial
issue of *Tempo*, ed. David
Drew
prem. Jane Manning,
Tunnell String Trio, BBC,
15.8.71

Never Talk to Strangers
(film)

Bassae (film)

1972
Op. 84 Voice of Quiet Waters
(Wordsworth, Conrad et al.)
for chorus and orchestra
dur. 16′
comm. BBC Northern
Symphony Orchestra
prem. BBC Northern Singers,
Leeds Festival Chorus, BBC
Northern Symphony
Orchestra, cond. Bryden
Thomson, Huddersfield
Town Hall, 14.4.73

Op. 85 Counting Your Steps
(poems of the Gabon
pygmies) for chorus, four
flutes and four percussion
dur. 17′
comm. BBC
prem. BBC Chorus, cond.
Michael Gielen, Round
House, 22.5.72

Op. 86 Chimes and Cantos
(Herrick) for baritone and
instrumental ensemble
dur. 7′
comm. The Globe Playhouse
Trust
prem. Michael Rippon,
London Sinfonietta, cond.
John Pritchard, Southwark
Cathedral, 23.4.72

Op. 87 Plenum I for piano
dur. 12′
prem. Katharina Wolpe,
1972

Op. 88 Dialogo (Quasimodo) for
tenor and lute
dur. 14′
comm. Wynford Evans, Carl
Shavitz/Arts Council
prem. Wynford Evans, Carl
Shavitz, Purcell Room,
12.11.72

Op. 89 The Linnet from the Leaf
(Lutyens) – music-theatre,
for five singers and two
instrumental groups
dur. 45′
comm. BBC
prem. Jane Manning, Sarah
Walker, Meriel Dickinson,
Brian Burrows, Michael
Rippon, BBC Symphony
Orchestra, cond. Lionel
Friend, BBC, 11.11.79

?Plenum for soprano and
piano

Paid On Both Sides, BBC

1973

Op. 90   **Rape of the Moon** –
divertimento for wind octet
dur. 14′
comm. Mayfair Ensemble/
Arts Council
prem. Mayfair Ensemble,
Purcell Room, 20.3.73

Op. 91   * **The Waiting Game**
(Lutyens) – three scenes for
mezzo, baritone, actor and
small orchestra
dur. 40′

Op. 92   **Plenum II** for oboe and
thirteen instruments
dur. 23′
comm. Janet Craxton
prem. Janet Craxton,
London Sinfonietta, cond.
Andrew Davis, Queen
Elizabeth Hall, 14.6.74

Op. 93   **Plenum III** for string
quartet
dur. 9′
prem. Chilingirian String
Quartet, Purcell Room, 6.5.74

Op. 94   **Tre** for clarinet
dur. 9′
prem. Alan Hacker, 27.2.77

Op. 95   **Roads** for two sopranos,
counter-tenor, tenor, baritone,
bass
dur. 14′
comm. Purcell Consort of
Voices
prem. Purcell Consort of
Voices, Cheltenham, 6.7.74

Op. 96   **Laudi** (Lutyens) for
soprano, three clarinets,
piano and percussion
dur. 16′
comm. Matrix/Arts Council
ded. Anne Macnaghten
prem. Matrix, University of
Nottingham, 11.11.74

?Divertimento for wind
ensemble

1973/4

Op. 97   **One and the Same**
(Lutyens) for soprano,
speaker, two female mimes,
male mime, two instrumental
ensembles
dur. 26′30″
comm. York Festival
prem. Jane Manning, Freda
Dowie, Vesuvius Ensemble,
Alexander Ray London
Ballet Theatre, York, 21.6.76

1974

Op. 98   **The Winter of the World**
for two orchestras
dur. 15′30″
comm. English Bach Festival
prem. Twentieth-Century
Ensemble of the Royal
College of Music, cond.
Edwin Roxburgh, St John's,
Smith Square, 5.5.74

Op. 99   * **Kareniana** for viola and
ten instruments
dur. 14′
ded. Karen Phillips

Op. 100   **Plenum IV** for organ duet
dur. 9′
comm. Nicholas and Stephen
Cleobury/Arts Council
prem. Nicholas and Stephen
Cleobury, Royal Festival
Hall, 5.3.75

**Two D. H. Lawrence
Songs** for unaccompanied
voice –
'*Shadows*'
'*The Song of a Man who has
Come Through*'
prem. ?Jane Manning ?John
Patrick Thomas

* **Of the Snow** (Martens –
'Voyage to Spitsbergen') for
three unaccompanied voices

* **The Hidden Power**
(Shelley) for two voices

Sloth – One of the Seven Deadly Sins for two counter-tenors, tenor, two baritones, bass
dur. 5′
comm. The King's Singers
prem. The King's Singers, Cheltenham 8.7.74

1974/5

Op. 101   **Eos** for small orchestra
dur. 10′
comm. Twentieth-Century Ensemble of London
prem. Twentieth-Century Ensemble of London, cond. Edwin Roxburgh, Nottingham, 24.2.75

1975

Op. 102   *** The Goldfish Bowl** (Lutyens) – ballad opera (scrapped)
dur. 120′

Op. 103   **This Green Tide** for basset horn and piano
dur. 10′
comm. Georgina Dobree
prem. recording by Georgina Dobree

Op. 104   **Pieta** for harpsichord
dur. 9′
comm. Colin Tilney
ded. 'in memoriam Luigi Dallapiccola'
prem. 6.2.77

Op. 105   **Go, Said the Bird** for electric guitar and string quartet
dur. 12′
comm. Bath Festival/Arts Council
prem. Mitchell Dalton, Chilingirian String Quartet, Bath, 2.7.76

Op. 106   **The Ring of Bone** (Beckett/Lutyens) for piano and optional speaking voice

dur. 10′
comm. Manchester New Music Forum
prem. Peter Lawson, Manchester 70th Birthday Concert, 12.5.76

Fanfare for a Festival for three trumpets and three trombones
dur. 4′
comm. York Festival/Arts Council
prem. Equale Brass, *c*. 5.6.76

1976

Op. 107   **Mare et Minutiae** for string quartet
dur. 16′30″
written for the Medici Quartet
prem. Medici Quartet, York, 12.6.76

Op. 108   **Rondel** for orchestra
dur. 15′
comm. Royal Liverpool Philharmonic Orchestra
prem. Royal Liverpool Philharmonic Orchestra, cond. Simon Rattle, 25.4.78

Op. 109   **Like a Window** (Van Gogh) for actor, actress, singers, flute, cello and drums
dur. 25′
comm. 'In Performance'
prem. Freda Dowie, Alan Dobie, Susan Milan, Olga Hegedus, Anne Collis, London Voices, cond. Malcolm Hicks, BBC, 24.11.77

Op. 110   **Constants** for cello and piano
dur. 15′
comm. Joan Dickson and Joyce Rathbone/Arts Council
prem. Joan Dickson and Joyce Rathbone, Wigmore Hall, 30.1.77

Op. 111   * **Nocturnes and
            Interludes** for soprano and
            piano
            dur. 18′

Op. 111a   **It is the Hour** (Byron) for
            two sopranos, tenor, bass
            dur. 5′30″
            comm. Yorkshire Derwent
            Trust/Arts Council
            prem. White Rose Singers,
            Malton Water Festival,
            29.9.76

Op. 112   * **Concert Aria** for female
            voice and orchestra
            dur. 12′

Op. 113   * **Six Bagatelles** for
            chamber orchestra
            dur. 14′

           1977
Op. 114   ***Fantasia** for alto
            saxophone and three
            instrumental groups (three
            bass clarinets, double bass,
            four claves: piano, string
            quartet, four triangles: two
            trumpets, two tenor
            trombones, four tam-tams)
            dur. 13′

Op. 115   **Variations – Winter
            Series: 'Spring Sowing'**
            (Ursula Vaughan Williams) –
            song cycle for soprano and
            piano
            dur. 40′ (revised version
            16′30″)
            comm. Jane Manning and
            Richard Rodney Bennett
            prem. Jane Manning,
            Richard Rodney Bennett,
            Royal Northern College of
            Music, 21.2.79

Op. 116   ***Five Impromptus** for
            piano
            dur. 10′
            comm. Roger Woodward

Op. 117   **Cascando** (Beckett) for
            contralto, violin and string
            orchestra
            dur. 10′
            comm. Katholieke Radio
            Omroep/Frans van Rossum
            prem. Susan Tyrrell, KRO
            Hilversum, 4.12.79

Op. 118   **Nox** for piano and chamber
            orchestra
            dur. 14′
            prem. Peter Lawson, City of
            London Sinfonia, cond.
            Richard Hickox, EL BBC
            Memorial Concert, 'Music In
            Our Time', 15.12.83

Op. 119   **Madrigal** for oboe and
            violin
            dur. 7′30″
            written in memory of
            Kenneth Heath
            prem. Janet Craxton, Perry
            Hart, Redcliffe Concert,
            21.1.81

Op. 120   **By All These** (Richard
            Jeffries) for soprano and
            guitar
            prem. Alison Horriben, Nick
            Hooper, British Music
            Information Centre, 30.3.81

Op. 121   ***Romanza** for guitar
            dur. 9′
            comm. David Starobin

Op. 122   **O Absalom** for violin,
            oboe/cor anglais, viola, cello
            dur. 12′
            comm. Perry Hart
            prem. London Oboe Quartet,
            Wigmore Hall, 14.6.78

Op. 123   * **Chorale, Prelude and
            Paraphrase** (Keats) for
            string quintet, tenor, piano
            and three percussion
            dur. 16′

1978

Op. 124   ***Tides** for orchestra
dur. 13´

Op. 125   **Doubles** for string quartet
dur. 10´
comm. Medici Quartet
prem. Medici Quartet,
Hampstead, 18.3.79

Op. 126   **Seven Preludes** for piano
dur. 22´
prem. Jeremy Brown,
Wigmore Hall, 4.9.78

Op. 127   **Elegy of the Flowers**
(Cavafy) for tenor and three
instrumental groups
dur. 13´
comm. Philip Langridge
prem. Philip Langridge, City
of London Sinfonia, cond.
Richard Hickox, 26.1.80

Op. 128   **Footfalls** for flute and piano
(with optional spoken words)
dur. 8´
comm. Ann Cherry and
Jeremy Brown/Vaughan
Williams Trust
prem. Ann Cherry, Jeremy
Brown, Purcell Room, 7.2.79

1979

Op. 129   **Echoi** (Thomas Merton) for
mezzo and orchestra
dur. 13´
prem. Elise Ross, BBC
Scottish Symphony
Orchestra, cond. Simon
Rattle, 1.7.80

Op. 130   **Cantata** (Ursula Vaughan
Williams) for soprano and
instrumental ensemble
dur. 16´

Op. 131   **She Tells Her Love**
While Half Asleep (Graves)
for solo voice
dur. 5´

ded. Hazel Thomas
prem. Dorothy Dorow, BBC,
18.1.83

Op. 132   **The Great Seas** for piano
dur. 20´
prem. Michael Finnissy,
British Music Information
Centre, 18.12.79

Op. 133   **Prelude** for violin
dur. 11´
comm. Perry Hart
prem. Perry Hart, Redcliffe
Concert, 21.1.81

Op. 134   ***Cantata** (Baudelaire) for
soprano, alto, baritone,
instrumental ensemble
dur. 13´
ded. Robert Saxton

Op. 135   **Trio** for clarinet, cello and
piano
dur. 13´
comm. Muhlfeld Trio
prem. Muhlfeld Trio, 22.5.80

Op. 136   **The Roots of the World**
(Yeats) for chorus and cello
obbligato
dur. 11´30´´
prem. Ionian Singers, cond.
James Wood, 14.4.88

Op. 137   **That Sun** (Flaubert) for
contralto and piano
dur. 11´
prem. Susan Tyrrell, David
Owen Norris, Purcell Room,
7.1.80

Op. 138   **Echoes** (Hiromi Sudo) for
contralto, alto flute, cor
anglais and string quartet
dur. 11´
prem. Susan Anderson,
Suoraan, Bracknell, 28.6.81

Op. 139   **String Quartet**
dur. 10´
comm. Edinburgh Quartet
prem. Edinburgh Quartet,
Edinburgh, 9.11.80

Op. 140 **Morning Sea** for oboe/oboe d'amore and piano
dur. 12′30″
comm. Elizabeth and Robin Canter
prem. Robin Canter and Lynn Hendry, Wigmore Hall, 18.12.81

Op. 141 **Three Books of Bagatelles** for piano
dur. 31′15″
prem. (Book I) Michael Finnissy, 75th Birthday Concert given by the Vesuvius Ensemble, Wigmore Hall, 10.7.81

1980
Op. 142 **Concert Aria – Dialogo** (Quasimodo) for high soprano and orchestra
dur. 13′
comm. City of London Sinfonia/Arts Council, for EL's 75th birthday
ded. Richard Hickox
prem. ?Eiddwen Harrhy, City of London Sinfonia, February 1981? or Deborah Cook, City of London Sinfonia, cond. Richard Hickox, Cheltenham, 12.7.81

Op. 143 **Mine Eyes, My Bread, My Spade** (Tanner) for baritone and string quartet
dur. 13′
comm. Ian Caddy for EL's 75th birthday
prem. Ian Caddy, Delme String Quartet, Wigmore Hall, 22.7.81

Op. 144 **Rapprochement** for horn, harp and instrumental ensemble
dur. 12′
comm. Lontano
prem. Anthony Halstead, Frances Kelly, Lontano, cond. Lionel Friend, New Macnaghten Concert, St John's, Smith Square, 3.11.81

Op. 145 ***Deroulement** for oboe and guitar
dur. 10′30″

Op. 146 **String Quartet – Diurnal**
dur. 15′
comm. Medici Quartet/Arts Council
prem. Medici Quartet, Altrincham, 21.12.81

Op. 147 **Six** for clarinet, trumpet, piano, violin, double bass and percussion
dur. 15′
prem. Lysis, Purcell Room, 16.5.81

Op. 148 **Soli** for clarinet and double bass
dur. 7′
prem. Lysis, Purcell Room, 13.12.80

Op. 149 **Wild Decembers** for orchestra
dur. 12′
comm. February Festival, Milton Keynes
prem. Philharmonia Orchestra, cond. Sir Charles Groves, Bletchley, 14.3.82

Op. 150 **Fleur de Silence** (Remy de Gourment) for tenor and seven instruments
dur. 14′
written for Philip Langridge
prem. Philip Langridge, London Sinfonietta, cond. Ronald Zollmann, Round House Prom, BBC, 2.8.81

Op. 151 ***The Singing of Birds** (Yeats, Plato/ Mary Silverthorne) for speaker and solo viola
dur. 10′

1981

Op. 152 **Music for Orchestra IV** for chamber orchestra without violins
dur. 13′
prem. City of London Sinfonia, cond. Richard Hickox, BBC Memorial Concert, 'Music In our Time', 15.12.83

Op. 153 **Branches of the Night and of the Day** for horn and string quartet
dur. 8′
comm. South Hill Park Arts Centre
prem. Locrian Quartet, 9.10.81

Op. 154 **La Natura Dell 'Acqua** for piano
dur. 9′
prem. Michael Finnissy, Purcell Room, 28.10.84

Op. 155 **String Quartet XII**
dur. 9′
comm. Harrogate Festival/ Yorkshire Arts Association
prem. Medici Quartet, Harrogate, 5.8.82

Op. 156 **The Living Night** for solo percussion or brass and cello
dur. 12′30″
comm. James Wood
prem. James Wood, Park Lane Group Festival, St Bartholomew the Great's, 23.6.82

Op. 157 **Echo of the Wind** for solo viola
dur. 7′
written for Paul Silverthorne
prem. Paul Silverthorne, Tribute Concert, St John's, Smith Square, 19.7.84

?Gone Like A Sea-Covered Stone for orchestra

?String Quartet (scrapped)

1982

Op. 158 **String Quartet XIII**
dur. 11′
comm. Edinburgh Quartet
prem. Edinburgh Quartet, Wigmore, 16.3.83

Op. 159 **Encore – Maybe** for piano
dur. 8′30″
prem. Thalia Myers, Wigmore Hall, 7.3.83

Op. 160a **Triolet I** for clarinet, mandolin and cello
dur. 10′
prem. Roger Heaton, James Ellis, Alexander Baillie, New Macnaghten Concert, Wigmore Hall, 4.12.84

Op. 160b **Triolet II** for cello, marimba and harp
dur. 9′
prem. Alexander Baillie, Gregory Knowles, Helen Tunstall or Rachel Masters, New Macnaghten Concert, Wigmore Hall, 4.12.84

*Fanfare – Jubilato** for viola

A Married Man theme tune (scrapped)

Miscellaneous works, undated (in Lutyens Collection in the British Library)

Fantaisie in C sharp minor for piano, violin, cello and horn

Scherzo for violin, vioila, cello and piano

Trio for clarinet, cello and piano (?draft for Op. 135)

Wendy: Her Dream for
flute, violin, piano, cello and
tuba (including 'Susie's
Song' and 'Homage à les
Sonnenbergs') – ? mid–6os.

Barcarolle for piano

Berceuse for piano

La Chasse for piano

Chorale Prelude for organ

Dance Souvenance for
piano

Piano Sonata

**Praeludium e Fuga of
Bach** arr. horn and harp

Trivia for viola and piano

Electra for two choruses and
piano

**'All and all the dry
world's lever'** for chorus

Anthem 'Eternal Father'
for choir

Balade of Bon Counseill for
chorus

'Lenten ys Come' for
chorus

'Nightingales' for chorus

**'Proud Music of the
Storm'** for chorus (TATB)

'Rose Kissed Me Today'
for chorus (SAT)

'Sweet Day' for chorus

**'Welcome Maids of
Honour'** for chorus (SCTB)

**'After the Songless Rose
of Evening'** for soprano and
quartet

**'Gently, Sorrowfully Sang
the Maid'** for voice and
quartet

'Nuits de Juin' for contralto
and quartet

'Perhaps' for mezzo,
clarinet, bassoon and quartet

'Recueillement' for voice
and quartet

Songs from Shakespeare –
Stephano's Song from *The
Tempest* for baritone, cello,
guitar and strings
Feste's Song from *Twelfth
Night* for soprano, oboe,
guitar and cello (see 1933–4)

'Song in the Songless' for
contralto and quartet

'Stay O Sweet' for voice
and quartet

'Amoretti' for speaker and
viola

Dirge for voice and piano

Fantasy for voice and piano

'I Sat With Love' for tenor
and piano

'I Sent A Wreath' for voice
and piano

'Liza' for voice(s) and piano

'Mary Anne' for voice and
piano

Nursery Rhyme – 'Three
Little Children' for voice
and guitar

'O Blandos Oculos' for voice and harp

'O Yet Forgive' for voice and piano

'Rondeaux' for voice and piano

Stanzas from 'Thyrsis' for mezzo/baritone and piano –
'Thief in the Night' (?D. H. Lawrence, 1933–4?)
'To Sea'

'D'Un Vanneur de Ble aux Vents'
'Weathers'

'A Wet Day – Four Seasonal Songs whilst a Plumber Fetched his Tools' for voice and piano

'Winter Returns' for tenor and piano

Fanfare Finale for orchestra

Highlife for orchestra

Sources

EL – Elisabeth Lutyens

ELL – Letters of Elisabeth Lutyens

ELP – Papers of Elisabeth Lutyens

URP – Papers of Ursula Ridley

RIBA – Letters of Sir Edwin and Lady Emily Lutyens, in the Library of the Royal Institute of British Architects

BBC Cav – BBC Written Archives, Caversham, Reading

GB – *A Goldfish Bowl*, the autobiography of Elisabeth Lutyens

Br. Lib. – British Library, Elisabeth Lutyens Collection

Prologue

1. Arthur Koestler, 'The Birth of a Myth' [on Richard Hillary], *Horizon*, April 1943. Reprinted in *The Yogi and the Commissar*, Jonathan Cape, 1945: quoted in Robert Hewison, *Under Siege: Literary Life in London 1939–45* (revised edition Methuen, 1988), p. 48.
2. *A Goldfish Bowl*, Cassell, 1972.
3. *Evening Standard*, 18.10.82.
4. Br. Lib. Add. Mss. 64456. Draft insert for *Time Off? Not a Ghost of a Chance!*
5. Cyril Connolly, *Enemies of Promise* (Penguin, 1961), p. 157.
6. Katharina Wolpe, interview with the authors, 9.3.88.

Chapter One

Our principal sources in this chapter, used *passim*, have been: the letters of Elisabeth Lutyens to her mother, 1906–22; the correspondence between her parents over the same period, in RIBA and as reproduced in *The Letters of Sir Edwin Lutyens to his wife, Lady Emily*, edited by Clayre Percy and Jane Ridley (Collins, 1985); *A Goldfish Bowl*; Mary Lutyens, *To Be Young* (Hart-Davis, 1959), *Krishnamurti: The Years of Awakening*, (Farrar, Straus and Giroux, 1975), and *Edwin Lutyens* (John Murray, 1980); Lady Emily Lutyens, *A Blessed Girl* (*Memoirs of a Victorian Girlhood Chronicled in an Exchange of Letters, 1887–1896* (Rupert Hart-Davis, 1953) and *Candles in the Sun* (Hart-Davis, 1957); Robert Lutyens, *Fragment of Autobiography*, (unpublished, 1942); Christopher Hussey, *The Life of Sir Edwin Lutyens* (Country Life, 1950);

E. Neill Raymond, *Victorian Viceroy – The Life of Robert, the First Earl of Lytton* (Regency, 1980); Elizabeth Longford, *A Pilgrimage of Passion: the Life of Wilfrid Scawen Blunt* (Weidenfeld, 1979).

Interviews with Mary Lutyens, Constance 'Annie' McKerrow, Lady Eve Balfour.

1. Robert Lutyens, 'Notes on Sir Edwin Lutyens', lecture to the Art Workers' Guild 18.6.69.
2. RIBA, Edwin/Emily, 22.8.10.
3. RIBA, Edwin/Emily, 27.9.14.
4. ELP, Betty Balfour/Emily, 9.7.06.
5. ELP, Diary for 1918.
6. RIBA, Emily/Edwin, 13.1.21.
7. Quoted in Mary Lutyens, *Edwin Lutyens*, p. 170.
8. RIBA, Emily/Edwin 11.8.11; Edwin/Emily, 14.8.11.
9. RIBA, Emily/Edwin, 21.5.12.
10. RIBA, Edwin/Emily, 1913.

Chapter Two

Sources as in Chapter 1
1. ELP, 'Goldfish Bowl', Anriette Malet, 'The Lutyens Family'.
2. ELP, School Reports.
3. ELP. 'Correspondence', Irene Martin/EL, 26.11.62.
4. ELP, 'Notebooks'.
5. Daphne Pollen, *I Remember, I Remember* (privately published, 1983), p. 140.

Chapter Three

Principal sources: letters of Elisabeth Lutyens to Lady Emily, 1922–6; correspondence of Lady Emily and Sir Edwin, 1922–26; *A Goldfish Bowl*; Mary Lutyens, *To Be Young* and *Krishnamurti: the Years of Awakening*; Lady Emily Lutyens, *Candles in the Sun*; Robert Lutyens, *Fragment of Autobiography*. Interviews with or letters from Mary Lutyens, Anne Glock, Sally Swing Shelley, Helen Knothe/Nearing, Rosalind Rajagopal.

1. RIBA, Emily/Edwin, 3.8.10.
2. ELP, 'Goldfish Bowl'.
3. Cecil Gray, *A Survey of Contemporary Music* (O.U.P., 1924), p. 112.
4. Stuart Scott, 'John Foulds 1880–1939', *Composer*, Winter 1981.
5. Scott, *op. cit.* p. 9.
6. ELP, 'Goldfish Bowl', early draft *From Here To Maternity, c.* 1956.
7. Pollen, *op. cit.* p. 184.
8. ELP, 'Theosophical diary', 1924/5.
9. BBC Radio 4, 'The Mischief Makers', 12.4.86.
10. ELP, 'Theosophical diary', 1924–5.
11. *Ibid.*
12. URP, Emily/Ursula, 9.4.29.
13. ELP, 'Talks, Lectures and Articles', *All In A Work's Day*, 1971.

Chapter Four

Principal sources: letters of Elisabeth Lutyens to her mother, 1926–38; correspondence of Sir Edwin and Lady Emily, 1926–38; *A Goldfish Bowl*; ed. Jane Bowers and Judith Tick, *Women Making Music: The Western Art Tradition 1150–1950* (Macmillan, 1986); Louise Collis, *Impetuous Heart – the story of Ethel Smyth* (William Kimber, 1984); Margaret Stewart, *English Singer – the life of Steuart Wilson* (Duckworth, 1970). Interviews with Mary Lutyens, Ian Glennie, Anne Glock, Wendy Toye, Anne Macnaghten, Iris Lemare, Elizabeth Maconchy, Lady Eve Balfour, Sarah Tenant-Flowers, Jessie Hinchliffe.

1. Peter J. Pirie, *The English Musical Renaissance* (Gollancz, 1979), p. 133.
2. ELP, 'Notebooks', notes for lecture 'Style and Integrity', delivered at ?Dartington Summer School of Music.
3. Constant Lambert, *Music Ho!* (Penguin, 1948), p. 125.
4. *Ibid.*, p. 25.
5. ELP, 'Talks, Lectures and Articles'; fifth in the series 'Contemporary English Music'. EL quotes Vaughan Williams as quoting Parry.

6. ELP, 'Goldfish Bowl', *From Here To Maternity.*
7. URP, Ursula/Emily, 7.5.26.
8. Igor Stravinsky, *Chronicle of My Life*, Chapter 4. Quoted in Bruno Monsaingeon, *Mademoiselle: Conversations with Nadia Boulanger* (Carcanet, 1985).
9. ELP, 'Goldfish Bowl', *From Here To Maternity.*
10. Quoted in Christopher Hussey, *The Life of Sir Edwin Lutyens* (Country Life, 1950), p. 438.
11. URP, Emily/Ursula, 1.3.29.
12. Quoted in Jack Barbera and William McBrien, *Stevie* (Heinemann, 1985), p. 63.
13. ELP. 'Goldfish Bowl', first typed draft, Chapter 3.
14. Iris Lemare, interview with the authors, 17.2.87.
15. ELP, 'Talks, Lectures and Articles', fragment of autobiography, 1940s.
16. Boswell, *Life of Samuel Johnson*, Vol. 1, p. 463, 31.7.1763.
17. Virginia Woolf, *A Room of One's Own* (Hogarth Press, 1929), p. 128.
18. ELP, 'Talks, Lectures and Articles', notes for lecture.
19. Virginia Woolf/Vanessa Bell, May 1931. Quoted in Louise Collis, *Impetuous Heart: the story of Ethel Smyth*, p. 177.
20. Iris Lemare, interview with the authors, 17.2.87.

Chapter Five

Principal sources: *A Goldfish Bowl*; ELP 'Edward Clark'; BBC Written Archives, Caversham; British Library, Add. Mss. 52256–7; Robert Henderson, draft monograph 'Edward Clark' (unpublished), 1960s; Nicholas Kenyon, *The BBC Symphony Orchestra: the first fifty years 1930–80* (BBC, 1981).

Interviews with or letters from James Clark, Ian Glennie, Sidonie Goossens, Norman Del Mar, Shula Doniach.

1. ELP, 'Edward Clark', lecture by Edward Clark, *A Modern French Composer – Claude Debussy*, 17.2.08.
2. Michael Kennedy, *Adrian Boult*, (Hamish Hamilton, 1987), p. 56.
3. ELP, 'Edward Clark', talk by Edward Clark, *Arnold Schoenberg in Berlin*, 5.1.52.
4. Schoenberg, diary entry 10.2.12, quoted in H. H. Stuckenschmidt, *Arnold Schoenberg: his life, world and work* (Calder, 1977).
5. Constant Lambert, *op. cit.* p. 36.
6. And see *Westminster Gazette* 9.4.21, *Standard* 21.4.21, and *Manchester Guardian* 28.4.21.
7. Letter from David Lyness, Assistant Manager of the Duke of York's Theatre, to the authors, 20.7.88.
8. Virgil Thomson, *Virgil Thomson* (Weidenfeld, 1967).
9. Quoted in Kennedy, *op. cit.*
10. Br. Lib. Add. Mss. 52256–7.
11. *The Times* 9.4.21.
12. Denis ApIvor, 'Edward Clark', unpublished memoir, *c.* 1983.
13. BBC radio talk, *c.* 8.4.32.
14. Sir William Glock, interview with the authors, January 1987.
15. BBC Cav. R27/55, 'Music General – Commissioned Works'.
16. ELP, 'Correspondence', Walton/EL 15.7.73.
17. ELP, 'Edward Clark', tribute on his death, Boult/EL, *c.* 1.5.62.
18. 8.2.32. Quoted in Kenyon, *op. cit.*
19. Leon Goossens, in eightieth-birthday tribute to Boult, BBC Radio Three, 3.4.69.
20. *Sunday Referee*, *c.* 24.11.31.
21. Quoted in Kenyon, *op. cit.* p. 83.
22. Br. Lib. Add. Mss. 52256–7. Van Dieren/Clark, 28.12.31.
23. Br. Lib. Add. Mss. 52256–7. Schoenberg/Clark, 16.9.49.
24. ELP, 'Goldfish Bowl', letter Kenneth Wright/EL incorporated in early draft.
25. BBC Cav. Newspaper Cuttings – Edward Clark. *News Review* 11.6.36.
26. See e.g. Roger Milner, *Reith: the BBC Years* (Mainstream, 1983).
27. W. J. West, *Truth Betrayed* (Duckworth, 1987) and James Clark, letter to the authors, 5.2.89.
28. BBC Cav. R27/432, 'Music General

– Public Concert Policy', Boult/DP, 12.5.33.

29. Information compiled by Benjamin Frankel as evidence for presentation in court in June 1955.
30. *News Chronicle, c.* 30.3.36.
31. Kennedy, *op. cit.*
32. ELP 'Edward Clark'.

Chapter Six

Principal sources: *A Goldfish Bowl*; index to Edward Clark papers in Moldenhauer Archive, NorthWestern University, Chicago.

Interviews with Rose Abdalla, Sarah Tenant-Flowers, Anthony Payne.

1. Br. Lib. Add. Mss. 52256–7. e.g. Newman/Clark, 11.12.29.
2. Yolanda Sonnabend, interview with the authors, 29.5.88.
3. ELP, 'Goldfish Bowl', second typed draft.
4. Schoenberg/Rene Leibowitz, 1.10.45 in *Arnold Schoenberg: Letters*, tr. Wilkins and Kaiser (Faber, 1974).
5. Sarah Tenant-Flowers, interview with the authors, 11.5.88.
6. ELP, 'Talks, Lectures and Articles', EL interview with Stephen Plaistow, 5.7.71.
7. Sarah Tenant-Flowers, interview with the authors, 11.5.88.
8. ELP, 'Talks, Lectures and Articles', fourth in series of six lectures in Brighton on 'Contemporary English Music'.
9. Denis ApIvor, interview with the authors, 14.3.88.
10. 'The Composer and His Audience', in ed. Rollo Myers, *Twentieth-Century Music* (Calder and Boyars, 1968), p. 83.
11. URP, Ursula/Emily, 9.5.41.
12. Alban Berg, 'Why is Schoenberg's Music So Hard to understand?', tr. Anton Swarowsky and Joseph H. Lederer, *The Music Review* XIII/2, May 1952. Reprinted in Elliott Schwartz and Barney Childs, *Contemporary Composers on Contemporary Music* (Holt, Rinehart and Winston, 1967).
13. 'On the Twelve-Note Road' in *Music Survey IV*, 1.20.51 (reprint Faber, 1981), p. 321.
14. Quoted in Schoenberg/unknown correspondent, 22.4.14, in *Arnold Schoenberg: Letters* (Faber, 1974), p. 50.
15. Quoted in Nicolas Slonimsky, *Music Since 1900* (Cassell, 1972), pp. 424–5, 724.

Chapter Seven

Principal sources: EL's letters to her mother, 1939–43; the correspondence of Sir Edwin and Lady Emily; the letters of Ursula Ridley to Lady Emily, 1940–43; *A Goldfish Bowl*; ELP, 'Edward Clark' – NERO, Music for the People.

Interviews with Mary Lutyens, Clayre Percy, Constance 'Annie' McKerrow, Ian Glennie, Sebastian Glennie.

1. Br. Lib. Add. Mss. 52256–7. Dent/Clark, 5.4.39.
2. Brigid McConville, *Sisters: Love and Conflict Within the Lifelong Bond* (Pan, 1985), p. 18.
3. Interview with the authors, 18.3.88.
4. ELP, 'Goldfish Bowl', first typed draft, Chapter 5.
5. ELP, 'Correspondence', Adolph Hallis/EL. 24.8.39.
6. George Braithwaite, letter to the authors, 10.12.88.

Chapter Eight

Principal sources: *A Goldfish Bowl*; Hugh David, *The Fitzrovians* (Michael Joseph, 1988); Andrew Motion, *The Lamberts* (Chatto and Windus, 1986); Paul Ferris, *Dylan Thomas* (Hodder and Stoughton, 1977); Jack Barbera and William McBrien, *Stevie* (Heinemann, 1985); Nina Hamnett, *Is She A Lady? A Problem in Autobiography* (Allen Wingate, 1955); Denise Hooker, *Nina Hamnett, Queen of Bohemia* (Constable, 1986); Barbara Coulton, *Louis MacNeice in the BBC* (Faber, 1980); Robert

Hewison, *Under Siege: Literary Life in London 1939–45* (revised edition Methuen, 1988).

Interviews with or letters from Conrad Clark, Rose Abdalla, James Clark, Isabel Rawsthorne, Jessie Hinchliffe, Denis ApIvor, Francis Bacon, Ken Cameron.

1. ELP, 'Notebooks', draft letter, not sent, *c.* 1971.
2. Quoted in Anthony Powell, *Messengers of Day* (Heinemann, 1978).
3. Quoted by Robert Hewison, *Under Siege.*
4. ELP, 'Copyright', Thomas/EL, 14.6.72.
5. Peter Heyworth, interview with the authors, 2.3.88.
6. Gwen Watkins, *Portrait of a Friend* (Gomer Press, 1983), pp. 128–30.
7. Barbera and McBrien, pp. 266–7.
8. Smith/James Laughlin, 25.10.63, quoted in Barbera and McBrien, p. 244.
9. ELP, 'Goldfish Bowl', *From Here To Maternity*, p. 19.
10. James Clark, letter to the authors, 5.2.89.
11. ELP, 'Talks, Lectures and Articles', interview with Stephen Plaistow, 1971.
12. Quoted in Arthur Bliss, *As I Remember* (Faber, 1970), p. 104.
13. BBC Cav R19/314 C147, 'Enter Caesar', MacNeice/Director of Features, 3.7.46.
14. Br. Lib. Add. Mss. 64731.
15. ELP, 'Talks, Lectures and Features', Editor of COAL, Central Office of Information/EL, 5.8.47.
16. *A Goldfish Bowl*, p. 156.
17. URP, Emily/Ursula, 19.5.47.
18. ELP, 'Talks, Lectures and Articles', *Daily Herald*, 'Chanticleer', 21.8.47.
19. ELP, 'Talks, Lectures and Articles', *A Working Lifetime*, *c.* 8.7.71.

Chapter Nine

Principal sources: *A Goldfish Bowl*; EL's letters to her mother 1948–52; BBC

Caversham; BBC Sound Archives, Broadcasting House; British Film Institute.

Interviews with John Amis, Denis ApIvor, Jill Craigie, Miron Grindea, Iain Hamilton, Howard Hartog, Mary Lutyens, Joyce Rathbone, Donald Swann.

1. BBC Cav. 'Edward Clark', Contributor's File I, Kenneth Wright/Clark, 19.10.36.
2. BBC Cav. R27/66/1 'Music General – Conductors', 31.12.42.
3. BBC Cav. 'Edward Clark' Contributor's File I, Victor Hely-Hutchinson/Clark, 15.2.45.
4. BBC Cav. R27/66/1.
5. Schoenberg/National Institute of Arts and Letters, 22.5.47, tr. Wilkins and Kaiser, *op. cit.*
6. Conversations with the authors, 1984–9.
7. ELP, 'Goldfish Bowl', first typed draft, Chapter 9.
8. ELP. 'Libretti and Scripts', *Rhadamanthus.*
9. *Music Survey*, III/2 Dec. 1950, New Series 1949–52 ed. Donald Mitchell and Hans Keller (reprinted Faber, 1981).
10. Virginia Woolf, *A Room of One's Own* (Hogarth Press, 1929), p. 79.
11. BBC Cav. R19/984.
12. Jill Craigie, conversation with the authors, August 1988.
13. Claude Steiner, *Games Alcoholics Play: The Analysis of Life Scripts* (Grove Press, 1971) pp. xvi-xvii; Doreen Birchmore and Rodeen Walderman, 'The Woman Alcoholic: A Review', in ed. David Robinson, *Alcohol Problems* (Macmillan, 1979), pp. 116–17.
14. Donald Swann, telephone conversation with the authors, 1988.
15. Henry Reed, *Hilda Tablet and Others*, (BBC, 1971).
16. Caitlin Thomas with George Tremlett, *Caitlin: A Warring Absence* (Secker, 1986).
17. Thomas/Margaret Taylor, ?Oct. 1951, in *The Collected Letters of*

Dylan Thomas ed. Paul Ferris (Dent, 1985), pp. 815–16.

18. *The Paris and New York Diaries of Ned Rorem 1951–61* (North Point Press, 1983), p. 310.

19. J. Yerbury Dent, 'Anxiety and its Treatment', pp. 33–4, quoted in Frederick B. Rea, *Alcoholism: Its Psychology and Cure* (Epworth Press, 1956).

20. ELP, 'Problems – Health', notebook recording details of cure.

Chapter Ten

Principal sources: BBC Sound Archives; ELP, 'Talks, Lectures and Articles' and 'Libretti and Scripts'.
 Interviews with or letters from Phil Martell, Mrs Hermione Mathieson, Ken Cameron.

1. ELP, 'Talks, Lectures and Articles.'
2. *ADAM*, nos. 235–7, 1953.
3. BBC Cav. EL Contributor's File, Tiller/EL, 18.9.52.
4. British Film Institute catalogue.
5. ELP, 'Films and Theatre'.
6. Hanns Eisler, *Composing for the Films* (Dobson, 1951), pp. 33–43.

Chapter Eleven

Principal sources: EL letters to William Glock 1953–8; *A Goldfish Bowl*; archives of the Macnaghten Concerts.
 Interviews with or letters from Sir William Glock, Lady Glock, Anne Macnaghten, Shula Doniach, Dorothy Morland, Georgina Dobree, Malcolm Williamson, Richard Rodney Bennett, Alexander Goehr, Iain Hamilton, Frank Hauser, Yolanda Sonnabend, Kenneth Waller.

1. *Daily Telegraph*, 'Composers in a changing society', 18.3.72.
2. ELP, 'Talks, Lectures and Articles', on *Valediction*, c. 1953/4.
3. ELP, 'Correspondence', Dallapiccola/EL, 11.5.57.

4. Shula Doniach, interview with the authors 22.4.88.
5. ELP, 'Talks, Lectures and Articles', c. 1953/4.
6. ELL, EL/Alwyn, 22.1.74.
7. ELP, 'Talks, Lectures and Articles', lecture in Brighton, 1971.
8. ELP, 'Correspondence', Downes/EL, 23.4.56, 19.10.56.
9. BBC memorial concert, December 1983: introduction to *Music for Orchestra IV*.
10. Richard Rodney Bennett, interview with the authors, 18.2.88.
11. Georgina Ivor, letter to the authors 13.5.88.
12. Mentioned in authors' conversations with Hugh Wood, Stephen Plaistow, Brian Elias.
13. Barbera and McBrien, *op. cit.* pp. 233–4.
14. ELL, EL/William Glock, 29.3.58.
15. ELP, 'Talks, Lectures and Articles', notes for lecture, undated.
16. Brian Elias, interview with the authors, 1.12.87.
17. Interview on *Music Weekly*, BBC Radio Three, 10.4.88.
18. Constant Lambert, *Music Ho!*, p. 178.
19. Letter to authors, 15.6.88.
20. ELP, 'Correspondence', Williamson/EL, 11.11.77.
21. ELP, 'Correspondence', Bennett/EL, c. 1966.
22. Dorothy Morland, conversation with the authors, 1988.
23. *New Sounds, New Personalities: British Composers in the 1980s* (Faber, 1985), pp. 130–1.
24. ELP, 'Articles about EL', Payne – draft Grove entry, c. 1973.

Chapter Twelve

Principal sources: ELP, 'Edward Clark'; Benjamin Frankel Papers; *A Goldfish Bowl* – early drafts; transcript of Mr Justice Hilbery's Summing-Up, 17.6.55; BBC Caversham – ISCM papers.
 Interviews with or letters from Xenia Frankel, Bertha Stevens, Lord Scarman,

Buxton Orr, Milein Keller, James Gibb, Howard Hartog, Sydney Giebel, Malcolm Williamson, Alexander Goehr, Sir William Glock.

1. ELL, EL/John Patrick Thomas, 29.1.76.
2. ELP, 'Goldfish Bowl', miscellaneous draft, quoting a letter of Edward Clark to Alan Rawsthorne.
3. BBC Cav. R27/157/1, Isaacs/Murrill, 24.10.50.
4. Malcolm Williamson, conversation with authors, 6.4.88.
5. BBC Cav. R27/157/II, Minutes of ICA Music Section Sub-Committee, 10.4.53.
6. Article in *Tempo*, Autumn 1952.
7. Malcolm Williamson, conversation with authors, 6.4.88.
8. ELP. 'Goldfish Bowl', first typed draft, Chapter 10.
9. ELP. 'Goldfish Bowl', first typed draft, Chapter 11.
10. BBC Cav. R27/157/II, Minutes of ICA Music Section Sub-Committee, 31.3.54.
11. Benjamin Frankel Papers, Frankel/Goffredo Petrassi, 15.11.55, and deposition of Stanley Glasser, 25.5.54.
12. *The Times* Law Report, 14.6.55.
13. ELP, 'Edward Clark', article by Dent on ISCM.
14. Frankel Papers, List of Contributors, July 2–23, 1955.
15. Rose Abdalla, interview with the authors, 3.11.88.
16. ELP, 'Goldfish Bowl', early draft.
17. Article in ed. Ronald Stephenson, *Time Remembered: Alan Bush – An 80th Birthday Symposium* (Bravura, 1981).
18. ELP, 'Correspondence', Alwyn/EL, 14.2.73.
19. Rose Abdalla, interview with authors, 3.11.88.
20. ELP, 'Goldfish Bowl', first typed draft, Chapter 4.
21. ELL, EL/Alwyn, 13.6.73.
22. Lambert, *Music Ho!*, pp. 153–4.

Chapter Thirteen

Principal sources: BBC Caversham; *A Goldfish Bowl*.

Interviews with Conrad Clark, Hugh Wood, Malcolm Williamson, Sir William Glock, Tony Burton.

1. Peter J. Pirie, *The English Musical Renaissance* (Gollancz, 1979), p. 202.
2. Robert Hewison, *In Anger: Culture in the Cold War 1945–60* (Weidenfeld and Nicolson, 1981), p. 171.
3. Nicholas Kenyon, *The BBC Symphony Orchestra*, pp. 200ff.
4. Quoted in Stewart, *English Singer – the life of Steuart Wilson*.
5. BBC Cav. R27/157/I. Isaacs/Murrill, 21.6.51.
6. Kenyon, *op. cit.*, p. 238.
7. BBC Cav. 'Music General – Conductors III 1955–72', RMC 003556. Johnstone/Val Gielgud, 12.12.55.
8. BBC Cav. 'Music General – New Music Committee II 1955–7', RMC 003570. Simpson/HMP, 13.4.56.
9. BBC Cav. 'Music General – Conductors III 1955–72', RMC 003556. Johnstone/Gielgud, 12.12.55.
10. BBC Cav. Edward Clark – Contributor's File, Lambert et al./BBC, 3.8.50.
11. BBC Cav. Edward Clark – Contributor's File, Wilson memo, 19.8.50.
12. BBC Cav. Edward Clark – Contributor's File, Howgill/Murrill, 11.9.50.
13. BBC Cav. 'Music General – Conductors III 1955–72', RMC 003556. Johnstone/Howgill, 11.10.55.
14. BBC Cav. 'Music General – Conductors III 1955–72', RMC 003556. Lionel Salter/Johnstone, 11.11.55.
15. BBC Cav. 'Music General – Conductors III 1955–72', RMC 003556. Smith/Gielgud, 5.12.55.
16. ELL, EL/Alwyn, 31.3.73.

17. BBC Cav. EL – Contributor's File, Wade/Howgill, 25.11.53.
18. BBC Cav. EL – Contributor's File, Wade/Howgill, 24.2.54.
19. BBC Cav. EL – Contributor's File, Salter/Johnstone, c. 17.10.53.
20. BBC Cav. EL – Contributor's File, Howgill/EL, c. 25.11.53.
21. BBC Cav. EL – Contributor's File, EL/Howgill, 19.2.54.
22. BBC Cav. EL – Contributor's File, Isaacs memo, c. Feb. 1954.
23. BBC Cav. R27/46/ Johnstone/Frankel, 28.10.55.
24. ELP, 'Copyright', Mary Lutyens/EL, 10.12.72.
25. Jessie Hinchliffe, interview with the authors, 18.3.88.
26. Peter Heyworth, interview with the authors, 2.3.88.
27. Denis ApIvor, interview with the authors, 14.3.88.
28. ELP, 'Correspondence', EL/Alwyn, 17.3.73.
29. Malcolm Williamson, conversation with the authors, March 1988.
30. Interview with the authors, 22.4.88.
31. Anna Phillips, letter to the authors, 20.6.88.

Chapter Fourteen

Principal sources: EL's letters to William Alwyn; *A Goldfish Bowl*; ELP, 'Programme Notes'.

Interviews with Conrad Clark, Katharina Wolpe, Sir William Glock, Antony Hopkins.

1. ELP, 'Correspondence', Davenport/EL, 5.5.62.
2. ELL, EL/John Patrick Thomas, 12.11.77.
3. Conrad Clark, interview with authors, 11.5.84.
4. ELL, EL/Alwyn, 17.3.73.
5. Igor Stravinsky, *Chronicle of My Life*, Chapter 4, quoted in Monsaingeon, *op. cit.*
6. *GB*, p. 272.
7. Denby Richards, *Hampstead and Highgate Express*, August 1976.

8. *The Times*, 5.8.76.
9. Kenyon, *op. cit.*, pp. 290–5.
10. BBC Cav. R27/55. 'Music General – Commissioned Works'.
11. Kenyon, *op. cit.*, p. 300.
12. Conversation EL/John Alldis/Katharina Wolpe, 'Composer's Portrait', BBC, 1966.
13. e.g. Peter Heyworth in the *Observer*, Desmond Shawe-Taylor in the *Sunday Times*, Colin Mason in the *Guardian*, week of 10.12.63.
14. ELP, 'Talks, Lectures and Articles', notes for 'The language of music today'.
15. Malcolm Williamson, conversation with the authors, March 1988.
16. Joyce Rathbone, interview with the authors, 17.3.88.
17. ELP, 'Programme Notes'.
18. ELP, 'Programme Notes'.
19. *Financial Times*, 21.2.72.
20. ELL, EL/Alwyn, 1.6.73.
21. Princess Daihaku, 7th century; Yakamichi, d. 785. Tr. Eiko Nakamura.
22. Arthur Bliss, *As I Remember* (Faber, 1970), p. 66.
23. Review of seventieth Birthday Concert, July 1976.
24. 'Talking About Music/ 37', BBC Radio 4, broadcast 7.6.70.

Chapter Fifteen

Principal sources: ELP, 'Libretti and Scripts'.

Interviews with Anthony Besch, Susan Bradshaw.

1. *Grove's Dictionary of Music and Musicians* (Macmillan, 1979), entry on 'Elisabeth Lutyens', pp. 375–6.
2. ELL, EL/John Wenham.
3. ELP, 'Notebooks', c. 1967.
4. Robert Saxton, interview with authors, 27.10.87.
5. ELL, EL/Alwyn, 31.3.73.
6. Salvatore Quasimodo, *Collected Poems*, tr. Jack Bevan, (Penguin Modern European Poets, 1965).
7. 'The Mi'raj of Abu Yasid', quoted

in R. C. Zaehner, *Hindu and Muslim Mysticism* (Athlone Press)
8. Donne 'Devotion' – 'A man cannot injure Man'.
9. ELP, 'Programme Notes'.
10. EL/Brian Elias, 16.9.70.
11. Georgina Dobree, letter to the authors, 5.5.88.
12. ELP, 'Correspondence', Alwyn/EL, 19.3.73.
13. *Financial Times*, 16.1.71.
14. *Financial Times*, 8.6.71.
15. Interview with the authors, 9.5.88.
16. Interview with the authors, 1.12.87.
17. ELP, 'Articles about EL', interview with Stephen Plaistow, 1971.
18. *GB*, p. 178.
19. Robert Hewison, *Too Much: Art and Society in the Sixties 1960–75* (Methuen, 1986), p. 52.
20. Richard Findlater, *Banned! A Review of Theatrical Censorship in Britain* (MacGibbon and Kee, 1967), p. 170.
21. Letter to the authors, 14.7.88.
22. EL/Elias, 13.11.67.
23. ELL, EL/Leon Lovett, 28.7.70.
24. ELL, EL/Leon Lovett, 21.9.71.
25. *The Times*, review of Monod, *Chance and Necessity*.
26. 'Harold's Leap', in *Collected Poems* (Penguin).
27. R. D. Smith, 'Castles on the Air', in *Time Was Away: the World of Louis MacNeice* (Dolmen, 1974), p. 92.
28. ELP, 'Libretti and Scripts', early draft of *Time Off*.
29. EL radio interview with John Amis, 'Talking About Music – Words, Music and the Stage', BBC, 16.4.73.
30. ELP, 'Correspondence', Alison Bauld/EL, 8.3.72.

Chapter Sixteen

Interviews with or letters from Carol Barratt, Alison Bauld, Michael Blake Watkins, Robin Bone, Richard Deering, Brian Elias, Janet Graham, Jonty Harrison, Stuart Jones, Glyn Perrin, Robert Saxton, Andrrw Thomson, Anne Balfour-Fraser, Freda Dowie, David Thompson.

1. Conrad Clark, tape sent to the authors, February 1989.
2. *Ibid.*
3. EL interview with Jeffrey Kemp, 'Write What the Film Needs', *Sight and Sound* Autumn 1974, quoted in Deborah Price, *The Perceptibility of the Compositional Procedures of Elisabeth Lutyens*, M. Phil. thesis, Lancaster 1974.
4. ELP, 'Talks, Lectures and Articles', *Divide and Misrule*, November 1972.
5. ELP, 'Goldfish Bowl', *From Here To Maternity*.
6. ELP, 'Talks, Lectures and Articles', *Composers on Criticism*, 1971.
7. Interview with the authors, 13.3.88.
8. Norman Del Mar, interview with the authors, 2.5.88.
9. Interview with the authors, 1.7.88.
10. Katharina Wolpe, interview with the authors, 9.3.88.
11. Carol Barratt, interview with the authors, 14.4.88.
12. Iain Hamilton, interview with the authors, 15.4.88.
13. EL/Elias, 5.5.71.
14. EL/Elias, 2.11.71.
15. Norman and Pauline Del Mar, interview with the authors, 2.5.8.
16. Stephen Plaistow, interview with the authors, 15.10.87.
17. ELL, EL/Alwyn, 4.3.73.
18. And c.f. Isabel Rawsthorne, interview with the authors, 1987.
19. Barbera and McBrien, pp. 266–7.
20. Jane Manning, interview with the authors, 25.3.88.
21. ELP, 'Correspondence', Benjamin Sonnenberg/EL, 1966.
22. Stephen Plaistow, interview with the authors, 15.10.87.

Chapter Seventeen

Principal sources: EL's letters to John Patrick Thomas, William Alwyn and Brian Elias; ELP – 'King Henry's Road'.

1. Quoted in Victoria Glendinning, *Rebecca West – A Life* (Weidenfeld, 1987), p. 109.
2. Nicholas Nabokov, 'Twentieth-Century Makers of Music', introduction to Robert Layton and Humphrey Searle, *Twentieth-century Composers III: Britain, Scandinavia and the Netherlands* (Weidenfeld and Nicolson, 1972), p. xv.
3. Gerhard/William Glock, quoted in *GB*, p. 304.
4. John Patrick Thomas, tape to authors, June 1988.
5. URP, Ursula/Emily, 9.5.41.
6. Anthony Gilbert, interview with the authors, 13.3.88.
7. EL/Elias, 5.5.71.
8. ELP, 'King Henry's Road'.
9. ELP, 'Notebooks', notes for lectures *c.* 1958/9.
10. ELP, 'Articles about EL', interview with Clare Colvin, *Observer* 1.11.81.
11. ELL, EL/Michael Graubart, 10.11.72.
12. Susan Sontag, 'Have You Lied About Your Age Today?', *Nova*, September 1973.
13. Glendinning, *op. cit.*, p. 66.
14. ELP, 'Address Books'.
15. Mary Lutyens, conversations with the authors, February 1989.
16. Lytton/Mrs Earle, 25.1.1881. Quoted in Betty Balfour, *Personal and Literary Letters of Robert Lytton*, Vol. II, p. 224.
17. *A Blessed Girl*, p. 8.
18. Robert Lutyens, *Fragment of Autobiography*, p. 176.
19. ELP, 'Goldfish Bowl', first typed draft, Chapter 9.
20. Interview with the authors, 1987.
21. ELP, 'Goldfish Bowl', *From Here To Maternity*.
22. EL/Elias, 23.11.70.
23. *The Collected Poems of D. H. Lawrence* (Heinemann).

Chapter Eighteen

Principal sources: EL's letters to John Patrick Thomas and William Alwyn; ELP, 'Notebooks' and 'Libretti and Scripts'.

Interviews with or letters from Rose Abdalla, Sebastian Glennie, Anthony Gilbert, Sally Groves, Michael Vyner, Bill Colleran, David Drew, Wilfred Mellers, Ursula Vaughan Williams, Susan Tyrrell, Brian Elias, Sir Michael Tippett, Michael and Ellen Graubart, Mike Ashman.

1. ELL, EL/John Patrick Thomas, 12.11.77.
2. Letter to the authors, 1988.
3. Interview with the authors, 16.2.89.
4. *GB*, p. 308.
5. ELL, EL/John Patrick Thomas, 29.1.75.
6. John Patrick Thomas, letter to the authors, 3.2.89.
7. Interview with the authors, 16.6.88.
8. Salvatore Quasimodo, *Selected Poems* tr. Jack Bevan (Penguin Modern European Poets, 1965).
9. Interview with the authors, 17.3.88.
10. Eric Berne, *Games People Play – the Psychology of Human Relationships* (Penguin, 1967), p. 15.
11. Interview on *Music Weekly*, 10.4.88.
12. Virginia Woolf, *A Room of One's Own* (Hogarth, 1929), p. 141.
13. *GB*, p. 306.
14. Sue Stedman-Jones, *Studio International* 1973, quoted in Hewison, *Too Much: Art and Society in the Sixties 1960–75* (Methuen, 1986), p. 241.
15. ELP, 'Talks, Lectures and Articles', *Composers on Criticism*.
16. EL/Elias, 29.4.72.
17. Smith/Naomi Mitchinson, quoted in Barbera and McBrien, p. 185.
18. Alan Peacock and Ronald Weir, *The Composer in the Marketplace* (Faber, 1975), p. 162.
19. Ernst Roth, *The Business of Music: Reflections of a Music Publisher* (Cassell, 1969), p. 96.
20. *Sunday Telegraph*, 21.2.69.
21. Michael Vyner, interview with the authors, 22.4.88.
22. ELL, 'Publishers', EL/Colleran, 5.10.73.

23. Quoted in Michael Kennedy, *Britten* (Dent, 1981), p. 61.

24. 'On Winning the First Aspen Award', *Sunday Review*, 22.8.64. Reprinted in ed. Elliott Schwartz and Barney Childs, *Contemporary Composers on Contemporary Music* (Holt, Rinehart and Winston, 1967), p. 118.

25. Cyril Connolly, *Enemies of Promise* (Penguin, 1961), p. 92.

26. ELL, EL/Alwyn, 17.3.73.

27. Quoted in Kennedy, *Britten*, p. 63.

28. ELP, 'Talks, Lectures and Articles', Brighton 1971.

29. Ursula Vaughan Williams, interview with the authors, 4.3.88.

30. Covent Garden programme for memorial performance of *Peter Grimes*, 24.3.77. Quoted in Kennedy, *Britten*, p. 54.

31. Murray Schafer, *British Composers in Interview* (Faber, 1963), p. 98.

32. Andrew Thomson, letter to the authors, 16.1.87.

33. Geoffrey Grigson, *Recollections – Mainly Writers and Artists* (Chatto and Windus, 1984), p. 154.

34. ELP, 'Goldfish Bowl', *From Here To Maternity*.

35. Interview with the authors, 25.3.88.

36. Interview with the authors, 18.2.88.

37. ELL, EL/John Patrick Thomas, 12.6.72.

38. ELP, 'Goldfish Bowl,' correspondence with Cassell & Co.

39. *Ibid.*

40. EL/Elias, April 1970.

41. EL interview, *Classical Music Weekly*, 20.11.76.

42. Elizabeth Forbes, *Financial Times*, 29.11.76.

43. ELP, 'Talks, Lectures and Articles', *All in a Work's Day*.

44. Meirion Bowen, *Guardian*, 27.11.76.

45. Paul Griffiths, *Musical Times*, January 1977.

46. ELL, EL/Frans van Rossum, June 1976.

47. Mary Lutyens, conversation with the authors, 1988.

Chapter Nineteen

Principal sources: ELP, 'Notebooks'; EL's letters to John Patrick Thomas, William Alwyn and Brian Elias.

Interviews with, or letters from Mary Lutyens, Sebastian Glennie, Rose Abdalla, Tess Glennie, Glyn Perrin, Brian Elias, Ian Caddy, Paul and Mary Silverthorne, John Patrick Thomas, Sydney and Hazel Giebel, Bill Colleran, Kenneth Waller.

1. Schoenberg/National Institute of Arts and Letters, 22.5.47, in *Arnold Schoenberg: Letters*, tr. Wilkins and Kaiser.

2. Igor Stravinsky with Robert Craft, *Dialogues and a Diary* (Doubleday, 1963).

3. *The Times*, 13.7.81.

4. Henri Matisse, quoted in ELP, 'Talks, Lectures and Articles', *A Working Lifetime* (*Listener*, 8.7.71.)

5. ELL, EL/Alwyn, 31.3.73.

6. ELL, EL/Alwyn, 22.1.74.

7. Dylan Thomas/Trevor Hughes, Feb. 1933, in *The Collected Letters of Dylan Thomas*, ed. Paul Ferris (Dent, 1985), p. 14.

8. EL/Elias, 18.6.71.

9. ELL, EL/John Patrick Thomas, 29.1.76.

10. Paul Silverthorne, interview with the authors, 26.2.88. John Amis, interview with the authors, 24.4.88.

11. ELP, 'Programme Notes', and cf. *GB*, p. 267.

12. Paul Griffiths, conversation with the authors, 22.1.88.

13. Review of Seventieth Birthday Concert, July 1976.

14. Anthony Gilbert, interview with the authors, 13.3.88.

15. ELP, 'Talks, Lectures and Articles', fragment of autobiography written in the 1940s.

16. ELP, 'Correspondence', Mary Lutyens/EL, 22.5.79.

17. Neville Braybrooke, letter to the authors, 10.11.87.

18. Mary Lutyens, conversation with authors, 4.6.86.

19. Freda Dowie, interview with the authors, 1.7.88.
20. Alison Bauld, interview with the authors, 16.6.88.
21. Jessie Hinchliffe, interview with the authors, 18.3.88.
22. E. Neill Raymond, *Victorian Viceroy – The Life of Robert, the first Earl of Lytton* (Regency, 1980).
23. Ursula Vaughan Williams, interview with the authors, 4.3.88.
24. *GB*, p. 303.
25. *The Collected Poems of D. H. Lawrence* (Heinemann).
26. Telephone conversation with the authors, 1988.
27. ELL, EL/ John Patrick Thomas, 5.7.82.
28. Interview with the authors, 26.2.88.
29. Sally Groves, interview with the authors 22.2.8.
30. Candia Lutyens, letter to the authors, 4.2.89.
31. Interview with the authors, 2.11.88.
32. *Country Life*, 4.3.82.
33. ELP, 'Correspondence', John Davies, LWT/EL, 28.1.83.

34. *International Herald Tribune*, 9–10.1.82, interview with Mary Blume.
35. Programme note for Lutyens concert in Macnaghten – Lemare series, 4.12.84.
36. ELL, 'Correspondence', Smith/EL, 28.11.69.
37. e.g. David Cairns, *Sunday Times*, 17.4.83; Bayan Northcott, *Sunday Telegraph*, 17.4.83.
38. Interview on *Music Weekly*, 10.4.88.
39. Virginia Woolf, *A Room of One's Own* (Hogarth Press, 1929), p. 95.
40. See Nicola LeFanu, 'Master Musician: an Impregnable Taboo?', *Contact*, 1987.
41. Hugh Wood, interview with the authors, 22.4.88.
42. ELP, 'Articles about EL', *My Brilliant Career*, interview with Nicola Tyrer, *Daily Express*, Woman's Page, 26.10.82.
43. Phil Martell, interview with the authors, 28.3.88.

Index